Java™ and XML

Your visual blueprint for creating
Java-enhanced Web programs

by Paul Whitehead, Dr. Ernest Friedman-Hill,
and Emily Vander Veer

Visual

From

maranGraphics®

&

Wiley Publishing, Inc.

Java™ and XML: Your visual blueprint for creating
Java-enhanced Web programs

Published by
Wiley Publishing, Inc.
909 Third Avenue
New York, NY 10022

Published simultaneously in Canada

Library of Congress Control Number: 2002102421

ISBN: 0-7645-3683-4

Manufactured in the United States of America

10 9 8 7 6 5 4 3 2 1

1V/RZ/QW/QS/IN

Trademark Acknowledgments

Important Numbers

For U.S. corporate orders, please call maranGraphics at 800-469-6616 or fax 905-890-9434.

For general information on our other products and services or to obtain technical support, please contact our Customer Care Department within the U.S. at 800-762-2974, outside the U.S. at 317-572-3993 or fax 317-572-4002.

Permissions

Originally built in 1803 with an addition in 1853, North Carolina's Cape Hatteras Lighthouse stands 193 feet tall, making it the tallest brick lighthouse in the United States. To find out more about the Cape Hatteras Lighthouse and the Cape Hatteras National Seashore, check out *Frommer's® The Carolinas & Georgia, 5th Edition,* available wherever books are sold or at Frommers.com.

Wiley Publishing, Inc.

is a trademark of
Wiley Publishing, Inc.

Java™ and XML

maranGraphics is a family-run business located near Toronto, Canada.

At **maranGraphics**, we believe in producing great computer books — one book at a time.

maranGraphics has been producing high-technology products for over 25 years, which enables us to offer the computer book community a unique communication process.

Our computer books use an integrated communication process, which is very different from the approach used in other computer books. Each spread is, in essence, a flow chart — the text and screen shots are totally incorporated into the layout of the spread. Introductory text and helpful tips complete the learning experience.

maranGraphics' approach encourages the left and right sides of the brain to work together — resulting in faster orientation and greater memory retention.

Above all, we are very proud of the handcrafted nature of our books. Our carefully chosen writers are experts in their fields, and spend countless hours researching and organizing the content for each topic. Our artists rebuild every screen shot to provide the best clarity possible, making our screen shots the most precise and easiest to read in the industry. We strive for perfection, and believe that the time spent handcrafting each element results in the best computer books money can buy.

Thank you for purchasing this book. We hope you enjoy it!

Sincerely,

Robert Maran

President

maranGraphics

Rob@maran.com

www.maran.com

CREDITS

**Acquisitions, Editorial,
and Media Development**

Project Editor
Maureen Spears

Acquisitions Editor
Jen Dorsey

Product Development Supervisor
Lindsay Sandman

Copy Editor
Marylouise Wiack

Technical Editor
Dr. Ernest Friedman-Hill

Editorial Manager
Rev Mengle

Permissions Editor
Laura Moss

Media Development Specialist
Travis Silvers

Manufacturing
Allan Conley
Linda Cook
Paul Gilchrist
Jennifer Guynn

Production

Book Design
maranGraphics®

Production Coordinator
Dale White

Layout
Melanie DesJardins, LeAndra Johnson,
Kristin McMullan, Laurie Petrone

Screen Artists
Mark Harris, Jill A. Proll

Cover Illustration
David E. Gregory

Proofreader
Christine Pingleton

Quality Control
John Bitter

Indexer
Johnna VanHoose

Special Help
Cricket Franklin, Jill Mazurcyzk,
Jade Williams

ACKNOWLEDGMENTS

Wiley Technology Publishing Group: Richard Swadley, Vice President and Executive Group Publisher;
Bob Ipsen, Vice President and Executive Publisher; Barry Pruett, Vice President and Publisher; Joseph Wikert,
Vice President and Publisher; Mary Bednarek, Editorial Director; Mary C. Corder, Editorial Director;
Andy Cummings, Editorial Director.

Wiley Production for Branded Press: Debbie Stailey, Production Director.

TABLE OF CONTENTS

Java™ and XML:
Your visual blueprint for creating
Java-enhanced Web programs

5) XML DOCUMENT TYPE DEFINITIONS

6) XML SCHEMAS

7) THE SAX API

TABLE OF CONTENTS

8) THE DOM

9) JDOM

Java™ and XML:
Your visual blueprint for creating
Java-enhanced Web programs

10) JAXP

APPENDIX A

APPENDIX B

APPENDIX C

APPENDIX D

INDEX

CD-ROM INSTALLATION INSTRUCTIONS

INTRODUCING THE JAVA PHENOMENON

Well suited for developing modern, Internet-enabled and XML-aware applications, developers often find that the Java computer programming language allows them to write software more quickly, and with better quality, than other languages they know. Java allows you to build applications that you can safely use in a wide range of different environments and that you can construct with widely recognized, and highly efficient, programming techniques.

THE BIRTH OF JAVA

First released by Sun Microsystems in 1994 as part of the Hot Java Web browser, Java featured several types of downloadable dynamic content. Java's safe nature made this kind of dynamic content possible without posing any threat of data loss or compromise to the user. The dynamic content included special handlers for new network protocols as well as small graphical modules that were embedded on a Web page. These modules were called *applets,* and applets gave Java its first wave of visibility. In the fall of 1995, version 2.0 of the Netscape Navigator Web browser was the first mainstream application to include applet support. Other browsers soon followed suit.

James Gosling and others originally conceived Java as a simple, portable, safe, object-oriented, dynamic, and mobile environment for developing consumer electronics software, specifically set-top TV boxes. Each of these goals greatly contributed to Java's popularity.

A Simple Language of Least Surprise

Although it contains powerful and sophisticated features, Java is simple in the sense that it is a small and consistent language. This language does not have a long list of rules and special cases. The average Java programmer can understand and use it easily. A simple language lets you concentrate on *what* your program should do, rather than *how* to do it. Java also embodies the *principle of least surprise*. Java programs always behave the way you expect them to. You cannot redefine the meanings of the basic components of the language, as you can with C++, and you cannot perform surprising textual substitutions, as you can with the preprocessor in C. These properties make Java programmers more productive because you do not waste your time puzzling over difficult-to-understand code.

Portable Programs

Java is a portable language in which you can write a program once and run it on any computer that supports Java. While you must distribute programs written in many languages in special versions for Microsoft Windows, Macintosh, Linux, and other platforms, the same Java program can run on each of these systems without change. Java programs cannot only run on every operating system, but they run the same way on different operating systems. Java is a precisely specified language. That is, Java spells out every aspect of the language — the sizes of data types, the order of evaluation of function arguments, the behavior of floating-point arithmetic — in its formal language specifications. Most other computer languages do not specify these details, which makes other languages difficult to use to write programs that run on more than one kind of computer.

Java programs are also portable across international boundaries because Java supports translation of programs for international use. Java represents text in *Unicode*, a special system that can represent the characters of almost every alphabet in current use around the world. Furthermore, Java includes libraries that enable you to work with and store foreign-language translations of the text that appears in the user interface of your software.

THE BIRTH OF JAVA (CONTINUED)

Object-Oriented Language

In an *object-oriented language*, a program is divided into many separate units called *objects*. You can program and understand each type of object in isolation. Breaking a program into small, well-defined pieces in this way makes object-oriented programs easier to write, to understand, and to change.

An object typically includes two parts. First, it includes *information*. Just as each object in the real world has a color, a size, and a weight, Java objects contain their own unique data. Secondly, objects include *instructions* for working with this data; for example, a Button object might include instructions for drawing a button on the computer screen and for reacting to mouse clicks. Each set of instructions is termed a *method*. In general, doing useful work in Java consists mainly of asking objects to perform methods for you. An object responds to such a request by following the instructions that the method contains.

Having all the instructions and data broken up into objects makes Java software *modular*, and thus easier to understand one piece at a time. Object-oriented languages also promote software reuse — that is, you may define a kind of object and use it in several different programs unchanged.

Safe Programs

Java prevents faulty or malicious programs from crashing your computer. Such crashes often come about due to language constructs that allow access to raw memory or other hardware features. Java's architecture allows you to control access to your computer's resources and to protect your data.

Because Java is safe, downloading Java software onto your computer presents little risk. You may find downloading a document, or a bit of software, to your computer dangerous, but there is no such thing as a Java virus. Likewise, Java applets embedded in a Web page can safely run on your desktop computer. Java runs the applets inside a protected environment to prevent them from accessing any of your files, network servers, or other resources.

Dynamic Language

Because Java is a *dynamic language*, you can upgrade Java-based applications without shutting them down. You can add new code or remove old code from a running Java application at any time. You may find this an enormously powerful feature in a network environment in which you must have certain services available 24 hours a day, 7 days a week. For example, as technology evolves, an electronic commerce Web site can add new features, modify its presentation style, and patch its existing code. The dynamic nature of Java enables you to upgrade the server without interrupting service.

INTRODUCING THE JAVA PHENOMENON (CONTINUED)

JAVA ON THE SERVER

The safety and dynamic qualities of Java make it an excellent choice for around-the-clock application deployment, while Java's portability and ease-of-use make it a winner for developing server-side Web applications. As a result, Java's Web presence includes more than just the applets you see on Web pages. Many

Web sites use Java to perform non-graphical tasks behind the scenes. You have access to the data that Web servers store and reference in databases and in XML format. Java's ability to easily work with these technologies reinforces its position on the server.

JAVA VIRTUAL MACHINE

The characteristics of Java are all natural consequences of its *virtual machine architecture*. Programs in the Java language run on an idealized computer called the *Java Virtual Machine*, or JVM. Although hardware engineers have built hardware implementations of the JVM, most often you simulate the JVM in software on another computer. Real or simulated, all JVMs execute the same instructions in the same way, so that every Java program runs properly on every JVM. Several independent implementations of the JVM in software include JVMs from Sun Microsystem, Microsoft, IBM, and the GNU project. Hardware vendors and academic groups have ported Sun Microsystem's implementation to many systems. You have software JVMs available to you for essentially every kind of computer.

The virtual machine architecture is an excellent choice for implementing a safe environment to run a suspicious program from an unknown source. Although you may find it difficult or impossible to disconnect your hard drive from the computer before running a suspicious program, you can disconnect simulated JVM effortlessly. Similarly, you can prevent programs running in a JVM from accessing other peripherals and other parts of your computer, as necessary. When you trust an application, however, it can have the same access to your computer as do any other programs you run.

JAVA PROGRAM STRUCTURE

The Java language organizes its programs in a hierarchical fashion, making them easier to read and understand. The fundamental unit of Java software is the *class*. A class is a description of a type of object, and includes a collection of data and the code that operates on that data. A typical Java program consists of dozens or hundreds of classes, some written specifically for that program, and many others culled from Java's extensive library of useful standard classes.

Classes reside in groups called *packages*. Java typically categorizes the classes in a package by their function. For example, the Java libraries contain a package specifically devoted to classes for formatting text. Although the classes written in the exercises of this book are not collected into packages, you should always collect real code that you write into packages.

All Java code appears inside of classes. Furthermore, all executable statements appear inside of methods, which reside in classes. No global variables or functions may appear outside of any class, as happens in C++. You cannot write a single isolated line of Java code the way that you can write a single line of Perl or JavaScript. Java's rigorous structural rules might not seem worth the effort for short programs, but for substantial software — anything more than a few dozen lines — the benefits of a more structured language immediately become clear.

INTRODUCING XML

An efficient and effective way of storing and sharing information, XML (Extensible Markup Language) enables you to share data along with information that describes the data. XML makes it possible for a wide range of technologies, devices, and applications to easily share data in a controlled and consistent manner. Being a simple yet powerful markup language, you can use XML to store information, which you can access on a wide variety of platforms with a multitude of differing applications. You can rapidly develop XML programs at a low cost and facilitate communication of organized and accessible data between users.

THE WORLD WIDE WEB CONSORTIUM

XML is a specification laid down by the World Wide Web Consortium, more simply known as the W3C. The primary purpose of the W3C includes specifying and promoting standards for technology and software that programmers use with the World Wide Web. The W3C consists of many different companies, but the products that they support do not tie in to any specific company and are freely available for any individual or company to use or otherwise implement. The W3C is a truly international organization, with members from companies and educational institutions around the world.

MARKUP LANGUAGES

A *markup language* consists of programming code that you use to describe information. For example, you may call the name of the document *title*, which allows any program — such as a word processor — that processes the information to easily determine the title of the document. The markup language consists of tags, which identify pieces of information. A tag typically consists of a tag name, which you precede with a less-than symbol (<) and follow with a greater-than symbol (>). For example, a tag that identifies the title of a document would resemble <title>. Tags typically consist of a start and an end tag, both tags being identical except for the end tag that includes a forward slash, as in </title>. You identify the information, generally known as the content of the tag, by enclosing it within the start and end tags. HTML (Hypertext Markup Language) is probably the most widely known markup language.

XML is a subset of SGML (Standard Generalized Markup Language) and is similar to HTML, which is itself a subset of SGML.

SGML

XML is based on SGML. You use SGML to structure information, or more specifically, to create your own markup languages, which you can then use to structure data. In existence for many years, large organizations, such as governments, have used SGML within proprietary software. SGML makes it easy to store information, which you can transform, reformat, and output to different devices, such as printers and screens. You use HTML, the most popular example of an SGML-based markup language, to format information that you want to make available on the World Wide Web so that HTML-compatible applications, such as Web browsers, can access it.

HTML

Because they do not find HTML as complex as SGML, many people use HTML as a markup language to format their data. Unfortunately, HTML is not an appropriate method for storing many different types of information, such as image or audio information. Because HTML evolved to contain tags that you use solely for formatting the display of information, using HTML to format the structure of information may present problems. For example, HTML contains a font tag that describes which font to use when displaying text. You may find this type of formatting information helpful if you intend to display the information in a Web browser, but unnecessary when you store the information in a database. For this reason, you primarily use HTML to format information that a Web browser displays, and other markup languages to format the information for other purposes such as storing data and data analysis. For example, programmers use Wireless Markup Language, WML, to format information for display on wireless communication devices. In many cases you use another markup language, such as XML, to format and structure information. You can then easily convert that information to HTML for displaying within a Web browser.

XML

Initially developed in an effort to focus more on the content of information rather than on the formatting and displaying of that information, document authors can use the XML markup language to create their own tags to describe the information in their documents. The document authors can use these tags with their own applications to interpret the information correctly, as well as in conjunction with other markup languages, to format the information for display. Unlike HTML, which uses a specific set of tags to describe the formatting of information, XML does not contain any tags that describe how to format the information for display. XML merely lays out how you can create your own markup language to describe your information.

XML DOCUMENTS

An XML document contains data as well as additional information, which you represent with XML markup tags and which describes the data in the document. You specify these tags within the document itself. For example, if you want to use a tag called manager to describe the person who oversees a project, you define the manager tag within the XML document. You can then use the manager tag throughout the XML document to specify the name of anyone who manages a project. Although XML documents are rarely similar, you base them on specifications, which you must always follow when creating and using the markup tags that describe the information within XML documents. You do not require any special XML applications to create XML documents; in fact, you can create very simple XML documents with a basic text editor. Although text based, you are not intended to read the information in an XML document as you would with a word processing document. You usually access information in XML documents via XML-compatible applications, such as Web browsers, or via an application that you have created yourself.

INTRODUCING XML (CONTINUED)

VERSIONS

To standardize the way you use XML, the W3C created the XML specification, which consists of a set of rules and guidelines that details exactly how to implement XML. Known simply as the XML specification, it ensures compatibility between the applications and code that work with XML information, and the other XML applications and information. The current version of the XML specification is 1.0.

COMPATIBLE

Because it is *platform independent,* you can use XML on computers that utilize different operating systems. For example, when you create an XML document on a computer with UNIX, and then transfer that document to a computer running the Windows XP operating system, the XML applications can access the document without any conversion. Programs that you create with different programming languages can also access XML; you can create an application with Java, and another application with Perl, and both applications can just as easily access the same XML document. Because a wide range of vendors and applications now support XML, you can use different applications to process your XML documents. For example, you may use an XML-based spellchecker to check the spelling of the text in your XML document and then use another XML application to display the information.

COST

You can take your information and structure it into an XML document without having to pay a license or registration fee to use that document with XML applications. The XML specification is freely available to anyone who wants to access it. You can create documents and applications, or transfer information using the XML specification. This does not mean that XML-based applications are free; for example, you have to pay for most XML applications, but you do not have to pay for using the XML specification to build those applications.

XML-BASED TECHNOLOGIES

Apart from the XML specification, which details how to create XML documents, you also have a multitude of technologies and XML-related specifications available to you. For example, Extensible Stylesheet Language (XSL) is an XML-based technology that formats XML information for display. The W3C creates and controls many of these companion technologies and modules.

STABLE

A very stable technology, once you have structured your information with XML, you do not have to alter that information to accomplish different tasks. For example, if you have documents that contain information structured with XML, you can create an application that can display the embedded information in the XML document. If at a later date you want to display the information differently, such as on a cellular phone display, you can simply use another application, or alter your existing application; you do not have to alter the information in the XML document.

EASY TO LEARN

Formatting your information with XML is a very simple process to learn. Basic XML documents contain information enclosed in tags that you can easily create yourself. You do not require special tools, applications, or prior programming knowledge to create XML documents that can store information. Although you must follow rules and guidelines, XML is highly structured, making it very easy to acquire knowledge incrementally, so you can learn different aspects of XML as the need arises. You can create and save a simple XML document for the first time in less than an hour. If you are already familiar with programming or using another markup language such as HTML, then you will find learning XML even easier.

INTRODUCING XML (CONTINUED)

RESOURCES

Due to XML's wide implementation and acceptance, you have a collection of XML-related information available to you on the Internet. Many Web sites, newsgroups, and mailing lists exist that provide a wide variety of information for people learning to use XML, as well as information for more experienced developers. When looking for XML-related information on the Internet, a good place to start is the W3C Web site, http://www.w3.org/XML/.

VIEWING XML

People who work with an XML document generally want to view the information stored within the document. This may cause a problem because the XML tags in the XML document do not actually specify how to display the information. You can view the XML document itself, sometimes color-coded and formatted to make it easier to read, but the information itself is not formatted solely for display — you typically must view the information along with the tags inside the XML document. If you want to view information within an XML document and want that information to be formatted in a specific way, you must create an application that accesses and then formats the information for display. Because each XML document can use different tags and contain different types of information, no one application can view information in a variety of XML documents.

NETWORKS

Text based, just like HTML, XML makes it easy to transfer information across networks. Besides local area networks and the Internet, programmers increasingly use XML for wireless networks. Because of its platform independence, XML can format information for transfer via wireless networks — a benefit because the platforms of the devices on a wireless network typically differ greatly. For example, you can transfer a list of your daily meetings via a wireless network to your personal digital assistant, your home computer, or your cellular phone, which can all display the same information.

EXCHANGE INFORMATION

People primarily use XML to structure information because of XML data's ability to communicate efficiently with different applications. For example, a network application may need to keep track of users and passwords and in turn exchange that information with other computers on the network. XML provides a very efficient way to structure that information so that you can transfer and process it between the different applications on the different networks.

BUSINESS DATA

Almost all businesses must now exchange information with clients, suppliers, contractors, and other companies. XML allows businesses to construct their own markup languages, which they can use to transfer information to other businesses and clients. For example, a business that sells cleaning products might create a markup language to describe their products. The company can then exchange information with both their clients and suppliers using information about their products, and format this information with their own custom XML. This ensures that both client and company have the same methods when referring to products, such as serial numbers and product numbers. This leads to more efficient, effective, and error-free exchange of information.

LOCATING INFORMATION

Structuring information with XML usually involves identifying and labeling individual parts of the information. For example, you may need to examine and identify a person's address, street name, country, and ZIP code. Identifying and labeling information makes it easier to search for data instead of searching a complete text document to locate a street name; now you can simply search the part of the document that contains the addresses because you have identified the addresses using markup tags.

JAVA AND XML COMBINED

A side from the immense popularity that both Java and XML enjoy, you should consider combining the Java and XML technologies when creating applications or working with information because together, these

technologies give you portability, well-defined standards, extendibility, Internet compatibility, a variety of applications, and the option of reusing code.

PORTABILITY

One of Java's strengths is its ability to run on multiple platforms. Because programmers have adapted the Java environment to run on a wide variety of operating systems and devices, you can execute the Java programs you created on a UNIX computer on a computer that uses the Microsoft Windows XP operating system. Because the information you store in XML format is also platform independent, you can easily transfer it across different networks, operating systems, and applications. Wherever Java programs can run, you can also access

XML information. This enables both Java and XML information to interoperate efficiently and effectively on a wide variety of platforms. Where you once commonly developed applications so that you could port them to different operating systems with different programming languages, you can now create Java applications, and store the applications' data with XML. You can create your application and data once and run it on any mainstream operating system without having to alter the code of the application or your data.

STANDARDS

Because W3C details the XML specification and Sun Microsystems controls the specification for the Java programming language, and because a multitude of developers make changes to the standards and specifications of Java and XML only after thorough testing and investigation, both Java and XML have well-defined specifications. This leads to a longer lifetime for

any Java applications and any information you store with the XML specifications guidelines. Changes to the Java and XML specifications are also more infrequent than newer technology specifications. This means you do not have to worry about rapidly changing specifications or that the code you write today may become incompatible with future specifications.

EXTENSIBLE

You can consider code that you create using Java and information that you store using XML documents to be very extensible. From its conception, one of the Java programming language's strengths lies in its ability to create extensible applications. As a truly object-oriented programming language, you can improve, modify, or even completely rewrite portions of code without having to alter any other parts of an application that use that code. Information that you store within an XML document has access to an unlimited number of

markup tags. The document's author completely controls the makeup and nature of these tags. You can rearrange, sort, or otherwise modify the information in whatever manner suits the applications which access that data. At a future date, you can easily add features to any application that uses the Java programming language and stores its application data in an XML format with minimal impact on the existing code. This further ensures the longest possible lifetime for the applications and the data you create.

INTERNET COMPATIBLE

One of the most popular programming languages for creating network applications, the Java programming language lets you build both large and small networks, particularly those you want to place on the Internet. You have a wide range of resources, developers, and tools available to help create Java applications for the Internet. Likewise, XML information is fast becoming one of the most popular methods of storing data on the Internet, particularly on the World Wide Web and applications related to the World Wide Web. Because XML is derived from SGML, the same source from whence HTML was derived, many Java developers familiar with HTML can easily make the transition to Java- and XML-structured information.

INTEROPERABILITY

A large number of technologies allow XML data and Java programs to work together efficiently. You can easily create a Java application that can access XML documents. Many Java developers and corporations contribute to various tools and utilities that make it easy for Java applications to work with XML information. While most of these technologies—such as some Application Programming Interfaces (APIs)—which access XML information, lack full maturity, they are still stable enough to use in a production environment. As time progresses, you can anticipate even more integration between Java and XML with new and improved tools and applications. Because stable standards and specifications govern both Java and XML, interoperability between the two technologies can only increase in the future. Because XML is vendor neutral, meaning that no one corporation controls XML, developers of new applications and technologies are more receptive to the concept of using XML to structure their data. XML data in itself is very easy to process; an application you create with Java can access XML documents as easily as it can access any other file, if not more easily. Both Java and XML can use *Unicode character encoding*, a system that makes it easy to exchange data and information between your XML applications and your Java code.

APPLICATIONS

Applications are now available that use both XML and Java technologies. For example, you can use very popular XML parsers, which Java code can easily access, to work with XML documents. Many XML parsers include the Java code necessary to communicate with the XML parsers. Newer Java development tools also feature full support for XML information. Given the advantages of storing information using XML, such as easier information manageability and identification, you can only expect more applications to start using XML to format their data. Having a wide range of XML-compatible applications gives you a wider choice of tools when you create Java applications. From within your Java application you can easily access specialized XML applications. For example, you can use one XML application to generate XML tags and document markup, and use another more specialized application to display or save that data.

REUSABILITY

Another useful feature for application development is the concept of *reusable code*. If you create code in a modular fashion, then you have those code modules available for reuse in other applications. This allows for more efficient, more reliable, and faster creation of applications. Once you create a number of modules, each of which performs a specific task, you can combine them to create a new application. You can create both Java applications and XML documents using a modular design, allowing for the reuse of both Java code and XML information. This code and information reusability allows developers to quickly create flexible, more efficient applications using Java and XML.

INSTALL THE JAVA SDK

You use the Java Software Development Kit, simply known as the SDK, or the JDK, to compile and execute Java programs. You need to install the Java SDK to create Java programs and to access an XML parser with Java.

In addition to accessing version 1.3.1 of the Java SDK on the CD-ROM that accompanies this book, you can obtain the latest version of the Java SDK from the main Java Web site at java.sun.com. The Web site includes downloading and installation instructions. Sun Microsystems regularly updates the Java SDK with new features and improvements. Always check for and use the latest version of the Java SDK. See Appendix D for more information on the CD-ROM that accompanies this book.

On the Windows platform, you install the Java SDK using a standard Windows installer program. The Java SDK also currently has versions for the Solaris and Linux platforms available on the Sun Java Web site. Follow the instructions on the Web site to download and install these versions.

During the installation process, Java SDK suggests a default directory to which Sun Microsystems recommends you install the program. You can select which components of the Java SDK to install. Unless you have a reason not to, you should install all the components available.

After you install the Java SDK, you should restart your computer, particularly if you are upgrading from an older version of the Java SDK.

After the installation is complete, you can view a file that displays any last-minute changes to the documentation. Always carefully review this file when installing a new Java SDK. Besides listing changes to the Java files themselves, you may find that the Java SDK installation procedure requires that you make changes to your computer's configuration when you install later versions of the Java SDK.

INSTALL THE JAVA SDK

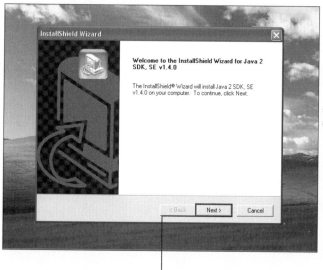

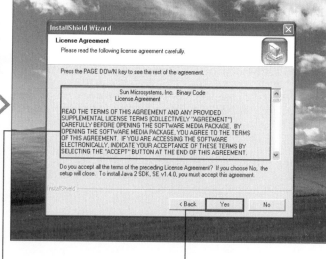

1 Insert the Java SDK CD-ROM and double-click the icon for the Java SDK installation program to start installing the Java SDK.

■ A setup screen appears.

2 Click Next to continue.

■ A software license agreement displays.

3 Click Yes to accept the agreement.

Extra

The Java SDK has a large quantity of documentation available. Due to its large size, you can download the Java SDK documentation, available in a separate package, from the same Web site that carries the Java SDK, http://java.sun.com. It is recommended that you install the Java SDK documentation, particularly if you want to create your own Java applications. If you install the documentation, you have a quick way to reference up-to-date information about your Java SDK installation.

The Java SDK is over 20MB in size. If you use a modem to connect to the Internet, it can take a few hours to download. For convenience and slightly increased speed, you can start the Internet download and let it continue through the night.

Consider placing the location of the Java SDK in the path of your operating system. Adding the location to the path enables you to compile and run Java programs without always having to specify the location of the Java SDK. Refer to the Java SDK installation documentation and your operating system's documentation for information about changing the path.

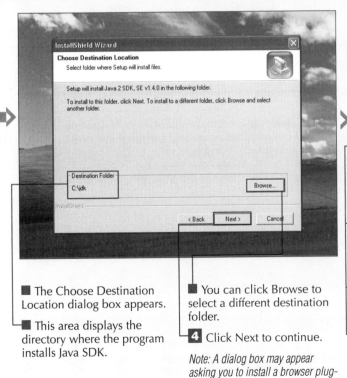

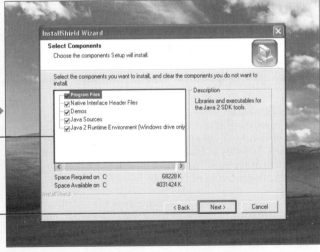

■ The Choose Destination Location dialog box appears.

■ This area displays the directory where the program installs Java SDK.

■ You can click Browse to select a different destination folder.

4 Click Next to continue.

Note: A dialog box may appear asking you to install a browser plug-in. Click Next to continue.

■ Java installs each component in this area that displays a check mark.

5 Click Next to install the Java SDK on your computer.

■ A dialog box appears when the installation completes.

6 Click Finish to close the dialog box.

7 Restart your computer.

OBJECT-ORIENTED PROGRAMMING CONCEPTS

Java shares many concepts with other object-oriented programming languages, such as C++ and Python. While object-oriented programming languages use the same concepts, the terminology and coding systems sometimes differ. For example, in Perl, you refer to a single value in an object as a *property*. In Java, you refer to it as a *field*.

CLASSES

A *class* is the primary programming structure that you use to create applications. It consists of the Java code that serves as a template or plan for creating objects, which are the core features of object-oriented programming. You can use a single class to create many objects. For example, you can use a class with code that generates comments to create an object that inserts a comment at the start of an XML document. You can use the same class to create another object that inserts copyright information at the bottom of an XML document. Because more than one Java program can use and share classes, programmers can avoid constantly rewriting the same type of code.

OBJECTS

An *object*, a package of data and a set of procedures that make use of the data, has two primary functions: to store information and to perform tasks. Objects contain *fields* to store information, and *methods*, which you use to perform tasks. You can create objects to perform a single task or a range of related tasks. You can create multiple objects using the same class. When you create an object, you consider it an *instance* of the class that creates the object.

FIELDS

Fields, also known as data fields, consist of the properties or attributes associated with an object. In comparison to other programming languages, Java treats its fields as variables of the class. Fields can store different types of data, such as strings of text, integers, and references to other objects.

Changing the values of an object's fields usually affects the behavior of the object. For example, in an object that inserts a line break into the content of an XML element, you can create a field to specify how many line breaks you want to insert. With a field value of 1, Java inserts a single line break. When you change the field value to 10, Java inserts 10 new lines in the XML document.

When you create multiple objects using the same class, you make the objects the same, except for the values held in the object's fields.

METHODS

A *method* is the code that objects use to perform a specific task. A class that creates objects can contain multiple methods. The methods in a class usually perform related tasks. For example, in a class that creates an XML document, one method may format the data, while another method saves the information to a file. The values stored in the fields of the object may influence the behavior of methods.

ARGUMENTS

You may pass one or more values, called *arguments*, to a method to provide it with input data or additional information about how to perform a task. For example, when using a method that creates elements in an XML document, you may need to pass the number of required elements to the method. Some methods do not require any arguments.

RETURN VALUES

A method may return a value after performing a specific task. The return value may indicate the result of a calculation, or it could indicate whether the program performed the task successfully. For example, a method that writes information may return a `true` or `false` value depending on whether the program saved the information. The program can then use the information to determine the next code that it needs to execute.

DATA HIDING

By making the fields and methods of the classes inaccessible to other parts of the program, *data hiding* makes classes easier to use. The program only has to know how to access the class, not the internal workings of the class. You often hide data in programs to protect outside users from tampering with classes and to ensure that users apply the methods of the classes as you originally intended. A programmer can modify and maintain the code within the class without affecting the programs that use the class. This also helps ensure that objects developed by multiple people are compatible.

KEYWORDS

The Java programming language includes many keywords that you utilize to create applications. A *keyword* is a word reserved for use only by Java. You cannot use keywords as variable names or values in your code. If you use a Java keyword inappropriately, the Java compiler detects the error and stops compiling the code. The following table displays a listing of Java keywords:

abstract	boolean	break	byte	case
catch	char	class	const	continue
default	do	double	else	extends
false	final	finally	float	for
goto	if	implements	import	instanceof
int	interface	long	native	new
null	package	private	protected	public
return	short	static	strictfp	super
switch	synchronized	this	throw	throws
transient	true	try	void	volatile
while				

THE JAVA CLASS LIBRARY

A *class*, the smallest unit of Java code that you can run, is the fundamental structure that Java applications use to group together related code. Java includes a collection of predefined classes, called the *Java class library*, also known as the *standard class library* or the *Java Application Programming Interface (API)*, for use in every Java program you create. You save time and effort creating programs by using the predefined classes in the Java class library because

you do not have to re-create the code every time you want to perform a common task, such as displaying a message on the screen. You use some predefined classes quite often, such as those that display output, while you may require others less frequently, such as the classes that help you create Graphical User Interfaces (GUIs).

JAVA CLASS LIBRARY INSTALLATION

When you install the Java SDK on your computer, the Java class library also automatically installs. Java stores the class library in a Java Archive (JAR) file named `rt.jar` in the lib subdirectory of the jre directory. You can find the jre directory in the main Java SDK directory. You do not need to adjust any settings on

your computer to specify the location of the Java class library before using a class from the library in your code. The Java compiler automatically knows where to locate the files that make up the Java class library.

VERSIONS

The Java standard class library is continually modified and appended by Sun Microsystems. Applications that you created with a later version of the Java standard class library may not work when the code compiles using an older version of the class library. Ensure that

any code you create works with the current version of the standard class library to which you have access. In almost all cases you want to use the very latest version of the Java class library.

PACKAGES

Java organizes the classes that make up the class library into packages. A *package* consists of a set of related classes that Java stores in a separate collection. For example, Java stores classes that generate output in a different package than classes that process data from a database. Generally, classes in the same package can easily access each other.

Java bases package names on the directory structure that stores the classes in the package. For example, Java stores the classes in the `java.util` package in the util subdirectory of the java directory.

IMPORT PACKAGES

You can import a package from the Java class library into a Java program. This allows you to efficiently use all the classes in the package. The `java.lang` package automatically imports into every Java program you create. For more information about importing a package, see Chapter 3.

CREATE PACKAGES

In addition to using predefined classes from Java class library packages, you can author your own classes and store them in packages you create. For example, if you create three classes to work with an XML document, you can store these classes in a package named `xmldoc`. You can then use the classes from the package when creating other Java applications. For more information about creating packages, see Chapter 3.

COMMONLY USED JAVA CLASS LIBRARY PACKAGES

The Java class library contains more than 70 packages. The following table lists some of the most commonly used packages in the library. For a more detailed list of the packages in the Java class library, see Appendix B.

PACKAGE	DESCRIPTION
`java.io`	Contains classes that allow Java programs to perform data input and output tasks.
`java.lang`	Contains the fundamental classes of the Java programming language. The Java compiler automatically loads this package.
`java.math`	Contains classes that allow Java programs to perform arbitrary-precision arithmetic.
`java.lang.ref`	Contains classes that allow Java programs to interact with the garbage collector, which performs memory management tasks.
`java.lang.reflect`	Contains classes that allow Java programs to obtain information about the variables and methods of loaded classes.
`java.security`	Contains classes that allow Java programs to carry out security procedures, such as controlling access and encrypting data.
`java.sql`	Contains classes that allow Java programs to access and process data from a database.
`java.text`	Contains classes that allow a Java program to manipulate strings, dates, numbers, and characters.
`java.util`	Contains utility classes that allow Java programs to perform various tasks such as date and time operations and random number generation.
`java.util.jar`	Contains utility classes that allow Java programs to read and write Java Archive (JAR) files.
`java.util.zip`	Contains utility classes that allow Java programs to read and write ZIP files.
`javax.swing`	Contains classes for creating Swing Graphical User Interface (GUI) components. You can use Swing GUI components on all platforms.

JAVA CONVENTIONS

To work effectively with the Java programming language, you should familiarize yourself with its conventions and understand how to follow them. This section lists the most common conventions. For more information about the conventions in Java, you can consult the Java SDK documentation.

SEMICOLONS

Most Java statements end with a semicolon (;). Java statements that include a block of code, known as the *body* of the statement, are the exception. Examples of these types of statements include methods, conditional statements, and statements that create a loop. The Java compiler stops compiling code and reports an error if it finds a required semicolon missing or if you include an unnecessary semicolon. When an error occurs due to the omission or misplacement of a semicolon, the Java compiler may mark the error in the statement following the actual location of the error. To avoid these types of errors, always review your Java code carefully before compiling the code. Some Java development tools automatically inform you if you omit a required semicolon in your code.

BRACES

Java statements that include a body use braces {} to indicate the beginning and the end of the body. A body often contains several statements. If a statement block contains only one statement, you typically do not need braces, but for consistency programmers often include them. You can include braces in one of two accepted formats in your Java code. No one braces format is more correct than the other. When making your decision about which style to use, consider who may review your code in the future and the format with which you are more comfortable. Choose one format and then use that format consistently throughout your code. Most Java development tools can automatically reformat existing code to reflect a particular style. You can use these tools to reformat your own, or other people's, Java code. A popular Java development tool that allows you to reformat code is SlickEdit, available at http://www.slickedit.com.

Brace on same line as statement:

The most widely used format places the opening brace on the same line as the Java statement. You place the closing brace on its own line and in the same column as the first character of the Java statement that uses the braces.

Example:

```
public static void main(String[] args) {
    System.out.println("Hello.");
    System.out.println("My name is Bob.");
}
```

Brace directly underneath the statement:

The second format places each brace on its own line. The braces are in the same column as the first character of the Java statement that uses the braces. Although easier to read, the format adds more lines to your Java code.

Example:

```
public static void main(String[] args)
{
    System.out.println("Hello.");
    System.out.println("My name is Mary.");
}
```

INDENTING

When working with a Java statement that includes a body, always indent the code within the body. Indenting makes your code easier to read. To keep your Java programs consistent, you should use the same indenting style in all of your code. You can use either tabs or spaces to indent code.

Code without indents:

```java
public static void main(String[] args)
{
int counter = 1;
while (counter <= 5)
{
System.out.println(counter);
counter++;
}
}
```

Code with indents:

```java
public static void main(String[] args)
{
    int counter = 1;
    while (counter <= 5)
    {
        System.out.println(counter);
        counter++;
    }
}
```

WHITESPACE

Whitespace is the term used to describe characters that do not display or print, such as spaces, tabs, and newlines. Using whitespace in your Java code can greatly improve the readability of your code. For example, a user may find `x + 1 / age` easier to read than `x+1/age`. Java removes whitespace in your code before it compiles. This means that including whitespace does not affect the speed at which the Java code compiles, nor does it affect the performance of the application using the code.

COMMENTS

You can include comments in your Java code to explain important or difficult sections of code. A good programming practice, adding comments can help make the code easier to understand. Comments are particularly useful if you or someone else will need to modify or troubleshoot the code in the future. Using descriptive names for items such as classes, methods, and variables can also make your code easier to understand. To learn how to add comments to your Java code, see Chapter 4.

CREATE A SOURCE FILE

After installing the Java SDK, you can begin to build Java programs. The first step involves class creation. A *class*, the smallest unit of Java code that you can run, is the fundamental structure that Java applications use to group together related code. For example, a class called CheckText may contain all the code it needs to analyze and validate a string of text. You can also use the CheckText class on its own in a program, or in conjunction with other classes. All Java applications must include at least one class. For more on Java classes, see the section "The Java Class Library."

You define Java classes using the keyword class followed by a space and then the class name. You should make the class name easy to understand and include the purpose of the class. You follow the class name with a pair of braces {}. You must place all methods and Java code in the class

between the braces. The code between the braces, called the body of the class, consists of methods, which are structures that contain the Java code for specific actions. For more information about defining a method, see the section "Create a Method."

You must make the class name the same as the filename you use to save the program. For example, if you call the class in your Java program DisplayText, you must save the program with the filename DisplayText.java. Please also note that Java is a case-sensitive language. Therefore, continuing the previous example, if you save the program with the filename displaytext.java, an error may occur when you attempt to compile the program.

After you save the code that creates the class in the file, the file is referred to as a source file. Java applications can use single or multiple source files.

CREATE A SOURCE FILE

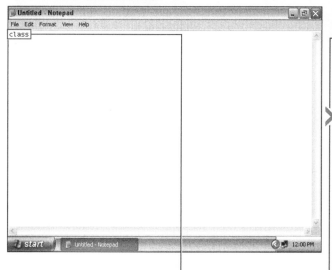

1 Start the text editor you want to use to create a Java program.

2 Type **class**.

3 Type the name of the class you want to create.

Extra

Class names can begin with any letter, an underscore (_) or the symbols $, £ or ¥. Class names cannot begin with a number or contain any punctuation, such as a period or a comma. You cannot make class names the same as any of the Java reserved words, such as do, while, or public. These naming rules also apply to the naming of methods, fields, and parameters in Java code.

You should always include comments to make your Java code easier to understand. Comments are helpful if you or other people need to modify or troubleshoot the code. Any code you write should include comments that indicate the author's name and the main purpose of the program. You precede comments with //, which you can include at the end of a line of code or on a separate line.

Example:
```
// Author: Martine Edwards
class DisplayWelcome  // This class displays a welcome
message
{
     // The body of the class is placed here
}
```

You may want to add comments that span multiple lines to your Java code. To do so, type /* before the first line of the comment and */ after the last line of the comment.

Example:
```
/*
This Java application
displays a welcome message when
the program is executed
*/
```

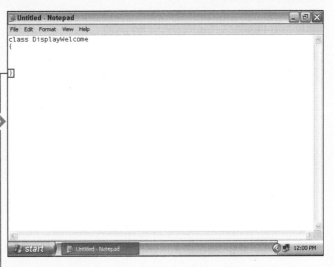

4 Type an opening brace to mark the beginning of the body of the class.

5 Press Enter to create blank lines where you type the body of the class.

6 Type a closing brace to mark the end of the body of the class.

■ Your source file is complete and ready for a method.

Note: To define methods for the classes you create, see "Create a Method" in this chapter.

CREATE A METHOD

After you create a class, you can create methods for the class. Similar to subroutines and functions that you find in other, non-object-oriented programming languages, *methods* contain lines of code that perform a specific task, such as displaying an invoice number or calculating the final total of an invoice. Using methods allows you to re-use sections of code and to group lines of code into smaller, more manageable sections. This makes it easier for people to understand and troubleshoot the code.

You can use *method modifiers*, such as `public` and `static`, to tell Java how you want to utilize a method. An access modifier, the `public` method modifier indicates that other classes can use this method. A `static` method modifier means that any program can use the method without having to create an object of the class to declare the method.

A method declaration should also include a return type. A *return type* specifies the type of value the method returns.

If a method does not return a value to the code, you should make the return type `void`. For more information about return values in methods, see Chapter 3.

You follow the name of a method with parentheses, as in the example:

```
DisplayInvoice()
```

Every Java application must have a method called `main`, which Java calls when the application starts up. You must place the argument `String[] args` within the parentheses at the end of the method name for a `main` method. This argument indicates that the method can accept strings passed from the command line when the Java program executes.

The method declaration ends with a pair of braces. You place the code that makes up the body of the method inside the braces.

CREATE A METHOD

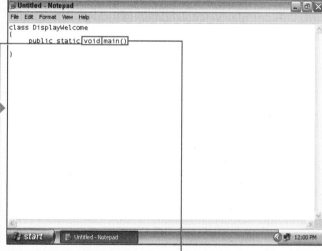

1 In the body of a class, type the method modifiers for the method you want to declare.

■ A main method must include the **public** and **static** method modifiers.

2 Type the return type of the method.

■ A method that does not return a value must include the **void** return type.

3 Type the name of the method and follow it with ().

Extra

Consisting of multiple words, the method's name should indicate its purpose. To make the name easier to read, you can capitalize the first letter of each word except the first, for example:

`displayMyName`

You can use different access modifiers when declaring a method, depending on how Java accesses it. Any class within any package can access the `public` access modifier. Any class within the same package and any subclass of the class that contains the method within a different package can access the `protected` access modifier. Only the class that contains the method can access the `private` access modifier.

A method can generate a result, which it then returns to the calling code. You can make the return type any valid data type in Java, such as `String`, `byte`, or `boolean`. The body of a method that returns a value must also include a `return` statement. An error may occur if the data type of the returned value does not match the specified method declaration return type.

You must precede every `main` method with the `public` and `static` keywords. If you do not specify these keywords, the compiler may generate an error message.

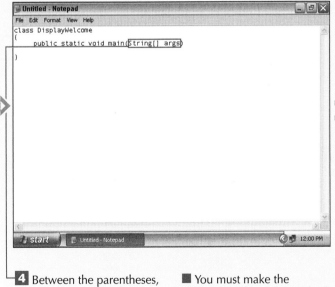

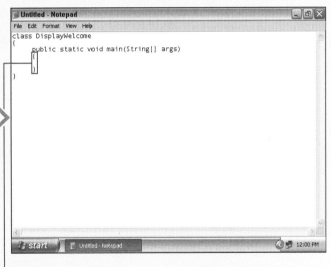

4 Between the parentheses, type any arguments the method requires.

■ You must make the arguments of a `main` method `String[] args`.

5 Type the opening and closing braces that will contain the body of the method.

Note: To create the body of the method, see the section "Create the Method Body" in this chapter.

■ Your method is complete.

CREATE THE METHOD BODY

You must create the body of a method, which contains the Java code that performs a task, within the method's braces {}. Java often uses the code in the body of a method to call, or access, another method. You can define the called method in the same class or in a different class. Re-using methods saves you time and effort when writing Java programs. For example, if you create a method that displays your name and e-mail address, you can use the same method in any Java application you create.

You can apply many classes and methods within the Java SDK to perform a wide variety of common tasks. For example, the Java SDK includes a class called Math, which contains several methods that perform mathematical calculations. To determine the square root of a number, you can simply call the sqrt method from the Math class.

You can use methods, for example System.out.print, to display information on a user's screen. Java automatically creates the system class, included in the Java SDK, when it executes the program. You use the out field to send information to the standard output device, typically the screen. The print member takes an argument, which you must enclose in parentheses. Use System.out.print to display any type of data in Java. When using System.out.print to display a string of text, you must enclose the string in quotation marks.

After you create the code for your Java program, save it as a text file with the .java extension. You must make the name of the file the same as the name of the first class defined in the code.

CREATE THE METHOD BODY

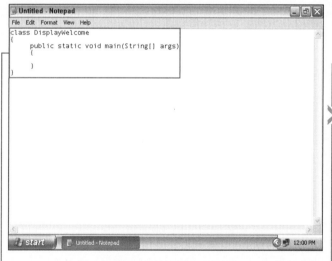

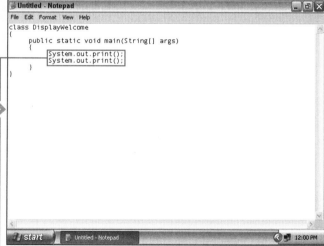

CREATE THE METHOD BODY CODE

1 Type the code that defines the class and the method you want to use.

2 In the body of the method, type the code for the task you want to perform.

■ This example uses **System.out.print** to display output.

Apply It

To start a new line at the end of a line of text when it displays, you can use the escape sequence \n. This escape sequence \n allows you to display text over multiple lines. You can also use System.out.println to start a new line.

TYPE THIS:

```
class MyIntroduction
{
    public static void main(String[] args)
    {
        System.out.println("My name is Andrew.");
        System.out.print("\nThis is my first Java program." + "\n");
    }
}
```

RESULT:

```
My name is Andrew.

This is my first Java program.
```

The classes and methods within the Java SDK are collectively known as the Java class library, also called the Java Application Programming Interface (API). The Java SDK documentation describes all the classes and methods available in the Java class library. If you have not already installed the Java SDK documentation, you can obtain the documentation on the Web at java.sun.com.

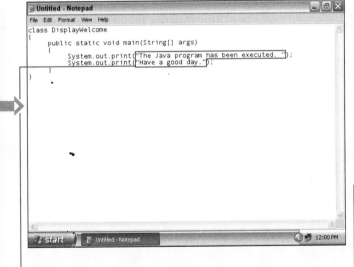

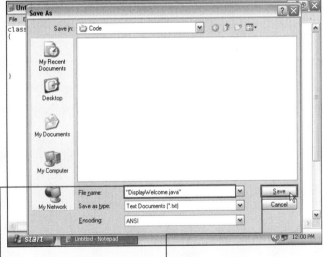

3 Type any arguments the code requires.

■ You must enclose string arguments within quotation marks.

SAVE JAVA CODE

1 Click File ➪ Save to open the Save As dialog box.

2 Type the name of the file.

■ Use the same name as that of the first class in the code and include the .java extension.

■ You may need to place quotation marks around the name of the file.

3 Click Save.

■ Notepad saves your code.

Note: You can now compile the Java code. See the section "Compile a Java Program" for more information.

COMPILE A JAVA PROGRAM

B y compiling Java code you can convert previously saved source code in a text file into bytecode. Bytecode contains instructions that the Java interpreter executes.

You need a Java compiler to compile Java code. The Java SDK includes a Java compiler application called `javac`, which you can execute from the command prompt. If you have a Windows operating system, you need to open a Command Prompt window to use `javac`.

To compile Java source code, you enter the name of the Java compiler, such as `javac`, at the command prompt, followed by the name of the file that stores the code you want to compile. The filename must have the `.java` extension. Depending on whether you have added the location of the Java SDK programs to your operating system's path variable, you may need to specify the full path to the Java compiler, which is typically c:\jdk1.3\bin\javac.

For information about setting the path variable, refer to the Java SDK installation instructions or your operating system's documentation.

Before compiling Java code, the Java compiler checks the code for errors. If it finds an error, the code does not compile and an error message displays.

If the Java code compiles successfully, Java saves the resulting bytecode in a new file with the `.class` extension. Java takes the name of the new file from the name of the file that stores the source code. For example, when Java compiles the code in a file named `Program.java` that contains a class called Program, it saves the bytecode in a file called `Program.class`. The filenames of Java programs are case sensitive on most platforms. After Java compiles the source code, you can execute the Java program. For more on executing the Java program, see the section "Execute a Java Program."

COMPILE A JAVA PROGRAM

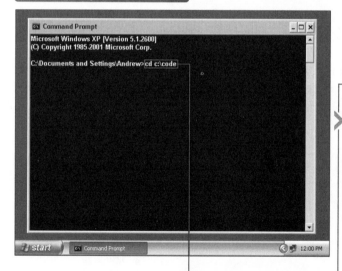

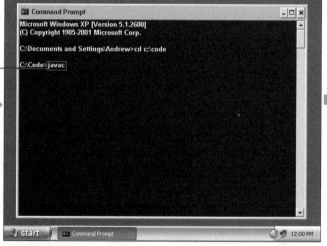

1 Open the window that allows you to work at the command prompt.

2 Navigate to the directory that stores the Java code you want to compile.

3 To compile the Java code using the `javac` compiler, type **javac**.

■ If you did not add the location of the `javac` compiler to your operating system's path variable, you need to type the full path of the `javac` program.

Extra

When compiling Java source code, you may see one of two main types of errors:

Java SDK Errors

If your operating system cannot locate the Java compiler, you may have experienced a problem during the Java SDK installation. Java SDK errors usually result in an error message such as "bad command or file name." To correct this type of error, first determine the correct path to the compiler. If you cannot locate the Java compiler, try re-installing the Java SDK. If you still cannot confirm the path to the compiler, check that you have not made any typing mistakes in the path.

Source Code Errors

A wide variety of errors can occur in Java source code. When the Java compiler finds an errorcode, it displays an error message that usually specifies the error type and where the compiler detected the error. For example, the error "Program.java:5: invalid method declaration" indicates that an error involving a method declaration was generated at line 5 in the `Program.java` file. It is important to note that the line number indicates the line that the compiler was processing when it detected the error, which is not necessarily the line that contains the error.

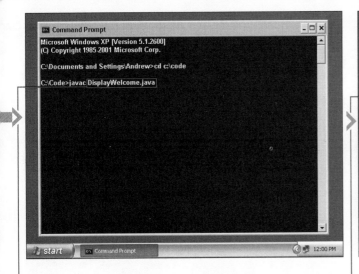

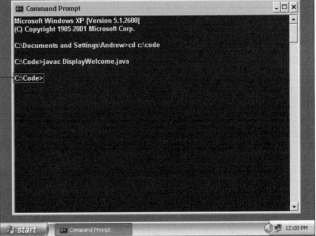

4 Type the name of the file that stores the Java code you want to compile, including the `.java` extension.

5 Press Enter to compile the Java code.

■ If the Java code successfully compiles, the command prompt reappears.

■ If an error message appears, the Java code did not successfully compile.

■ The Java program is now ready for execution.

Note: See the section "Execute a Java Program" for more information.

EXECUTE A JAVA PROGRAM

A fter the Java compiler converts the source code for a Java program into bytecode, you can execute, or run, the program. Executing an application enables the computer to read and process your code. The computer, in conjunction with the operating system, then performs the actions that you specify in the program. Some applications execute a task and then terminate, while others may continue executing until a user, or other condition, causes the application to cease execution.

The Java interpreter must process the bytecode before you can execute the code. The Java interpreter first checks the bytecode to ensure the code is safe to execute, and then it interprets and executes the instructions within the bytecode.

The Java interpreter executes the instructions in the bytecode in the *Java Virtual Machine*, or JVM, which is a controlled environment.

The Java interpreter, called `java`, comes with the Java SDK and is typically stored in the c:\jdk1.3\bin directory. Like the Java compiler, you must run the Java interpreter at the command prompt. Although a standalone program, you can integrate the Java interpreter into other programs, such as Web browsers. This allows you to execute your Java programs on different platforms.

To evoke the Java interpreter, you include the name of the interpreter and follow it with the name of the bytecode file. You should not include the `.class` extension. For example, to execute the instructions in the `Program.class` file, type **java Program**.

If the Java program executes successfully, the results of the program display. If the Java interpreter encounters any errors, it stops executing the program. Most of the errors that you encounter at this stage usually relate to the use of incorrect filenames or paths.

EXECUTE A JAVA PROGRAM

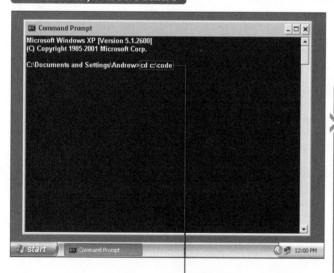

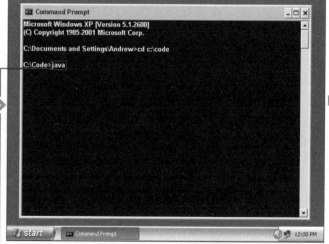

1 Open the window that allows you to work at the command prompt.

2 Navigate to the directory that stores the bytecode for the Java program you want to execute.

3 To execute the instructions in the bytecode using the Java interpreter, type **java**.

■ If you did not add the location of the Java interpreter to your operating system's path variable, you need to type the full path of the Java interpreter.

Apply It

Some text editors you use to create Java programs allow you to bind commands to unused keystrokes. Binding allows you to add commands that insert small templates for parts of Java syntax, increasing the speed and efficiency with which you can create Java code.

Example: Ctrl+C for a class:
```
public class Example {

}
```

Example: Ctrl+M for an empty main method:
```
public static void main(String[] argv) {

}
```

Example: Ctrl+P for a println statement:
```
System.out.println();
```

TYPE THIS:
```
Ctrl+C up-arrow,Ctrl+M up-arrow,Ctrl+P
```

RESULT:
```
public class Example {
   public static void main(String[] argv) {
       System.out.println();
   }
}
```

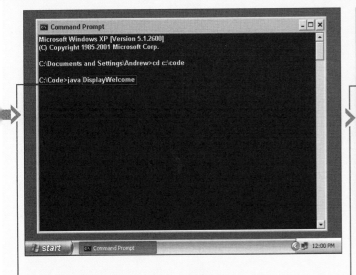

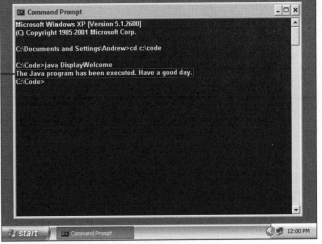

4 Type the name of the file that stores the bytecode for the Java program you want to execute.

5 Press Enter to execute the program.

■ The results of the program display on the screen.

CREATE AN OBJECT

When a class file exists, you can create an object that takes on the characteristics of the specifications laid out in the class file. For example, if a class file specifies the code for a method "displayName", then any object you create using that class file has a method called "displayName". For more information about creating a class file, see Chapter 2.

The first step in creating a simple object requires you to build a class file that contains a method. A simple class file includes a class and method declaration within the class file. The method body can include code that returns some information. In this section's example, the method simply returns a string that contains an e-mail address. You must compile the class file before you can use it to create an object. Because you do not execute the class file like a

standalone application, it does not need to use the main method. The second step entails building a standalone Java application that you then use to create, or *instantiate*, the object with the newly created class file. Because the purpose of this program is to make it an executable standalone application, you must include the method main.

A class file can create an object by using the new operator. The statement to create the new object starts with the name of the class. You follow this with the name you want to give to the object. The name you use for the object accesses the different characteristics of the object.

After you create the object, or *instantiate* the object, you can access the method in the object and then retrieve the information in the method.

CREATE AN OBJECT

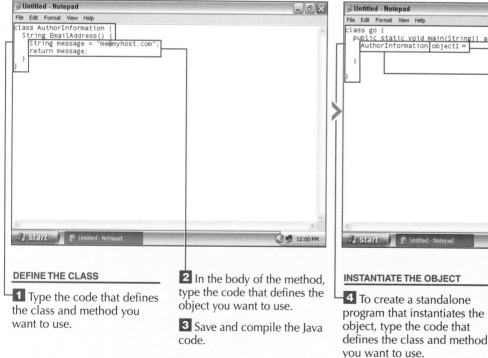

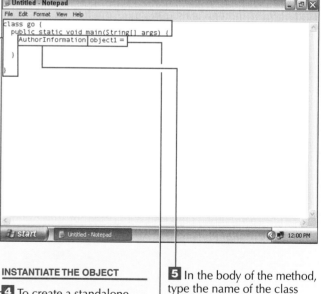

DEFINE THE CLASS

1 Type the code that defines the class and method you want to use.

2 In the body of the method, type the code that defines the object you want to use.

3 Save and compile the Java code.

INSTANTIATE THE OBJECT

4 To create a standalone program that instantiates the object, type the code that defines the class and method you want to use.

5 In the body of the method, type the name of the class you defined in step 1.

6 Type a name you want to use for the object, and follow it with **=**.

Extra

The directory you create to store files for your Java programs may depend on the setup of your computer and the tools, such as a Java development application, that you use to create your Java applications. In most cases, you can set up a specific directory dedicated to Java program development. When first learning to create Java applications, you may find it easier to store the class file that defines an object and the file that instantiates the object in the same directory. You often use packages to access class files that exist across multiple directories. For more information about using packages, see the section "Import a Package" in this chapter.

You very rarely find an object consisting of only a single method. In most cases, objects are more complex, containing a wide range of related methods and fields that dictate the behavior of the object.

The methods and fields of an object are also referred to as *members*. Methods and fields that are available when you instantiate an object and are unique to that object are called *instance members*.

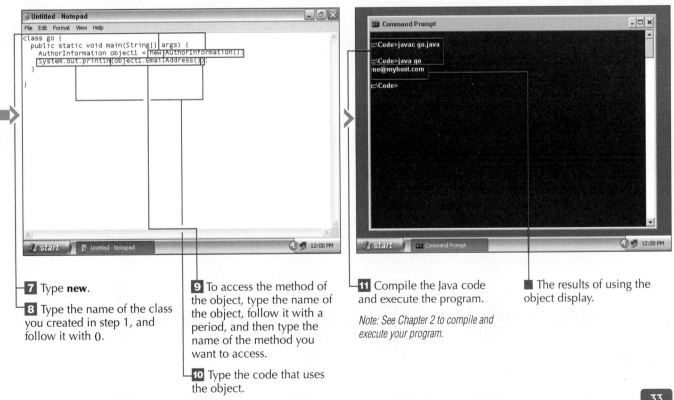

7 Type **new**.

8 Type the name of the class you created in step 1, and follow it with ().

9 To access the method of the object, type the name of the object, follow it with a period, and then type the name of the method you want to access.

10 Type the code that uses the object.

11 Compile the Java code and execute the program.

Note: See Chapter 2 to compile and execute your program.

■ The results of using the object display.

WORK WITH OBJECT FIELDS

You can create an object field, also referred to as a *data field*, to hold information that typically relates to the object. The information you contain in an object's fields determines the properties and attributes of the object.

When you create objects of the same class, the objects have the same methods, but some or all of the object fields may hold different information. For example, each object you create from the `Employee` class may have an object field called `empNumber` that stores the unique employee number for each object.

You must declare object fields in the class body outside of any methods. This allows you to use the field as soon as you create the object. You can specify an access modifier for an object field you create, as well as the storage field's data type. The access modifier determines what code has access to the field.

You create most object fields with an initial value. You can later change the value of an object field as you would change the value of a variable. Changing the value of an object field may alter the way some of the methods of the object behave. Object fields may also hold constant data, which you cannot change.

You can use the `dot` operator (`.`) to access an object field in a program. When specifying the object field, you separate the field name from the object name by a dot, such as `object.field`. The object name is the name that you gave the object when you first created it.

Unlike methods, you do not follow object field names with parentheses. You can have object fields and methods that share the same name in a program.

WORK WITH OBJECT FIELDS

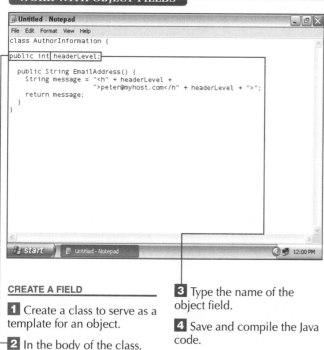

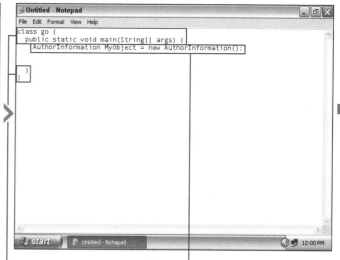

CREATE A FIELD

1 Create a class to serve as a template for an object.

2 In the body of the class, type the access modifier and data type for the object field you want to create.

3 Type the name of the object field.

4 Save and compile the Java code.

USING AN OBJECT FIELD

5 To create a standalone Java program, type the code that declares the class and `main` method.

6 In the body of the `main` method, type the code to create an object using the class you created in step 1.

Extra

You can set a default value for an object field by using a *constructor*. A constructor is a special type of method that always executes each time you create an object. This makes constructors useful in performing initialization tasks for new objects, such as setting up a connection to a database. A constructor method must have the same name as the class for which it is the constructor.

Example:
```java
class AuthorInformation {
  public int headerLevel;

  public AuthorInformation() {
    headerLevel = 3;
  }
  public String EmailAddress() {
    String message = "<h" + headerLevel +
                            ">sandman@myhost.com</h" + headerLevel + ">";

    return message;
  }
}
```

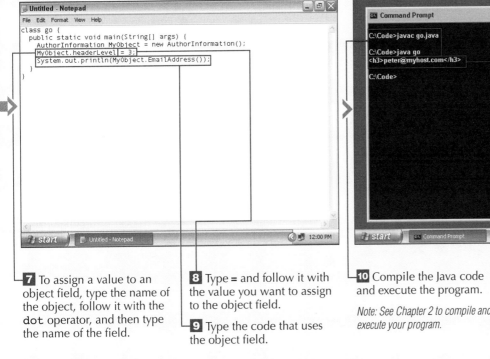

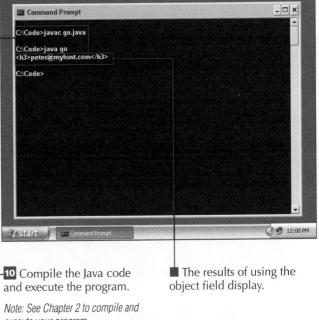

7 To assign a value to an object field, type the name of the object, follow it with the **dot** operator, and then type the name of the field.

8 Type **=** and follow it with the value you want to assign to the object field.

9 Type the code that uses the object field.

10 Compile the Java code and execute the program.

Note: See Chapter 2 to compile and execute your program.

■ The results of using the object field display.

SPECIFY THE DATA TYPE FOR A VARIABLE

Java is a "strongly typed language," which means that you must specify a data type for each variable that you use in a Java program. This distinguishes Java from many other programming languages, such as Perl, which do not require you to assign variables to data types.

Variables can use eight basic data types, called *primitive types*. The data type you specify for a variable determines the range of values that the variable can store and the amount of memory, measured in bits, that the variable requires. For example, a variable with the `byte` data type can store a number between -128 and 127, and requires 8 bits of memory.

Each primitive data type has a default value. If you declare a variable as an object field without assigning a value, Java assigns the default value for the variable's data type to the variable.

The operating system or compiler that you use does not affect the specifications for data types in Java, such as

memory requirements and default values. This ensures that a data type has the same meaning when a user executes a program on different computers.

Specifying the data type for a variable requires that you know in advance the types of values that you want to store in the variable throughout your program. Once you declare a variable, you cannot change the data type for the variable. If you want to convert the value in a variable to a different data type, you must assign the value to a new variable that uses the desired data type. This process is called *casting*. When converting a value to a new data type, make sure that the conversion does not result in an unintended loss of data. For example, converting the number 13.56 to an integer value, which does not allow any numbers after the decimal, results in a new value of 13.

Variable names can consist of any number of letters, numbers, or underscore characters and must start with a dollar symbol, underscore, or a letter.

SPECIFY THE DATA TYPE FOR A VARIABLE

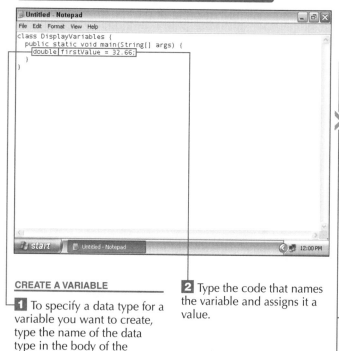

CREATE A VARIABLE

1 To specify a data type for a variable you want to create, type the name of the data type in the body of the method.

2 Type the code that names the variable and assigns it a value.

CONVERT A VALUE TO A DIFFERENT DATA TYPE

3 Type the code that declares a variable, which stores the converted value.

4 Type the name of the variable you created in step 3, and follow it with a =.

5 Type the data type to which you want to convert the value enclosing it in parentheses.

6 Type the name of the variable that stores the value you want to convert.

Extra

You can use eight primitive data types as the value for a variable.

PRIMITIVE DATA TYPES			
TYPE	SIZE IN BITS	DEFAULT VALUE	POSSIBLE VALUES
boolean	1	false	'true' or 'false'
char	16	\u0000	unicode character, '\u0000' to 'uFFFF'
byte	8	0	-128 to 127
short	16	0	-32,768 to 32,767
int	32	0	-2,147,483,648 to 2,147,483,647
long	64	0	-9,223,372,036,854,775,808 to 9,223,372,036,854,775,807
float	32	0.0	±1.4E-45 to ±3.4028235E+38
double	64	0.0	±4.9E-324 to ±1.7976931348623157E+308

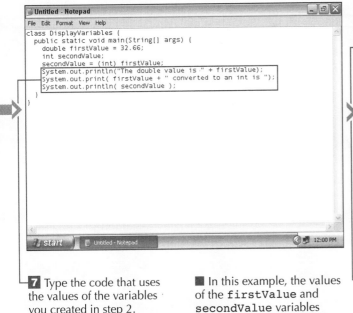

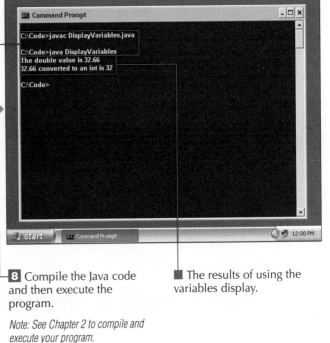

7 Type the code that uses the values of the variables you created in step 2.

■ In this example, the values of the `firstValue` and `secondValue` variables display.

8 Compile the Java code and then execute the program.

Note: See Chapter 2 to compile and execute your program.

■ The results of using the variables display.

WORK WITH STRINGS

Almost all Java applications require you to create and work with string values. A *string* contains textual data. A collection of characters, a *string* contains any combination of letters, numbers, and special characters, such as $, & or #.

Before you can use a string variable in a Java program, you must declare the string variable, a process similar to that of declaring other types of variables. To declare a string variable, use the name String, and follow it with the variable name. The capital S at the beginning of the keyword String indicates that a string variable is an object of the String class. The String class is contained in the java.lang package available to all Java programs as part of the standard class library.

After you declare a string variable, you can assign it a value using the assignment operator (=). You must enclose a string value in double quotation marks ("), which identify

the beginning and end of the string and allow Java to work with the string as one piece of information.

You can use the concatenation operator (+) to join multiple strings together. You can also use the concatenation operator to join other types of variables and values together.

You can insert special characters called *escape sequences* into a string. Escape sequences allow you to include special characters in the string. Commonly used escape sequences include \t, which inserts a tab, and \n, which starts a new line.

If you installed the documentation package available for the Java Software Development Kit (JDK or SDK), you can find more information about the String class under the main JDK directory at \docs\api\java\lang\String.html. You can also find documentation for JDK at the java.sun.com Web site.

WORK WITH STRINGS

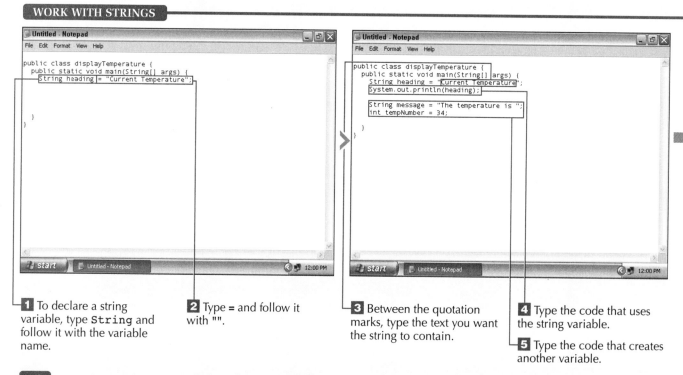

1 To declare a string variable, type **String** and follow it with the variable name.

2 Type = and follow it with "".

3 Between the quotation marks, type the text you want the string to contain.

4 Type the code that uses the string variable.

5 Type the code that creates another variable.

Apply It

You can determine the number of characters a string contains by using the `length` method of the `String` class.

TYPE THIS:

```java
class DisplayVariables {
  public static void main(String[] args) {
    String message = "The temperature is ";
    System.out.print("The length of the string is ");
    System.out.println(message.length());

  }
}
```

RESULT:

```
The length of the string is 19
```

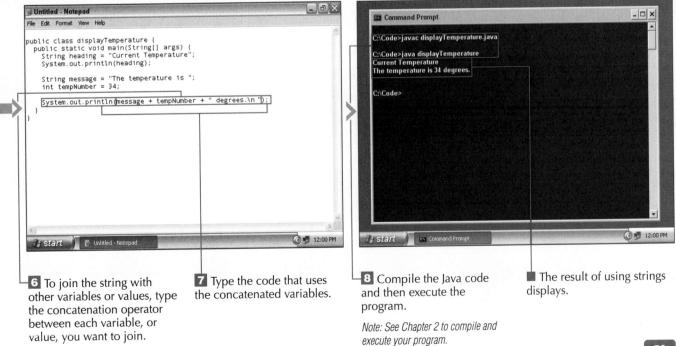

6 To join the string with other variables or values, type the concatenation operator between each variable, or value, you want to join.

7 Type the code that uses the concatenated variables.

8 Compile the Java code and then execute the program.

Note: See Chapter 2 to compile and execute your program.

■ The result of using strings displays.

CALL A METHOD

Once you create a method, you need to *call* it, a process by which Java accesses and executes the code in the method. The code in a method does not execute until you call the method.

To call a method in the same class in which you declared it, you can create an object of the class and then type the name of the object followed by a period and then the name of the method followed by a set of parentheses. Make sure you type the method name exactly as you type it in the code that declares the method.

Some methods require you to include arguments within the parentheses that follow the method name. For information about passing arguments to methods, see the section "Using Return Values and Arguments." For more on creating a method, see Chapter 2.

When you call a method, the code within the method executes as if you had typed the code in the location where

you called the method. Once Java finishes processing the code in the method, it continues execution from the line following the method call.

In some programs, you may need to call a method that you have declared in a different class. The access modifiers you use in method declaration determine the locations from which you can call the method.

You can also group classes that contain methods into a package. You may need to specify the package in which the class containing the method is located. For more information about packages, see the section "Create a Package."

In addition to calling methods you have created, you can also call methods that the Java class library provides. For example, `System.out.println()` calls a Java class library method, which you can use to display data. For more information about the Java class library, see Chapter 2.

CALL A METHOD

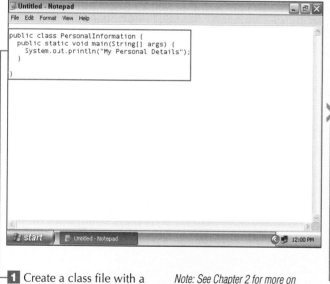

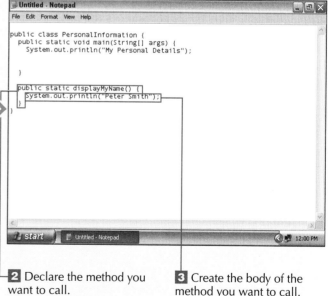

1 Create a class file with a `main` method.

Note: See Chapter 2 for more on creating a class file.

2 Declare the method you want to call.

3 Create the body of the method you want to call.

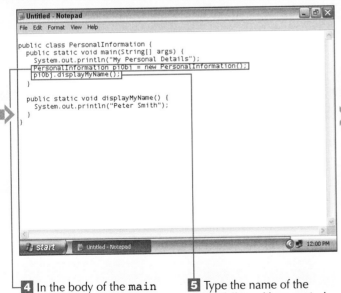

Apply It

A *static method* is a method that is the same for each object that uses the method. You denote a static method by the keyword static in the method declaration. If you declare a static method that you want to call in a different class, you must specify the class that contains the method you want to call. You use the dot operator (.) to link the class name and the method name. You must create any methods you intend to call from another class with the public access modifier. You can create a class that accesses the methods of the created class in the example that follows.

TYPE THIS:

```
public class CallingClassMethods {
  public static void main(String[] args) {
    System.out.println("My Personal Details");

    PersonalInformation.DisplayMyName();
  }
}
```

RESULT:

```
My Personal Details
Peter Smith
```

4 In the body of the **main** method, create an object from the class.

5 Type the name of the object followed by a period and the name of the method you want to call, and follow it with a set of parentheses.

6 Compile the Java code and then execute the program.

Note: See Chapter 2 to compile and execute your program.

■ The result of executing the code in the method displays.

USING RETURN VALUES AND ARGUMENTS

You can have a method return a value to the code. You might make a return value the result of a calculation or procedure, or make it indicate whether Java successfully completed a process.

When you declare the method, you must specify the return value's data type. You can make return values any valid data type in Java, such as `String`, `byte`, or `boolean`. An error may occur if the returned value's data type does not match the specified return type in the method declaration. The Java compiler generates an error when you attempt to compile the Java code that contains the mismatched data types.

Java returns information from a method using the keyword `return`. Once the `return` statement executes, the processing of the method ends and the value in the `return` statement passes back to the calling statement.

You can use a method with a return value as if it were a variable. For example, you can display the value that a

method returns using `System.out.print`. You can also assign the value that the method returns to a variable.

You can also pass one or more values, called *arguments*, to a created method. Passing arguments to a method allows you to use one method throughout a program to process different data.

To define a method that accepts an argument, you include a data type and variable name in the parentheses at the end of the method name in a method declaration. When you call the method, you include the data you want to pass in the parentheses following the method name.

You can pass any type of data to a method, but it must match the data type you specify in the method declaration. For example, if a method expects an integer value for calculation, passing a string value to the method causes an error to occur.

USING RETURN VALUES AND ARGUMENTS

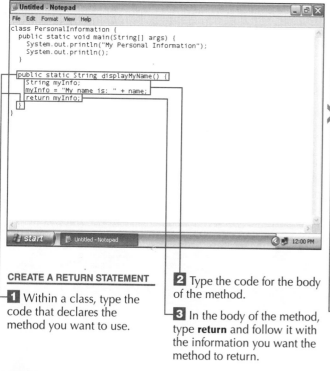

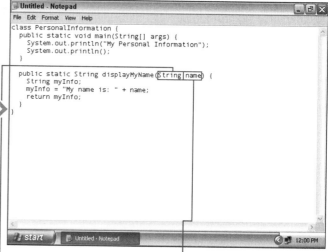

CREATE A RETURN STATEMENT

1 Within a class, type the code that declares the method you want to use.

2 Type the code for the body of the method.

3 In the body of the method, type **return** and follow it with the information you want the method to return.

PREPARE A METHOD TO ACCEPT ARGUMENTS

4 Between the parentheses, following the method name in the method declaration, specify the data type of the argument that the method will accept.

5 Type the name of the variable that will store the value of the argument.

■ When preparing a method to accept multiple arguments, you must separate each data type and variable pair with a comma.

A method can have more than one `return` statement. You commonly find this in methods that use conditional statements. Although a method can have more than one `return` statement, Java only executes one `return` statement. When Java encounters a `return` statement, it terminates the execution of the method.

TYPE THIS:

```java
class MakeList {
  public static void main(String[] args) {
    System.out.println(CheckAge(29));
  }
  static String CheckAge(int age) {
    if (age > 21) {
      return "You may take the survey";
    } else {
      return "You are too young to take the survey";
    }
  }
}
```

RESULT:

```
You may take the survey
```

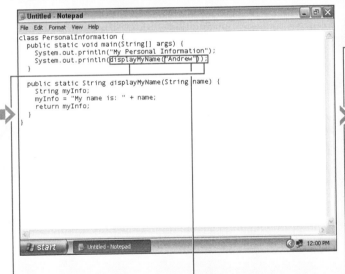

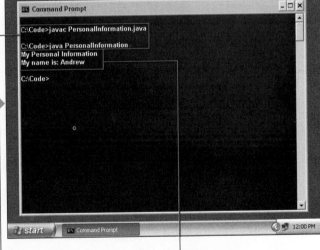

CALL A METHOD USING ARGUMENTS

6 In the body of the `main` method, type the code that calls the method you want to use.

7 Between the parentheses following the method name, type the arguments you want to pass to the method.

■ When passing multiple arguments, you must separate the arguments with a comma.

8 Save the Java code.

9 Compile the Java code and then execute the program.

Note: See Chapter 2 to compile and execute your program.

■ The result of passing arguments to a method using a return value displays.

USING THE IF STATEMENT

Y ou can use an `if` statement to determine whether a condition is true or false. You can make the condition as complex as you want provided that it always produces either a true or false value. With a true condition, the section of code directly following the `if` statement executes. For example, you can create a program that displays a "Good Morning" message when a user runs the program between 5:00 AM and 11:59 AM. With a false condition, code from the `if` statement does not execute.

If the code consists of more than one line, you must enclose the section of code you want to execute in braces { }, referred to as a *statement block*. You must enclose the condition for an `if` statement in parentheses ().

If you want an `if` statement to execute a block when a condition remains false, you must include an `else` clause. Using an `if` statement with an `else` clause allows you to

execute one of two sections of code, depending on the outcome of testing the condition. If the condition is true, the statement block directly following the `if` statement executes. If the condition remains false, the statement block directly following the `else` clause executes. Using an `else` clause ensures that a section of code executes regardless of the testing condition's outcome. For example, you can have a program display a "Good Morning" message or a "Good Evening" message, depending on the time set on the computer that executes the program.

To make your code easier to read and understand, always indent the statement block that contains the code that you want to execute. Many programmers also use spaces within statements to make the statements easier to read. The Java compiler ignores whitespace characters, such as tabs and blank lines, so these characters do not affect the function or performance of your Java program.

USING THE IF STATEMENT

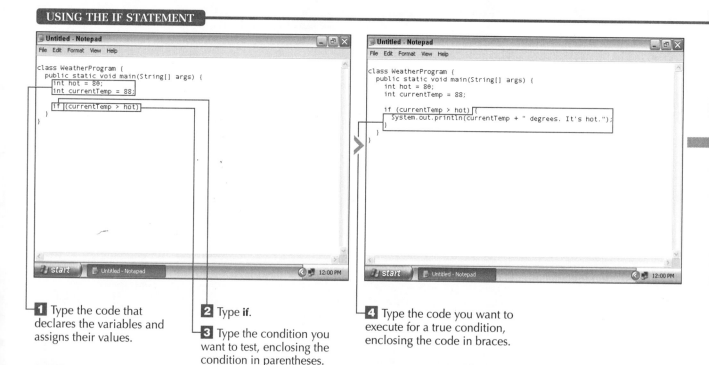

1 Type the code that declares the variables and assigns their values.

2 Type **if**.

3 Type the condition you want to test, enclosing the condition in parentheses.

4 Type the code you want to execute for a true condition, enclosing the code in braces.

Apply It

If you need to execute only one line of code based on a condition being true, you can place the code that you want to execute on the same line as the `if` statement. You can also place the condition code on the next line without the braces {}.

YOU CAN TYPE THIS:

```
if (currentTemp > hot) {
   System.out.println("It's hot.");
}
```

AS THIS:

```
if (currentTemp > hot) System.out.println("It's hot.");
```

Nested `if` statements allow you to specify multiple conditions for an `if` statement at the same time. Java evaluates each `if` statement only if the previous `if` statement is true. If all of the `if` statements remain true, a section of code executes. If any of the `if` statements are false, code from the `if` statements does not execute.

TYPE THIS:

```
int hot = 80, veryHot = 85, currentTemp = 88;
if (currentTemp > hot) {
   System.out.print(currentTemp + " degrees. It's ");
   if (currentTemp > veryHot) {
      System.out.print("very, very ");
   }
   System.out.println("hot.");
}
```

RESULT:

```
88 degrees. It's very, very hot.
```

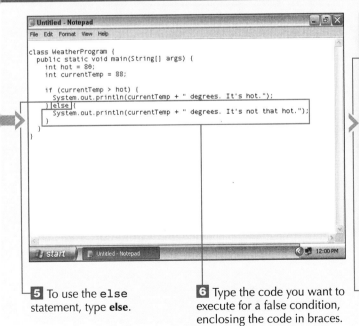

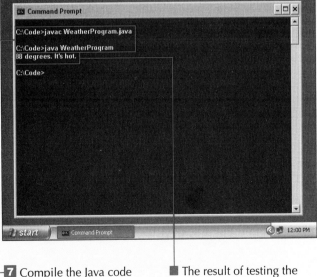

5 To use the `else` statement, type **else**.

6 Type the code you want to execute for a false condition, enclosing the code in braces.

7 Compile the Java code and then execute the program.

■ The result of testing the condition displays on the screen.

Note: See Chapter 2 to compile and execute your program.

USING THE FOR STATEMENT

Programmers often need to execute the same statement or block of statements several times. The `for` statement allows you to create a loop that repeats the execution of code a specific number of times. For example, you may want to create five line breaks in an XML document. Instead of typing the code that creates a line break five times, you can create a loop that executes the code to create a line break and then repeats the loop until the value of a counter reaches five.

When creating a `for` statement, you usually use a variable, called an *iterator*, which acts as a counter for the loop. You use an *initialization expression* to specify a starting value for the iterator.

You must also specify a condition that evaluates the value of the iterator. For true conditions, the loop executes and processes the block of code you specify. For false conditions, the block of code does not execute and the loop ends.

You use the re-initialization expression to modify the value of the iterator. For example, if you use the increment operator (++) in the re-initialization expression, the value of the iterator increments by one each time Java executes the loop. The expression `i++` functions the same as `i = i + 1`.

You place the block of code, known as the *body* of the loop, you want to execute between braces `{}`. You should indent the code in the body of a loop to make the code easier to read and understand. The code in the body of a `for` loop can include any valid Java statements, such as calls to other methods. You may also place another loop within the body of a `for` loop, a process referred to as *nesting*. You should avoid having too many nested loops because it makes the program difficult to read and troubleshoot.

USING THE FOR STATEMENT

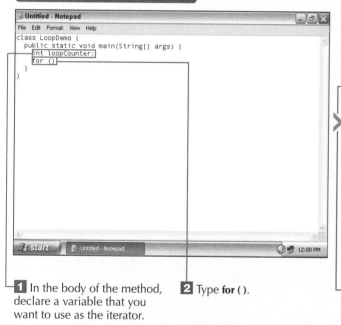

1 In the body of the method, declare a variable that you want to use as the iterator.

2 Type **for ( )**.

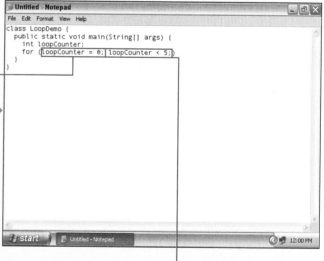

3 Type the initialization expression that specifies the starting value of the iterator and follow it with a semicolon.

4 Type the condition that evaluates the value of the iterator and follow it with a semicolon.

Extra

Java can still execute a loop even if you omit one or more expressions from the `for` statement. However, you must specify any expressions you omit from the `for` statement elsewhere in the code. For example, if you specify the starting value of the iterator in another part of your code, you do not need to include an initialization expression in the `for` statement. Remember to still include all the necessary semicolons in the `for` statement.

Example:
```
int loopCounter = 3;
for (; loopCounter < 5; loopCounter++) {
  System.out.println(loopCounter);
}
```

If a `for` statement has no condition and you do not specify a condition in the body of the loop, Java assumes that the condition is always true and creates an infinite loop, a situation that you want to avoid.

Example:
```
int loopCounter;
for (loopCounter = 1; ; loopCounter++) {
  System.out.println(loopCounter);
}
```

If you have a single line of code in the body of a `for` loop, you forego enclosing the line in braces. Although optional in this situation, most programmers use the braces to keep their code consistent.

Example:
```
for (loopCounter = 0; loopCounter < 10; loopCounter++)
    System.out.println(loopCounter);
```

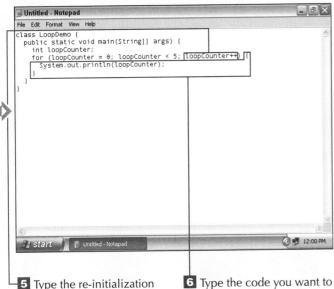

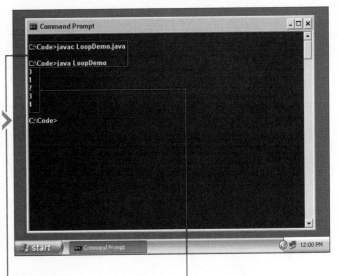

5 Type the re-initialization expression that modifies the value of the iterator each time the loop executes.

6 Type the code you want to execute as long as the specified condition remains true, enclosing the code in braces.

7 Compile the Java code and execute the program.

Note: See Chapter 2 to compile and execute your program.

■ The result of using the `for` statement displays.

USING THE WHILE OR DO WHILE LOOP

The `while` statement allows you to create a conditional loop that executes a section of code as long as a specified condition remains true. Conditions often test the value of an iterator. For example, you may want to process a pay statement for each of the 100 employees in a company. Instead of typing the code that processes a pay statement 100 times, you can create a loop to process the pay statement for each employee. The condition checks how many pay statements Java has processed. After the 100th pay statement, the condition evaluates as false and the loop ends.

You enclose the body of a `while` loop, which contains the section of code you want to execute, in braces `{ }`. If the condition tests the value of an iterator, the loop body also contains code to alter the value of the iterator. You can increase or decrease the value of an iterator. As long as the condition remains true, the section of code within the body of the loop executes. When Java reaches the end of the

loop body, it re-evaluates the condition. If the condition still holds true, the section of code executes again. If the condition turns false, the section of code in the loop body does not execute and the loop ends.

When creating a loop using the `while` statement, you make sure that Java evaluates the testing condition as false at some point. If the condition always remains true, the code in the loop body executes indefinitely. This kind of never-ending loop is known as an *infinite loop*. If you create an infinite loop, you must forcibly stop the execution of the Java program.

Depending on the result of the condition to be tested, the code within the `while` loop may never execute. If you need the code in the `while` loop to execute at least once, regardless of how Java evaluates the condition, you can use a `do while` loop.

USING THE WHILE OR DO WHILE LOOP

```
class WhileDemo {
  public static void main(String[] args) {
    int loopCounter = 1;
  }
}
```

```
class WhileDemo {
  public static void main(String[] args) {
    int loopCounter = 1;
    while (loopCounter <= 5)
  }
}
```

1 In the body of the method, type the code that creates an iterator and assigns it a value.

2 Type **while ()**.

3 Type the condition you want to evaluate.

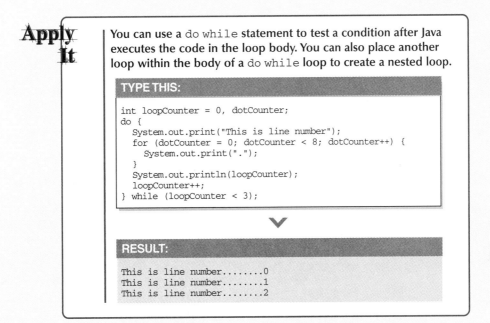

You can use a `do while` statement to test a condition after Java executes the code in the loop body. You can also place another loop within the body of a `do while` loop to create a nested loop.

TYPE THIS:

```
int loopCounter = 0, dotCounter;
do {
  System.out.print("This is line number");
  for (dotCounter = 0; dotCounter < 8; dotCounter++) {
    System.out.print(".");
  }
  System.out.println(loopCounter);
  loopCounter++;
} while (loopCounter < 3);
```

RESULT:

```
This is line number........0
This is line number........1
This is line number........2
```

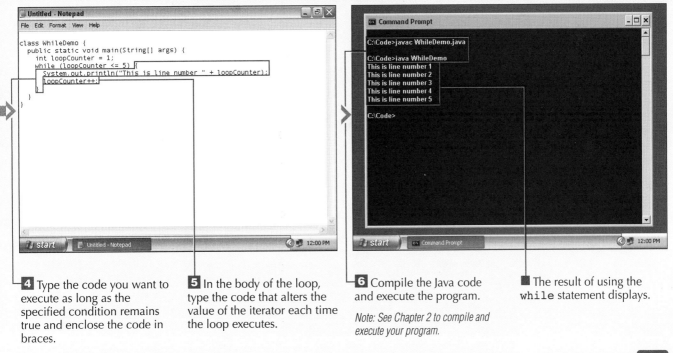

4 Type the code you want to execute as long as the specified condition remains true and enclose the code in braces.

5 In the body of the loop, type the code that alters the value of the iterator each time the loop executes.

6 Compile the Java code and execute the program.

Note: See Chapter 2 to compile and execute your program.

■ The result of using the `while` statement displays.

USING THE SWITCH STATEMENT

The `switch` statement allows you to execute a section of code, depending on the value of an expression you specify. When Java executes a `switch` statement, it compares the value of the expression against a number of possible choices, called `case` *values*. If the value of the expression matches a `case` value, the section of code following the `case` value executes. For example, you can create a `switch` statement that displays a specific message, depending on information that a user enters.

To use the `switch` statement, you must first specify the expression you want to use. The value of the expression must have a `char`, `byte`, `short,` or `int` data type. After specifying the expression, you must create the `case` values against which Java compares the expression. The expression must match the `case` value exactly. You cannot use an indefinite expression, such as `x > 10`, for a `case` value. Using an indefinite expression results in your code generating an error.

The `switch` statement compares the value of the expression to each `case` value in order, from top to bottom. You can place the `case` statements in any order, but to make your program more efficient, you should place the most commonly used `case` values first.

To prevent the `switch` statement from testing the remaining `case` values after Java finds a match, you should use the `break` statement to skip the remaining `case` statements and continue processing the code after the closing brace of the `switch` statement. You should use the `break` statement as the last statement for each `case` statement. Although the last `case` statement does not require a `break` statement, some programmers include it to be consistent. Including a `break` statement helps you remember to include the `break` statement if you later add another `case` statement to the `switch` statement.

USING THE SWITCH STATEMENT

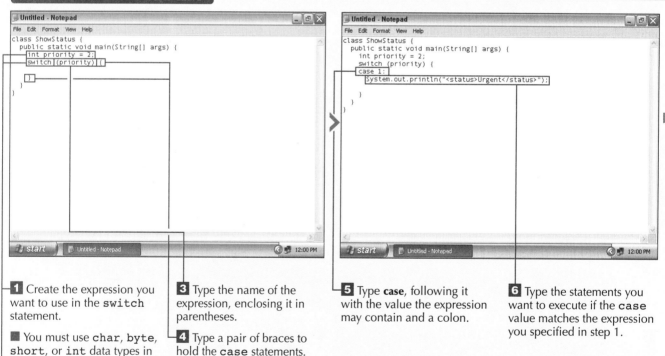

1 Create the expression you want to use in the **switch** statement.

■ You must use **char**, **byte**, **short**, or **int** data types in the expression.

2 Type **switch**.

3 Type the name of the expression, enclosing it in parentheses.

4 Type a pair of braces to hold the **case** statements.

5 Type **case**, following it with the value the expression may contain and a colon.

6 Type the statements you want to execute if the **case** value matches the expression you specified in step 1.

Extra

You can execute one section of code for multiple `case` statements, which allows you to use multiple conditions for the `case` values. You must follow each `case` statement you want to match with a colon.

Example:
```
switch (gender)
{
        case M: case m:
                System.out.println("Male");
                break;
        case F: case f:
                System.out.println("Female");
                break;
}
```

You can include a default statement in a `switch` statement if you want to execute specific code when none of the other `case` values match the specified expression. You must place the default statement last in the `switch` statement structure.

Example:
```
switch (priority)
{
        case 1:
                System.out.println("Urgent");
                break;
        case 2:
                System.out.println("Not Important");
                break;
        default:
                System.out.println("Ignore");
}
```

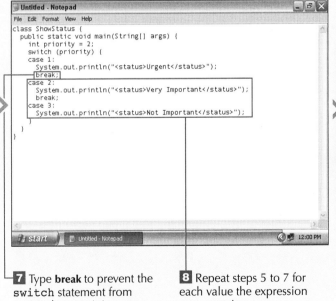

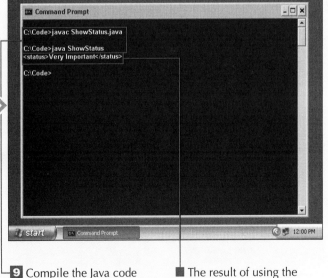

7 Type **break** to prevent the `switch` statement from testing the remaining **case** values after a section of code executes.

8 Repeat steps 5 to 7 for each value the expression may contain.

9 Compile the Java code and then execute the program.

Note: See Chapter 2 to compile and execute your program.

■ The result of using the `switch` statement displays.

CREATE AN ARRAY

An array stores a set of related values, called *elements*, that are of the same data type. For example, an array can store the name of each day of the week. Using an array allows you to work with multiple values at the same time.

The first step in creating an array involves declaring an array variable. You do this by specifying the data type of the values that you want the array to store and following it with brackets [ ]. For more information about data types, see the section "Specify the Data Type for a Variable." You must also give the array a name. As with variable names, array names can consist of any number of letters, numbers or underscore characters and must start with a dollar symbol, underscore, or a letter.

Next, you can define the array. You do this using the new operator, which indicates that you want to set aside space in memory for the new array. You must also specify the number of elements that you want the array to store.

Java identifies each element in an array with an index number, which starts at 0, not 1. For example, an array that you define as items = new int[6] contains six elements indexed from 0 to 5.

You can specify the values you want each element to store. You must enclose string values in quotation marks.

To access an individual element in an array, you use the name of the array followed by the index number for the element enclosed in brackets. When you use brackets in this context, you refer to them as the *array access operator*. You can use an array element in a Java program as you would use a variable. For more information about using variables, see the section "Specify the Data Type for a Variable." Changing the value of an element does not affect the other elements in the array.

CREATE AN ARRAY

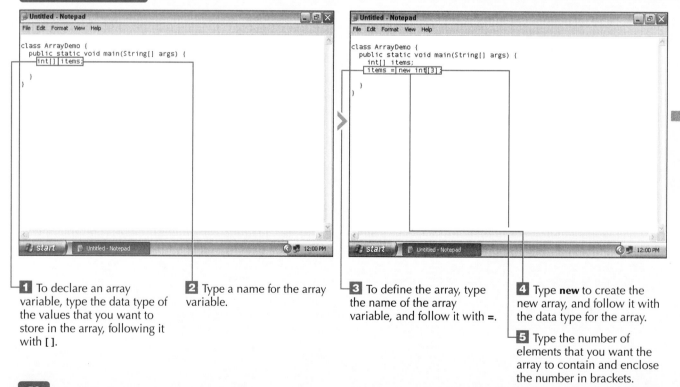

1 To declare an array variable, type the data type of the values that you want to store in the array, following it with [ ].

2 Type a name for the array variable.

3 To define the array, type the name of the array variable, and follow it with =.

4 Type **new** to create the new array, and follow it with the data type for the array.

5 Type the number of elements that you want the array to contain and enclose the number in brackets.

Apply It

Because it is a truly object-oriented programming language, Java treats arrays as objects. The `length` member of the array object allows you to determine the number of elements in an array.

TYPE THIS:

```
class ArrayLength {
  public static void main(String[] args) {
    int[] items;
    items = new int[3];

    items[0] = 331;
    items[1] = 324;
    items[2] = 298;

    int total = items.length;
    System.out.print("Number of items = " + total);
  }
}
```

RESULT:

```
Number of items = 3
```

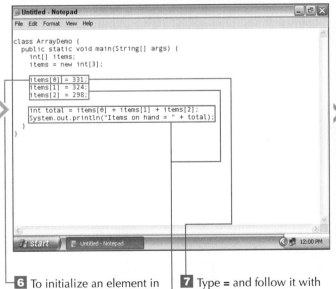

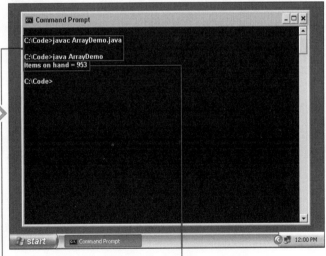

6 To initialize an element in the array, type the name of the array, and follow it with the element's index number, enclosing the number in brackets.

7 Type = and follow it with the value for the element.

8 Repeat steps 6 and 7 for each element in the array.

9 Type the code that accesses elements in the array.

10 Compile the Java code and then execute the program.

Note: See Chapter 2 to compile and execute your program.

■ The results of creating an array and accessing elements display.

CREATE A PACKAGE

If your Java program contains a large number of class files, you can organize the files by grouping them into *packages*. Keeping your files organized allows you to more efficiently locate needed information in those files. A package stores a collection of related classes. For example, you can group all the shipping-related classes in a program into a package called shipping.

Packages allow you to use classes with identical names in the same Java program. To prevent naming conflicts, Java normally does not permit you to use classes with the same name in one program. However, when you place classes with the same name in different packages, you can use the classes in a single application without conflict.

When creating a package, you must build a directory to store all the classes for the package. The name of the directory you create should describe the classes the

package will store. You must also make the name of the directory the same as the added package name. You must save all the classes belonging to a package in the same directory.

You add a package statement to a class file to specify the name of the package to which you want the class to belong. The package statement must match the first line of code in the class file. If the package name consists of multiple words, separate the words with dots. Each word in the name must represent an actual directory on your computer. For example, Java stores classes that you place in a package called `myapps.internet` in a directory called `internet`, located within the `myapps` directory.

To use a class stored in a package in an application, you specify the package name and the class name.

CREATE A PACKAGE

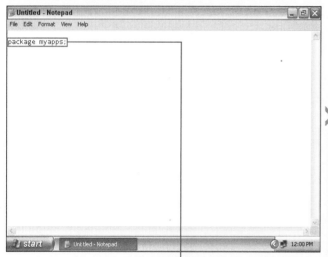

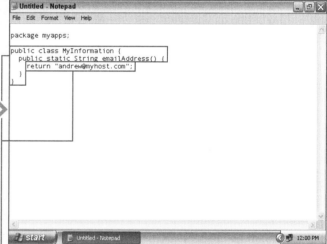

STORE A CLASS

1 Create a directory to store classes for the package.

2 On the first line type **package** and follow it with the name of the package you want to create.

Note: You must name the package with the same names as the directory you created in step 1.

3 Type the code that declares a class and a method that you want to use in other Java programs.

4 In the body of the method, type the code for the task you want to perform.

5 Save the code in the directory you created in step 1.

■ Java saves the code.

Extra

Java specifies that every class must belong to a package. If you do not specify a package for a class, it always belongs to the default package, whose name is the empty string " " .

If you use a Java development tool, such as an Integrated Development Environment (IDE), Java may have already set up package directories within a main class directory for you. You can usually change the configuration of the program to specify another directory as the main class directory.

The method you employ to create directories depends on the type of operating system you have on your computer. If you have a UNIX-based operating system, such as Linux, you might use the `mkdir` command to create directories in a terminal window. If you have an operating system with a Graphical User Interface (GUI), such as Macintosh or Windows, you can utilize program-provided graphical tools to create directories.

When you use a stored class in a package, you must specify the name of the package in addition to the class name. To avoid specifying the package name each time you use the class, you can import the package into your program. For more information on importing packages, see the section "Import a Package."

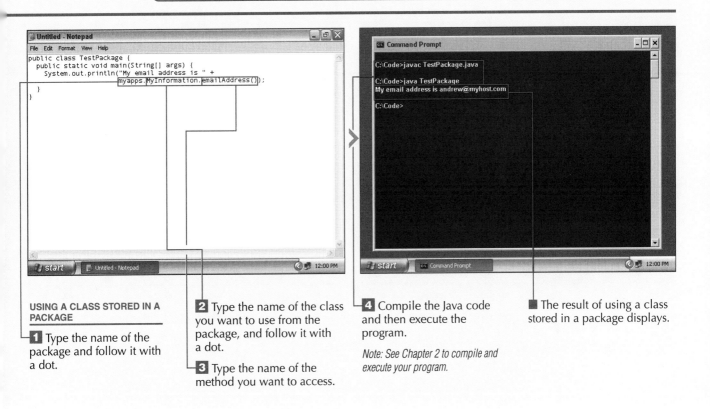

USING A CLASS STORED IN A PACKAGE

1 Type the name of the package and follow it with a dot.

2 Type the name of the class you want to use from the package, and follow it with a dot.

3 Type the name of the method you want to access.

4 Compile the Java code and then execute the program.

Note: See Chapter 2 to compile and execute your program.

■ The result of using a class stored in a package displays.

IMPORT A PACKAGE

To reduce the amount of typing required to create a Java application, you can import a class from a previously created package into a Java program. You may find this helpful if you plan to use the class several times in the program. You must first create the package you want to import. For more information about creating a package, see "Create a Package" in this chapter. Once you import a package and a class, you do not need to specify the name of the package each time you want to access the class.

You use the `import` statement to import a package and usually place it at the beginning of your Java program. If your program contains a package statement, you must place the `import` statement after the package statement. You can import several packages and classes into one Java program. Each package you want to import must have its own `import`

statement. To prevent naming conflicts, you should not import two classes with the same name into one program.

To avoid generating an error during code compilation, you must check the availability of the package directory and the class that you want to import. Although not a concern in most situations, availability becomes important if you develop programs on different computers or different platforms.

When importing a class from a package, you must specify the name of the class you want to import.

In addition to packages and classes that you create, you can import packages and classes from the Java class library. For more information about the packages included in the Java class library, see Chapter 2.

IMPORT A PACKAGE

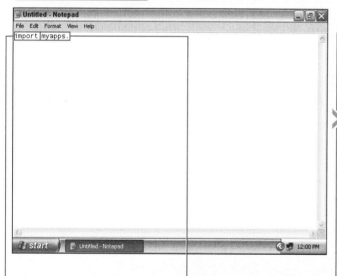

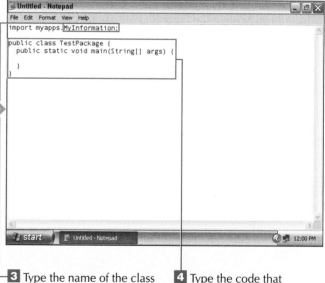

■1 To import a package, type **import** in the first line of code.

■2 Type the name of the package you want to import and follow it with a dot.

■ This example uses the package created in the section "Create a Package."

■3 Type the name of the class you want to import.

■4 Type the code that declares the class and the method you want to use.

Extra

You can use the wildcard character * to have Java import all the classes a package contains. You may find this useful if you want to access several classes in a package. For example, to import all the classes in the `myapps.webutils` package, use the statement `import myapps.webutils.*`

When using the wildcard character *, remember that only the classes in the named package import. For example, the `import myapps.webutils.*` statement only imports the classes it finds in the `myapps.webutils` package and does not import any classes it finds in the `myapps.webutils.text` package. To import classes from the `myapps.webutils.text` package, you must use the `import myapps.webutils.text.*` statement.

Java can automatically import certain packages when you compile code. The `java.lang` package, a part of the Java class library, automatically imports whenever you compile code. If your code contains classes that do not belong to a package, Java imports the default package " " and assigns the classes to that package. If your Java code contains a package statement, the named package also automatically imports.

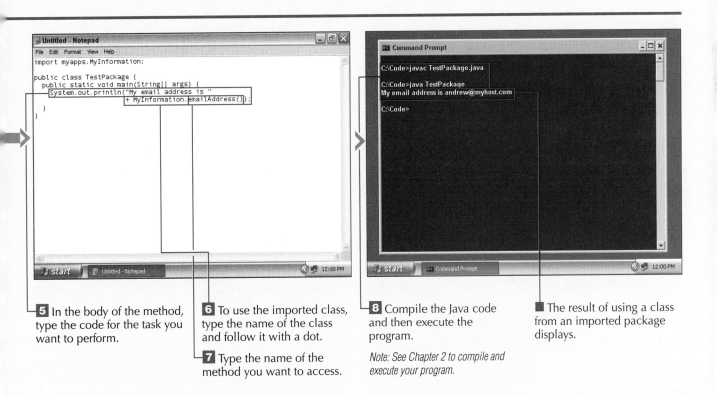

5 In the body of the method, type the code for the task you want to perform.

6 To use the imported class, type the name of the class and follow it with a dot.

7 Type the name of the method you want to access.

8 Compile the Java code and then execute the program.

Note: See Chapter 2 to compile and execute your program.

■ The result of using a class from an imported package displays.

EXTEND A CLASS

If a class you create relates to a previously created class, you can make the new class an extension of the original class. For example, you can make a new class that performs tasks using a database, making it an extension of the class that connects to the database. This allows you to re-use Java code in the original class without having to retype the code in the new class.

When you extend a class, you usually refer to the original class as the *superclass*, while you call the new class the *subclass*.

When declaring a class for use as a subclass, you must include the `extends` keyword to specify the name of the class that you want to act as the superclass. You must make the class you specify with the `extends` keyword a valid class and accessible to the subclass when the subclass compiles.

The ability of a method within a superclass to access a subclass depends on the access modifier the method uses.

Any other class can access a method with the public access modifier, while no other class can access a method with the private modifier. A method that does not have a specified access modifier is said to have default access, which means any class in the same package as the defining class can access it, while classes outside of the package cannot access it. The protected modifier is like the default, but all subclasses can access a protected method no matter what the package to which they belong is.

Once you create a subclass as an extension of a superclass, you can produce a new class that accesses the subclass. For example, a new class can create an object using the subclass. The class information from both the subclass and the superclass combines to form a single object, with methods from both the subclass and the superclass available to the object.

Many of the classes included with the JDK extend other classes. For information about the JDK classes, refer to the JDK documentation that accompanies the JDK.

EXTEND A CLASS

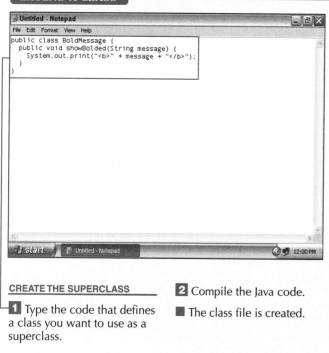

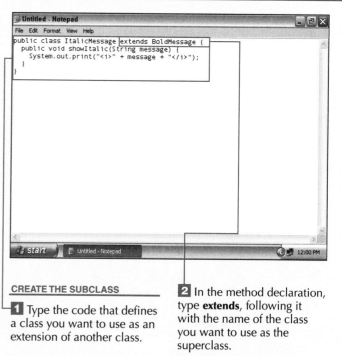

CREATE THE SUPERCLASS

1 Type the code that defines a class you want to use as a superclass.

2 Compile the Java code.

■ The class file is created.

CREATE THE SUBCLASS

1 Type the code that defines a class you want to use as an extension of another class.

2 In the method declaration, type **extends**, following it with the name of the class you want to use as the superclass.

3 Compile the Java code.

■ The class file is created.

Extra

As with methods, fields within a superclass also become available to a subclass, depending on the access modifier a field uses. Subclasses have access to all the public and protected fields of their superclass; they may also use the fields with default protection, if the subclass and superclass are in the same package.

You can override methods in a superclass. To override a method in the superclass, create a method in the subclass that has the same name as the method you want to override. You must make the access modifier of the method in the subclass the same or less restrictive than the access modifier of the method in the superclass. When you create an object using the subclass, the method in the subclass becomes available instead of the method in the superclass.

You can also make a subclass a superclass of another class. This allows you to create a chain of subclasses and superclasses. You call a class that extends directly from a superclass a *direct subclass* of the superclass. You refer to a class that is an extension of another subclass as an *indirect subclass* of the superclass.

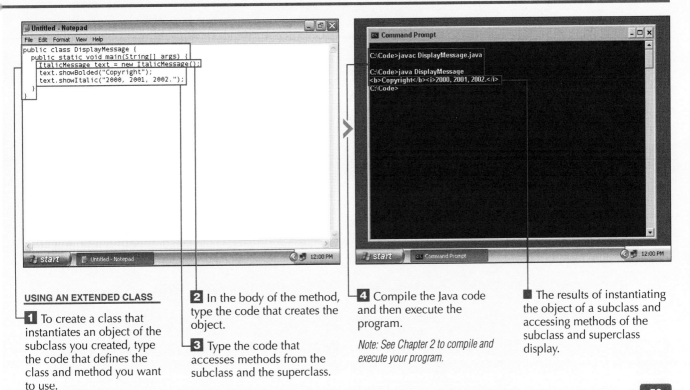

USING AN EXTENDED CLASS

1 To create a class that instantiates an object of the subclass you created, type the code that defines the class and method you want to use.

2 In the body of the method, type the code that creates the object.

3 Type the code that accesses methods from the subclass and the superclass.

4 Compile the Java code and then execute the program.

Note: See Chapter 2 to compile and execute your program.

■ The results of instantiating the object of a subclass and accessing methods of the subclass and superclass display.

CREATE AN EXCEPTION

An exception, which occurs when Java encounters a problem during the execution of a Java program, causes Java to create an object that stores information about the problem. You handle errors by accessing the properties of an exception object. The type of exception object that Java creates depends on the kind of problem that occurs. For example, an error in a mathematical calculation may generate an `ArithmeticException` object.

Encountering an exception does not necessarily mean that the processing of a Java program must stop. You can handle some errors within the Java code of a program; it all depends on the type and severity of the error. For example, you can create a `try` block and a `catch` block to handle exceptions that could potentially arise when a section of code processes, allowing your code to recover from an exception. For information about creating a `try` block and a `catch` block, see the section "Handling Errors."

For more information about the different types of exception classes and the kinds of errors that create them, refer to the Java Application Programming Interface (API) documentation or to Appendix B.

To troubleshoot the error-handling capabilities of your Java applications, consider having your Java code generate exceptions. One of the easiest ways to generate an error in any programming language involves creating a mathematical calculation where zero divides into a number, which generates a 'division by zero' error. Within your Java code, a division by zero error generates an `ArithmeticException` object, which you can then use to create the code that handles the error.

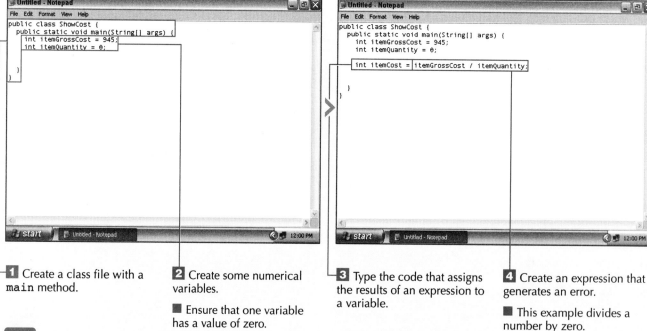

1 Create a class file with a `main` method.

2 Create some numerical variables.

■ Ensure that one variable has a value of zero.

3 Type the code that assigns the results of an expression to a variable.

4 Create an expression that generates an error.

■ This example divides a number by zero.

One of the most common sources of exceptions is the interpretation of user input. You can use `NumberFormatExceptions` to determine if a user entered a number as an integer, a floating-point number, or not a number at all.

TYPE THIS:

```java
public class NumberFormat {
  public static void testNumber(String number) {
    try {
        new Integer(number);
        System.out.println(number +
                          " is an integer.");
        return;
      }
    catch (NumberFormatException notAnInt) {
        try {
          new Double(number);
          System.out.println(number +
                            " is a floating-point number.");
          return;
        }
        catch (NumberFormatException notAFloat) {
          System.out.println(number +
                            " is not a number at all.");
        }
      }
  }
  public static void main(String[] argv) {
    testNumber("1v");
    testNumber("2.3");
    testNumber("ABC");
  }
}
```

RESULT:

```
1 is an integer.
2.3 is a floating-point number.
ABC is not a number at all.
```

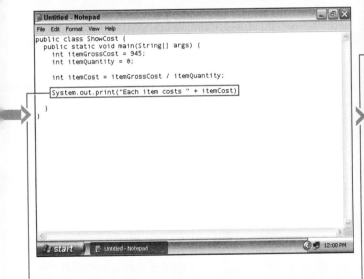

5 Type the code that generates a message.

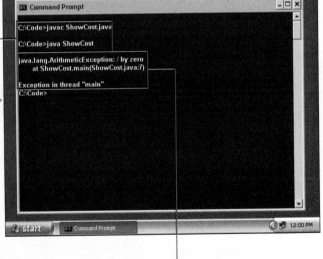

6 Compile the Java code and then execute the program.

Note: See Chapter 2 to compile and execute your program.

■ An error message displays.

HANDLE ERRORS

I f a section of code in a Java program may possibly generate an error, you can create a try block and a catch block to handle the error.

A try block detects if an exception occurs in a section of code. To create a try block, use the keyword try and enclose the code that may cause an exception in braces.

A catch block contains the code that executes when the try block detects an error. The catch block must immediately follow the try block. To create a catch block, use the keyword catch and enclose the code you want to execute in braces. You follow the catch keyword with a parameter enclosed in parentheses. The parameter specifies the class of the exception and a name for the object that Java creates when the error occurs.

A catch block can only catch the type of exception that a parameter specifies. If the try block generates a different type of exception, the code in the catch block does not execute. Usually the exceptions you catch consist of *checked exceptions*, which the compiler forces you to catch. Checked exceptions indicate an unexpected but recoverable condition.

When an exception occurs in a line of code, the line of code is said to *throw an exception*. When a line of code in a try block throws an exception, the processing of code in the try block stops immediately and any remaining statements in the try block do not execute. The catch block catches the error that a try block throws and Java continues processing on the first line of code in the catch block.

You can make the code in a catch block display a customized error message to notify a user of an error occurrence. You should make the customized error message easy to understand as well as specific to the error.

HANDLE ERRORS

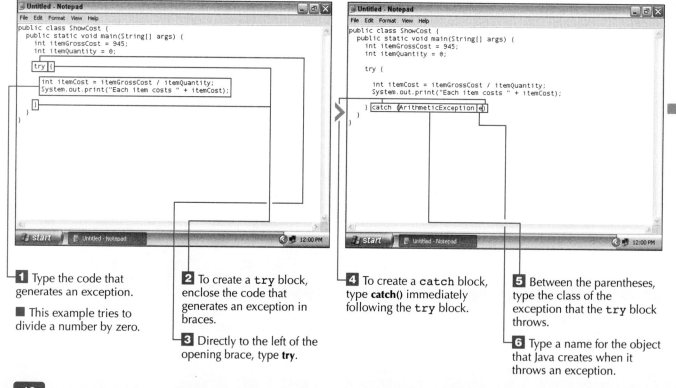

-1 Type the code that generates an exception.

■ This example tries to divide a number by zero.

-2 To create a **try** block, enclose the code that generates an exception in braces.

-3 Directly to the left of the opening brace, type **try**.

-4 To create a **catch** block, type **catch()** immediately following the **try** block.

-5 Between the parentheses, type the class of the exception that the **try** block throws.

-6 Type a name for the object that Java creates when it throws an exception.

Extra

As with any Java code, you have strict rules governing the scope of variables that you use in `try` and `catch` blocks. Java does not make variables that you declare in a `try` block available for use in the `catch` block. In the following example, the code does not compile because the `locationMessage` variable is not available in the `catch` block.

Example:

```
try {
  String locationMessage = "determining item cost";
  int itemCost = itemGrossCost / itemQuantity;
  out.print("Each item costs " + itemCost);
} catch (ArithmeticException e) {
  out.print("Error has occurred at " +
locationMessage);
}
```

Make your `try` blocks as large as possible, ideally encompassing virtually all the code in a method. This has the effect of placing all the functional code inside the `try` block, and all the error handling code at the end of a routine. Separating the two kinds of code makes them both easier to understand and troubleshoot.

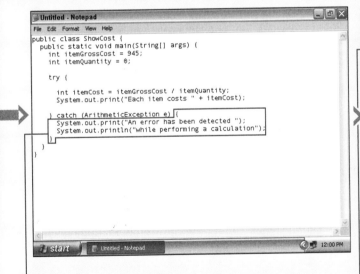

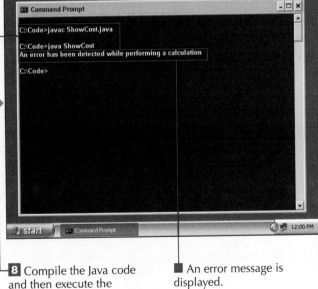

7 Type the code you want to execute when the `catch` block processes and enclose the code in braces.

8 Compile the Java code and then execute the program.

Note: See Chapter 2 to compile and execute your program.

■ An error message is displayed.

UNDERSTANDING VARIABLE SCOPE

The scope of a variable determines the part of a program that can access the variable and use its value. Java has strict guidelines governing variable scope, which it refers to as *scoping rules*.

You determine the scope of a variable by the position of the variable declaration within a block of code. An opening brace and a closing brace denote a block of code. The scope of a variable runs from the line of code containing the variable declaration to the closing brace of the block.

If you declare a variable in the body of a class, outside of any method, the variable becomes accessible to all the methods in the class. You refer to a variable that you declare in a class body as a *member variable*.

A variable that you declare within a method is referred to as a *local variable*. A local variable only becomes accessible

within the method in which you declared it. Other blocks of code created within the method can access the local variable.

You can use the same name to declare a member variable and a local variable in one class. When you use the same name to declare two variables of different scopes, Java treats the variables as distinct. Although variables with different scopes can have the same name, using unique variable names makes your code easier to understand. For example, instead of using a variable named counter for all your counting functions, you should use variations of the name, such as loopCounter for counting loop iterations or processCounter for counting the number of times a particular process executes.

UNDERSTANDING VARIABLE SCOPE

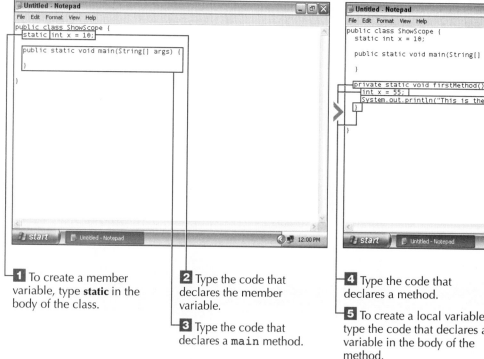

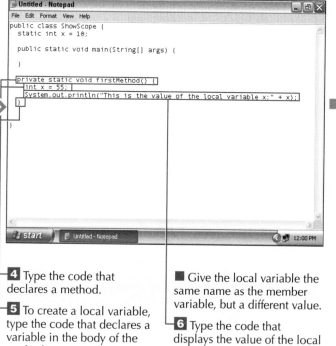

1 To create a member variable, type **static** in the body of the class.

2 Type the code that declares the member variable.

3 Type the code that declares a main method.

4 Type the code that declares a method.

5 To create a local variable, type the code that declares a variable in the body of the method.

■ Give the local variable the same name as the member variable, but a different value.

6 Type the code that displays the value of the local variable.

Apply It

To prevent errors, you must not reference variables declared in other blocks of code. Java restricts the scope of a variable to the block of code that contains the variable declaration. If you declare a variable in a block of code that an `if` statement or a statement that produces a loop creates, the variable becomes a local variable.

TYPE THIS:

```
if (2+2 == 4) {
   int x = 3;
}

System.out.print(x);
```

RESULT:

```
Scope.java:12: cannot resolve symbol
symbol  : variable x
location: class Scope
          System.out.print(x);
                           ^
1 error
```

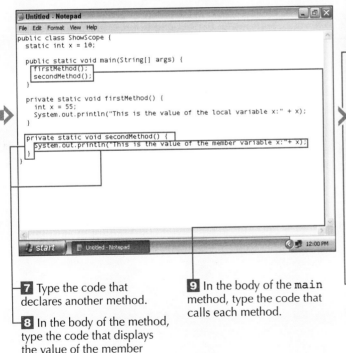

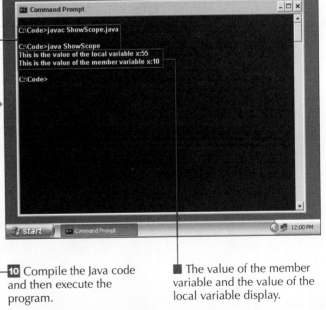

7 Type the code that declares another method.

8 In the body of the method, type the code that displays the value of the member variable.

9 In the body of the **main** method, type the code that calls each method.

10 Compile the Java code and then execute the program.

Note: See Chapter 2 to compile and execute your program.

■ The value of the member variable and the value of the local variable display.

CREATE AN XML DOCUMENT

XML documents are text documents that contain information which conforms to the XML specification. Because XML documents use plain text, you can employ any simple text editor to easily create them.

A simple XML document starts with an XML declaration. An *XML declaration* provides basic information concerning the XML document to any application that processes the document. You must make the XML declaration the very first line of an XML document. For simple XML documents, the following line is the XML declaration:

```
<?xml version="1.0" standalone="yes"?>
```

This XML declaration tells the processing application that this is an XML document that should conform to the XML 1.0 specification and that it is a standalone document. A *standalone document* does not need to access any other documents or files for information.

The bulk of XML documents consist of sections of information called *elements*. Elements have a start tag and an end tag, and typically contain some content, which you place between the start and end tags. For example, the element <name>Andrew</name> consists of a start and an end tag, and as the content — in this example, the word 'Andrew'. You call the first element in an XML document the *root* element.

When saving a previously created XML document using a word processor, you must ensure that you save the XML document as a plain text document. By default, most word processors save documents in a proprietary format that XML-reading applications cannot read. You save the XML document with the file extension .xml.

Once you save an XML document, you can load it into an application capable of processing XML documents. Microsoft's Internet Explorer is a popular Web browser that you can use to view simple XML documents.

CREATE AN XML DOCUMENT

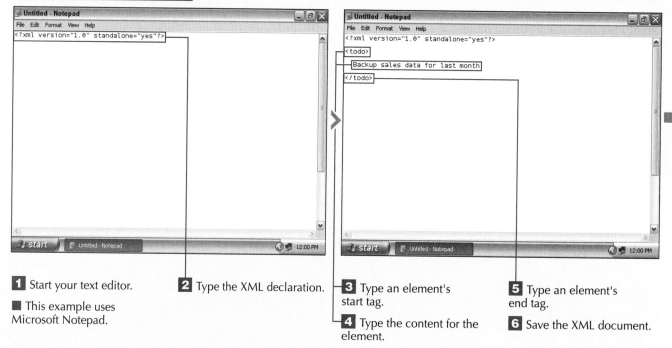

1 Start your text editor.

■ This example uses Microsoft Notepad.

2 Type the XML declaration.

3 Type an element's start tag.

4 Type the content for the element.

5 Type an element's end tag.

6 Save the XML document.

Apply It

If you make a mistake in your XML document, the Web browser generates an error message and may even give you detailed information about the type and location of that error.

TYPE THIS:

```
<?xml version="1.0" standalone="yes"?>
<todo>
   Backup sales data for last month
</todonow>
```

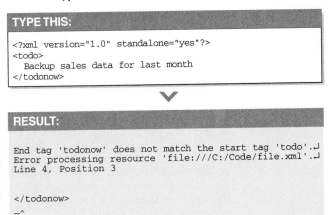

RESULT:

```
End tag 'todonow' does not match the start tag 'todo'.⏎
Error processing resource 'file:///C:/Code/file.xml'.⏎
Line 4, Position 3


</todonow>
_^
```

When you use a Web browser to view an XML document, the Web browser may reformat the information prior to displaying it. For example, it may insert indents and new lines into the XML code to make the code easier to read. You can always view the original source code file by using the View Source feature of your Web browser.

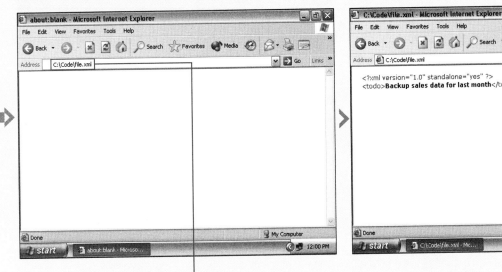

7 Start the application that you want to process the XML document.

■ This example uses Microsoft Internet Explorer 6.

8 In the address bar, type the name of your XML document and press Enter.

■ The content of the XML document displays.

VERIFY WELL-FORMEDNESS

Before you can consider something an XML document, you must ensure that the XML code in the document is well-formed. The *XML specification* is a collection of rules, or constraints, that specifies how you should construct an XML document. Part of the XML specification dictates the structure of an XML document, as well as how you should format the individual items in the document. These syntax and structure constraints, detailed in the XML specification, determine if an XML document is well-formed. If an XML document follows all the rules and guidelines in the XML specification, then you can call the XML document well-formed. You cannot call a document that is not well-formed an XML document.

Checking if an XML document is well-formed requires the use of an XML application that can analyze the XML document and verify the document's well-formedness. Many applications exist that allow you to verify well-formedness.

For example, although primarily designed to display HTML documents, some Web browsers also check the XML document's well-formedness. While you may find Web browsers a quick and convenient way to check for well-formed XML documents, if you intend to work with a number of XML documents, you should use an application designed primarily to work with XML documents.

Many XML applications that you utilize to develop XML documents only allow you to perform certain actions, such as spell checking your document or reformatting the code to make it easier to read, if the document is well-formed. For this reason you should continually check your XML document to ensure that the XML document is well-formed as you develop the document. If you check your XML document and it is not well-formed, an error message displays to indication the portion of the document causing the failure.

VERIFY WELL-FORMEDNESS

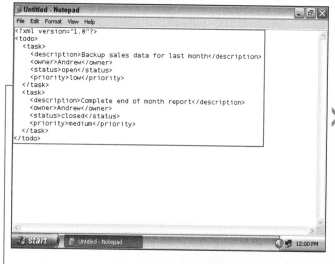

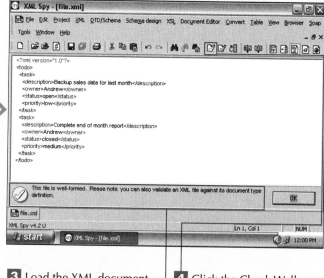

CHECK A WELL-FORMED DOCUMENT

1 Create or open a simple XML document.

Note: See the section "Create an XML Document" to create an XML document.

2 Save the XML document.

3 Load the XML document into the XML application.

Note: This example uses XML Spy, available on the companion CD-ROM.

4 Click the Check Well-Formedness button.

■ The application indicates that the document is well-formed.

Extra

The XML specification contains rules that identify what constitutes a well-formed XML document. The XML specification indicates the rules, or constraints, that apply to well-formed XML documents with the letters wfc. You can view the XML specification on the Internet at http://www.w3.org/TR/2000/REC-xml-20001006.html.

Besides monitoring an XML document for well-formedness, you must also verify the XML document's validity. You must create a valid XML document according to the exact rules laid out in the XML specification. If a document is a valid XML document, it is also well-formed. For more information about XML document validity, see Chapter 6.

The information in XML documents is always case sensitive. If you use the wrong case when typing start and end tags, a common error, you create code that generates an XML document that is not well-formed. For example, `<myName>Andrew</myName>` is correct, but the code `<MyName>Andrew</myName>` generates an XML document that is not well-formed.

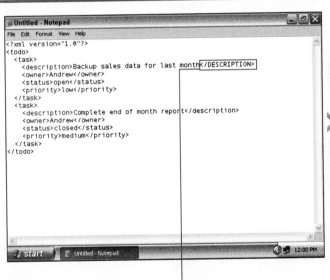

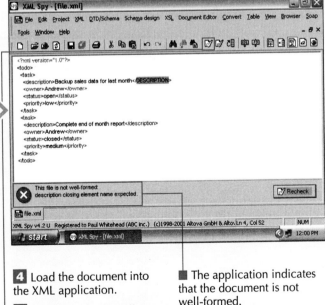

CHECK A NON-WELL-FORMED DOCUMENT

1 Create a simple XML document.

Note: See the section "Create an XML Document" to create an XML document.

2 Adjust the end tag so that it does not match the start tag.

3 Save the document.

4 Load the document into the XML application.

5 Click the Check Well-Formedness button.

■ The application indicates that the document is not well-formed.

CREATE ELEMENTS

You use an element within an XML document to identify information. An *element* consists of a start tag and an end tag. Between the start and end tags, you place the element's content. Tags start with the < delimiter and end with the > delimiter. You place the tag name between the delimiters. In the end tag, you must precede the element name with a /.

In many cases elements contain text information, but they can also contain other types of information including other elements. You call an element that you make a part of the content of another element a *child element*. You refer to an element that contains another element as the *parent element* of the child element. For more information about the different types of element content, see Chapter 5.

How you structure the elements in an XML document depends on the type of information that it contains. You have no rules governing how you place your elements so long as the document conforms to the XML specification.

However, you should try to structure the elements to match the structure of the information within the XML document.

You do not have to place information in elements to consider them valid; in fact, quite commonly the elements of an XML document contain no information.

You cannot use spaces in the name of an element. To make XML documents easier to read, the names of elements should specifically indicate the type of content within the elements.

You make the root element the first element in an XML document, placing all other elements within the start and end tags of the root element.

When adding elements to an XML document, you should verify that the XML document is well-formed. See the section "Verify Well-Formedness" in this chapter to verify your XML document.

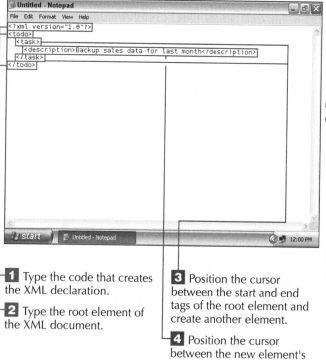

1 Type the code that creates the XML declaration.

2 Type the root element of the XML document.

3 Position the cursor between the start and end tags of the root element and create another element.

4 Position the cursor between the new element's start and end tags and type the content of the child element.

5 Type the code that creates additional child elements.

Extra

Element names can consist of any combination of alphanumeric characters, hyphens, underscores, periods, or colons. The name of any element must begin with a letter, a colon, or an underscore.

If an element contains no content, you call it an *empty* element. Instead of creating both a start and an end tag, you combine an empty element into one tag. This tag consists of the element name, which you follow with a /. For example, the element `<status></status>` is exactly the same as `<status/>`.

While you can nest elements together, you cannot allow the start and end tags of elements to overlap, as in the following example.

Example:

A Valid Element

`<person>Tom<age>33</age></person>`

An Invalid Element

`<person>Tom<age></person>33</age>`

You cannot use markup symbols in the text of an element's content. For example, you cannot define an element `<notes>I always make sure to use the <br> tag in my html code.</notes>` because it contains the markup tag `<br>` as part of the element's content.

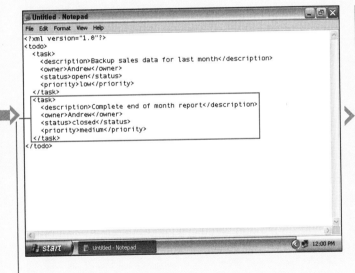

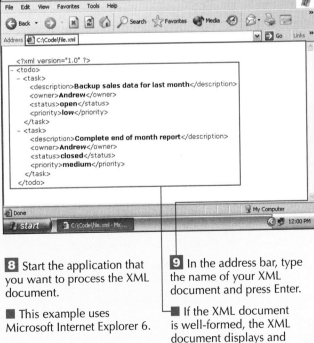

6 Type the code that creates additional child elements of the root element.

7 Save the XML document.

8 Start the application that you want to process the XML document.

■ This example uses Microsoft Internet Explorer 6.

9 In the address bar, type the name of your XML document and press Enter.

■ If the XML document is well-formed, the XML document displays and shows the elements.

71

ADD ATTRIBUTES

You use an *attribute* to provide additional information about an element's content. Most elements store data in the form of content between the start and end tags of the element. As well as content, elements may also have attributes, which hold data, associated with them.

An attribute consists of its name and value. You separate the attribute name and value with the = character. You must enclose an element's attributes and their values within the element's start tag. You must always enclose the value of an attribute within quotes, even if you use the attribute to indicate a numerical value. For example, the start tag `<alert level="3">` is valid while `<alert level=3>` is not valid.

An element can have multiple attributes. You can separate attributes from each other and from the element name by one or more spaces or line breaks. Using line breaks to separate attributes may make your XML document easier to read, especially if you have many attributes within a single start tag.

In many cases, elements that have attributes can also use child elements instead of attributes. Typically, you can use attributes even when you only have one option for a given value. For example, an element that describes a product in a warehouse may have an attribute that indicates whether you have the item in stock. This information makes a suitable attribute because you can only have one value, yes or no, depending on the item's availability. Conversely, you can place the name of the item's supplier in a child element because an item in the warehouse may have more than one supplier.

ADD ATTRIBUTES

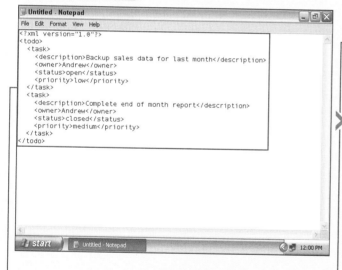

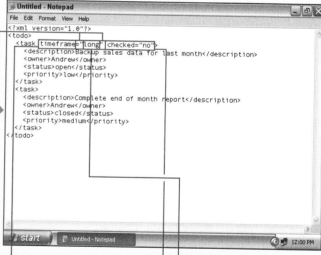

1 Create or open a simple XML document.

Note: See the section "Create an XML Document" to create an XML document.

2 Place the cursor within a tag and type the name of the attribute.

3 Type = "".

4 Position the cursor between the quotation marks and type the value for the attribute.

5 Repeat steps 2 through 4 for each attribute of the element you want to create.

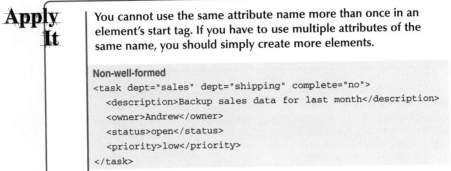

Apply It

You cannot use the same attribute name more than once in an element's start tag. If you have to use multiple attributes of the same name, you should simply create more elements.

Non-well-formed
```xml
<task dept="sales" dept="shipping" complete="no">
  <description>Backup sales data for last month</description>
  <owner>Andrew</owner>
  <status>open</status>
  <priority>low</priority>
</task>
```

Well-formed
```xml
<task complete="no">
  <dept>sales</dept>
  <dept>shipping</dept>
  <description>Backup sales data for last month</description>
  <owner>Andrew</owner>
  <status>open</status>
  <priority>low</priority>
</task>
```

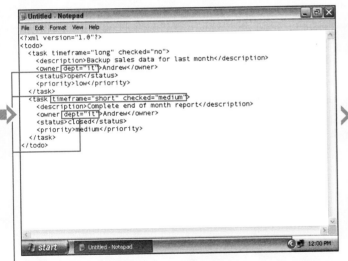

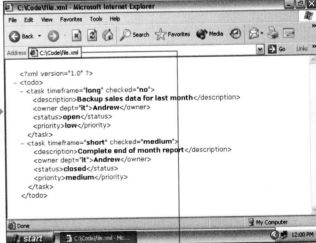

■ Repeat steps 2 through 5 for each element to which you want to add attributes.

6 Save the XML document.

7 Start the application that you want to process the XML document.

■ This example uses Microsoft Internet Explorer 6.

8 In the address bar, type the name of your XML document and press Enter.

■ If the XML document is well-formed, the XML document displays the elements' attributes.

ADD A COMMENT

You can add a *comment*, a helpful piece of inserted text, to an XML document. You typically insert comments as a reference for users who actually read the XML document. While you typically may find the overall structure of an XML document easy to read and understand, readers may not find specific details of your particular XML document apparent. By including a detailed comment, you help to ensure that anyone who reads your XML document will understand your reasons for constructing your document the way you did. Not only does this serve as an aid to people who may read your code, but it may also help you if you have to reread your own code after you have not read it for some time.

You denote the start of a comment with <!-- and end the comment with -->. You use this same method to insert comments in HTML documents. The application processing

the XML document ignores any comments you place in it. You must place comments outside of any tags in the XML document, preferably on their own line.

You can place any text information within a comment except a double hyphen. You can even include line breaks in your comments to make your comments easier to read.

You can only use comments after the XML declaration in an XML document, and you must place the XML declaration in the first line of your XML document.

Placing comments in your code is a good programming practice. At the very least, you should ensure that you use comments to include the author of the document and a method by which a reader can contact the author.

ADD A COMMENT

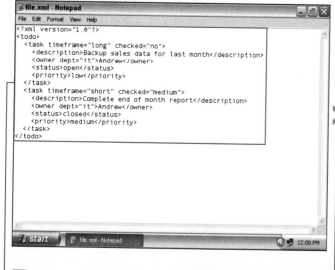

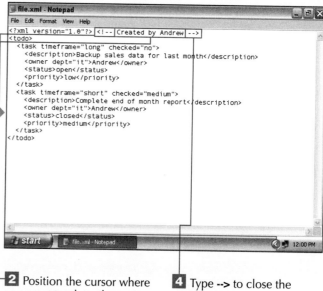

1 Create or open an XML document.

Note: You can use the XML document created in the section "Add Attributes."

2 Position the cursor where you want to place the comment and type **<!--**.

3 Type the remainder of the comment.

4 Type **-->** to close the comment tag.

Apply It

You can also use comments while developing your code to help eliminate errors. For example, you can use comments to isolate unfinished sections of code that would otherwise generate errors when you check them for well-formedness.

TYPE:

```
<?xml version="1.0"?>
<todo>
                <task dept="sales" complete="no">
                    <description>Backup sales data for last month</description>
                    <owner>&name;</owner>
                    <status>open</status>
                    <priority>low</priority>
                </task>
<!--
                <task dept="accounting" complete="no">
                    <description>
                    <owner>
                    <status>
                    <priority>
                </task>

-->
</todo>
```

RESULT:

```
This file is well-formed.
```

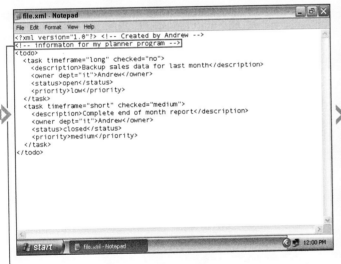

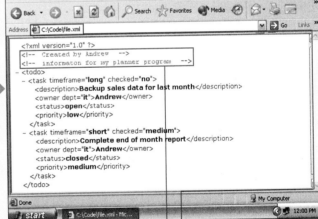

5 Position the cursor on a new line.

6 Repeat steps 2 through 4 to create another comment.

7 Save your XML document.

8 Start the application that you want to process the XML document.

■ This example uses Microsoft Internet Explorer 6.

9 In the address bar, type the name of your XML document and press Enter.

■ If the XML document is well-formed, the XML document displays the comments.

INCLUDE SPECIAL PROCESSING INSTRUCTIONS

Y ou can pass application-specific instructions from an XML document to an XML processor using a construct called a *processing instruction*. You only use processing instructions when working with an application that expects the instructions in an XML document.

When creating your own Java applications you can easily make applications that detect processing instructions in an XML document. You can then have the application perform a task, depending on the parameters you specify in the processing instructions.

The syntax for declaring a processing instruction is `<?spaceDelimitedInstructions?>`, where you replace `spaceDelimitedInstructions` with any valid XML name, and follow it with any required parameters. Because you aim processing instructions at specific applications, the first word in a processing instruction often represents the name of that specific application. You follow the name with any additional words, which represent the parameters that the target

application can interpret. If you create a Java application and call it printXML, you may specify printXML so that the processing instruction targets that application. You may use the data in the processing instruction to indicate whether the printXML application should print the document or perform some other functions on the XML document.

An application that processes XML documents ignores any processing instructions that do not target that application. Most XML applications do not make use of the processing instructions you place in XML documents.

You can insert a processing instruction anywhere in an XML document as long as you do not place it within a tag or make it the first line of the XML document. Where you place the processing instruction depends on the application at which you target the processing instruction and what task that application performs. Users commonly place processing instructions at the top of the XML document, after the XML declaration.

INCLUDE SPECIAL PROCESSING INSTRUCTIONS

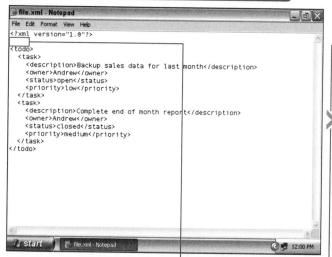

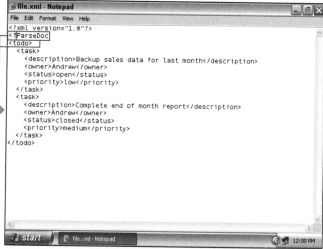

1 Open or create the XML file to which you want to add a processing instruction.

2 Position your cursor after the XML declaration.

3 Type the beginning tag, **<?**, for the processing instruction.

4 Type the name of the target application.

■ In this example, the target application is ParseDoc, which is a Java application.

Extra

Each word within a processing instruction must begin with a letter or underscore and can only contain the following:

- Letters
- Hyphens
- Digits
- Periods
- Underscores

You cannot make the first word in a processing instruction `xml`, which is a reserved word.

With a few exceptions, XML parsers ignore processing instructions. Recognizing and executing processing instructions appropriately is up to the processor — the application that extracts, manipulates, and displays XML.

The exception is the XML declaration itself (`<xml version="1.0">`). All XML parsers recognize and handle this processing instruction.

You have no limit to the number of parameters that you can specify for a processing instruction. For example, you can use:

Example:
```
<?ParseDoc check="yes" print="laser" compile?>
```

Any text after the target application name passes to the target application. The target application analyzes the parameters of the processing instruction and extracts the necessary information.

```
file.xml - Notepad
File  Edit  Format  View  Help
<?xml version="1.0"?>
<?ParseDoc check="yes"
<todo>
  <task>
    <description>Backup sales data for last month</description>
    <owner>Andrew</owner>
    <status>open</status>
    <priority>low</priority>
  </task>
  <task>
    <description>Complete end of month report</description>
    <owner>Andrew</owner>
    <status>closed</status>
    <priority>medium</priority>
  </task>
</todo>

start      file.xml - Notepad                    12:00 PM
```

```
file.xml - Notepad
File  Edit  Format  View  Help
<?xml version="1.0"?>
<?ParseDoc check="yes"?>
<todo>
  <task>
    <description>Backup sales data for last month</description>
    <owner>Andrew</owner>
    <status>open</status>
    <priority>low</priority>
  </task>
  <task>
    <description>Complete end of month report</description>
    <owner>Andrew</owner>
    <status>closed</status>
    <priority>medium</priority>
  </task>
</todo>

start      file.xml - Notepad                    12:00 PM
```

5 Type the text that you want to use as the parameters.

6 Type the ending tag, **?>**, for the processing instruction.

7 Save the file.

USING PREDEFINED XML ENTITIES

XML applications processing the XML document may incorrectly interpret some special characters that you place into element content XML markup tags. You can incorporate special characters into XML data using predefined XML entities.

XML parsers make certain assumptions about XML document syntax, for example, that a left angle bracket (<) begins a tag. However, you may need to include a left angle bracket in an element's value, for example:

```
<err_desc>If the system fails, you will see
this message: <error 101></err_desc>.
```

Because an XML parser has no way of determining that the second left angle bracket shown above is not the beginning of another tag, it generates an error when attempting to process this statement.

To define data containing special characters like angle brackets, XML uses predefined entities to differentiate between symbols that have special meaning in XML, such as the left angle bracket, and those same symbols embedded in a text string.

XML supports five predefined entities. Each of them includes a semicolon at the end of the entity:

- `&lt;`, which stands for the less-than character (<)

- `&gt;`, which stands for the greater-than character (>)

- `&amp;`, which stands for an ampersand (&)

- `&apos;`, which stands for an apostrophe (')

- `&quot;`, which stands for a quotation mark (")

USING PREDEFINED XML ENTITIES

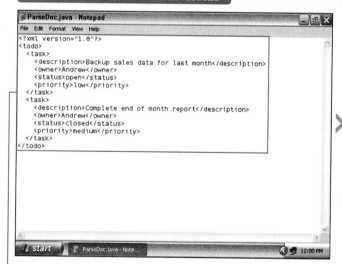

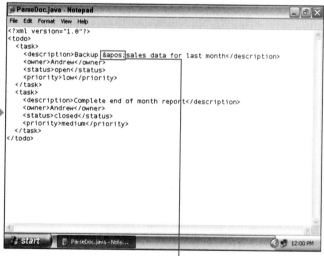

1 Open or create the XML file in which you want to reference a predefined entity.

2 Position your cursor at the point in the text where you want to add the predefined entity.

■ In this example, the reference will be added directly to an element's content.

3 Type the entity reference.

■ In this example, the entity referenced is the apostrophe, which you declare using `&apos;`.

Extra

Entities can appear inside attribute declarations as well as inside element values. For example, the following XML code is valid:

Example:
```
<wholesalers name="Biggs &amp; Tate"/>
```

The five entities in this example are sometimes referred to as predefined *internal* entities. Internet Explorer provides support for these five entities, which are available for both XML and HTML documents. See Chapter 5 to define custom entities, including external, parsed, and unparsed entities. Entities in XML can take one of four forms:

ENTITY	FORM
Internal general	Referenced from inside an XML document; you define substitute text inside a DTD.
External general	Referenced from inside an XML document; you define substitute text inside some external file.
Internal parameter	Referenced from inside a DTD document; you define substitute text inside a DTD.
External parameter	Referenced from inside a DTD document; you define substitute text inside some external file.

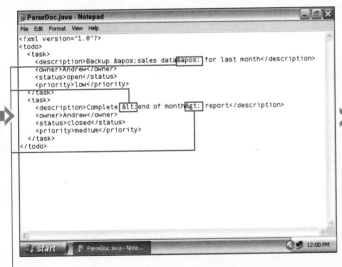

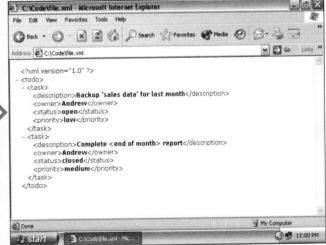

4 Type any other entity references.

5 Save the file.

6 Display the XML document in an XML application.

■ This example uses Microsoft Internet Explorer 6.

■ The predefined entities display as special characters.

INCLUDE NONSTANDARD TEXT

You can include a large amount of data in XML elements that may contain nonstandard text, such as HTML code. The section "Using Predefined XML Entities" earlier in this chapter shows you how to include special characters in your XML documents using predefined entities. Entities are fine for occasional use, and individual characters, but if you need to incorporate a large number of special characters, you can use another construct designed specifically for that purpose: the CDATA section.

The CDATA section enables you to incorporate large blocks of text containing special characters into an XML document without replacing each special character with an entity reference.

A CDATA section starts with the characters <![CDATA[and ends with the characters]]>. Within the tag, you

can include any text that may contain special characters. When an XML application processes this information, the XML parser does not check the text; instead, the text passes through the XML parser as the parser encounters it in the document. The XML application that processes the XML document then takes the responsibility to analyze or otherwise use the text containing special characters in a meaningful way.

You can make the information in the CDATA section almost anything. It can contain programming code, such as Java, or, more commonly, HTML. You often use HTML code in CDATA sections because an XML parser interprets the markup tags that you use in HTML as XML markup tags and generates parsing errors. You can include XML information in a CDATA section, but the XML parser does not check the XML code for validity or any other XML characteristic.

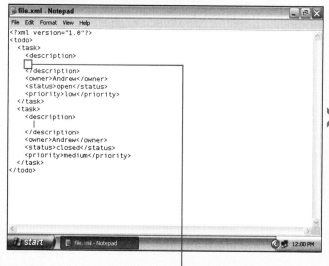

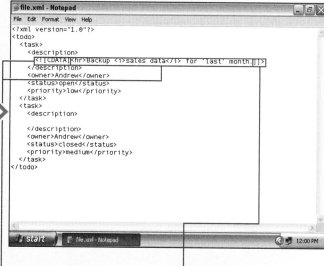

1 Open or create the XML document in which you want to declare a CDATA section.

2 Position your cursor where you want to declare the CDATA section.

■ In this example, the CDATA section will be declared as the content for an element.

3 Type the beginning CDATA tag, **<![CDATA[**.

4 Type the special character text.

5 Add the ending CDATA tag, **]]>**.

Extra

Because the CDATA section holds unrestricted character data, few syntax rules apply to CDATA contents. These rules are:

- You must represent CDATA sections as element values.

- You cannot use]] between the start and end CDATA tags.

You may find a CDATA section ideal if you want to pass a large block of text containing several special characters to your XML processing application. The following example incorporates a block of scripting code, which contains many special characters, into an XML document.

Example:

```
<![CDATA[
<SCRIPT LANGUAGE="JavaScript">
// Jamcracker, Inc. is providing this code as a service only;
// no warranties or fitness for use are implied. Please check ⏎
our
// service manual for instructions on coding additional ⏎
necessary
// functions and parameters.
function isUpToDate(downloadDate) {
// This function queries Jamcracker, Inc.'s database to ⏎
determine if
// there have been product updates since the last XML file ⏎
download.
var connectionUp=pingDatabase();
lastUpdated = queryDatabase();
if (downloadDate < lastUpdated && connectionUp) {
        display("Please download the latest XML file to ⏎
ensure up-to-date product information.")
    }
}
</SCRIPT>
]]>
```

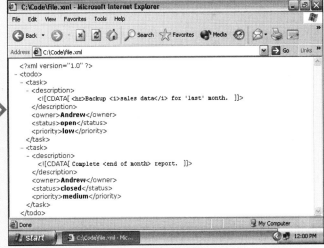

6 If required, add other CDATA sections.

7 Save the XML document.

8 Display the XML document in an XML application.

■ This example uses Microsoft Internet Explorer 6.

■ The special characters display.

DECLARE A DTD

You can create a set of rules for each XML document. This allows you to control the format of data that makes up your XML documents. For example, you can specify that an element called company contain only text, and no other type of information.

You can define the content make-up for components of an XML document by using a document type definition, or DTD. Comprised of plain text, *DTDs*, also called *vocabularies*, define a common set of structured elements and attributes, much like human vocabularies establish common words and syntax rules.

As with XML documents, you create the DTD using plain text, so you can include the text for a DTD inside your XML document. Referred to as *inline* DTDs, you use DTDs within an XML document for short XML documents as well as all XML documents that you are in the process of developing. To create element declarations for multiple XML documents, see the section "Create an External DTD File."

You place a DTD into an XML document in a tag. You make the opening characters of the tag <!DOCTYPE and follow the tag with the name of the root element. You make the root element the first element in the XML document. After the name of the root element, you enclose the DTD rules in square brackets, and follow the rules with a greater-than character (>).

The DTD rules can specify the type of data that a user can include as content for elements within the XML document. You call rules that apply to elements *element declarations*. An element declaration consists of a tag that starts with <!ELEMENT, the element name, and then the type of data that forms the element's content. You close the element declaration with a greater-than character (>). For elements that contain text data, the data type (#PCDATA) indicates that you must make the content of the element character data.

DECLARE A DTD

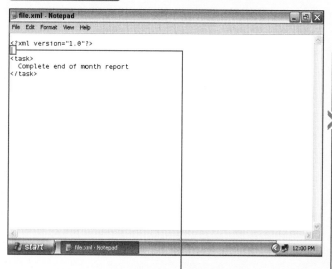

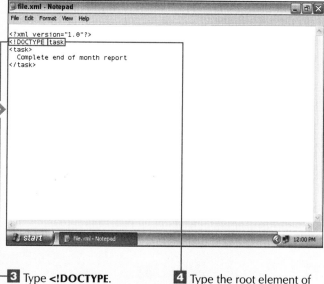

1 Open or create the XML file to which you want to add an inline DTD.

2 Position the cursor directly below the XML declaration and directly above the root element declaration.

■ This example uses the root element **task**.

3 Type **<!DOCTYPE**.

4 Type the root element of the XML document.

Extra When using a DTD with an XML document, you must associate all elements that you define in an XML file with a corresponding declaration in the DTD. You can declare the type of an XML element using any of the following:

ELEMENT DECLARATION TYPE	DESCRIPTION
(#PCDATA)	Character data.
(#PCDATA) *	Zero or more characters.
(anElement)	One instance of anElement.
(anElement+)	One or more instances of anElement.
(anElement?)	Zero or more instances of anElement.
(anElement, anotherElement)	One instance each of anElement and anotherElement.
(anElement | anotherElement)	One instance of anElement *or* one instance of anotherElement.
(#PCDATA | anElement) *	Either an instance of anElement *or* multiple characters. When you use this as one of multiple options, #PCDATA must appear first.
EMPTY	No content.

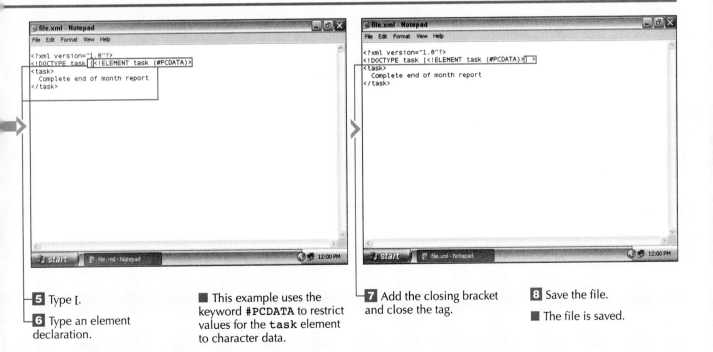

5 Type [.

6 Type an element declaration.

■ This example uses the keyword **#PCDATA** to restrict values for the **task** element to character data.

7 Add the closing bracket and close the tag.

8 Save the file.

■ The file is saved.

CREATE AN EXTERNAL DTD FILE

You can use the same DTD to create element declarations for elements located throughout multiple XML documents. For more on creating an inline DTD, see the section "Declare a DTD." If you want other XML documents to access your DTD, you can save the text of a DTD as a separate file and refer to the DTD file from inside your other XML documents. A DTD that you save in a separate file is an *external DTD*. Because using an external DTD separates validation rules from XML data, this external DTD approach promotes document reusability. Multiple XML documents can refer to the same DTD file without having to replicate validation rules within each XML document.

Because an external DTD is a text file, you can create it with any text editor. Java still considers an external DTD as an XML file and therefore requires an XML declaration as the first line of the DTD. After the XML declaration, you can specify the DTD element declarations for each element you use in the XML document. Unlike inline DTDs, you do not need to enclose the DTD rules in a DOCTYPE declaration or use other types of start and end tags to encompass the validation rules.

You must indicate the name and location of the external DTD file within the XML document to which you want the DTD to apply. As with inline DTDs, the DOCTYPE declaration indicates the root element name, but instead of containing the DTD rules, you use the SYSTEM keyword and follow it with the DTD filename. The SYSTEM keyword indicates that the local computer system can access the DTD file.

You can use any valid filename as the name of a DTD file. Consider using a name that indicates to what type of elements the DTD applies. By convention, all DTD files end with the file extension .dtd.

CREATE AN EXTERNAL DTD FILE

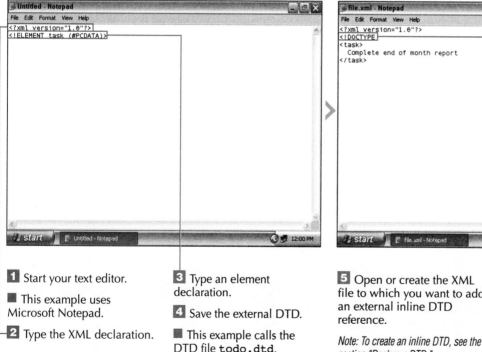

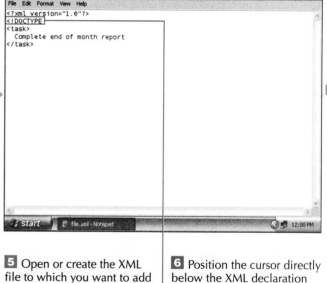

1 Start your text editor.

■ This example uses Microsoft Notepad.

2 Type the XML declaration.

3 Type an element declaration.

4 Save the external DTD.

■ This example calls the DTD file **todo.dtd**.

5 Open or create the XML file to which you want to add an external inline DTD reference.

Note: To create an inline DTD, see the section "Declare a DTD."

6 Position the cursor directly below the XML declaration and directly above the root element declaration.

7 Type **<!DOCTYPE**.

Extra

The XML parser assumes that an unqualified filename resides in the same directory as the referring XML document. If the DTD file resides in another directory, the value for this parameter must reflect the qualified DTD filename. For example, if the `file.xml` file resides in the c:\code directory, and the `todo.dtd` file resides one directory beneath it in the c:\code\DTDs directory, the `DOCTYPE` declaration of the `file.xml` XML document must appear as follows:

Example:
```
<!DOCTYPE tasks SYSTEM "/DTDs/todo.dtd">
```

To determine if your DTD works with your XML documents, check your XML documents with an application that can validate both XML documents and DTDs. You can find a trial version of one such application, XML Spy, at http://www.xmlspy.com/ as well as on the CD-ROM included with this book.

Using external DTDs presents you with the difficulty of transferring multiple files when you want to share your XML documents. Not only must you include your external DTD file with the XML documents that access them, you must also locate the DTDs in the correct directory when transferring them to another system. For more convenience, most developers store the DTD in the same folder as the XML documents that use the DTD.

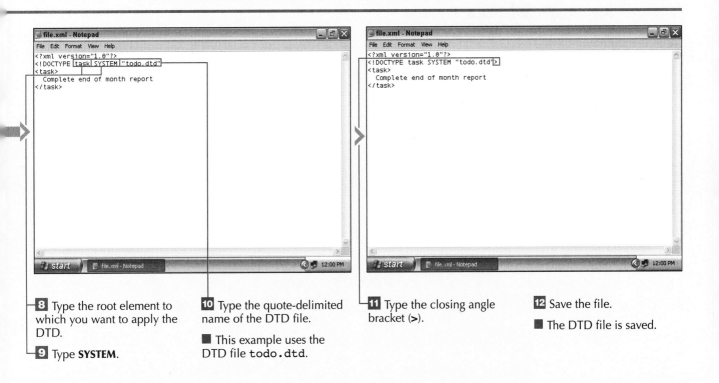

8 Type the root element to which you want to apply the DTD.

9 Type **SYSTEM**.

10 Type the quote-delimited name of the DTD file.

■ This example uses the DTD file **todo.dtd**.

11 Type the closing angle bracket (**>**).

12 Save the file.

■ The DTD file is saved.

DECLARE A CONTAINER ELEMENT

Y ou can create element declarations in the DTD that specify rules for simple elements that hold only textual data. You can also create element declarations in the DTD that define a more complex element structure, such as elements that contain other elements. A *container element* is what you call any element that contains another element.

Programmers commonly create XML documents that nest elements within other XML elements. Enforcing container relationships enables you to model complex relationships between XML data. For example, you can model relationships between repeating, related groups of elements, such as employees and projects, customers and orders, and products and retailers.

Similar to a declaration containing character data, when you declare an element containing other elements, you specify

the name of the element instead of a data type. An element you contain within another element must still have its own element declaration elsewhere in the same DTD.

You can also create container elements that contain other elements. As long as you declare them all properly in the DTD with the appropriate element declarations, you can endlessly nest levels of elements. Elements can contain just one other element or multiple elements. Almost every XML document contains at least one container element. In most cases, an XML document consists of many container elements. In all but the very simplest XML documents, you make the root element a container element that has no textual data, just elements.

You can also define elements to contain a combination of text and one or more other elements. For more information about defining other element types, see the section "Define the Structure of Elements" in this chapter.

DECLARE A CONTAINER ELEMENT

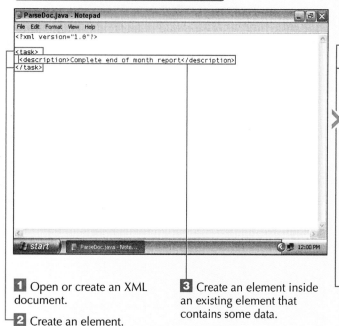

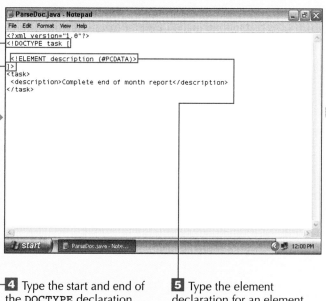

1 Open or create an XML document.

2 Create an element.

Note: For information on how to create an element, see Chapter 4.

3 Create an element inside an existing element that contains some data.

4 Type the start and end of the `DOCTYPE` declaration.

5 Type the element declaration for an element that has some content.

Extra

While you do not need to declare contained elements in the same order in the DTD as you have them in the XML document, doing so is good programming practice, making your code easier to read and troubleshoot. Indenting each contained element makes identifying the relationships between elements much easier.

DTD

```
<!ELEMENT description (#PCDATA)>
<!ELEMENT who (#PCDATA)>
<!ELEMENT task (description, who)>
```

XML Code

```
<task>
    <description>Backup sales data</description>
    <who>Andrew</who>
</task>
```

You must reference elements that belong to namespaces in DTDs by their fully qualified names. For example, the following specifies that the `retailers` element associated in the corresponding XML file with the `r` namespace is contained by the `marketing_info` element. For more information about namespaces, see the section "Using Namespaces" in this chapter.

Example:

```
<!ELEMENT marketing_info
(unique_characteristics, rank, r:retailers)>
```

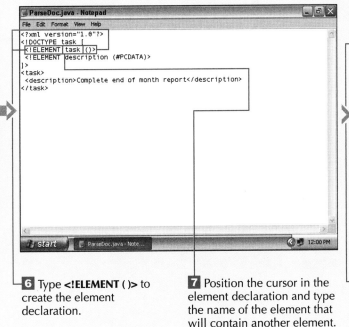

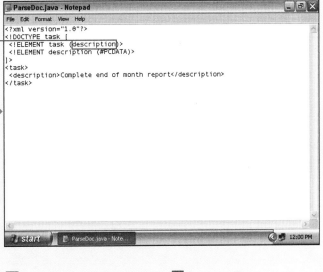

6 Type **<!ELEMENT ( )>** to create the element declaration.

7 Position the cursor in the element declaration and type the name of the element that will contain another element.

8 Type the name of the contained element.

9 Save the file.

■ The DTD file is saved.

DEFINE THE STRUCTURE OF ELEMENTS

Y ou can specify the function of elements in the XML document. Constraining what type of data an element contains ensures the proper formatting of information in the XML document — a format that an XML application may require. For example, you can specify an element that stores a person's name may only contain other elements that represent the first and last name of the person. This helps ensure the integrity of the data in that element when you use an XML application that verifies the validity of the data in the XML document.

Defining the content of an element to ANY allows you to make the content of the element virtually any text. You can make the content of the element another element or allow the content of the element to contain markup such as HTML tags.

You can define an element as *empty*. Although empty elements cannot hold any content, they can still have attributes you define within the element's start tag. For more information about attributes, see the section "Define Element Attributes."

You can also define an element to only allow the element to contain other specific elements. For example, an address element may contain the element street and the element city. When defining an element that contains other elements, you must define the listed elements elsewhere in the DTD within their own element declarations.

When specifying a list of elements that you want to contain within an element in an XML document, you can group the element names together by enclosing them in parentheses.

If an XML document uses an element, and that element does not comply with the specified validation rules in the DTD, an XML application may consider the document invalid and may not process it. You can verify that the structure of elements within an XML document conforms to the validation rules set out in the DTD by using an XML validation application such as XML Spy. For more information about using an XML validation application, see Chapter 4.

DEFINE THE STRUCTURE OF ELEMENTS

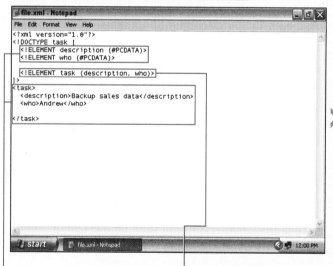

1 Create or open an XML document that contains child elements.

2 Type code to create the element declarations for the child elements.

3 Type code to create the element declaration for the parent element.

Note: For information on how to create an element, see Chapter 4.

4 Add the name for the new element to the list of values in the element declaration.

Extra

You can use additional symbols to further define the contents of an element. Depending on the symbol, you can increase or restrict the type of content for an element. For example, you can specify that an element, or parenthesized group of elements, may appear more than once by using the plus symbol (+).

Example:
```
<!ELEMENT task (description | who | reserved)+>
```

SYMBOL	DESCRIPTION
|	A single element from a list of elements separated by a | .
*	Allows multiple elements or no element to appear.
+	Requires at least one or more elements to appear.
?	Allows an optional selection of one choice.
,	Specifies the sequence in which the elements must appear.
( )	Groups all or some of the elements together.

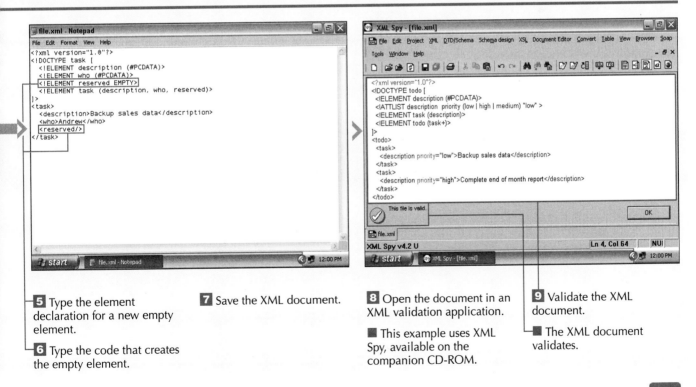

5 Type the element declaration for a new empty element.

6 Type the code that creates the empty element.

7 Save the XML document.

8 Open the document in an XML validation application.

■ This example uses XML Spy, available on the companion CD-ROM.

9 Validate the XML document.

■ The XML document validates.

DEFINE ELEMENT ATTRIBUTES

XML elements can contain *attributes*, name and value pairs in the form of strings, that can store additional information about an element. Attributes give you another choice, other than elements, for storing data. You declare attributes in the DTD using the `<!ATTLIST>` tag. When declaring an attribute for an element, you must specify the element with which you associate the attribute, as well as the type of data that you want to contain as the value of the attribute. The most commonly specified type for an attribute, `CDATA`, uses normal text as a value for an attribute. When specifying the `CDATA` attribute type, you cannot include markup, such as HTML tags, within the attribute value. For a list of other attribute types, see Appendix C.

A DTD can specify a default value for an attribute, to be used if a given element in an XML document does not specify a value for that attribute. You typically define the attribute declaration within the DTD immediately after the element to which the attribute applies. See the section "Declare a DTD" for more information on DTDs.

While multiple elements of differing names can use attributes that have the same name, you must have a separate attribute declaration for each element that uses the attribute of the same name. For example, you may have two attribute declarations that specify the attribute name `title`; one declaration specifies the attribute with the element `book`, while another declaration specifies the element `position`.

Whether you consider an empty element or one that contains data, you can still specify attributes for that element in the DTD.

After you create the attribute declaration in the DTD, you can save your file or check that you have defined the attributes properly by using an XML validation application. The companion CD-ROM has an XML validation application, called XML Spy, which validates XML documents.

DEFINE ELEMENT ATTRIBUTES

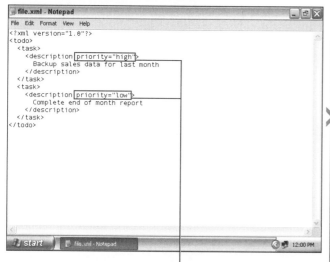

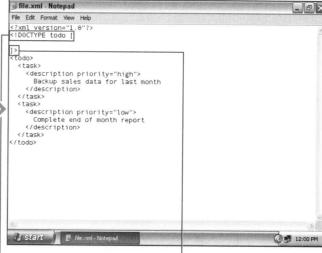

1 Open or create an XML document that contains elements.

2 Type attributes for the elements.

Note: For more information about adding attributes, see Chapter 4.

3 Type the opening characters of an inline DTD declaration.

4 Type the characters that close the DTD declaration.

Apply It

You can declare multiple attributes for a single element in the DTD.

TYPE THIS:

```
<!DOCTYPE todo [
<!ELEMENT description (#PCDATA)>
<!ATTLIST description priority CDATA "low"
              status CDATA "open"
              owner CDATA "non assigned"
>
<!ELEMENT task (description)>
<!ELEMENT todo (task+)>
]>
```

RESULT:

```
<todo>
  <task>
    <description priority="high" status="open" owner="Andrew">
      Backup sales data for last month
    </description>
  </task>
  <task>
    <description priority="low" status="open" owner="Andrew">
      Complete end of month report
    </description>
  </task>
</todo>
```

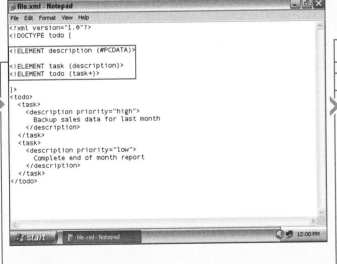

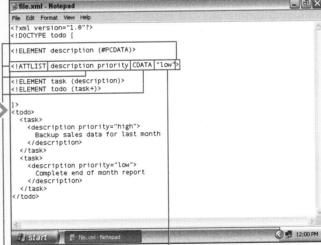

5 Type the code that creates the element declarations for the elements in the XML document.

6 Type the attribute declaration tag.

7 Type the name of the element and the name of the attribute.

8 Type the attribute type.

■ This example uses the most common attribute type, **CDATA**.

Note: See Appendix C for a list of other attribute types.

9 Type the default value for the attribute.

10 Save the file.

■ The XML document is saved.

91

DECLARE ATTRIBUTES AS WORDS

You can define an attribute validation rule to constrain the value of an XML attribute to a single word, or *token,* to help ensure the integrity of the data in the XML document. For example, an attribute you call name may have a value of John, while the same attribute may not have a value of John Smith if you only make the value a word. To define an attribute validation rule that constrains the value of an XML attribute to a single word, you must define the attribute type as NMTOKEN.

You can make the single word any valid XML name. You always start with a letter or an underscore. The remaining characters in a valid XML name can include letters, numbers, periods, hyphens, and underscores. Valid XML names can also contain colons, although you want to avoid colon usage because they cause confusion when you work with namespaces. You cannot use whitespace, such as tabs and spaces, in a valid XML name.

If you define an attribute with an attribute type of NMTOKEN and the attribute's value contains more than a single word, your XML document will fail validation. You can still specify a default value for an NMTOKEN type attribute, but you must make the default value for the attribute a single word; otherwise the document will fail validation.

As with all validation rules in the DTD, specifying that an attribute can only have a single word is useful as long as the application that processes the XML document containing the DTD understands and implements the validation rule. If you create your own applications, you need to ensure that any data that uses the value for an attribute in an XML document conforms to the validation rules laid out in the DTD. The companion CD-ROM has an XML validation application on it called XML Spy that you can use to validate XML documents.

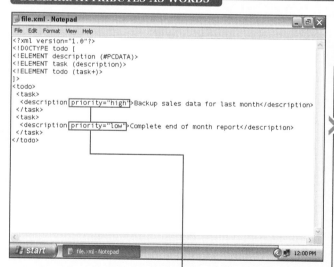

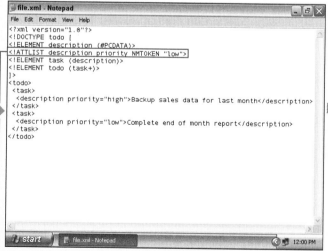

1 Open or create an XML document that contains elements.

2 Type attributes that use a single word as a value to the elements.

Note: For more information about adding attributes, see Chapter 4.

3 Type the code that creates the attribute declaration, setting the attribute type as NMTOKEN.

4 Save the XML document.

Apply It

You can define an attribute validation rule to constrain the value of an XML attribute to multiple words by specifying the NMTOKENS attribute type instead of NMTOKEN.

TYPE THIS:

```
<?xml version="1.0"?>
<!DOCTYPE todo [
<!ELEMENT description (#PCDATA)>
<!ATTLIST description priority NMTOKENS "very low">
<!ELEMENT task (description)>
<!ELEMENT todo (task+)>
]>
<todo>
  <task>
    <description priority="somewhat high"> Backup sales data for last month </description>
  </task>
  <task>
    <description priority="very low">Complete end of month report</description>
  </task>
</todo>
```

RESULT:

This file is valid.

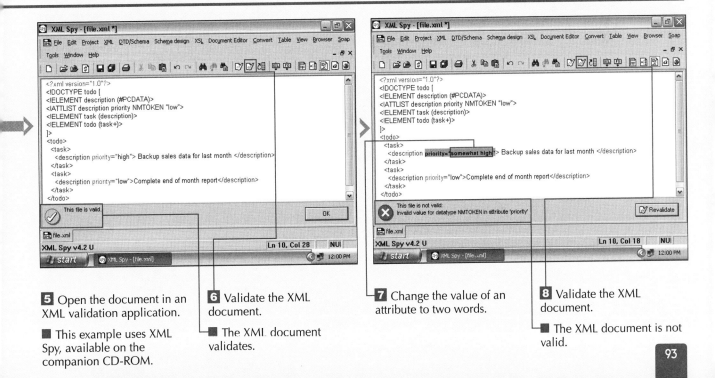

5 Open the document in an XML validation application.

■ This example uses XML Spy, available on the companion CD-ROM.

6 Validate the XML document.

■ The XML document validates.

7 Change the value of an attribute to two words.

8 Validate the XML document.

■ The XML document is not valid.

RESTRICT ATTRIBUTES TO A LIST OF VALUES

Y ou can define a validation rule to constrain the value of an XML attribute to one in a list of predefined values. In other words, you can declare an attribute of type *enumerated list*. Declaring attributes in this way helps reduce input errors and serves as a good approach for fields, where you already know all the possible values during XML document creation. For example, you may have state or province codes available to you when you create the XML document and can easily incorporate this information into a list.

You must separate each option within the list with a vertical bar (|). On most keyboards, you find the vertical bar key to the left of the backspace key, and you commonly use it when programming to symbolize the keyword OR. You can specify any number of values within the enumerated list, although lists with a large number of values can make your declarations harder to read. You enclose the list of possible values that a user can choose in parentheses.

You must give each value within the list of options a valid XML name. Although you must start XML names with a letter or an underscore, the remaining characters can include letters, numbers, periods, hyphens, and underscores.

You can also specify a default value for an attribute that uses an enumerated list. You must make the default value one of the words in the list of possible values.

If you intend to create the code that sets the values for an attribute, and you have those values available in a DTD validation rule, you must also create the code that can parse the attribute declaration and select a valid value from the enumerated list.

The companion CD-ROM has an XML validation application on it called XML Spy that you can use to validate XML documents.

RESTRICT ATTRIBUTES TO A LIST OF VALUES

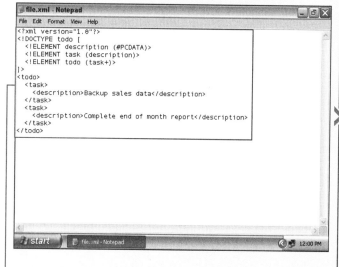

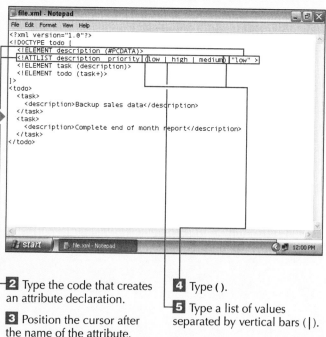

1 Open or create an XML document that contains elements and a DTD.

2 Type the code that creates an attribute declaration.

3 Position the cursor after the name of the attribute.

4 Type ( ).

5 Type a list of values separated by vertical bars (|).

Apply It

Remember that any values you specify within an attribute declaration are always case sensitive; as with most things to do with XML documents, mismatching the case of attribute values results in an error when you validate the XML document.

TYPE THIS:

```
<?xml version="1.0"?>
<!DOCTYPE todo [
<!ELEMENT description (#PCDATA)>
<!ATTLIST description priority (low | high | medium) "low">
<!ELEMENT task (description)>
<!ELEMENT todo (task+)>
]>
<todo>
  <task>
    <description priority="Low">
      Backup sales data for last month
    </description>
  </task>
  <task>
    <description priority="high">
      Complete end of month report
    </description>
  </task>
</todo>
```

RESULT:

```
This file is not valid:
Unexpected choice "Low" for
attribute "priority": (low |
high | medium) expected
```

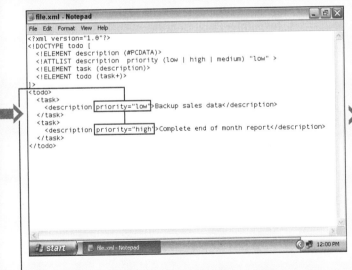

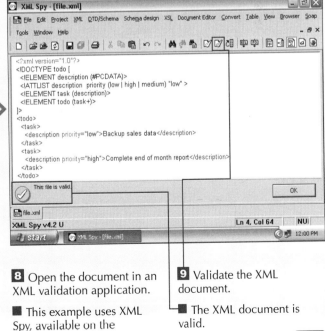

6 Type the code that creates the attributes for the elements as specified in the DTD.

7 Save the XML document.

8 Open the document in an XML validation application.

■ This example uses XML Spy, available on the companion CD-ROM.

9 Validate the XML document.

■ The XML document is valid.

CREATE INTERNAL GENERAL ENTITIES

You can describe a single section of data, called a *general entity*, which you refer to repeatedly inside an XML document. Defining entities saves you from having to constantly repeat long or difficult passages of text inside an XML file. You often define general entities to represent sections of code for information such as addresses, phone numbers, company names, or disclaimers. Apart from reducing the size of the XML document, using general entities also makes it easier to update the information throughout an XML document or, indeed, multiple XML documents. When information changes, for example a phone number, you only have to update the information where you declare the general entity, and not the potentially numerous locations throughout your XML document.

You declare general entities in the DTD. You start an entity declaration in the DTD with <!ENTITY and follow it with

the name for the entity as well as its value. You must enclose the value of an internal general entity within quotation marks (" "). Whenever you include the name of the general entity in the XML document, XML substitutes the values you specify in the DTD for the entity name. When specifying an entity name in an XML document, you precede the name of the general entity with an ampersand (&). You immediately follow the name of the general entity with a semicolon (;).

Most XML applications, including most XML parsers, automatically substitute the value for the general entity name before your code can access the XML document. If you create a Java application that uses an XML parser that does not resolve the entities, you need to create the code that substitutes the specified value for the general entity name throughout the XML document.

CREATE INTERNAL GENERAL ENTITIES

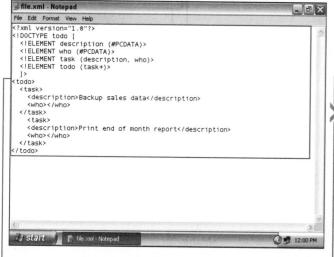

1 Open or create an XML document that contains elements and a DTD.

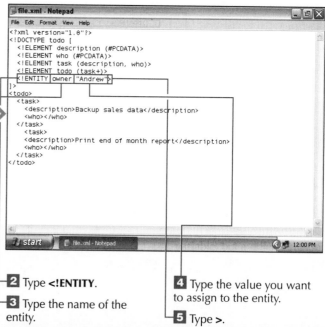

2 Type **<!ENTITY**.

3 Type the name of the entity.

4 Type the value you want to assign to the entity.

5 Type **>**.

Apply It

You do not have to use general entities only in the content of elements; you can also use them to provide information for other parts of an XML document, such as attribute values.

TYPE THIS:

```
<?xml version="1.0"?>
<!DOCTYPE todo [
  <!ELEMENT description (#PCDATA)>
  <!ATTLIST description
  who CDATA #REQUIRED
>
  <!ELEMENT task (description)>
  <!ELEMENT todo (task)>
  <!ENTITY owner "Andrew">
]>
<todo>
  <task>
    <description who="&owner;">Backup sales data</description>
  </task>
</todo>
```

RESULT:

```
- <todo>
  - <task>
      <description who="Andrew">Backup sales data</description>
    </task>
  </todo>
```

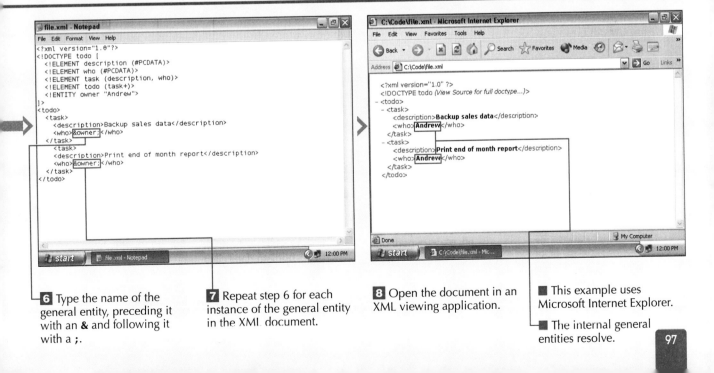

6 Type the name of the general entity, preceding it with an **&** and following it with a **;**.

7 Repeat step 6 for each instance of the general entity in the XML document.

8 Open the document in an XML viewing application.

■ This example uses Microsoft Internet Explorer.

■ The internal general entities resolve.

CREATE A NOTATION

XML documents may contain information other than straight text. You can use an XML document to store, or reference, many different types of data. You use a notation declaration to notify the application that the XML document may contain non-XML data. *Non-XML data* includes information such as a word-processing file, an image file or some other proprietary file type. For example, an XML document that stores information about employees of a company might need to reference an image that contains a picture of an employee.

A notation declaration specifies the name of the notation. It starts with <!NOTATION followed by the name of the notation. You must make the name of a notation a valid XML name consisting of letters, digits, periods, underscores, and hyphens. After the name of a notation, the notation declaration can indicate the file type of the data. You can indicate the file type by including the SYSTEM keyword and following it with the data type of the information that you

want to reference within the XML document. You enclose the data type in quotation marks (" ").

XML applications do not typically support the processing of non-XML data; if you create your own code to process the XML data, you must create code that can handle the data types in the XML document as specified in a notation declaration. Typically, XML applications, such as an XML parser, do not verify or otherwise check the validity of a notation declaration. The XML parser checks the notation declaration for correct formatting, but only to ensure the validity of the DTD and XML documents.

You use notation declarations with external unparsed entities. For more information about external unparsed entities, see the section "Create External General Entities" in this chapter. After you create a notation declaration, you can use an XML validation application to verify the validity of the notation declaration.

CREATE A NOTATION

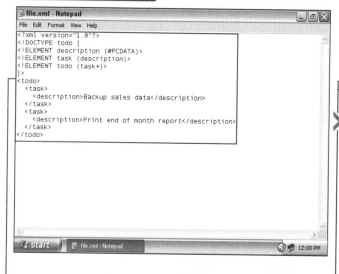

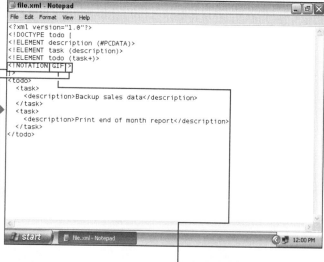

1 Open or create an XML document that contains a DTD.

2 Position the cursor on a new line within the DTD.

3 Type **<!NOTATION>**.

4 Position the cursor within the tag and type the name of the notation.

■ In this example, the notation name is GIF.

Extra

Similar to XML entities and processing instructions, notations enable developers to incorporate non-XML data into XML applications. The difference among these three approaches is as follows:

- *Entities* provide links to the physical location of non-XML data; for example, `<!ENTITY name SYSTEM "http://www.someDomain.com/someURL">`.

- *Processing instructions* provide programmatic instructions for accessing and viewing non-XML data; for example, `<?gcc helloWorld.c?>`.

- *Notations*, in contrast, describe the format of non-XML data files; for example, `<!NOTATION PDF SYSTEM "application/pdf">` or `<!NOTATION PDF PUBLIC "someUrl">`.

You use notation declarations to identify information that requires the use of another application to process the information. The applications that can process the information are called *helper applications*. For example, you may consider an image-editing program a helper application that prints image data stored in an XML document. When dealing with notation declarations and helper applications, you have no guarantee that a specific helper application exists on the computer system processing your XML documents. If you intend to process your XML documents on multiple computers on which you do not have the helper application available, the notation declaration's information may not process as you intend.

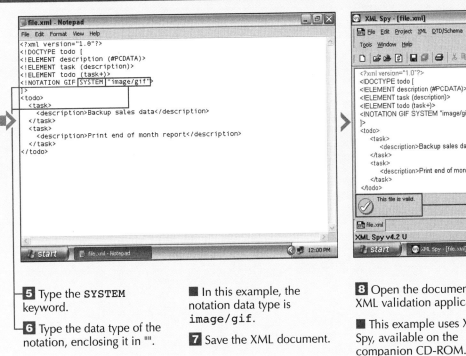

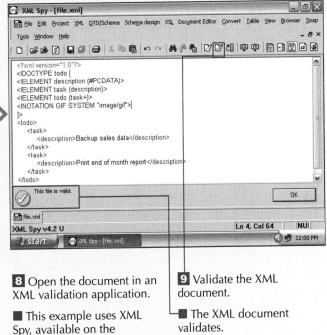

5 Type the SYSTEM keyword.

6 Type the data type of the notation, enclosing it in "".

■ In this example, the notation data type is `image/gif`.

7 Save the XML document.

8 Open the document in an XML validation application.

■ This example uses XML Spy, available on the companion CD-ROM.

9 Validate the XML document.

■ The XML document validates.

CREATE EXTERNAL GENERAL ENTITIES

Y ou can declare an external general entity to reference an external data source, such as a JPG or PDF file, in your XML-based application. You define an external data type as any non-XML data type, such as a picture or word-processing document. While you can store different data types in an XML document, programmers more commonly reference an external file that contains the data.

As with internal general entities, you precede an external general entity declaration with an exclamation point (!) and the ENTITY keyword. You must also specify the name of the external general entity that you want to use. You can indicate the location of the data file by specifying the SYSTEM keyword and following it with the path and filename of the XML data file. You must enclose the filename in quotation marks (" ").

When you reference an external data file in an external entity declaration, and that data file is not another XML document, you must specify the NDATA keyword. You

follow the NDATA keyword with a notation name that you have previously specified in a notation declaration within the DTD. For information about notation declarations, see the section "Create a Notation" in this chapter.

To declare an external general entity that you want to include as an external data source, you must first create a notation declaration in a DTD. To do so, see the section "Create a Notation."

Most XML applications do not automatically process the files to which an external general entity refers. For this reason, when creating your own code, make sure your code can process the files that the general entity indicates. While XML does not require this, you typically use the information in the related notation declaration to process the external general entity. After you create a general entity, you can use an XML validation application to verify the validity of your general entities.

CREATE EXTERNAL GENERAL ENTITIES

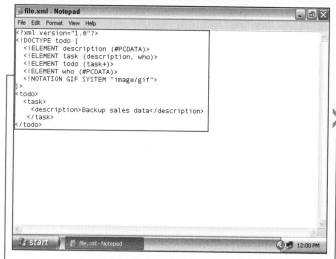

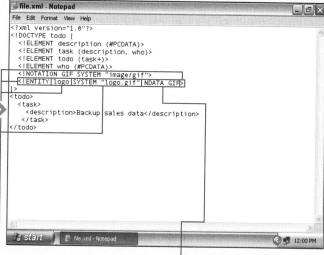

1 Open or create an XML document that contains a DTD.

2 Type **<! ENTITY>**.

3 Position the cursor in the tag and type the name of the entity.

4 Type the **SYSTEM** keyword and follow it with the name of the external file.

5 Type the **NDATA** keyword and follow it with the previously defined notation attribute.

Note: For information about notation declarations, see the section "Create a Notation."

Extra

You can specify an external filename using absolute or relative URLs. For example, the following are all valid entity declarations:

Example:
```
<!ENTITY P1 SYSTEM "product1.gif" NDATA GIF>
<!ENTITY P1 SYSTEM "http://www.someDomain/product1.gif" NDATA GIF>
<!ENTITY P1 SYSTEM "../product1.gif" NDATA GIF>
<!ENTITY P1 SYSTEM "/xml/product1.gif" NDATA GIF>
```

Notation attributes describe non-XML data formats, while external entities reference notation attributes and describe the logical location of a non-XML data file. You must define a notation attribute before you can reference it. A good design practice is to define both notation attributes and notation references (entity declarations) in the same DTD file, such as:

Example:
```
<!NOTATION GIF SYSTEM "image/gif">
<!ENTITY P1 SYSTEM "../product1.gif" NDATA GIF>
```

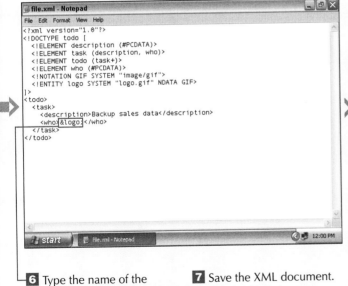

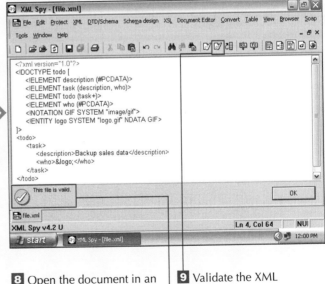

6 Type the name of the general entity, preceding it with an **&** and following it with a **;**.

7 Save the XML document.

8 Open the document in an XML validation application.

■ This example uses XML Spy, available on the companion CD-ROM.

9 Validate the XML document.

■ The XML document validates.

USING NAMESPACES

A common problem with most programming languages and large XML documents is that you can unintentionally have names that conflict. For example, you may have an element called name that refers to the title of a book, and in another part of the XML document, you may have another element called name, which refers to the name of a company. Naming conflicts commonly occur when you merge two or more XML documents into a single XML document. With programming languages such as Java, you can use scoping rules to prevent naming conflicts between various method, variable, and class names. Scoping rules define in what area of your code you can safely use named items.

In XML documents, you can use namespaces to prevent naming conflicts by associating each name with a namespace. You indicate what name belongs to which namespace by preceding each name with a prefix and following it with a colon.

You can create your own prefix names by simply preceding the name with the prefix. When you do so, the prefix name

should make sense within the context of the XML document. For example, you can create a prefix name that represents the section or element that encompasses the section of the XML document where you want to use the namespace. You may find that this makes your XML documents easier to read, understand, and troubleshoot.

In XML documents, using namespaces prevents naming conflicts. Because you can use the colon in any valid XML name, XML applications do not need to recognize namespaces to process XML documents that define namespaces with prefixes. The XML applications can simply interpret the namespace name, the colon, and the element name as a single word, which it can use as the element name. For code that needs to recognize namespace usage within an XML document, you must create the code that determines when, where, and how to use namespaces. You can configure most XML parsers to ignore or recognize the usage of namespaces within an XML document.

USING NAMESPACES

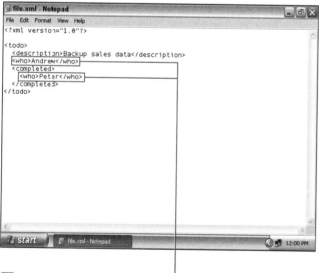

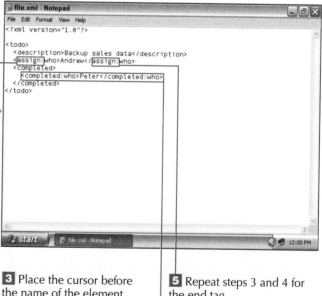

■1 Open or create an XML document.

■2 Create two or more elements of the same name.

■3 Place the cursor before the name of the element.

■4 Type the prefix name followed by a colon (:).

■5 Repeat steps 3 and 4 for the end tag.

■6 Repeat steps 3 to 5 for the element of the same name.

Apply It

Both elements and attributes can use a prefix to indicate that the subsequent name of the element or attribute belongs to a specific namespace.

TYPE THIS:

```
<?xml version="1.0"?>
<!DOCTYPE todo [
  <!ELEMENT assign:who (#PCDATA)>
  <!ELEMENT completed (completed:who)>
  <!ELEMENT completed:who (#PCDATA)>
  <!ATTLIST completed:who
    completed:dept CDATA #REQUIRED>
  <!ELEMENT description (#PCDATA)>
  <!ATTLIST description
    dept CDATA #REQUIRED>
  <!ELEMENT todo (description, assign:who, completed)>
]>
<todo>
  <description dept="sales">Backup sales data</description>
  <assign:who>Andrew</assign:who>
  <completed>
    <completed:who completed:dept="support">Peter</completed:who>
  </completed>
</todo>
```

RESULT:

```
This file is valid.
```

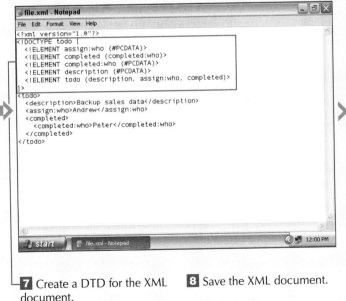

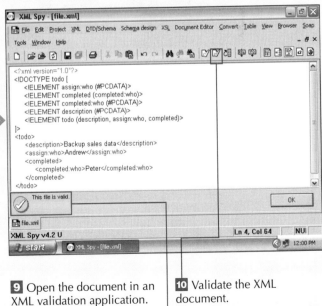

7 Create a DTD for the XML document.

8 Save the XML document.

9 Open the document in an XML validation application.

■ This example uses XML Spy, available on the companion CD-ROM.

10 Validate the XML document.

■ The XML document validates.

USING THE XML NAMESPACE ATTRIBUTE

You can use namespaces to guarantee the uniqueness of names within an XML document and prevent naming conflicts. Although a prefix identifies different namespaces, you must also make sure that the prefixes themselves remain unique.

You can specify the name or address of a URI that identifies a namespace and thus the associated prefix. The XML namespace attribute specifies the URI you associate with a namespace. You typically make the URI in the form of an Internet address such as http://www.company.com/xml/ns. As with all attributes, you specify the XML namespace attribute within the start tag of an element. The name of the XML namespace attribute as specified in the tag is xmlns. You call the URI that targets the XML namespace attribute the *namespace name*.

Although not required, you can have the XML namespace attribute, which targets the URI, provide information about that namespace. Most XML applications do not access the specified URI in the XML namespace attribute. You use the

namespace name primarily to guarantee uniqueness; to ensure uniqueness, no namespaces should ever share the same namespace name.

You can use the XML namespace attribute in XML documents that XML applications, unaware of namespaces, can parse. This ensures compatibility of XML documents that use namespaces with older XML applications, which programmers may have developed before the introduction of namespaces.

You specify the XML namespace attribute just like any other element attribute: you follow the word xmlns with a colon and then the name that you want to use as the namespace prefix. The value of this attribute becomes the namespace name. You must enclose the namespace prefix in quotation marks.

As with the addition of any attribute to an XML document that uses a DTD, you need to alter the DTD to reflect the changes in the XML document when you use namespaces.

USING THE XML NAMESPACE ATTRIBUTE

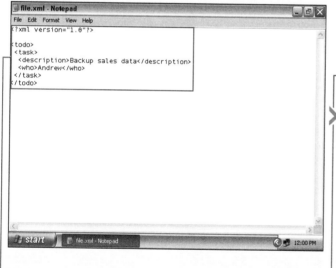

1 Open or create an XML document that contains elements.

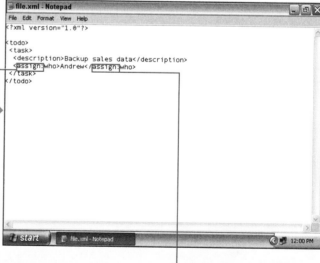

2 Type a prefix to an element name in the element start tag.

3 Type a prefix to an element name in the element end tag.

Extra

You can specify that XML use a default namespace whenever it encounters an unspecified prefix in the XML document. You specify the default namespace within the start tag of the root element. You define the default namespace using the attribute `xmlns` without following the word with a colon and a prefix name.

Example:
```
<!DOCTYPE todo [
<!ELEMENT description (#PCDATA)>
<!ELEMENT task (description, who)>
<!ELEMENT todo (task)>
<!ATTLIST todo xmlns CDATA #REQUIRED>
<!ELEMENT who (#PCDATA) >    ]>
<todo xmlns="http://www.company.com/ns">
  <task>
    <description>Backup sales data</description>
    <who>Andrew</who>
  </task>
</todo>
```

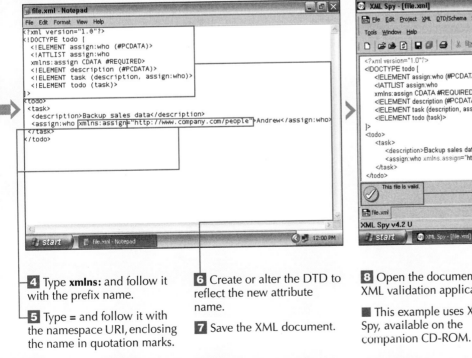

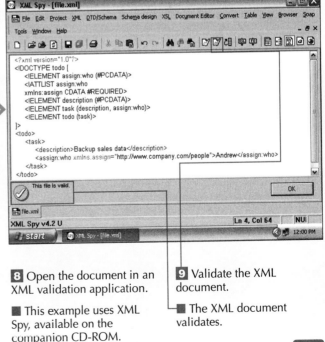

4 Type **xmlns:** and follow it with the prefix name.

5 Type **=** and follow it with the namespace URI, enclosing the name in quotation marks.

6 Create or alter the DTD to reflect the new attribute name.

7 Save the XML document.

8 Open the document in an XML validation application.

■ This example uses XML Spy, available on the companion CD-ROM.

9 Validate the XML document.

■ The XML document validates.

INTRODUCING XML SCHEMAS

XML Schema, an XML document that you create with XML syntax, allows you to describe and constrain both the structure and the data within an XML document. Having well-defined and easily described XML documents using XML Schemas makes it easier and more efficient to exchange the XML documents with other applications. Although you can accomplish many of the same tasks with DTDs, XML Schemas offer many more advantages than DTDs. In fact, XML Schemas are intended to replace the use of DTDs.

WHY NOT DTDS?

Non-Standard Format

Programmers who are unfamiliar with Standardized Generalized Markup Language (SGML) may find the keywords, coding styles, and structure of DTDs somewhat confusing. DTDs are unlike most programming languages as well as XML, so beginners must learn a new method of coding prior to creating XML documents if they want to use DTDs with their XML documents. You find this less likely with XML Schemas, which use a standard XML coding style in their creation.

Inflexibility

You may find DTDs limited in their ability to describe the actual content of the XML documents. For example, you cannot use a DTD to limit the content of an element to a numerical value. DTDs allow you to specify a number of data types, which you can use to restrict the type of content in an XML document, but you cannot use DTDs to restrict data to more complex data types, such as a `string` that consists of numbers. XML Schemas give you much better control over the type of information that you can place in an XML document.

Coexisting

You should know how to use, create, and modify both DTDs and XML Schemas; you use both when creating XML documents and both have valid methods for constraining and attempting to ensure the integrity of information in an XML document. For simpler XML documents, you may find DTDs more than adequate. For more complex documents, you may need to have more control over the content and structure of XML documents. For example, in XML documents that other people modify, you may want to use the more sophisticated aspects of an XML Schema to restrict the modifications that they can make.

ADVANTAGES OF XML SCHEMAS

Strong Data Typing

XML Schemas allow you to specify the content of the elements in an XML document. You can use XML Schemas to specify that the content of an element be a simple piece of data, such as a number, or you can even specify a more complex data structure that contains multiple elements, multiple data types, attributes, and structures. You can also constrain values to lists, making it harder for someone to inadvertently add incorrect data.

Modular Design

XML Schemas enable you to work with data structures, which you may find more familiar if you have previously worked with object-oriented programming languages. For example, XML Schemas allow you to modify, reuse, and replace previously created objects. As in any object-oriented programming language, modularity promotes more efficient and effective use of data. It also makes it much easier to modify, upgrade, or update your XML documents, making your information more extensible.

Namespaces Support

XML Schema fully supports the use of namespaces. Not only does XML Schema support a single namespace, but it also allows you to use multiple namespaces in a single XML document. This makes it much easier to reuse element definitions, freeing you from having to re-create the element rules each time you want to use them. As with namespaces in DTDs, you use prefixes to distinguish elements from other elements by referencing different namespaces.

Easy to Learn

Unlike DTDs, you create XML Schemas using XML tags. This means that programmers learning to create XML Schemas do not have to learn a new coding language at the same time. They can focus solely on creating the schemas themselves, and not on learning the syntax to create the schemas. The XML syntax that creates XML Schemas is the exactly same as the syntax you find in any standard XML document.

Efficient Data Exchange

Using XML Schemas allows applications to describe the information that they exchange with other applications. This allows applications that share data to understand this exchanged information. For example, XML Schema makes it possible to identify date and time information, which many applications also exchange. Before accessing the information in the XML document, the application can use the schema and determine where the information in the document is located as well as the format of the information within the XML document.

Fewer Errors

When using XML documents, including those that make use of DTDs, you could consider the document well-formed and valid, but you could still find errors in the data itself. For example, a telephone number may have a missing digit, or you may have omitted the address of a company. In both of these cases, the XML document reports any errors during validation. XML Schemas allow much more control over what can make up the content of an XML document, and this reduces the number of errors in the information stored in the XML document.

CREATE AN XML SCHEMA DECLARATION

You can create an XML Schema to describe the structure and content of an XML document. An XML Schema consists of an XML document that you can generate with XML syntax. You create the XML Schema using a schema declaration, which has a schema element. Because it uses XML syntax, the schema element must have a start and an end tag.

The XML Schema start tag contains the xmlns attribute, which targets the XML Schema namespace. The XML Schema namespace consists of an XML Schema containing the definitions for elements and attributes, which construct the schema. The xmlns attribute also allows you to specify the prefixes that identify the XML Schema namespace.

With namespaces, you can declare elements globally or locally. To declare an element globally, you must do so within the root element of the XML document. You declare locally declared elements within the content of another element, other than the root element.

You use the elementFormDefault attribute to mark a namespace prefix both as a globally and locally declared element. When you specify the value of the elementFormDefault attribute as unqualified, only global elements use the namespace prefix. Setting the elementFormDefault value to qualified means that you must use a namespace prefix for all elements within the XML document, whether global or local.

Because an XML Schema is still an XML document, you must include an XML declaration as the first line of the XML Schema. You can save XML Schemas as plain text files, typically with the extension .xsd. Once you have saved the XML Schema file, you can reference it from within the XML document that will use the XML Schema to constrain the structure and data in that XML document.

CREATE AN XML SCHEMA DECLARATION

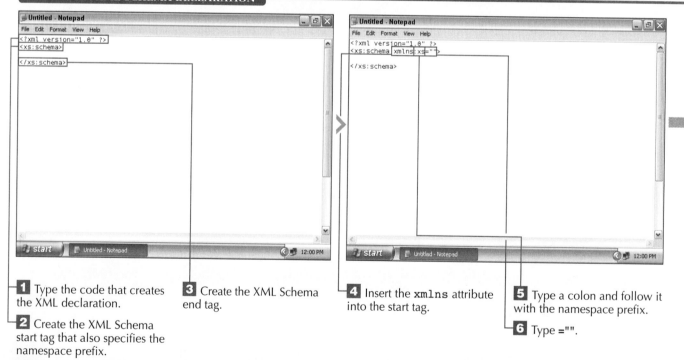

■1 Type the code that creates the XML declaration.

■2 Create the XML Schema start tag that also specifies the namespace prefix.

■3 Create the XML Schema end tag.

■4 Insert the xmlns attribute into the start tag.

■5 Type a colon and follow it with the namespace prefix.

■6 Type ="".

Extra

You may find it difficult to visualize the finished XML Schema file. An example of a simple XML Schema for a very basic XML document might look like this:

Example:

```
<xs:schema xmlns:xs="http://www.w3.org/2001/XMLSchema"
elementFormDefault="qualified">
  <xs:element name="description">
    <xs:complexType>
      <xs:simpleContent>
        <xs:extension base="xs:string">
          <xs:attribute name="priority" type="xs:string" use="required"/>
        </xs:extension>
      </xs:simpleContent>
    </xs:complexType>
  </xs:element>
  <xs:element name="owner" type="xs:string"/>
  <xs:element name="task">
    <xs:complexType>
      <xs:sequence>
        <xs:element ref="description"/>
        <xs:element ref="owner"/>
      </xs:sequence>
    </xs:complexType>
  </xs:element>
</xs:schema>
```

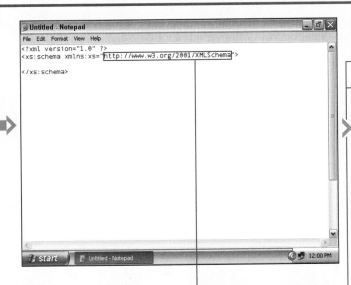

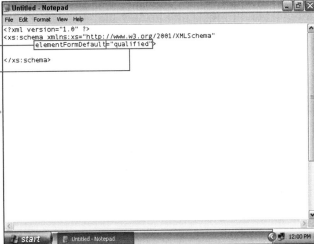

7 Position the cursor between the quotation marks.

8 Type the name of the XML Schema namespace.

9 Insert the `elementFormDefault` attribute into the start tag.

10 Assign the value `qualified` to the `elementFormDefault` attribute.

11 Save the XML Schema file.

■ The XML Schema is saved in a file.

DECLARE AN ELEMENT

You use elements, the most common type of items within an XML document, to identify information. A simple element consists of a start tag and an end tag with the content of the elements between the tags. Elements can also contain other elements; for more information, see the section "Declare a Container Element" in this chapter.

As with elements in DTDs and XML documents, you must declare the elements in the XML Schema that you declare within the XML document. A simple element declaration within an XML Schema specifies the name of an element and the type of data that you want the element to hold. You specify the name of an element within the start and end tags of that element in an XML document.

The element content's data type constrains the element content's value within the XML document. When the content of an element does not match the constraints as specified in the XML Schema, the XML document fails validation when you check it with a validation application. For information about validating XML documents that use an XML schema, refer to the section "Validate an XML Document" in this chapter. You must use valid XML documents when accessing XML documents from within a Java application you create, regardless of whether the XML document uses an XML Schema.

When specifying the data type of an element content that consists solely of text, you can use the value string in the element declaration. You must prefix the string value with the namespace name you use for the XML Schema namespace, previously defined within the same XML Schema.

When converting an XML document using a DTD to an XML document that utilizes an XML Schema, you can use a string data type to replace data that have a CDATA type.

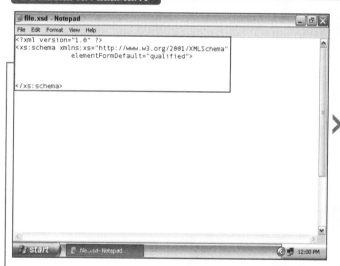

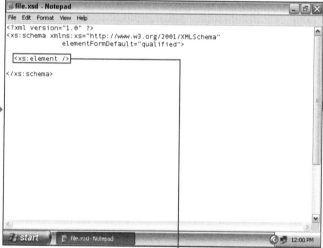

1 Open or create an XML Schema file that contains the XML Schema declaration.

Note: You can use the code from the section "Create an XML Schema Declaration."

2 Position the cursor between the start and end tags of the schema element.

3 Type the code that creates an empty element tag.

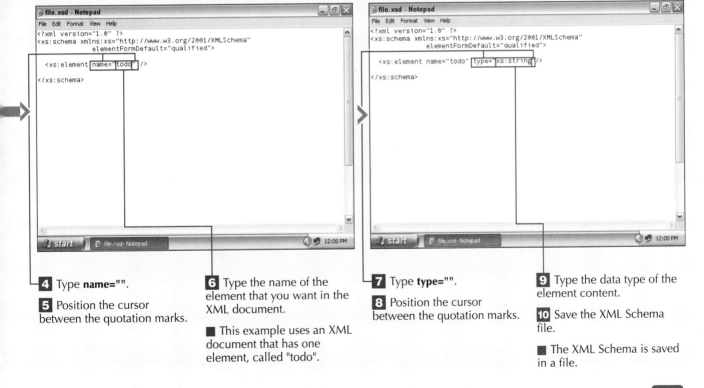

Apply It

If you use empty elements within your XML documents, you still must declare those elements within an XML Schema. To declare an element as 'empty' you must include the `complexType` element tag within the element's declaration. You do not have to specify the data type for an empty element. You do not consider the whitespace within an XML document between the element tags textual data.

XML Document
```
<todo>
</todo>
```

XML Schema
```
<xs:schema xmlns:xs="http://www.w3.org/2001/XMLSchema" elementFormDefault="qualified">
  <xs:element name="todo">
    <xs:complexType/>
  </xs:element>
</xs:schema>
```

-4 Type **name=""**.

5 Position the cursor between the quotation marks.

6 Type the name of the element that you want in the XML document.

■ This example uses an XML document that has one element, called "todo".

7 Type **type=""**.

8 Position the cursor between the quotation marks.

9 Type the data type of the element content.

10 Save the XML Schema file.

■ The XML Schema is saved in a file.

ASSIGN AN XML SCHEMA TO AN XML DOCUMENT

Once you create an XML Schema file, you can assign it to an XML document. To create an XML Schema file, see the sections "Create an XML Schema Declaration" and "Declare an Element." Assigning an XML Schema to an XML document involves specifying the location of the XML Schema file within the XML document. You do this by specifying the XML Schema file within the root element of the XML document that will utilize the XML Schema file.

The root element also uses the xmlns attribute to reference the location of the XML Schema namespace for instances. You must use this namespace if you intend to utilize the XML Schemas.

The prefix that you typically associate with the XML Schema namespace for instances is xsi. Only more sophisticated XML applications actually use the information in the xmlns attribute to locate and access the XML Schema namespace for instances. While most applications do not use the

information specified as the value for the xmlns attribute, you must define the xmlns attribute in order for your XML Schema and XML document to be valid. For information about validating XML documents that use an XML Schema, refer to the section "Validate an XML Document" in this chapter.

The noNamespaceSchemaLocation attribute of the XML Schema namespace for instances specifies the name of the XML Schema file for the element. For simple XML documents, only the root element uses the noNamespaceSchemaLocation attribute. The noNamespaceSchemaLocation attribute helps the XML application to recognize that it references an XML Schema file and not another namespace name.

You do not have to make any modifications that depend upon which XML document uses the XML Schema file. In this way, you can use the same XML Schema file with multiple XML documents.

ASSIGN AN XML SCHEMA TO AN XML DOCUMENT

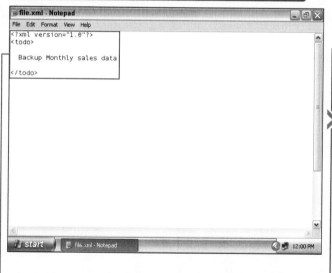

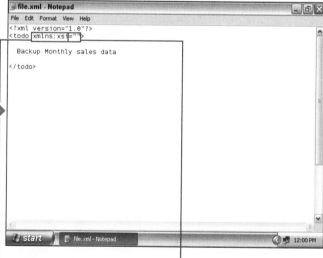

1 Open or create a simple XML document.

■ This example uses an XML document with a single element called "todo" that contains textual data.

2 Insert the **xmlns** attribute into the start tag.

3 Type **=""**.

Extra

You are not limited to using the `xsi` prefix when referring to the XML Schema namespace for instances. You can use any prefix you want as long as you use it consistently in the implementation of the prefix. Because `xsi` is the most commonly used prefix, you should not change it without good reason, as changing it may make your code harder to read by others.

Example:

```
<?xml version="1.0"?>
<todo xmlns:xmlNxInst="http://www.w3.org/2001/XMLSchema-instance"
    xmlNxInst:noNamespaceSchemaLocation="C:\Code\file.xsd">
<task priority="high">
    <description>Backup Sales Data</description>
    <owner>Andrew</owner>
  </task>
  <task priority="Low">
    <description>Backup Accounting Data</description>
    <owner>Andrew</owner>
  </task>
</todo>
```

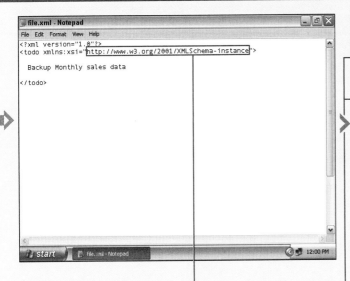

4 Position the cursor between the quotation marks.

5 Type the name of the XML Schema namespace for instances.

6 Insert the `noNamespace SchemaLocation` attribute into the start tag.

7 Assign the name of the XML Schema file to the `noNamespaceSchema Location` attribute.

8 Save the XML document.

■ The XML Schema is saved in a file.

VALIDATE AN XML DOCUMENT

You can validate an XML document to ensure that the contents of the referenced XML document conform to the rules as you specify them in an XML Schema. If the XML document contains information that does not conform to the specified XML Schema document rules, you consider the XML document invalid. During validation, the XML validation application checks each element in the XML document and compares it against the rules laid down for that element within the XML Schema document.

You can install an XML validation application on your computer. An XML validation application can check your XML documents to ensure that they conform to the defined rules in any previously created DTDs or XML Schema documents. As well as validating an XML document, you can also validate an XML Schema file itself. Because an XML

Schema document is also an XML document, it must conform to the rules of well-formedness and validity that apply to other XML documents. If your XML Schema document is not valid, you cannot check your XML documents against the XML Schema file for validity. When using an XML validation application, you must ensure that the application has the capability of validating documents using XML Schema documents and not just the capacity of validating the XML Schema documents themselves. Some older validation applications can only validate XML documents against a DTD and not an XML Schema document.

If the XML validation application finds an XML document invalid, the application typically indicates when and where the error occurred. You can use this information to correct the errors in your document or XML Schema file.

VALIDATE AN XML DOCUMENT

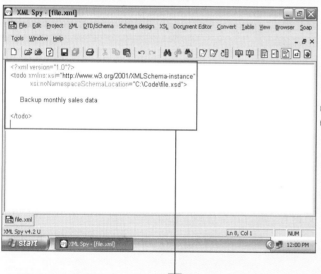

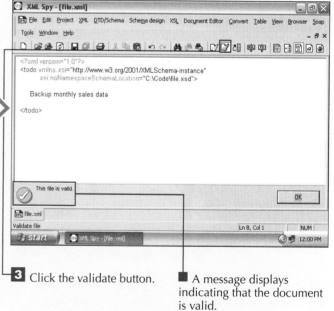

VALIDATE A VALID XML DOCUMENT

1 Start your XML validation application.

■ This example uses XML Spy, available on the companion CD-ROM.

2 Open or create an XML document that references an XML Schema.

Note: You can use the code created in the section "Assign an XML Schema to an XML Document."

3 Click the validate button.

■ A message displays indicating that the document is valid.

Extra

You can validate the actual XML Schema document by submitting it to a validation service on the World Wide Web. This enables you to create and check your XML Schema documents without having to install an XML validation application on your own computer. The most popular schema validation service is available from the World Wide Web Consortium, located at http://www.w3.org/2001/03/webdata/xsv. When you create XML documents and their related XML Schemas, or DTDS, an application called an XML parser accesses the XML documents from within your Java code. An XML parser can only process valid XML documents and make the information in those valid XML documents available to your Java application. To ensure proper XML parser operation, if possible, you should check your XML documents for validity before accessing them from within your Java applications.

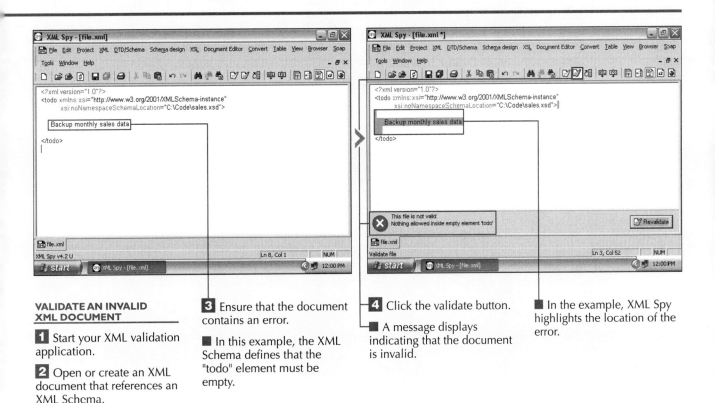

VALIDATE AN INVALID XML DOCUMENT

1 Start your XML validation application.

2 Open or create an XML document that references an XML Schema.

3 Ensure that the document contains an error.

■ In this example, the XML Schema defines that the "todo" element must be empty.

4 Click the validate button.

■ A message displays indicating that the document is invalid.

■ In the example, XML Spy highlights the location of the error.

DECLARE A CONTAINER ELEMENT

Apart from textual data, as shown in the section "Declare an Element," elements can also contain other elements. Creating elements within other elements allows you to build more complex XML document structures that can better organize information. You declare elements in an XML Schema that stipulates that the elements can only contain other elements. You use the `complexType` tag to declare the sub-elements of a container element and to create complex groups of data within an element.

You can specify in what order you want to create the sub-elements of a container element. When specifying the sequence of elements, you consider the XML document invalid if the sequence of elements in the XML document does not match the sequence of the elements in the XML Schema file.

When declaring a container element, you do not have to specify the element's data type in the same manner as you

would the data type for an element that contains information such as textual data. For more information about declaring elements that have textual data, see "Declare an Element" in this chapter.

The sequence of an element enforces the integrity of information within the XML document. For example, if you have an element that stores the address of a client, you can ensure that the information stores in a certain sequence; for example, you can specify the order: street, then city, and finally ZIP Code. As with all elements in an XML document, the sequence element must have a start and an end tag. For more information about start and end tags, see Chapter 4.

When a container element contains sub-elements, you must declare the sub-elements in the XML Schema. For simple elements that have only textual content, you can declare the elements with a data type of `string`. You must include a declaration for each separate element in the container element.

DECLARE A CONTAINER ELEMENT

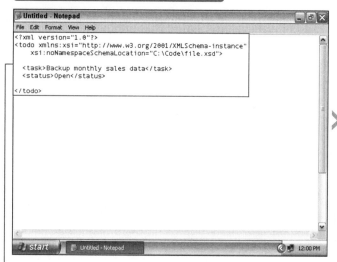

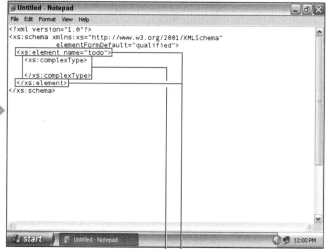

1 Create an XML document that contains a root element and two sub-elements.

2 Save the XML document.

3 Open or create an XML Schema file.

Note: You can use the code from the section "Create an XML Schema Declaration."

4 Type the code that declares the root element of the XML document.

5 Type the code that creates the `complexType` tags.

Apply It

You use the sequence tag known as a *compositor*, to ensure that you place the elements in an XML document in a precise order. To create a container element that contains other elements that you do not need to place in an ordered sequence, you use the 'all' compositor instead of the 'sequence' compositor when declaring the element. Unlike using DTDS, this feature makes XML Schemas very versatile when it comes to defining the structure of elements.

Example:

```
<xs:schema xmlns:xs="http://www.w3.org/2001/XMLSchema"
elementFormDefault="qualified">
  <xs:element name="todo">
    <xs:complexType>
      <xs:all>
      <xs:element name="task" type="xs:string"/>
      <xs:element name="status" type="xs:string"/>
      </xs:all>
    </xs:complexType>
  </xs:element>
</xs:schema>
```

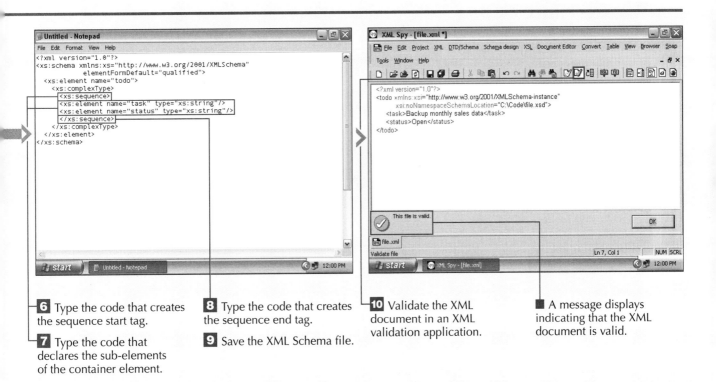

6 Type the code that creates the sequence start tag.

7 Type the code that declares the sub-elements of the container element.

8 Type the code that creates the sequence end tag.

9 Save the XML Schema file.

10 Validate the XML document in an XML validation application.

■ A message displays indicating that the XML document is valid.

DECLARE OPTIONAL ELEMENTS

You can declare elements in an XML Schema that you may or may not have present in the XML documents. When gathering data requirements for your XML document, you may find that the values for certain elements do not always exist at the time that you create the XML document. For example, in the case of an XML document that contains information about products, a newly introduced product may not have complete information about the product at the time of the product's introduction. Therefore, a product name and price might exist, but information such as units sold or supplier names may not. In cases such as these, you can define optional elements that you can add to an XML document as more information becomes available.

In the element declaration, you can use the `minOccurs` attribute to specify the minimum amount of occurrences of an element. You make the value of the `minOccurs` attribute the minimum number of times that the elements can appear, and express it as an integer. Although you use the value of the attribute as a numerical value, you must still enclose it, like all attribute values, in quotation marks.

When you specify a value of zero for the `minOccurs` attribute, the element is understood to be optional. The XML Schema sets the rule that the elements may appear in the XML document, or may not appear at all.

You still consider an empty element in an XML document an occurrence of an element, so an XML validation application can check the `minOccurs` attributes both for elements that have content, and elements that are empty. For more information about empty elements, see Chapter 4.

DECLARE OPTIONAL ELEMENTS

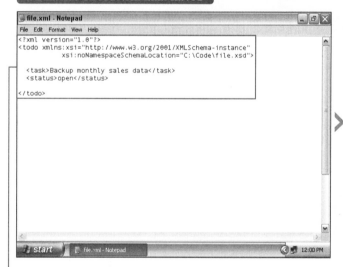

1 Open or create an XML document that contains elements.

Note: You can use the XML document from the section "Declare a Container Element."

2 Open or create an XML Schema document for the XML document created in step 1.

Note: You can use the XML Schema document from the section "Declare a Container Element."

3 Create an element declaration for an element that does not exist in the XML document.

You can specify the maximum amount of times that an element may appear by defining a value for the maxOccurs attribute. You can make the value for the maxOccurs attribute any positive integer value other than zero. To specify that an optional element can occur no more than once, set the maxOccurs attribute to one and the minOccurs attribute to zero.

Example:

```
<?xml version="1.0"?>
<xs:schema xmlns:xs="http://www.w3.org/2001/XMLSchema" elementFormDefault="qualified">
  <xs:element name="todo">
    <xs:complexType>
      <xs:sequence>
        <xs:element name="task" type="xs:string"/>
        <xs:element name="status" type="xs:string"/>
        <xs:element maxOccurs="1" minOccurs="0"
            name="priority" type="xs:string"/>
      </xs:sequence>
    </xs:complexType>
  </xs:element>
</xs:schema>
```

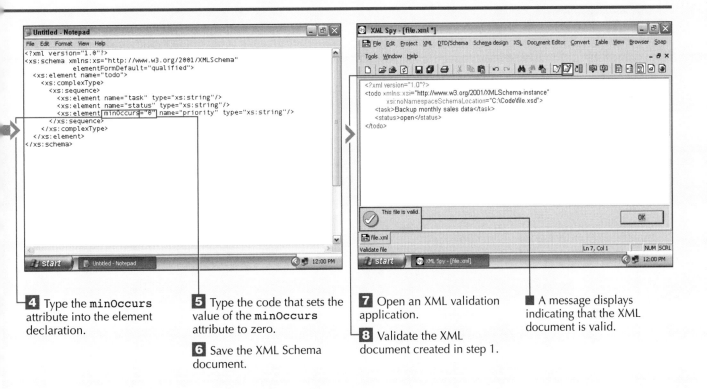

4 Type the minOccurs attribute into the element declaration.

5 Type the code that sets the value of the minOccurs attribute to zero.

6 Save the XML Schema document.

7 Open an XML validation application.

8 Validate the XML document created in step 1.

■ A message displays indicating that the XML document is valid.

SPECIFY DATA TYPES

Y ou can specify different data types for the content of elements. You refer to the data types that you can specify for an element as *primitive data types*. You can use elements that contain primitive data types as the basis for creating more complex data structures within your XML documents.

The ability to specify the data types for an element is another major advantage that using XML Schema documents has over using a DTD. Specifying the data type of the content of an element helps to ensure the integrity of the data that enters into an XML document. For example, you can set the data type of the content of an element as a number; thus, if someone modifies your XML document and inadvertently enters a string of text instead of a number for that element, the XML document fails validation, and the XML validation application should indicate the location

of the error. While most validation applications report the location of any errors, some validation applications may only report that an error occurred. If you create your own programs to validate XML documents, you should always generate as much information as possible about errors, including their location, in the event that errors occur.

You specify the data type in the element declaration using the type attribute. The value of the type attribute indicates the data type of the content that allows for that element. For textual data the data type is `string`. You have a number of data types for numerical data including `decimal` for decimal numbers and `float` for 32-bit floating numbers. For a list of data types that you can use when specifying the data type for an element, refer to Appendix C.

SPECIFY DATA TYPES

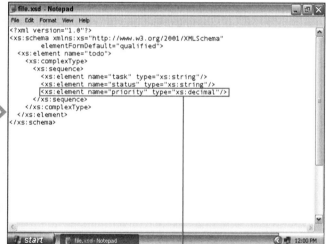

1 Open or create an XML document that contains **string** elements and uses an XML Schema.

Note: You can use the XML document from the section "Declare a Container Element."

2 Create an element that contains a decimal number.

3 Save the XML document.

4 Open or create an XML Schema document for the XML document created in step 1.

Note: You can use the XML Schema document from the section "Declare a Container Element."

5 Create an element declaration for the element that you created in step 2.

6 Save the XML Schema document.

Extra

You can use XML documents to store many different types of data; you can build even the most complex data structures in XML documents using elements consisting of simple data types. You have a wide range of data types that specify the content of an element. For a more complete list of element data types, please refer to Appendix C.

COMMON ELEMENT DATA TYPES	
DATA TYPES	**DESCRIPTION**
xs:string	Textual data such as names, addresses, and product descriptions
xs:decimal	Decimal numbers such as 3.0 and 4.27
xs:integer	Whole numbers like 27 and 502
xs:boolean	A true or false value
xs:date	A specific date such as 1998-09-19
xs:time	The time of day such as 13:34:01

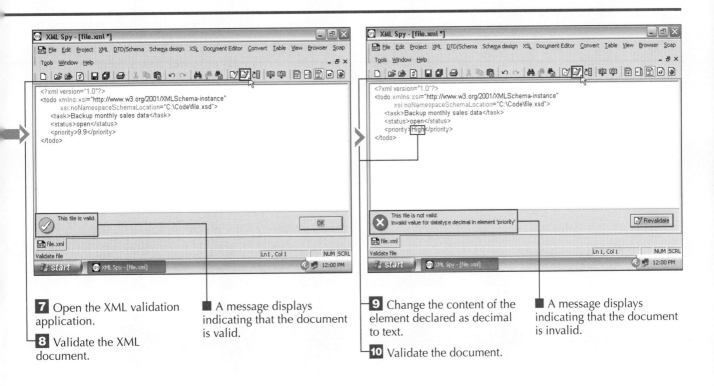

7 Open the XML validation application.

8 Validate the XML document.

■ A message displays indicating that the document is valid.

9 Change the content of the element declared as decimal to text.

10 Validate the document.

■ A message displays indicating that the document is invalid.

CONSTRAIN ELEMENT VALUES

Y ou can restrict the values of an element to ensure the integrity of the data in an XML document. You can define two types of information in an XML Schema: complex and simple.

You can restrict the characteristics, or facets, of information that become the content of an element. For example, in an element that contains textual data, you may want to limit the number of characters that make up that textual data, such as a 50-character limit for the number of characters in a person's name. You can also restrict the minimum length of characters of textual data; for instance, you may restrict an element that stores country location information to a minimum of two characters, thus ensuring that anyone modifying or adding information to the XML document stipulates at least an abbreviation for the country as the content of the element.

You restrict the information in the element using a simpleType definition. Once you create the simpleType element, you create a restriction element that details the restrictions on the type of data that makes up the content of the element. The restriction tag uses the base attribute to specify the data type of the element. Depending on the data type of the element, you can then specify the different kinds of restrictions that you want to apply to the data. Each facet has its own tag, which specifies the facet's name, as well as a value attribute, which specifies the value of the facet. For example, the string data type has a minimum length facet that you set to a number, which becomes the minimum required number of characters for the element in an XML document. For a list of data types and the applicable facets for those data types, refer to Appendix C.

CONSTRAIN ELEMENT VALUES

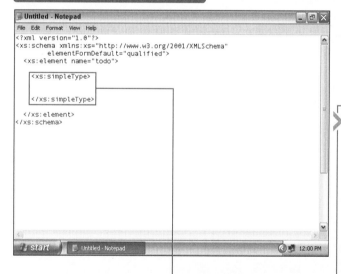

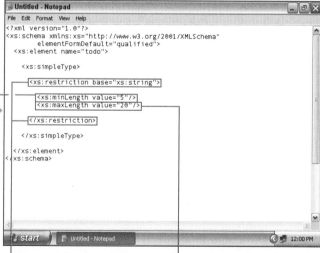

1 Create an XML Schema file element for an XML document that contains a single element.

■ This example uses an XML document with a root element called "todo" that will contain textual data.

2 Type the code that creates the opening and closing simpleType tags.

3 Type the code that creates a restriction tag, which imposes restrictions based on the string data type.

4 Type the code to specify the minimum length of the string content.

5 Type the code to specify the maximum length of the string content.

6 Save the XML Schema document.

Apply It

You can restrict the length of data of a `string` element to a specific number of characters by using the `length` facet. When using the `length` facet, be aware that any whitespace, such as a new line, is counted as a character.

To restrict the textual data of an element to precisely five characters, use the following code:

Example:
```
<?xml version="1.0"?>
<xs:schema xmlns:xs="http://www.w3.org/2001/XMLSchema"
        elementFormDefault="qualified">
  <xs:element name="todo">
    <xs:simpleType>
      <xs:restriction base="xs:string">
        <xs:length value="5"/>
      </xs:restriction>
    </xs:simpleType>
  </xs:element>
</xs:schema>
```

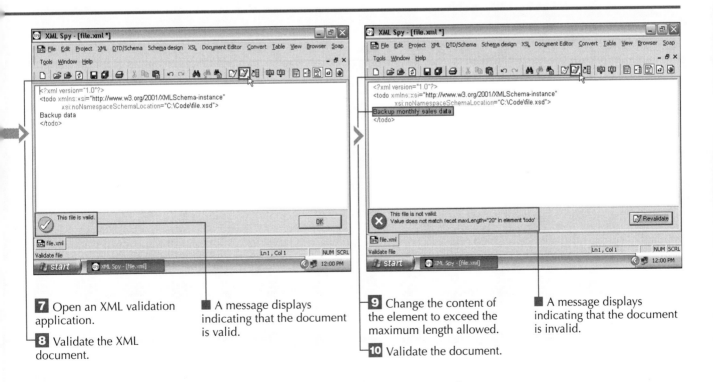

7 Open an XML validation application.

8 Validate the XML document.

■ A message displays indicating that the document is valid.

9 Change the content of the element to exceed the maximum length allowed.

10 Validate the document.

■ A message displays indicating that the document is invalid.

CONSTRAIN ELEMENT VALUES TO A LIST

You can restrict the value of an element in an XML document to a value that resides in a list, a capability you may find useful when creating XML documents. For example, you may constrain an element's value to a list of country codes, area codes, or product model numbers. Constraining values of an element to a list efficiently ensures the integrity of your data, particularly if a user may modify or otherwise alter that data.

The first step in restricting an element to a choice of values involves creating a simple type definition, which characterizes the restrictions of the element. The restriction element specifies the base data type of the element. If you create an element that stores a value chosen from a list of words, you define the base type, as specified in the restriction element, as a `string`. You can set the base type of the element to any valid type that allows you to specify values from a list.

Within the restriction element, the enumeration element specifies the actual values that you consider valid for that element. The data type that you specify within the enumeration element must match the data type as specified in the restriction element.

If you specify a value for an element in an XML document, and the value does not match any of the choices that the enumeration element in the XML Schema document indicates, the XML document will fail validation. The validation application typically indicates the nature and location of the error that causes the validation to fail. By default, you consider any whitespace within the content of the element as part of the textual data of the element.

CONSTRAIN ELEMENT VALUES TO A LIST

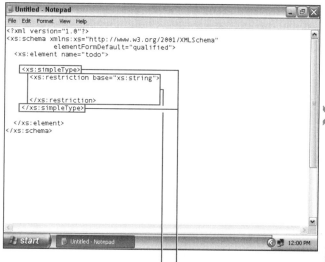

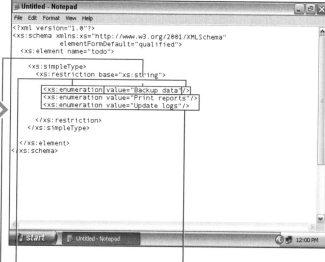

1 Open or create an XML Schema file.

■ This example uses an XML Schema file for an XML document that has a single element called "todo," which contains textual data.

2 Type the code that creates the `simpleType` element.

3 Type the code that creates the restriction element, setting the base data type to `string`.

4 Type the code that creates an enumeration element.

5 Type the code that sets the value of the value attribute to a list option.

6 Repeat steps 4 and 5 for each item in the list.

Apply
It

You can declare the elements in an XML Schema so validation applications can ignore any whitespace within the element. You often use whitespace within XML documents to make the XML document more readable. To specify that a validation application should ignore whitespace within an element when comparing the element's value to an enumerated list, use the `xs:whiteSpace` element.

Example:

```xml
<?xml version="1.0"?>
<xs:schema xmlns:xs="http://www.w3.org/2001/XMLSchema"
              elementFormDefault="qualified">
  <xs:element name="todo">
    <xs:simpleType>
      <xs:restriction base="xs:string">
        <xs:whiteSpace value="collapse"/>
        <xs:enumeration value="Backup data"/>
        <xs:enumeration value="Print reports"/>
        <xs:enumeration value="Update logs"/>
      </xs:restriction>
    </xs:simpleType>
  </xs:element>
</xs:schema>
```

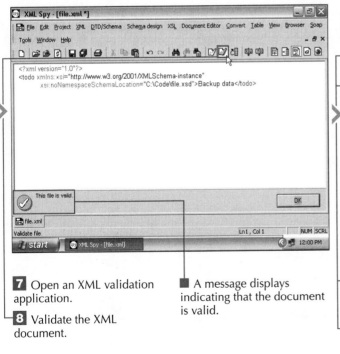

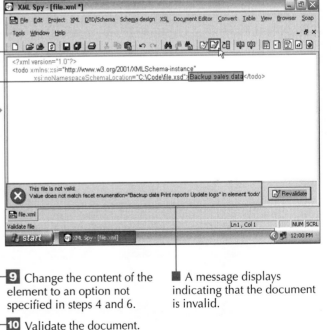

7 Open an XML validation application.

8 Validate the XML document.

■ A message displays indicating that the document is valid.

9 Change the content of the element to an option not specified in steps 4 and 6.

10 Validate the document.

■ A message displays indicating that the document is invalid.

DECLARE AN ATTRIBUTE

Y ou can declare elements in an XML document so that you can assign additional information to them in the form of attributes. For more information about element attributes, see Chapter 4. You can define elements that contain only values and no attributes or other elements as *simple types*. If you want to use attributes with elements in an XML document, you have to declare those attributes in the XML Schema document for that XML document.

Adding attributes to an element involves the creation of a complex type using a `complexType` definition. You can use complex types of data structures within an XML Schema to contain attributes, elements, or other complex-type data structures.

Each complex type must use a compositor element to indicate the sequence of items within the complex type. You can use the sequence compositor to specify the exact order of items within the complex type. For more

information about the sequence compositor, see "Declare a Container Element" in this chapter.

To define the attributes for an element, you must use the `simpleContent` and extension elements within the `complexType` element declaration.

You use the `simpleContent` element to indicate that the element does not contain other elements, and only textual data. The extension element indicates the data type of the elements.

The attribute declaration itself is very similar to an element declaration in that you must specify the data type of the attributes. You can make the data type any standard schema primitive data type. For textual values, you can specify the `string` data type. The attribute declaration also includes the name of the attribute as specified in the element tag within the XML declaration.

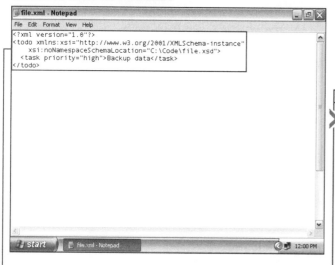

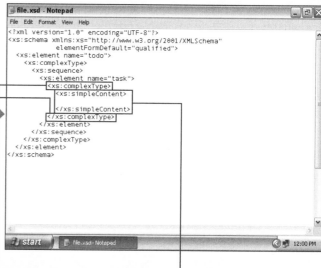

1 Open or create an XML document that uses an XML Schema and contains an element that has an attribute.

2 Open the XML Schema for the XML document you created in step 1.

3 Create the **complexType** element for the element for which you want to create the attribute.

4 Create the **simpleContent** element for the element you wish to create the attribute for.

Apply It

Just because you define an attribute in an XML Schema, does not mean you must use it in an XML document. To force an element to use an attribute, you can specify a value of `required` for the `use` attribute within the attribute's declaration.

Example:
```
<xs:schema xmlns:xs="http://www.w3.org/2001/XMLSchema"
                elementFormDefault="qualified">
  <xs:element name="todo">
    <xs:complexType>
      <xs:sequence>
        <xs:element name="task">
          <xs:complexType>
            <xs:simpleContent>
              <xs:extension base="xs:string">
                <xs:attribute name="priority"
                        type="xs:string" use="required"/>
              </xs:extension>
            </xs:simpleContent>
          </xs:complexType>
        </xs:element>
      </xs:sequence>
    </xs:complexType>
  </xs:element>
</xs:schema>
```

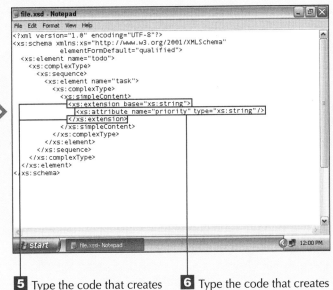

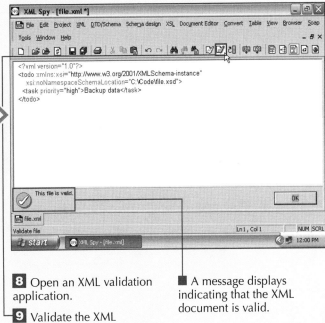

5 Type the code that creates the extension element, which specifies the element's data type.

6 Type the code that creates the attribute declaration, which specifies the name and data type of the attribute.

7 Save the XML Schema document.

8 Open an XML validation application.

9 Validate the XML document created in step 1.

■ A message displays indicating that the XML document is valid.

CONSTRAIN THE VALUES OF AN ATTRIBUTE

You can place limits and restrictions on the type and value of data that you use for an attribute in an element. Restricting or limiting the type of information of an attribute value helps to ensure the integrity of the attribute data within an XML document. When you use attribute values that do not meet the constraints as laid out in the XML Schema, the XML document fails validation when an XML validation application attempts to validate it.

You define the restrictions on the attribute values within the XML Schema document. As with any elements for which you want to restrict the values, you must create a simple type definition. The simple type definition allows you to specify the attribute's values.

When declaring an attribute with no restrictions, you specify the data type of the attribute within the attribute declaration. When creating restrictions on attributes, you specify the data type of the attribute within the restriction element. You specify the name of the attribute within the attribute declaration.

The type of restrictions you place on an attribute value depends on the type of data that becomes the value of the attribute. For `string` values, you can use restrictions such as maximum and minimum number of characters; for example, you may want to limit the number of characters in a person's name to no more than 30 characters. For numerical values you can specify the number of decimal places for a number, such as specifying two decimal places for currency data. For more information about the types of restrictions that you can apply to attribute data, refer to Appendix C.

CONSTRAIN THE VALUES OF AN ATTRIBUTE

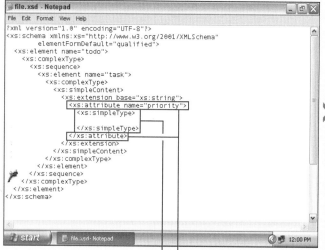

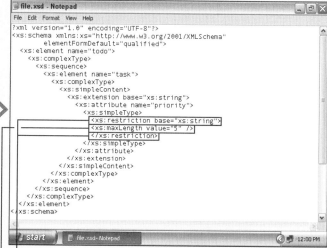

1 Open or create an XML Schema for an XML document that will contain an element, which has an attribute.

■ In this example, the XML document contains the element "todo," with the attribute named "priority."

2 Type the code that creates the attribute element, which specifies the name of the attribute.

3 Type the code that creates the simple type element for that attribute.

4 Type the code that creates the restriction element, which specifies the data type of the attribute.

5 Type the code that creates the elements, which restrict the type of data that you can use for the attribute.

■ This example restricts the length of the attribute to five characters.

6 Save the XML Schema document.

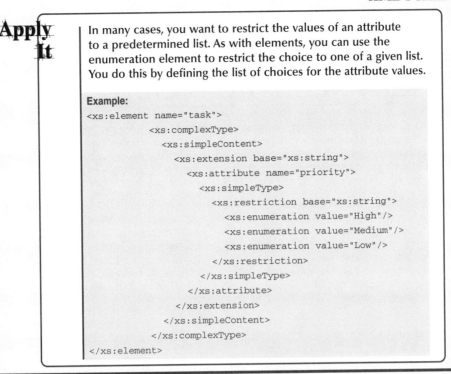

Apply It

In many cases, you want to restrict the values of an attribute to a predetermined list. As with elements, you can use the enumeration element to restrict the choice to one of a given list. You do this by defining the list of choices for the attribute values.

Example:

```
<xs:element name="task">
            <xs:complexType>
              <xs:simpleContent>
                <xs:extension base="xs:string">
                  <xs:attribute name="priority">
                    <xs:simpleType>
                      <xs:restriction base="xs:string">
                        <xs:enumeration value="High"/>
                        <xs:enumeration value="Medium"/>
                        <xs:enumeration value="Low"/>
                      </xs:restriction>
                    </xs:simpleType>
                  </xs:attribute>
                </xs:extension>
              </xs:simpleContent>
            </xs:complexType>
</xs:element>
```

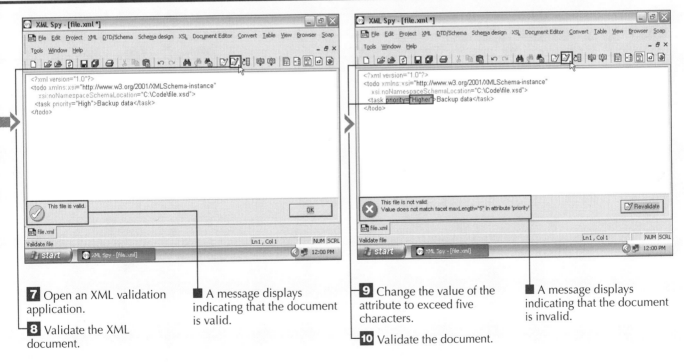

7 Open an XML validation application.

8 Validate the XML document.

■ A message displays indicating that the document is valid.

9 Change the value of the attribute to exceed five characters.

10 Validate the document.

■ A message displays indicating that the document is invalid.

REFERENCE PREDEFINED ELEMENTS

You can reference an element declaration from another section of an XML Schema. This allows you to group your element declarations together in a single section and simply reference those element declarations throughout the XML Schema.

Using a reference is similar to creating an element declaration. For more information about declaring elements within an XML Schema, see Chapter 4. The element declaration can contain an attribute called *ref*. You must assign a value to the ref attribute, and that value must have the name of the previously declared element. For example, if you have already declared an element called todo, you must make the value of the ref attribute in the element declaration todo.

Global element declarations are element declarations that you place within the start and end XML Schema tags, but

which other element declarations do not enclose. You can place element declarations within other elements or type definitions. You refer to these types of definitions as *local* definitions. Typically, within an XML Schema, the types of element declarations that you reference are either global or local element declarations.

Even when you reference a global element, if you place the element reference locally, that is, within an element or type declaration, and not in the actual schema declaration, you classify the referenced element as a local element declaration, even though it references a previously defined global element declaration.

You typically make references empty element declarations; they usually consist of one unified start and end tag. For more information about creating empty elements, see Chapter 4.

REFERENCE PREDEFINED ELEMENTS

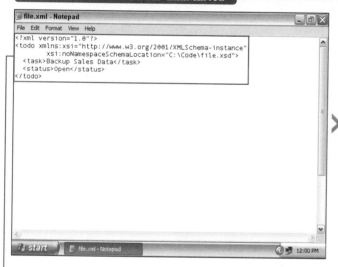

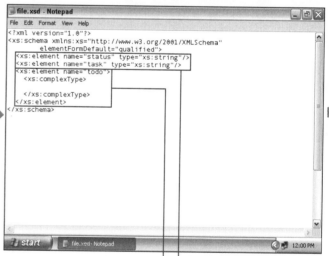

1 Open or create an XML document that uses an XML Schema document.

■ This example uses a simple XML document, which contains a root element and two sub-elements containing text.

2 Open the XML Schema document for the XML document referenced in step 1.

3 Type the code to create the element declarations for the elements that you want to contain text.

4 Type the code to create the element declaration for the container element.

Apply It

You can reference the same element declarations repeatedly throughout the XML Schema. This prevents you from having to repeatedly use the same element declarations, particularly when the declaration's element has a complex data structure. This example declares the status element once, and then references it twice.

Example:
```
<xs:schema xmlns:xs="http://www.w3.org/2001/XMLSchema"
               elementFormDefault="qualified">
  <xs:element name="status" type="xs:string"/>
  <xs:element name="task">
    <xs:complexType>
      <xs:sequence>
        <xs:element ref="status"/>
      </xs:sequence>
    </xs:complexType>
  </xs:element>
  <xs:element name="todo">
    <xs:complexType>
      <xs:sequence>
        <xs:element ref="task"/>
        <xs:element ref="status"/>
      </xs:sequence>
    </xs:complexType>
  </xs:element>
</xs:schema>
```

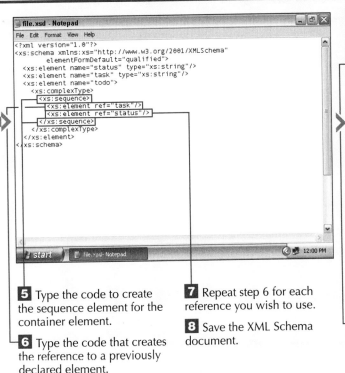

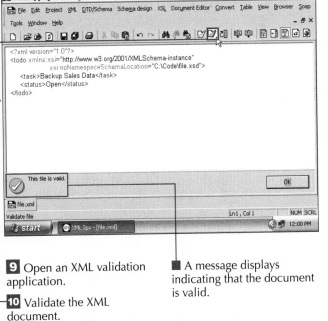

5 Type the code to create the sequence element for the container element.

6 Type the code that creates the reference to a previously declared element.

7 Repeat step 6 for each reference you wish to use.

8 Save the XML Schema document.

9 Open an XML validation application.

10 Validate the XML document.

■ A message displays indicating that the document is valid.

CREATE A GROUP OF ATTRIBUTES

You can create a declaration that defines a group of attributes to reduce the amount of typing you must perform when creating XML schemas. Defining an attribute group also allows for faster maintenance of XML schemas, should you need to update the XML schemas in the future.

You can create a group of attributes that multiple elements within an XML document can use. You use an attribute group element to declare which attributes you want to include within the attribute group. Within the attribute group element, the attribute declaration determines the characteristics of the attribute. The attribute group definition allows you to specify the name by which the elements reference that group of attributes.

The attribute declaration within an `attributeGroup` element is the same attribute declaration that you use when you want to declare the attribute within the element declaration. You may find creating an `attributeGroup` declaration helpful if you use the same attributes for

different elements throughout an XML document. The `attributeGroup` element allows you to specify the name and the characteristics of an attribute once. You can then simply reference that declaration when the element declarations in the XML Schema require it. Once you define the `attributeGroup`, you can reference it from within any complex type definitions.

You can only place an `attributeGroup` definition within the XML Schema element. You cannot nest it within another element declared in the XML Schema.

You make the actual reference to the `attributeGroup` with another `attributeGroup` element. The `ref` attribute of that element must reference the name of the attribute group. When using an `attributeGroup` element to reference a matching attribute group, the element must remain empty.

An `attributeGroup` definition can contain attribute declarations and references to other `attributeGroup` definitions.

CREATE A GROUP OF ATTRIBUTES

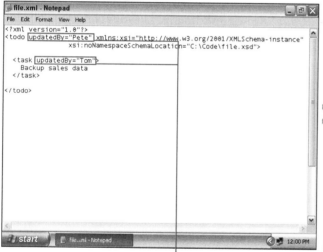

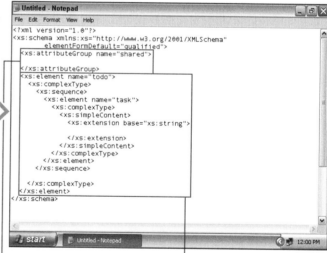

1 Open or create an XML document that contains multiple elements.

2 Create the same attribute for differing elements.

3 Open the XML Schema file for the document you created in step 1.

4 Type the code that creates the `attributeGroup` element declaration.

5 Type the code to create the remaining declarations for the elements in the XML document, without creating attribute declarations.

Apply It

You may find `attributeGroup` definitions a useful way to declare multiple attributes at the same time. You can combine different attribute types with different restrictions into one attribute group and then simply reference them throughout your XML Schema as required.

Example:

```
<xs:attributeGroup name="shared">
  <xs:attribute name="updatedBy" type="xs:string" use="required"/>
  <xs:attribute name="date" type="xs:string" use="required"/>
  <xs:attribute name="version" type="xs:decimal" use="required"/>
</xs:attributeGroup>
<xs:element name="todo">
  <xs:complexType>
    <xs:sequence>
      <xs:element name="task">
        <xs:complexType>
          <xs:simpleContent>
            <xs:extension base="xs:string">
              <xs:attributeGroup ref="shared"/>
            </xs:extension>
          </xs:simpleContent>
        </xs:complexType>
      </xs:element>
    </xs:sequence>
    <xs:attributeGroup ref="shared"/>
  </xs:complexType>
</xs:element>
```

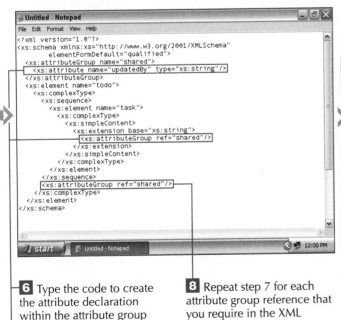

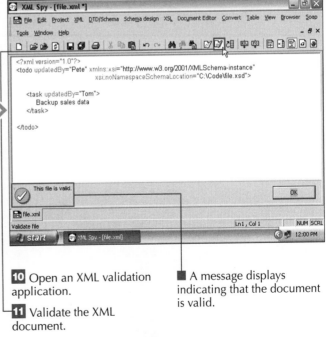

6 Type the code to create the attribute declaration within the attribute group element.

7 Type the code that references the attribute group definition.

8 Repeat step 7 for each attribute group reference that you require in the XML Schema.

9 Save the XML Schema document.

10 Open an XML validation application.

11 Validate the XML document.

■ A message displays indicating that the document is valid.

133

CONSTRAIN VALUES USING REGULAR EXPRESSIONS

You can specify that the value of the content of an element must conform to an existing set of rules using a *regular expression*. A regular expression is a series of symbols that allows you to specify the make up, or pattern, that a value must match. For example, you can use regular expressions to specify that a value must have textual data and that it must also have all uppercase characters. You can also use regular expressions to specify more complex patterns, for example, that a value must have a specific number of characters, that it must contain spaces, and that it must contain at least one space.

Many different programming languages have long used regular expressions to constrain values to a preset pattern. While each programming language may have slight deviations on the use of regular expressions, if you have previously used regular expressions with another programming language, you should have no problem using

regular expressions to specify a pattern for a value of an XML element.

The restriction element establishes the values that you want to constrain using regular expressions. The pattern element, within that element, then defines a regular expression that the XML validation application matches to the value of the data. You state the regular expression as a value of an attribute of the pattern element.

Regular expressions may initially seem very cryptic, but it is well worth the effort to understand how they work. When you become familiar with regular expressions, you may find yourself repeatedly using them to constrain the values of the data in your XML documents. Despite their simple implementation, you may find them a very powerful tool. For more information on regular expressions, refer to Appendix C.

CONSTRAIN VALUES USING REGULAR EXPRESSIONS

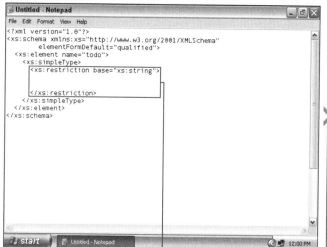

■ **1** Open or create an XML Schema for an XML document.

■ This example uses an XML Schema file for an XML document that contains one root element called "todo," which contains textual data.

2 Create the restriction tags for the element.

■ **3** Type any additional facets to constrain the value of the data.

■ This example uses whitespace within the element's content.

4 Type the code that creates the pattern element, which specifies the regular expression.

■ This example uses the regular expression "[A-Z,\s]*," which allows for a value that contains only uppercase characters and whitespaces, and any number of characters.

5 Save the XML Schema document.

Apply It

Not only can you restrict the value of elements using regular expressions, you can also use regular expressions to constrain the values of attributes.

Example:
```
<xs:element name="task">
  <xs:complexType>
    <xs:simpleContent>
      <xs:extension base="xs:string">
        <xs:attribute name="priority">
          <xs:simpleType>
            <xs:restriction base="xs:string">
              <xs:pattern value="[a-z]*"/>
            </xs:restriction>
          </xs:simpleType>
        </xs:attribute>
      </xs:extension>
    </xs:simpleContent>
  </xs:complexType>
</xs:element>
```

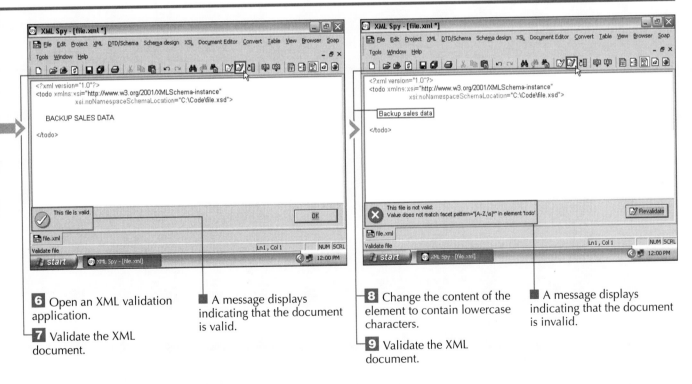

6 Open an XML validation application.

7 Validate the XML document.

■ A message displays indicating that the document is valid.

8 Change the content of the element to contain lowercase characters.

9 Validate the XML document.

■ A message displays indicating that the document is invalid.

AN INTRODUCTION TO THE SAX API

The SAX API allows the Java applications you create to communicate with an XML parser so that you can access XML documents from within your Java applications. SAX is an Application Programming Interface, or API, for XML parsers. The API consists of a set of rules and instructions for writing code that details how two applications communicate with each other. Originally developed in 1998 to become one of the first widely used XML parsers, the SAX API makes it easier for programmers to work with XML documents using multiple programming languages, such as Perl, C++, and Java.

SAX provides a way to communicate with an XML parser from within your Java code using straightforward Java instructions. Although not itself an XML parser, SAX contains a collection of code that you utilize within your own Java programs to access an XML parser of your choice. SAX only defines what code you must use to communicate with the XML parser. You can only use the XML parser, a separate program, with the SAX API if you configure it to understand and support the SAX API. An API allows you to create programs that you do not have to exclusively tie to specific applications. For example, if you use the SAX API to communicate with an XML parser that uses the SAX API—a *SAX-compliant XML parser*—you can upgrade the XML parser or switch to one from another vendor as long as the new XML parser can use the SAX API. You can make these changes to the XML parser without having to change your code. Using an API instead of communicating directly with an application also makes your code easier to maintain and troubleshoot.

VERSIONS

The SAX API has two major versions, both commonly in use: the older version 1.0, and the current version 2.0, also known as SAX 2, which will eventually replace SAX 1.0. Unlike SAX 1.0, SAX 2.0 has the capability to work with XML documents that use namespaces. If given a choice, you should use SAX 2.0 along with an XML parser that supports SAX 2.0. You can also work with different versions, such as beta versions, released during the development of the SAX API. For example, there is presently a beta version of SAX called SAX 2.0 beta 2. When obtaining the SAX API, you should ensure that you have a current and stable release. If the SAX API came with an XML parser, then you can be assured that the accompanying XML parser supports the SAX API.

EVENTS

When you parse an XML document, the XML parser processes specific characteristics of the XML document, such as the beginning of the document or the start and end of an element within the XML document. You refer to these characteristics as *events*. In an event-based XML parser, Java applications that communicate with the XML parser execute specific code when the XML parser encounters one of these events. Because the SAX API was developed for use with event-based parsers, you refer to it as an event-based API. Using the SAX API to develop your application allows you to create Java code that can execute whenever a specific event happens. The major benefit of event-based parsers stems from their ability to work efficiently with very large XML documents. Other types of parsers typically access an XML document after placing the XML document in memory. Event-based parsers that must first load the entire XML document into memory can easily run out of available memory, and run much slower when accessing very large XML documents.

You usually have multiple types of XML parsers for a Java application to use, depending on the nature of the XML document and the task you require it to perform.

SEQUENTIAL

You use event-based parsers, and in turn the SAX API, to access the contents of an XML file sequentially. A parser reads an XML document from its start through to its end. Any actions that the parser must take when it encounters specific content within an XML document must wait until the parser processes the preceding

content of the XML document. This sequential access of event-based parsers differs from other types of parsers, which load the entire XML document into memory and then allow a Java application to access the XML document at random locations.

COST

Because the files that make up the SAX API are public domain software, anyone can access the SAX API free of charge. The SAX API requires no licensing fee or other remuneration for developing personal or commercial applications. Some commercial products, which may

use and include the SAX API with the software application, may have a cost. You can find many applications, such as a wide range of SAX-compliant XML parsers that include the SAX API, readily available at no cost.

CLASS FILES

Although not a parser itself, SAX consists of a collection of Java classes and interfaces that you access within your Java code and that allows you to access a SAX-compliant XML parser. You must configure the XML parser in a way that allows SAX classes and interfaces to use it. Any XML parser that you can use with the SAX API typically includes the SAX class and interface files

with the parser. Although the SAX file is available separately, you should always use the SAX file that came with your current XML parser. This allows you to avoid compatibility or version conflicts between the SAX files and the XML parser. You may have to configure your computer to automatically locate the SAX class files after you copy them to your computer.

DOCUMENTATION

As with any type of API, current, error-free documentation on how to use the API is essential. If you obtain the SAX API with an XML parser, the parser almost always includes SAX documentation as well as very helpful documentation and programming examples that relate to using SAX with that particular parser. If the documentation did not come with the

XML parser, you can still access the documentation via the main SAX Web site at `http://www.saxproject .org`. You should always ensure that the documentation refers to your version of the SAX API. For this reason, consider using the SAX documentation that came with the SAX files and XML parser rather than the documentation available on the Internet.

INSTALL THE XERCES XML PARSER

The SAX API allows the Java applications you create to communicate with an XML parser so that you can access XML documents from within your Java applications. The Xerces XML parser is a popular, SAX-compliant parser that you can find on the companion CD-ROM, or via the Internet at http://xml.apache.org/. Once you obtain the Xerces XML parser, you can install it on your computer so that you can access it from your Java programs using the SAX API.

You can find the files that comprise the Xerces XML parser together in a *Java Archive* (JAR) file called xerces.jar. Placing the parser files into a single file makes it more convenient and efficient to transfer and copy the large amount of files that the Xerces XML parser requires. The Java Development Kit (JDK) consists of the files needed to create Java applications. The JDK can access any of the files within a JAR file as long as you place the JAR file in a directory that the JDK can access.

Installing the Xerces XML parser entails copying the xerces.jar file to a folder that holds Java class files. The process of copying the xerces.jar file varies depending on the operating system in use. For computers that utilize the Microsoft Windows operating system, you can copy files with the Windows Explorer application.

The special directory to which you copy the xerces.jar file holds class files that create Java programs. As a matter of convenience, you can also use the same directory to store any class files that you write or obtain elsewhere.

Once you copy the xerces.jar file to a class file directory, you must ensure that you can access the xerces.jar file and its contents from your Java programs by setting the CLASSPATH environment variable. For more information, refer to the section "Set the CLASSPATH Environment Variable."

INSTALL THE XERCES XML PARSER

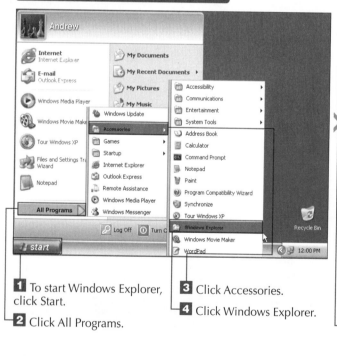

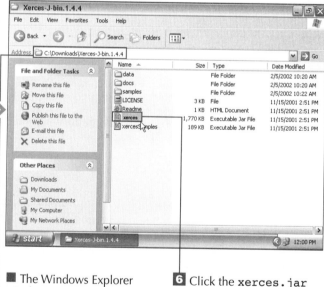

1 To start Windows Explorer, click Start.

2 Click All Programs.

3 Click Accessories.

4 Click Windows Explorer.

■ The Windows Explorer window appears.

5 Type the name of the folder that contains the Xerces files and press Enter.

6 Click the xerces.jar file.

Note: Depending on the display configuration of Windows Explorer, the file extension may not display.

Extra

If you have a version of Xerces designed for use on the Windows operating system, you usually find the Xerces XML parser and its companion files packaged into a single zip file. A zip file conveniently collects together multiple files into one package and then compresses them to save storage space. This saves you time when transferring the files over a network, such as the Internet. It also conserves storage space, an important consideration when you must store the files on a medium with limited space, such as a hard drive. To work with the files, you must first extract them from the zip file.

Many operating systems, such as Windows XP, can work directly with zip files, allowing you to easily extract some or all of the files from the zip file. Older operating systems, such as Windows 98, require you to install an application specifically for the zip files.

You can download an evaluation version of WinZip, a very popular application for working with zip files, from the Internet at http://www.winzip.com. WinZip is available for most versions of Windows.

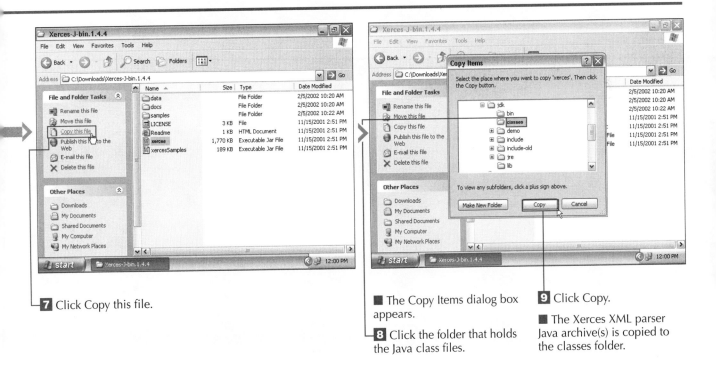

7 Click Copy this file.

■ The Copy Items dialog box appears.

8 Click the folder that holds the Java class files.

9 Click Copy.

■ The Xerces XML parser Java archive(s) is copied to the classes folder.

SET THE CLASSPATH ENVIRONMENT VARIABLE

To allow the Xerces XML parser to communicate within your Java code, you must change the CLASSPATH environment variable to include the location of the Xerces Java Archive (JAR) file. The computer's operating system uses an *environment variable* to hold a piece of information. The most common environment variable, the PATH environment variable, specifies where the operating system looks for files when you do not specify a location for a file. The CLASSPATH variable tells the Java Development Kit where to look for class files that you may require when creating your Java code.

The CLASSPATH environment variable usually indicates the location of many class and JAR files. You can specify different locations and JAR files within the CLASSPATH environment variable by separating each particular location with a semicolon (;) on Windows, or a colon (:) on UNIX. You can use the CLASSPATH environment variable to specify the location of JAR files, directories, or both JAR files and directories.

When creating a new environment variable, you must specify the name of the variable and a value that you want to assign to the environment variable. You specify the name of the environment variable in uppercase letters.

On Windows-based computers, you find *user environment variables* and *system environment variables*. You can only make user environment variables available to specific users, while any user who logs onto the computer can access system environment variables. Users typically create their own environment variables as they need them. Normally, you must log onto your computer as an administrator to add or change system environment variables.

As well as the location of commonly accessed class and JAR files, the CLASSPATH environment variable also specifies the current directory in which the Java file resides. You can accomplish this by specifying a path denoted by a single period (.).

SET THE CLASSPATH ENVIRONMENT VARIABLE

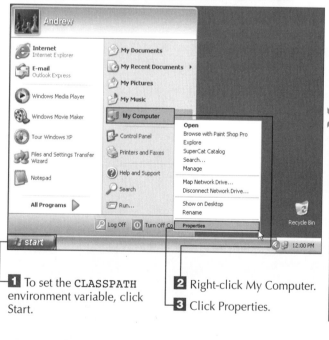

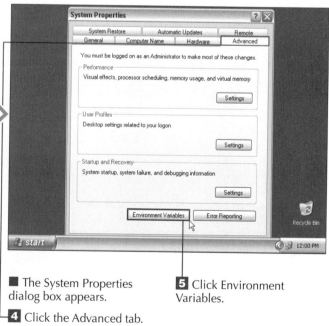

1 To set the CLASSPATH environment variable, click Start.

2 Right-click My Computer.

3 Click Properties.

■ The System Properties dialog box appears.

4 Click the Advanced tab.

5 Click Environment Variables.

Extra

You can also set the CLASSPATH environment variable from the command prompt with the Windows set command. You can then only access the CLASSPATH environment variable within the Command Prompt window where you set it. Opening another Command Prompt window requires you to reset the CLASSPATH environment variable.

Example:
```
set CLASSPATH =.;c:\jdk\classes\xerces.jar
```

For most Windows operating systems, you use the Windows set command to set the CLASSPATH environment variable for all Command Prompt windows. To do so, place the set command in the autoexec.bat file in the root directory of the computer, and then restart the computer. The new CLASSPATH replaces the previously specified CLASSPATH environment variable. You can append a new location to the existing CLASSPATH environment variable with %CLASSPATH% in the new CLASSPATH environment value. Never replace the existing content of the CLASSPATH environment variable, as it may hinder the operation of other applications.

Example:
```
set CLASSPATH =%CLASSPATH%;.;c:\jdk\classes\xerces.jar
```

Depending on the operating system, you may need to set the CLASSPATH environment variable. Some operating systems, such as UNIX, allow you to separate the different locations within the CLASSPATH environment variable, but you separate each location with a colon rather than the semicolon you use in Windows. To determine the correct configuration changes to make to your operating system, and the syntax to set the CLASSPATH environment variable, see the installation documentation that came with the XML parser for your operating system.

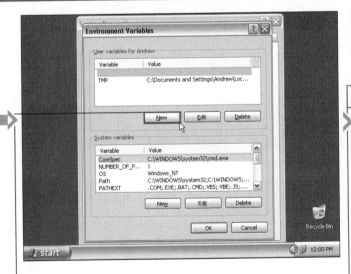

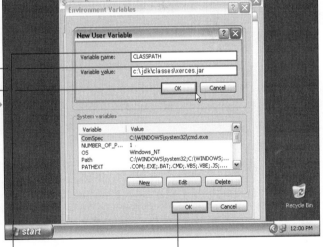

■ The Environment Variables dialog box appears.

6 Click New.

■ The New User Variable dialog box appears.

7 Type **CLASSPATH**.

8 Type the location of your class file directory.

9 Click OK.

10 Click OK.

11 Click OK in the System Properties dialog box.

■ The CLASSPATH environment variable changes.

CREATE AN EVENT HANDLER CLASS

Before you parse XML documents using the SAX API, you must create a special class file. You do this because using the SAX API to parse an XML document requires that you create a class that implements an interface. You use this interface much like a class.

The class that you want to use must implement the ContentHandler interface. You typically refer to the class you create as the event handler class, because the parser uses the class to execute code in response to specific events, such as when it encounters the end of an XML document during processing.

Before you can use the ContentHandler interface, you must import the org.xml.sax package, which contains the interface, into your code. You must define each method of an interface in any class that implements an interface. If you do not define a method of an interface within the class that extends the interface, your code generates an error when you compile it.

The ContentHandler interface has 11 methods that you must define in the class, which becomes the event handler class. The methods are characters, endDocument, endElement, endPrefixMapping, ignorableWhitespace, processingInstruction, setDocumentLocator, skippedEntity, startDocument, startElement and startPrefixMapping. For a list of the parameters for each method, see Appendix A.

Once you create the event handler class, you can compile your code to check for errors. You cannot perform any work with the event handler class until you create the code that actually parses an XML document. To use the event handler class while parsing an XML document, refer to the section "Parse an XML Document" in this chapter.

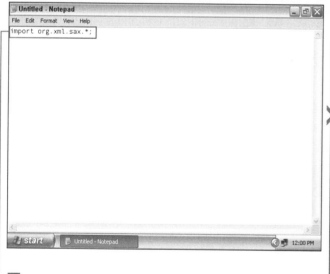

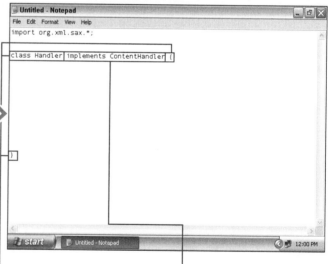

1 Type the code that imports the org.xml.sax package.

2 Type the code that creates a class.

3 Type the code that implements the ContentHandler interface.

Extra

When compiling the Java code that defines the handler class, the Java compiler may generate a message stating that you should declare your class as `abstract`. This message appears when you do not define the correct methods required in your handler class. If you receive a message about declaring your class as `abstract`, recheck the method names in your handler class to ensure that they are correct and that you have specified the correct number and type of parameters.

The SAX API defines the interface and methods that you must use when creating an event handler class. You can verify the required method names and their parameters by checking the SAX API documentation.

Documentation about the SAX API and the methods of the handler class are typically included with any SAX-compliant XML parser. If you do not have access to the SAX API documentation on your own computer, you can find it at http://www.saxproject.com. You should ensure that any documentation you reference matches the version of the SAX API that you are using.

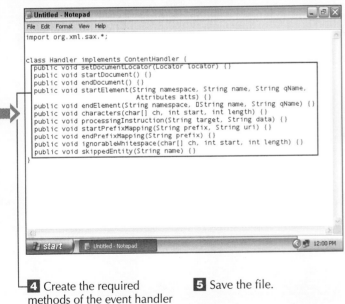

4 Create the required methods of the event handler class.

Note: For a list of parameters, see Appendix A.

5 Save the file.

6 Compile your Java code.

Note: For instructions on compiling, see Chapter 2.

■ If you have no errors, the code compiles.

PARSE AN XML DOCUMENT

Once you create the event handler class, you need to associate it with the XML parser using the SAX API. This process registers the handler with a *reader*, an instance of the XMLReader interface that you find in the org.xml.sax package and which you use to decipher the actual XML document. The SAXParser class, part of the org.apache.xerces.parsers package, allows the SAX API to communicate with the Xerces XML parser.

Employing a series of callbacks, you use the XMLReader interface to create an object that reads the information within an XML document. A *callback* occurs when an application calls the methods in your code. In this case, the XML parser calls the methods in the event handler class that you have created. The method that the parser calls depends on the type of information it encounters within an XML document. For more information about the methods that you must create in your event handler class, refer to the section "Create an Event Handler Class."

Once you create the XMLReader object, you must register the event handler class with the setContentHandler method. When you create the code that employs the setContentHandler method, the method uses the name of the event handler class as its only argument.

You use the parse method of the XMLReader object to start the parsing of an XML document. The parse method occurs when you specify the name of the XML document that you want to parse.

The parser calls the methods in the event handler class whenever it encounters the corresponding event. To make a method useful, you must create the code that specifies what you want the method to do. For testing purposes, you can simply assign code that displays a message to the startDocument method of the event handler class. This code executes when the XMLReader detects the start of the XML document.

PARSE AN XML DOCUMENT

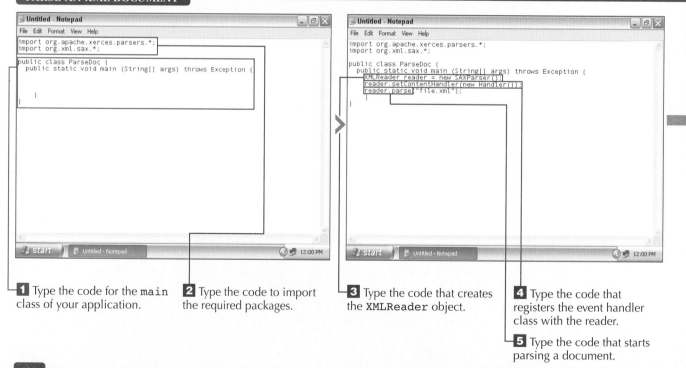

1 Type the code for the main class of your application.

2 Type the code to import the required packages.

3 Type the code that creates the **XMLReader** object.

4 Type the code that registers the event handler class with the reader.

5 Type the code that starts parsing a document.

Extra

You can only access the `org.apache.xerces.parsers` package when you use the Xerces SAX-compliant XML parser. If you use a different XML parser, consult that parser's documentation for instructions on how to communicate with the parser using the SAX API. For more information about obtaining and installing the Xerces XML parser, refer to the section "Install the Xerces XML Parser" in this chapter. You must have a well-formed XML document for the XML parser to parse it. For more information about well-formed XML documents, see Chapter 4.

An Example of a Well-formed XML Document:
```xml
<?xml version="1.0"?>
<todo>
  <task>
    <description>Backup sales data for last month</description>
    <owner>Andrew</owner>
    <status>open</status>
    <priority>low</priority>
  </task>
  <task>
    <description>Complete end of month report</description>
    <owner>Andrew</owner>
    <status>closed</status>
    <priority>medium</priority>
  </task>
</todo>
```

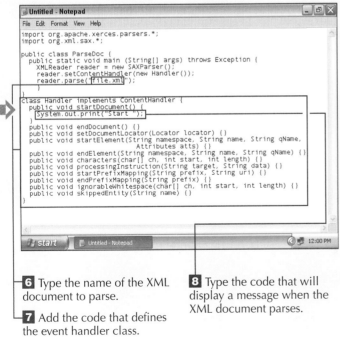

■6 Type the name of the XML document to parse.

■7 Add the code that defines the event handler class.

Note: Make sure the name of the class matches the name specified in step 4.

■8 Type the code that will display a message when the XML document parses.

■9 Compile and run your program.

Note: See Chapter 2 for instructions on compiling and running Java programs.

■ A message displays indicating that the document was parsed.

DETECT ELEMENTS IN AN XML DOCUMENT

lement declarations make up the majority of content in an XML document. Elements can have a start and an end tag, and may or may not have some content between the tags.

One of the first steps in processing an XML document in an application involves locating specific elements in the XML document. Once the parser detects an element in an XML document, it makes a callback to the appropriate method of the event handler class. You should place these methods of the SAX handler class in the Java code that you want to execute when the parser detects an element.

The parser calls the startElement method of the event handler class whenever the XMLReader detects a tag that it identifies as the start tag of an element. Likewise, the parser calls the endElement method of the event handler class whenever the XMLReader detects a tag that it identifies as the end tag of an element. The name of the element to

which the tag belongs passes to the method as a string. You can use this string value to determine the name of the element in your code.

Note that the startElement and endElement methods of the event handler class do not differentiate between a child and a parent element. The parser calls the appropriate method of the event handler class regardless of the position of the element in the XML document. Therefore, for nested elements, the parser may call the startElement method repeatedly before it calls the endElement method. If you have a situation where the parser must differentiate between a child and a parent element, you must write the code that makes that determination.

As with any document that you intend to parse, you should make the XML document well-formed to ensure that it processes. For more information about well-formed XML documents, refer to Chapter 4.

DETECT ELEMENTS IN AN XML DOCUMENT

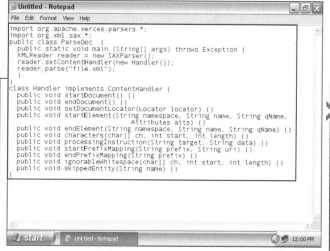

1 Open or create the code that parses an XML document.

Note: You can use the code created in the section "Parse an XML Document."

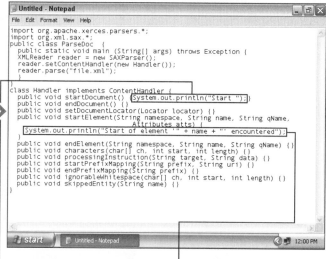

2 Type the code that you want to display a message when the parser starts to parse the document.

3 Type the code that displays the element name when a parser detects a start tag.

Apply
It

You may have some empty elements in an XML document that omit the closing element tag as long as the start tag ends with `/>`. For example, `<name></name>` is the same as `<name />`. The XML parser understands this, and it still calls both the `startElement` and `endElement` methods even if it sees only one tag. This is illustrated in the following example:

Process the XML document:
```xml
<?xml version="1.0"?>
<todo>
  <task />
  <task />
</todo>
```

RESULT:
```
Start
Start of element 'todo' encountered
Start of element 'task' encountered
End of element 'task' encountered
Start of element 'task' encountered
End of element 'task' encountered
End of element 'todo' encountered
```

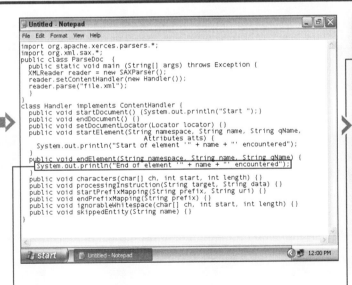

4 Type the code that displays the element name when the parser detects an end tag.

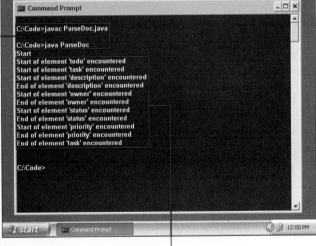

5 Compile and run your program.

Note: See Chapter 2 for instructions on compiling and running Java programs.

■ A message displays each time the parser encounters a start or end tag.

EXTRACT TEXTUAL ELEMENT CONTENT

You can use the event handler class file to extract the content of elements in an XML document. The content of an element consists of the data between the start and end tags of the element. Text data typically comprises the majority of the content of elements you find in an XML document.

An XML parser can determine the text content of an element and return the content to your Java code using the SAX API. The parser returns the text data with the `character` method of the event handler class.

The `character` method of the event handler class makes the text data of an element available in the form of a character array. Along with the character array, the `character` method also passes the character location within the array where the text data starts, and the number of characters that make up the text data of the element.

Given the character array that contains the element's content, along with the start location and number of characters, you can easily transfer the element data into a `String` variable. Converting the text data to a `String` makes the data easier to handle.

When working with an element's content, you typically identify the name of the element that contains the data. When displaying the content of elements, you can use the `startElement` and `endElement` methods of the event handler class to place the corresponding start and end tags on either side of the element's content.

What happens to the text data that makes up the content of an element in an XML document depends on what you want your application to do with it. Some applications may simply display or print the text data while other applications may want to execute other code depending on the actual content of the text data.

EXTRACT TEXTUAL ELEMENT CONTENT

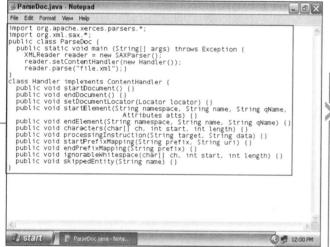

1 Open or create the code that parses an XML document.

Note: You can use the code created in the section "Parse an XML Document."

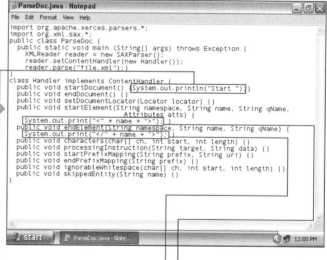

2 Type the code that you want to display a message when the parser starts to parse the document.

3 Type the code that displays the element name when the parser detects a start tag.

4 Type the code that displays the element name when the parser detects an end tag.

148

Extra

The character method of the event handler class passes the data to your application in the form of a character array. The character array does contain data other than the actual textual content of the element. The character method also returns the start location within the array and the number of characters of the element content, which you can use to extract the element content from the character array. You must always use the start location and number of characters data to extract the element content from the character array. If you try to access any other data in the character array other than what the values of the character method arguments specify, an error may occur.

In some cases the parser may call the character method of the event handler class repeatedly for one element. The content of the element passes to the character method in separate sequential sections. The number of times that the parser calls the character method when it retrieves element data depends on the type of XML parser in use, as well as the type of computing environment. You should take this repeated calling of the character method into account when working with element data.

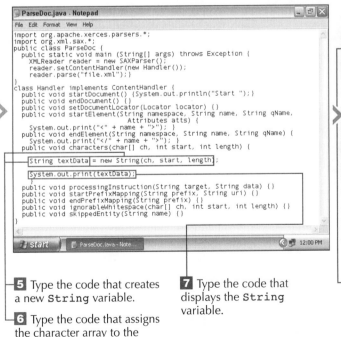

```
ParseDoc.java - Notepad
File Edit Format View Help
import org.apache.xerces.parsers.*;
import org.xml.sax.*;
public class ParseDoc {
  public static void main (String[] args) throws Exception {
    XMLReader reader = new SAXParser();
    reader.setContentHandler(new Handler());
    reader.parse("file.xml");}
}
class Handler implements ContentHandler {
  public void startDocument() {System.out.println("Start ");}
  public void endDocument() {}
  public void setDocumentLocator(Locator locator) {}
  public void startElement(String namespace, String name, String qName,
                           Attributes atts) {
    System.out.print("<" + name + ">");}
  public void endElement(String namespace, String name, String qName) {
    System.out.print("</" + name + ">"); }
  public void characters(char[] ch, int start, int length) {

    String textData = new String(ch, start, length);

    System.out.print(textData);
    }
  public void processingInstruction(String target, String data) {}
  public void startPrefixMapping(String prefix, String uri) {}
  public void endPrefixMapping(String prefix) {}
  public void ignorableWhitespace(char[] ch, int start, int length) {}
  public void skippedEntity(String name) {}
}
```

```
Command Prompt
C:\Code>javac ParseDoc.java

C:\Code>java ParseDoc
Start
<todo>
  <task>
    <description>Backup sales data for last month</description>
    <owner>Andrew</owner>
    <status>open</status>
    <priority>low</priority>
  </task>
  <task>
    <description>Complete end of month report</description>
    <owner>Andrew</owner>
    <status>closed</status>
    <priority>medium</priority>
  </task>
</todo>
C:\Code>
```

5 Type the code that creates a new **String** variable.

6 Type the code that assigns the character array to the **String** variable.

7 Type the code that displays the **String** variable.

8 Compile and run your program.

Note: See Chapter 2 for instructions on compiling and running Java programs.

■ The element content displays along with the start and end tags.

DETERMINE THE NUMBER OF ELEMENT ATTRIBUTES

You can associate an attribute — an additional item of information that provides more details about an element or the element content — with an element. For example, an element called 'fax' may have an attribute called 'code' that you use to indicate the area code of the fax number that makes up the content of the fax element. You need to determine the number of attributes an element contains in order to access the information in the attributes.

The first step in accessing the attributes of an element involves determining the number of attributes an element has. Elements may have multiple attributes or they may have no attributes at all. Next, you can determine the name of the attributes and any values associated with those attributes. The XML parser encounters element attribute information when it processes the start tag of an element. Information about any attributes of an element passes as an `Attributes` object to the `startElement` method of the event handler class. You can easily create code in the

`startElement` method to determine the number of attributes an element may have.

Because the `Attributes` interface is a part of the `org.xml.sax` package, you must import the `org.xml.sax` package into your program. For more information about importing a package, see Chapter 3.

As with most other objects, you can use methods to determine properties of an object. The method that determines the number of attributes of an `Attributes` object is the `getLength` method. The `getLength` method returns the exact number of attributes that you have specified for an element within an XML document.

Attributes of an element in an XML document may or may not have a value assigned to them. Regardless of whether you have specified the value for the attribute, the `getLength` method of the `Attributes` object counts the attribute.

DETERMINE THE NUMBER OF ELEMENT ATTRIBUTES

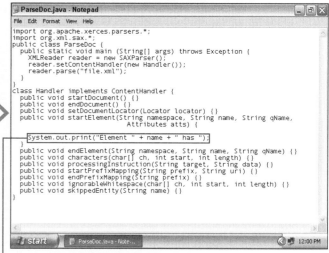

```
ParseDoc.java - Notepad
File Edit Format View Help
import org.apache.xerces.parsers.*;
import org.xml.sax.*;
public class ParseDoc {
  public static void main (String[] args) throws Exception {
    XMLReader reader = new SAXParser();
    reader.setContentHandler(new Handler());
    reader.parse("file.xml");
  }
}
class Handler implements ContentHandler {
  public void startDocument() {}
  public void endDocument() {}
  public void setDocumentLocator(Locator locator) {}
  public void startElement(String namespace, String name, String qName,
                           Attributes atts) {}
  public void endElement(String namespace, String name, String qName) {}
  public void characters(char[] ch, int start, int length) {}
  public void processingInstruction(String target, String data) {}
  public void startPrefixMapping(String prefix, String uri) {}
  public void endPrefixMapping(String prefix) {}
  public void ignorableWhitespace(char[] ch, int start, int length) {}
  public void skippedEntity(String name) {}
}
```

```
ParseDoc.java - Notepad
File Edit Format View Help
import org.apache.xerces.parsers.*;
import org.xml.sax.*;
public class ParseDoc {
  public static void main (String[] args) throws Exception {
    XMLReader reader = new SAXParser();
    reader.setContentHandler(new Handler());
    reader.parse("file.xml");
  }
}
class Handler implements ContentHandler {
  public void startDocument() {}
  public void endDocument() {}
  public void setDocumentLocator(Locator locator) {}
  public void startElement(String namespace, String name, String qName,
                           Attributes atts) {
    System.out.print("Element " + name + " has ");
  }
  public void endElement(String namespace, String name, String qName) {}
  public void characters(char[] ch, int start, int length) {}
  public void processingInstruction(String target, String data) {}
  public void startPrefixMapping(String prefix, String uri) {}
  public void endPrefixMapping(String prefix) {}
  public void ignorableWhitespace(char[] ch, int start, int length) {}
  public void skippedEntity(String name) {}
}
```

1 Open or create the code that parses an XML document.

Note: You can use the code created in the section "Parse an XML Document."

Note: You also need an XML document that contains elements with attributes. See Chapter 4 for more information.

2 Type the code that displays the name of the element.

If you want to access the attribute information from any method of the event handler class, you must retrieve it from the startElement method.

TYPE THIS:

```
private Attributes atts;
public void startElement(String namespace, String name,
                                String qName, Attributes atts) {
    this.atts=atts;
 }
 public void characters(char[] ch, int start, int length) {
    String textData = new String(ch, start, length);
    System.out.print("Element content: ");
    System.out.println(textData);
    System.out.println(atts.getLength() + " attributes\n");
 }
```

RESULT:

```
Element content: Backup Sales Data
2 attributes

Element content: Andrew
0 attributes

Element content: Print sales report
2 attributes

Element content: Mark
0 attributes
```

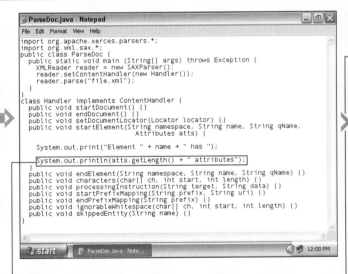

3 Type the code that displays the number of attributes.

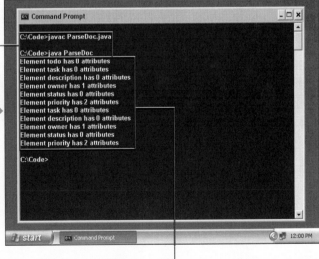

4 Compile and run your program.

Note: See Chapter 2 for instructions on compiling and running Java programs.

■ The name of each element and the number of attributes displays.

DETERMINE THE NAME OF ATTRIBUTES

You can determine the name of attributes that you specify for an element. As with all attribute details, the way to access the information is by using an `Attributes` object. The `Attributes` object passes to the `startElement` method of a previously created event handler class. For more information about event handlers, see the section "Create an Event Handler Class" in this chapter.

You use a specific method of the `Attributes` object to retrieve the name of elements' attributes. The `getLocalName` method requires that you specify an index number to indicate which attribute the name represents. The index number becomes the sole argument of the `getLocalName` method.

The `getLength` method determines the number of attributes that an element has. Once you determine the number of attributes, you typically use a loop to iterate through the attribute names. For more information about creating loops, see Chapter 3.

Before accessing the attributes of an element, you should determine if the element has any attributes associated with it. You can quickly check for the existence of attributes by using an `if` statement to determine if the number of attributes of an element is greater than zero. For more information about the `if` statement, see "Using the `if` Statement" in Chapter 3.

As the attribute information becomes available to the `startElement` method of the event handler, you can easily associate the correct element name with the corresponding attributes.

As with most indexes of numbers in Java, the index of the attributes starts with zero, not one, so that an element with two attributes must access them using the index numbers zero and one, not one and two. If you try to retrieve the name of an out-of-range attribute, the return value becomes a `null` value.

DETERMINE THE NAME OF ATTRIBUTES

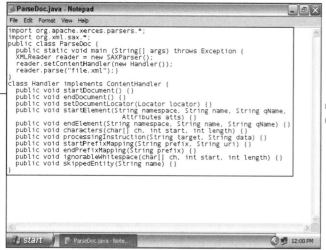

1 Open or create the code that parses an XML document.

Note: You can use the code created in the section "Parse an XML Document."

Note: You also need an XML document that contains elements with attributes. See Chapter 4 for more information.

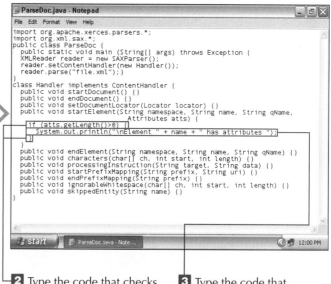

2 Type the code that checks for the existence of attributes.

3 Type the code that displays a message if the element has attributes.

The order in which a parser detects attributes is not necessarily the same order in which they become available using the `Attributes` interface. You should not write code that assumes a specific order for the attributes, as the order may change over time and on different platforms. Typically you create the code that reorders the attributes in a manner that makes it easy to work with your code, such as alphabetical order.

For example, using the code in the steps below may report the attributes of this element:

```
<priority ignore="no" checked="yes" level="3">medium</priority>.
```

First Parser
```
Element priority has attributes
ignore
checked
level
```

Second Parser
```
Element priority has attributes
level
ignore
checked
```

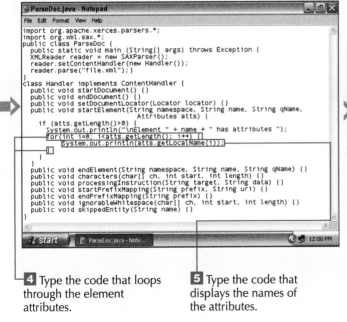

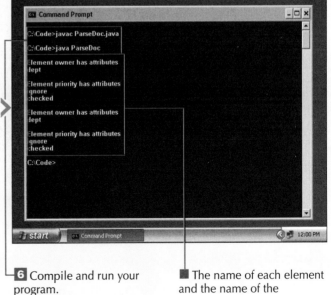

4 Type the code that loops through the element attributes.

5 Type the code that displays the names of the attributes.

6 Compile and run your program.

Note: See Chapter 2 for instructions on compiling and running Java programs.

■ The name of each element and the name of the element's attributes display.

DETERMINE THE VALUE OF ATTRIBUTES

You can determine the value of an element in order to retrieve the information from the element's attributes. An element's attributes consist of an attribute name and value. Once you determine the name of an attribute, you can retrieve its value and associate the name to the value. The `Attribute` object provides the `getValue` method, which utilizes an index number to access the value of an attribute. You can also use this same index number with the `getLocalName` method, to retrieve the attribute's name. In this way, the index number matches the attribute's name with its value. As attributes do not necessarily follow in the order that you specified them within the element, you typically use both the `getLocalName` and the `getValue` with the index number to access attribute values.

You can determine the number of attributes and values with the `getLength` method. Once you determine the number of attributes, you typically use a loop to iterate through the attribute names and values.

Attribute values are always returned as a string, even if the value of the attribute is a number. For example, if the attribute `age` has a value of 36, then 36 is the actual `string` value, not the number 36. Any mathematical calculations you perform on the value result in an error. To easily convert string data to numbers, see Chapter 3.

You must enclose the value of an attribute in single or double quotes when you specify the attribute value in an XML document. When the value passes to the event handler, the XML parser returns the value, without the quotes. For example, for the attribute name and value pair, `name="555-2230"`, only the text `555-2230` returns as the value of the attribute name. If you try to retrieve an out-of-range value of an attribute, then you receive the return value of `null`.

DETERMINE THE VALUE OF ATTRIBUTES

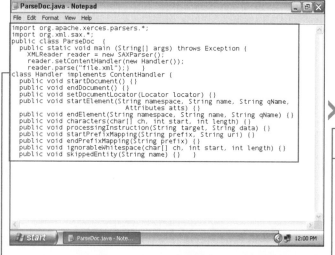

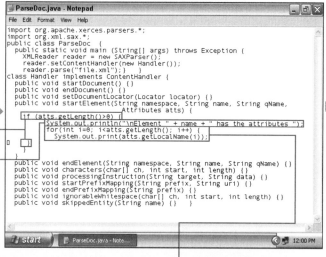

1 Open or create the code that parses an XML document.

Note: You can use the code created in the section "Parse an XML Document."

Note: You also need an XML document that contains elements with attributes. See Chapter 4 for more information.

2 Type the code that checks for the existence of attributes.

3 Type the code that displays a message if the element has attributes.

4 Type the code that displays the name of the attributes.

Apply It

You can use the `getType` method of the `Attributes` interface to determine the type of data of the attribute value. Unless you use a DTD or schema with your XML document, the data type is always `CDATA`.

TYPE THIS:

```
public void startElement(String namespace, String name, String qName,
                         Attributes atts) {
  if (atts.getLength()>0) {
    System.out.println("\nElement " + name + " has the attributes ");
    for(int i=0; i<atts.getLength(); i++) {
      System.out.print(atts.getLocalName(i));
      System.out.print(" which has a type of ");
      System.out.println(atts.getType(i));
    }
  }
}
```

RESULT:

```
Element owner has the attributes
dept which has a type of CDATA

Element priority has the attributes
ignore which has a type of CDATA
checked which has a type of CDATA
```

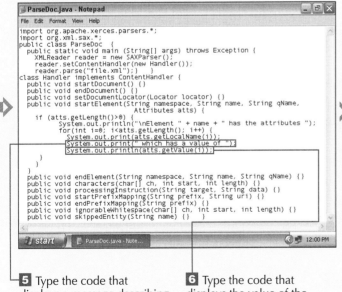

5 Type the code that displays a message describing the attribute value.

6 Type the code that displays the value of the attributes.

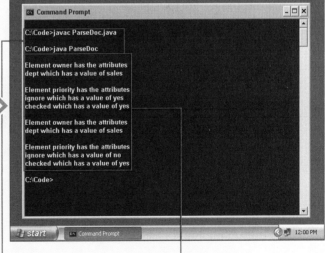

7 Compile and run your program.

Note: See Chapter 2 for instructions on compiling and running Java programs.

■ The name of each element, the name of the element's attributes, and the attribute's values display.

DETERMINE THE LINE NUMBER BEING PARSED

You can determine which line of an XML document a parser is currently processing when a specific event, such as a processing instruction, occurs. You use the `Locator` interface, part of the `org.xml.sax` package, to create an object. The object contains the location at which the XML parser is currently parsing in the XML document. For more information about importing a package, see Chapter 3.

The XML parser calls the `setDocumentLocator` method of the event handler class whenever the XML parser makes a callback to the event handler class, regardless of the type of event that triggers the callback or whether the XML parser intends to call any other method in the event handler. A `Locator` object passes to the `setDocumentLocator` method, which you can then use to determine the location that the XML parser is accessing. You use the `getLineNumber` method to return a value that represents the line number that the parser is currently parsing.

Because you cannot guarantee its accuracy, you should not access the `Locator` object outside of the event handler class. The `Locator` object passes to the `setDocumentLocator` method, and this limits its usefulness to code located within the `setDocumentLocator` method. To make it more useful, you should make the `Locator` object more accessible to other methods within the event handler class. The easiest way to do this involves creating a `Locator` object with a scope within the event handler class. This allows you to use the `Locator` object in the other methods of your class.

The `Locator` object and its data are only valid for the current event. As each event occurs, the data that a `Locator` object makes available changes. When working with the line numbers that the `Locator` object makes available, the line numbers start with number one and not zero.

DETERMINE THE LINE NUMBER BEING PARSED

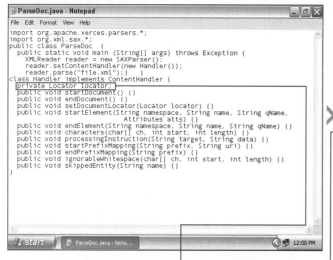

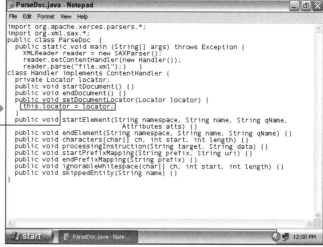

1 Open or create the code that parses an XML document.

Note: You can use the code created in the section "Parse an XML Document."

2 Type the code to create the variable that represents a **Locator** object with a scope within the event handler.

3 Type the code that assigns a **Locator** object to the **Locator** object you created in step 2.

Apply It

You can also use the `Locater` interface to locate the column number, the number of characters from the start of the line, that the XML parser is currently processing.

```
public void startElement(String namespace, String name, String qName,
                         Attributes atts) {
  System.out.print("On line " + locator.getLineNumber());
  System.out.print(" at column " + locator.getColumnNumber());
  System.out.println(" Start of element '" + name + "' detected ");
}
```

▼

```
On line 2 at column 7 Start of element 'todo' detected
On line 3 at column 9 Start of element 'task' detected
On line 4 at column 18 Start of element 'description' detected
On line 5 at column 12 Start of element 'owner' detected
On line 7 at column 13 Start of element 'status' detected
On line 8 at column 15 Start of element 'priority' detected
On line 10 at column 9 Start of element 'task' detected
On line 11 at column 18 Start of element 'description' detected
On line 12 at column 12 Start of element 'owner' detected
On line 13 at column 13 Start of element 'status' detected
On line 14 at column 15 Start of element 'priority' detected
```

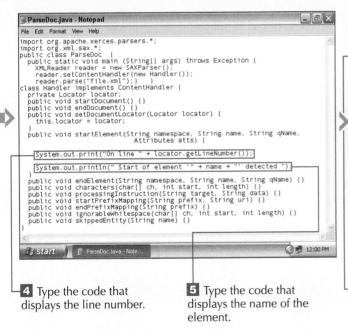

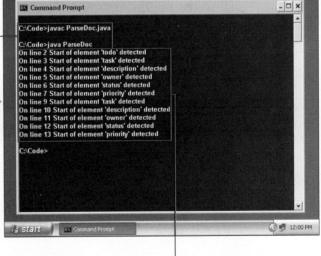

4 Type the code that displays the line number.

5 Type the code that displays the name of the element.

6 Compile and run your program.

Note: See Chapter 2 for instructions on compiling and running Java programs.

■ The name of each element, and the line number of the element in the XML document display.

DETERMINE IGNORABLE WHITESPACE IN AN ELEMENT

You can have the XML parser detect ignorable whitespace in your XML document to more efficiently identify what information the parser does not require when it processes an XML document. Most XML documents contain *whitespace*, which consists of non-displayable items such as a space character, tabs, or line breaks. Whitespace may include valid information, such as the spaces in text that compose an element's content. When you have valid whitespace as part of the textual content of an element, the XML parser detects it and then passes it to the application using the `characters` method of the event handler object. In that context you can consider the whitespace an actual part of the element content.

Some whitespace in an XML document may not form part of the content. The XML parser must detect it before it can perform a task, such as formatting an XML document for printing. You call this kind of whitespace *ignorable*

whitespace because it may not constitute a necessary part of the XML document, and therefore you can safely ignore it. For example, you may insert a line break between the end tag of one element and the start tag of the next element in an XML document. While making the XML document easier to read, the parser can safely ignore the line break without affecting the validity or contents of the XML document.

You detect ignorable whitespace with the `ignorableWhitespace` method of the event handler object. The `ignorableWhitespace` method works in the same manner as the `characters` method, in that the whitespace passes in a character array along with the start location and the length of the data in the array. You typically convert this character array into a string to make the information easier to manage.

DETERMINE IGNORABLE WHITESPACE IN AN ELEMENT

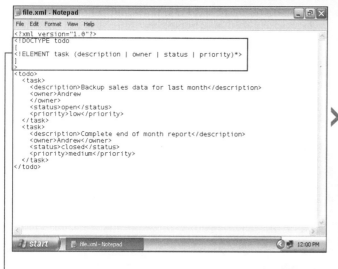

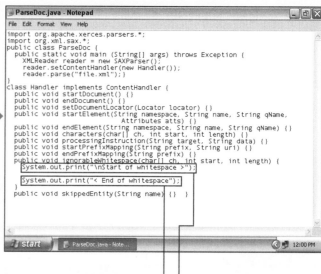

1 Open or create an XML document.

2 Create a DTD that defines an element that does not contain textual data.

Note: For more information about creating DTDs, see Chapter 5.

3 Save the XML document.

4 Open or create the code that parses the XML document saved in step 3.

Note: You can use the code created in the section "Parse an XML Document."

5 Type the code that displays a starting marker.

6 Type the code that displays an ending marker.

Apply It

You must include a valid DTD to determine which parts of the XML document constitute ignorable whitespace. The `ignorableWhitespace` method does not work unless you use a document type definition. You can test this by displaying a message whenever the parser detects ignorable whitespace. Try to detect whitespace in an XML document as in the example:

Example:
```
<?xml version="1.0"?>
<todo>
    <description>Backup sales data for last month</description>
</todo>
```

TYPE THIS:
```
public void ignorableWhitespace(char[] ch, int start, int length) {
        System.out.print("Detected ignorable whitespace");
}
```

RESULT:

No Result!

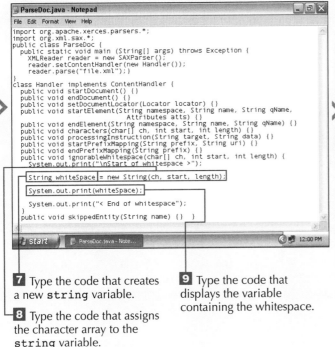

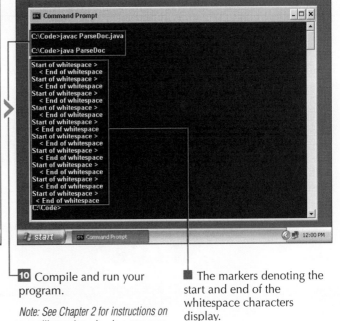

7 Type the code that creates a new **string** variable.

8 Type the code that assigns the character array to the **string** variable.

9 Type the code that displays the variable containing the whitespace.

10 Compile and run your program.

Note: See Chapter 2 for instructions on compiling and running Java programs.

■ The markers denoting the start and end of the whitespace characters display.

WORK WITH PROCESSING INSTRUCTIONS

You can use processing instructions to pass information to a specific application accessing an XML document. The application can then perform a task based on the values within the processing instruction or, if necessary, take no action at all.

Processing instructions in an XML document consist of two parts, the target and the value. The target is the first word of the processing instruction, while the value of the processing instruction consists of the remaining characters. Processing instructions within an XML document begin with <? and end with ?>.

You target the processing instruction at a specific application. For example, you may use <?Speller check=no?> as a processing instruction that notifies a text parsing application not to spell check the contents of the XML document.

Although you typically make the target name the name of the application for which you intend the processing instruction, you can also make it any valid word.

The XML parser detects processing instructions in an XML document using the processingInstruction method of the event handler class. The processingInstruction method passes two parameters as string data: the target name, and the value of the processing instructions as you specify them in the XML document.

Processing instructions have no impact on the document itself; an application only uses them when it processes the XML document to perform a task. Multiple processing instructions can exist in an XML document. If your application does not look for processing instructions in the XML document, then the application ignores any processing instructions that it encounters.

You must write your application so that it recognizes the processing instructions intended for it and then performs a task depending on the value of the processing instructions.

WORK WITH PROCESSING INSTRUCTIONS

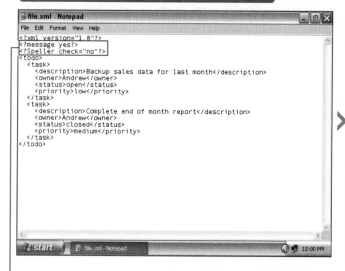

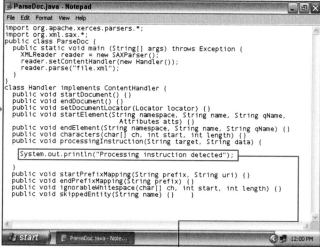

1 Open or create an XML document.

2 Insert one or more processing instructions.

Note: For more information about creating processing instructions, see Chapter 4.

3 Save the XML document.

4 Open or create the code that parses an XML document.

Note: You can use the code created in the section "Parse an XML Document."

5 Type the code that displays a message when the application detects a processing instruction.

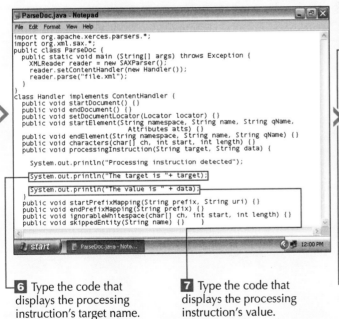

Apply It

If your application expects processing instructions in the XML documents that you process, you typically use multiple `if` statements to detect the processing instructions and then perform a specific task depending on the value in those instructions. If you include the processing instruction `<?myApp priority="high"?>` in your XML document, then you can change the code in the event handler's `processingInstruction` method to display a message when you flag an XML document as important.

TYPE THIS:

```
public void processingInstruction(String target, String data) {
    if (target.equals("myApp") {
        if (data.equals("priority=\"high\"")) {
            System.out.println("This document is of high priority. Review carefully");
        }
    }
}
```

RESULT:

```
This document is of high priority. Review carefully.
```

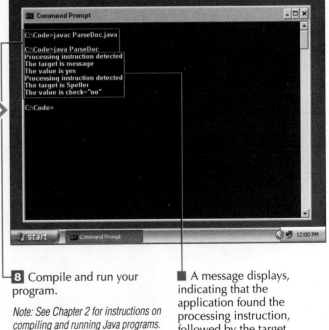

6 Type the code that displays the processing instruction's target name.

7 Type the code that displays the processing instruction's value.

8 Compile and run your program.

Note: See Chapter 2 for instructions on compiling and running Java programs.

■ A message displays, indicating that the application found the processing instruction, followed by the target and value.

PARSE MULTIPLE XML DOCUMENTS USING MULTIPLE EVENT HANDLERS

In many cases, an application needs to parse multiple XML documents. As with most Java objects, you can reuse the pre-existing, application-created objects — including objects created while parsing another document — to minimize memory usage and limit the use of resources on your computer. Reusing existing objects increases your application's efficiency, thereby improving the performance of your application.

You create an XMLReader object to parse an XML document using the SAX API. Once you create the XMLReader objects, you can use them to parse multiple XML documents. If possible, you should avoid creating a new instance of an XMLReader object if you can reuse an existing object.

Another advantage of reusing XMLReader objects involves not having to continually register the reader with an event handler class each time you want to parse an XML

document. Once you register the use of the event handler class, the application calls the methods of that handler class to correspond to the events that occur while the XML document parses. You can use the specified event handler on all subsequent parsed documents.

You can also reuse the XMLReader object to parse a previously parsed document, this time using a different event handler. For example, you may have one event handler that primarily checks for errors; if you find an error-free XML document, you can parse the document again, this time using an event handler that prints the information in the XML document.

Different APIs make use of reader objects like XMLReader. If you use other APIs to parse an XML document at the same time, you should ensure that you are using your SAX API event handlers with the appropriate reader objects.

PARSE MULTIPLE XML DOCUMENTS USING MULTIPLE EVENT HANDLERS

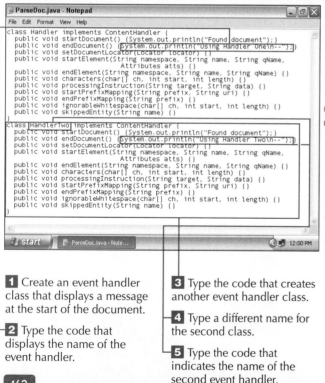

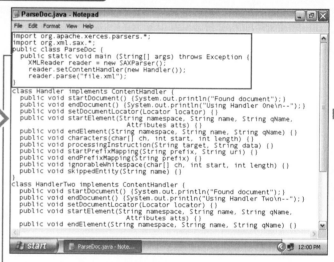

1 Create an event handler class that displays a message at the start of the document.

2 Type the code that displays the name of the event handler.

3 Type the code that creates another event handler class.

4 Type a different name for the second class.

5 Type the code that indicates the name of the second event handler.

6 Type the code that parses an XML document.

Extra

Regardless of how many event handler classes you use in your code, all must implement all the required methods of the `ContentHandler` interface, even if you do not use all of the methods. For more information about the methods you need when creating event handlers, see the section "Create an Event Handler Class."

While you can use the same `XMLReader` object to read multiple XML documents, you cannot reuse the `XMLReader` object while it is in the process of parsing a document. If you must parse two XML documents at the same time, you need to create another instance of the `XMLReader` object.

If necessary, you can create multiple instances of the `XMLReader` object so that each `XMLReader` object uses a different XML parser. You can then use the multiple `XMLReader` objects to process a single XML document. You may find this useful if you want to harness the benefits and strengths of individual parsers to process a complex XML document. Depending on the operating system environment and the file system that stores the XML document, you may only be allowed to access the XML document with one `XMLReader` object at a time.

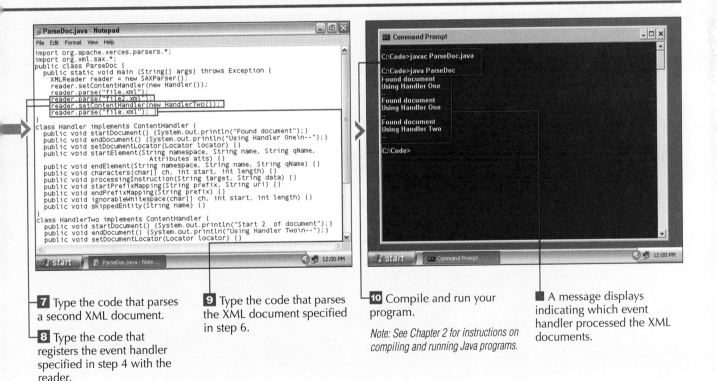

7 Type the code that parses a second XML document.

8 Type the code that registers the event handler specified in step 4 with the reader.

9 Type the code that parses the XML document specified in step 6.

10 Compile and run your program.

Note: See Chapter 2 for instructions on compiling and running Java programs.

■ A message displays indicating which event handler processed the XML documents.

CREATE AN ERROR HANDLER

You can use the SAX API to perform a specific task or tasks whenever it encounters an error when parsing a document. You can create code that can attempt to recover from the error, commit the error to an error log, or simply display a custom error message.

You can create an error handler class to handle SAX errors. The error handler class you create must implement the ErrorHandler interface of the org.xml.sax package.

In addition, it must also implement three methods: warning, error, and fatalError.

The SAX API calls each method whenever it generates the corresponding error while parsing an XML document. For example, the application calls the fatalError method of the error handler class whenever an error causes the XML parser to cease parsing the document. A SAXParseException object passes all methods of the error handler class. You can use a SAXParseException object to

determine more information about the causes of an error. For more information about SAXParseException, see the section "Create a Custom Error Message" in this chapter.

Once you have created the error handler class, you must register the error handler with the XMLReader object. You register the error handler using the setErrorHandler method of the XMLReader object.

Typically, you can include more that just the error-handling object to detect errors in your code. You should always develop applications that you create to handle any possible errors that the application generates when it is executed. If you do not have any error-handling capability built into your applications, your applications may abruptly halt and display a large amount of information upon encountering errors; they may even cause data loss. You typically create error handling code for all the methods in the error handling class. For more information about handling errors in Java code, refer to Chapter 3.

CREATE AN ERROR HANDLER

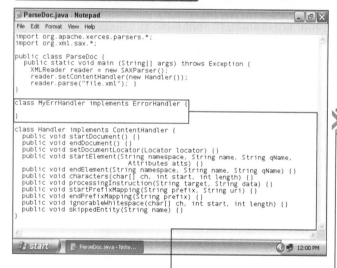

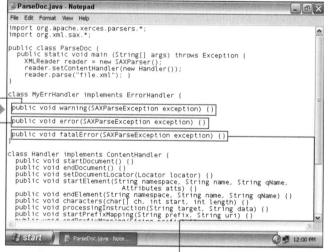

Note: To generate the required error, you need to parse an XML document that has an element with a missing end tag.

1 Open or create the code that parses an XML document.

Note: You can use the code created in the section "Parse an XML Document."

2 Type the code that creates the error handler class.

3 Type the code that creates the warning method.

4 Type the code that creates the error method.

5 Type the code that creates the fatalError method.

Extra

An application calls one of three required methods of the error handler class when it encounters the corresponding type of error. The XML specification defines the types of errors that the XML parser reports.

Warning

Warnings are errors that the `error` or `fatalError` methods do not catch. You can typically continue parsing an XML document after a warning generates.

Error

The parser uses the `error` method with the type of errors from which it can often recover. For example, the application calls this method if it finds the XML document an invalid XML document while parsing it.

FatalError

A call to the `fatalError` method often means that the application cannot properly parse an XML document, if, for example, the XML document does not have a required start or end element tag.

Fatal errors typically shut down any application that encounters them. To immediately terminate your application, you should call the `exit` method of the `System` class with an argument of -1.

Example:
```
public void fatalError(SAXParseException exception) {
   System.out.println("\n\n There has been a serious error\n\n");
   System.exit(-1);
}
```

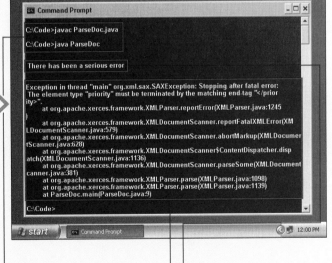

6 Type the code that displays a message when the application encounters a fatal error.

7 Compile and run your program.

Note: See Chapter 2 for instructions on compiling and running Java programs.

■ A message displays stating that the application encountered an error.

■ Depending on your parser and other error handling code, more error information may display.

CREATE A CUSTOM ERROR MESSAGE

You can create a custom error message to provide more information about the type of error a parser encounters. You can code this custom error message to display on screen, log to a file, or go into a database. Custom error messages make an application easier to troubleshoot and maintain.

When a parser encounters an error during the parsing of an XML document, it makes a call to a method in the error handler class. The method the XML parser calls depends on the type of error it encounters.

When the XML parser calls the method of the error handler, a SAXParseException object passes into the method. As with all exception errors, you commonly assign the name exception to the SAXParseException object.

The SAXParseException object allows you to access various methods to determine information about the error that caused the call to the method of the error handler. The getMessage method returns a string that may describe the exact nature of the error.

To locate the error in an XML document, you need to know the line at which the XML parser was parsing when it encountered the error. The getLineNumber method of the SAXParseException object determines this line. Similarly, the getColumnNumber method returns the column number at the time of the error. The column number is the number of characters from the beginning of the line. Because the values that the getLineNumber, getColumnNumber, and getMessage methods return are String values, you can easily display them. You typically create error-handling code for all the methods in the error-handling class.

The information passed to the SAXParseException object, such as the text of error messages, may change depending on the operating system environment, the XML parser that you use, and the version of Java that created the application.

CREATE A CUSTOM ERROR MESSAGE

Note: To generate the required error, you need to parse an XML document that has an element with a missing end tag.

Note: You can use the code created in the section "Create an Error Handler."

1 Open or create the code that parses an XML document and uses an error handler.

2 Type the code that displays a description of the error.

Apply It

You can use the `getSystemId` method of the `SAXParseException` object to access the name of the XML document that the parser parsed at the time of an error.

TYPE THIS:

```
public void fatalError(SAXParseException exception) {
  System.out.println("\n\n There has been a serious error\n");
  System.out.println("Error message\n" + exception.getMessage());
  System.out.println("\nAt Line: " + exception.getLineNumber());
  System.out.println("\nAt Column: " + exception.getColumnNumber());
  System.out.println("\nName: " + exception.getSystemId());
  }
```

▼

RESULT:

```
There has been a serious error

Error message
The element type "priority" must be terminated by the matching end-tag "</priority>".

At Line: 14

At Column: 9

Name: file:///C:/Code/file.xml
```

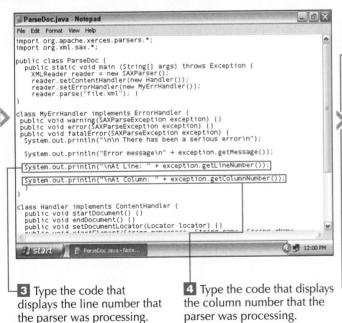

3 Type the code that displays the line number that the parser was processing.

4 Type the code that displays the column number that the parser was processing.

5 Compile and run your program.

Note: See Chapter 2 for instructions on compiling and running Java programs.

■ A detailed message displays.

■ Depending on your parser and other error handling code, more error information may display.

CREATE AN ENTITY RESOLVER

A n entity is a reference that allows you to use a string to represent a large amount of data in an XML document, thus saving you time when you write your code; instead of typing the same code repeatedly, you can simply insert a reference to an entity, which is a single line of code.

You can insert entities when you re-use a section of the same XML code within an XML document. For example, you can insert a company's address or a copyright warning message multiple times in the same document.

You can have either internal or external entities. *External entities* occur when you access information in a separate file from within your XML document. From within your Java code, you can determine what files resolve entities in the XML document that an application parses.

To determine the file name of an external entity reference, you create an entity resolver class file that implements the

EntityResolver interface. The EntityResolver interface is part of the org.xml.sax package, which you must import prior to using the interface. For more information about importing a package, see Chapter 3.

The entity resolver class must implement one method, called resolveEntity. The resolveEntity method has two arguments, the public ID and the system ID of the file the external entity references.

You can display the system ID string to determine the name of any file that your computer uses to resolve external entities in a parsed XML document.

The resolveEntity method has a return value of type InputSource, so unless you intend on returning an InputSource object for use elsewhere in your code, you must return a value of null from the resolveEntity method. For more information about return values, see Chapter 3.

CREATE AN ENTITY RESOLVER

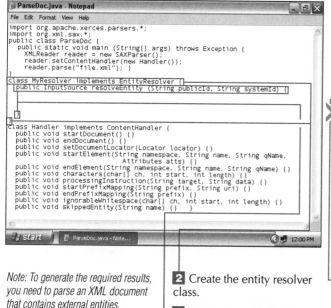

Note: To generate the required results, you need to parse an XML document that contains external entities.

1 Open or create the code that parses an XML document.

Note: You can use the code created in the section "Create an Error Handler."

2 Create the entity resolver class.

3 Create the **main** method of the class.

4 Type the code that displays the name of the referenced file.

168

Apply It

If you use multiple entity resolvers, you can easily determine the identification of the resolver registered with an XMLReader object by using the getEntityResolver method of the XMLReader object.

TYPE THIS:

```
public class ParseDoc {
  public static void main (String[] args) throws Exception {
    XMLReader reader = new SAXParser();
    reader.setContentHandler(new Handler());
    reader.setEntityResolver(new MyResolver());
    reader.parse("file.xml");
    System.out.print("The Current entity resolver is ");
    System.out.println(reader.getEntityResolver());
    }
}
```

RESULT:

```
Resolving entities using file:///C:/Code/who.xml
Resolving entities using file:///C:/Code/who.xml

The Current entity resolver is MyResolver@283b8a
```

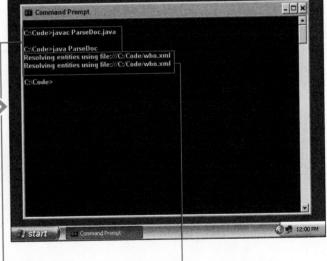

5 Type the code that causes the method to return a **null** value.

6 Type the code that registers the entity resolver with the **XMLReader** object.

7 Compile and run your program.

Note: See Chapter 2 for instructions on compiling and running Java programs.

■ The names of any referenced files display.

USING THE DEFAULT HANDLER

You can use a default handler class to speed up your development of Java applications that you create with the SAX API. Working with the SAX API and XML parsers requires many different types of handler classes to respond to many different events, such as errors and XML document parsing. These handler classes implement interfaces and may require that you define numerous methods whether you intend to use the methods in your application or not. The DefaultHandler class simplifies and reduces the amount of code you need to create for the various handler classes.

The DefaultHandler class implements many of the interfaces in the org.xml.sax package, including the ContentHandler, EntityResolver, and ErrorHandler interfaces. If you use any or all of these interfaces in your code, you can utilize the DefaultHandler class to create one multi-use class that can perform a variety of tasks. The DefaultHandler class is part of the org.xml .sax.helpers package, which you must import prior to using the class. For more information about importing a package, see Chapter 3.

The most common use of the DefaultHandler class involves replacing the classes that implement the ContentHandler interface. To employ the ContentHandler interface you must implement 11 methods, some of which you may not use. With the DefaultHandler class, you only have to define the methods that you actually intend to use.

As with any event handler class that implements the ContentHandler interface, you must register the class that extends the DefaultHandler class with the XMLReader object if you want to use a class based on the DefaultHandler class instead of the ContentHandler interface. Registering the event handler class with the XMLReader object enables the XMLReader object to call the appropriate methods in the event handler class when events occur, such as the detection of an element's start tag when an application parses an XML document.

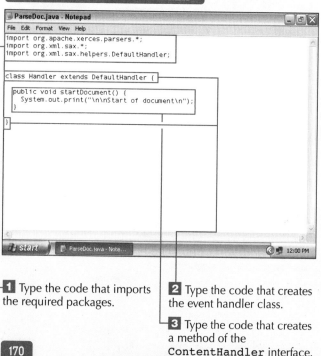

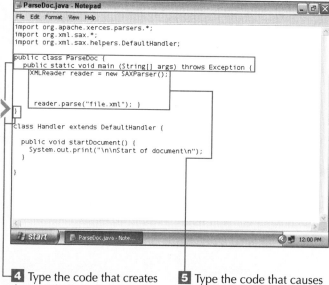

1 Type the code that imports the required packages.

2 Type the code that creates the event handler class.

3 Type the code that creates a method of the ContentHandler interface.

4 Type the code that creates the **main** class of your code.

5 Type the code that causes an application to parse an XML document.

Apply It

You can easily use the `DefaultHandler` class to implement the `EntityResolver` and `ContentHandler` interfaces.

TYPE THIS:

```
public class ParseDoc {
  public static void main (String[] args) throws Exception {
    XMLReader reader = new SAXParser();
    reader.setContentHandler(new BigHandler());
    reader.setEntityResolver(new BigHandler());
    reader.parse("file.xml"); }
}
class BigHandler extends DefaultHandler {
  public void startDocument() {System.out.println("\n\nStart of document\n");}
  public InputSource resolveEntity (String publicId, String systemId) {
    System.out.println("Resolving entities using " + systemId);
    return null; }
}
```

RESULT:

```
Start of document

Resolving entities using file:///C:/Code/who.xml
Resolving entities using file:///C:/Code/who.xml
```

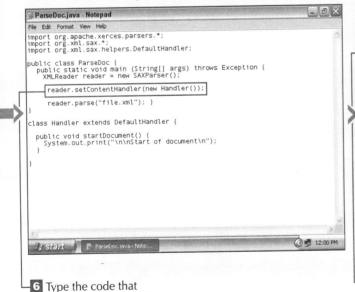

6 Type the code that registers the event handler with the `XMLReader`.

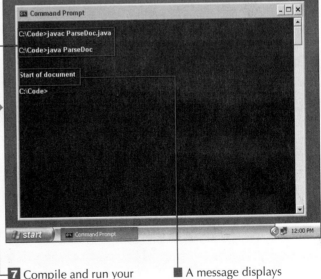

7 Compile and run your program.

Note: See Chapter 2 for instructions on compiling and running Java programs.

■ A message displays indicating that the application parsed the XML document.

DETERMINE FEATURE AND PROPERTY SETTINGS

XML parsers have their own settings, which you can check to determine if you have a specific function or feature available to your application. You refer to the settings of an XML parser as the features and properties of the parser.

The `getFeature` and `getProperty` methods of the `XMLReader` object read the features and properties of the parser. The `getFeature` and `getProperty` methods take one argument, which becomes the name of the feature. The name of the feature is usually a uniform resource identifier (URI). To make long URIs easier to manage, you commonly assign the URI to a string. Features return a `boolean` value, while properties return an object.

One feature that you may want to check is the feature at http://www.xml.org/sax/features/external-general-entities. This feature indicates whether text entities resolve when an XML parser parses an XML document that contains entities.

The SAX API specifies some features and properties which all SAX-compliant XML parsers must support. Other features and properties only become available when you use the SAX API with a specific XML parser. Only the SAX-specified features and properties are available on all SAX-compliant parsers.

Normally you do not depend too heavily on features or properties specific to one parser in your code. If you have to change the parser or even change to a different version of the same XML parser sometime in the future, you may find that the features and properties available in one version are not available in another. Other XML-parser-independent features can alter the configuration of an XML parser and achieve the same results as those that utilize features and properties. Before using the features and properties of an XML parser, refer to your specific XML parser's documentation for the best alternate methods.

DETERMINE FEATURE AND PROPERTY SETTINGS

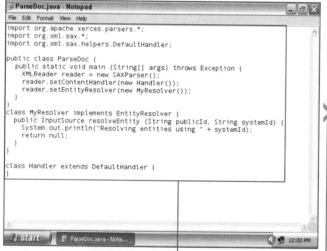

```
import org.apache.xerces.parsers.*;
import org.xml.sax.*;
import org.xml.sax.helpers.DefaultHandler;

public class ParseDoc {
  public static void main (String[] args) throws Exception {
    XMLReader reader = new SAXParser();
    reader.setContentHandler(new Handler());
    reader.setEntityResolver(new MyResolver());
  }
}

class MyResolver implements EntityResolver {
  public InputSource resolveEntity (String publicId, String systemId) {
    System.out.println("Resolving entities using " + systemId);
    return null;
  }
}

class Handler extends DefaultHandler {
}
```

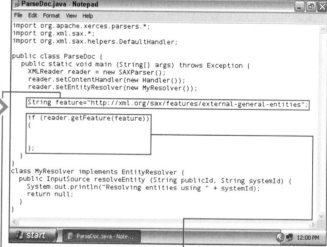

```
import org.apache.xerces.parsers.*;
import org.xml.sax.*;
import org.xml.sax.helpers.DefaultHandler;

public class ParseDoc {
  public static void main (String[] args) throws Exception {
    XMLReader reader = new SAXParser();
    reader.setContentHandler(new Handler());
    reader.setEntityResolver(new MyResolver());

    String feature="http://xml.org/sax/features/external-general-entities";

    if (reader.getFeature(feature))
    {

    };
  }
}

class MyResolver implements EntityResolver {
  public InputSource resolveEntity (String publicId, String systemId) {
    System.out.println("Resolving entities using " + systemId);
    return null;
  }
}
```

Note: To generate the required results, you need to parse an XML document that contains external entities.

1 Open or create the code that parses an XML document and implements an entity resolver class.

Note: You can use the code created in the section "Create an Entity Resolver."

2 Type the code that assigns a feature URI to a variable.

3 Type the code that tests the value of the feature.

Apply It

You can use the `setFeature` or `setPropery` methods of the `XMLReader` object to modify values, but not all XML parsers allow you to modify all features and properties. The XML parser may allow you to read, but not set, selected features and properties. If you attempt to modify a value when the XML parser disallows it, the parser generates an error.

TYPE THIS:

```
String feature="http://xml.org/sax/features/external-general-entities";
if (reader.getFeature(feature))
{
  System.out.print("The feature\n" + feature + "\nis enabled.\n\n");
  System.out.print("Now turning it off..\n\n");
  reader.setFeature(feature,false);
};
```

RESULT:

```
The feature
http://xml.org/sax/features/external-general-entities
is enabled.

Now turning it off..

Exception in thread "main" org.xml.sax.SAXNotSupportedException: http://xml.org/
sax/features/external-general-entities
        at org.apache.xerces.framework.XMLParser.setExternalGeneralEntities(XML
Parser.java:486)
```

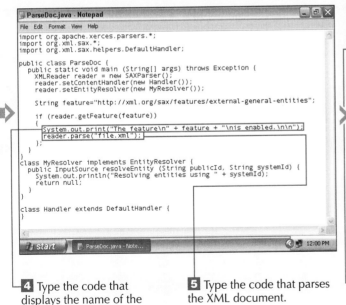

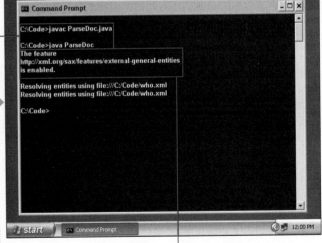

■-4 Type the code that displays the name of the feature.

■-5 Type the code that parses the XML document.

■-6 Compile and run your program.

Note: See Chapter 2 for instructions on compiling and running Java programs.

■ The name of the feature displays if the feature is enabled.

DETECT NOTATION DECLARATIONS

You can use a notation declaration to tell an application that an XML document contains information which an external application needs to process. You use the information in a notation declaration to determine what data or application your Java application may need to access and interpret the data. For example, if you parse an XML document on computers using different operating systems, you can access different image applications to interpret image data in an XML document. In many cases, the information indicates the actual file name of the application that you can use to process the data, such as spellcheck.exe for a spell-checking application. Or it may only return the type of information, such as image/gif. In cases where only the data type returns, you can configure the operating system to choose the application that best suits the date you want to process. You must ensure that you create the code that correctly processes the information.

You use the DTDHandler to access interface notation information. You must create a DTD handler class that implements the DTDHandler interface. Once you create the DTD handler class, you register the class with the XMLReader object, using the setDTDHandler method.

The DTDHandler interface requires you to define two methods, the notationDecl method and the unparsedEntityDecl method. The notationDecl method accesses any declared notation in the DTD of an XML document. When the notationDecl method finds a notation declaration, it passes it to the name of the notation, the public ID, and the system ID of the external ID. For more information about notation declaration of an external ID, see Chapter 5.

You can use notation declaration with processing instructions to instruct your application to perform a specific task.

DETECT NOTATION DECLARATIONS

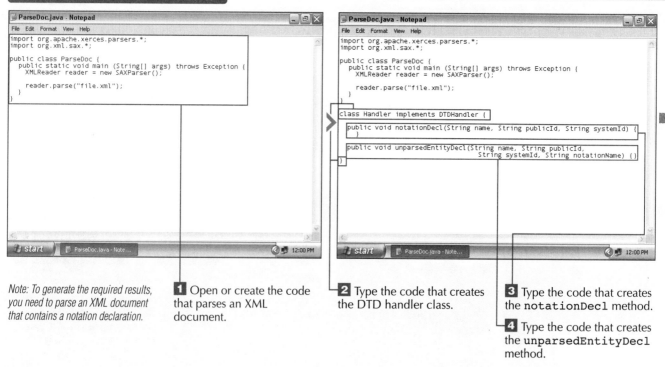

Note: To generate the required results, you need to parse an XML document that contains a notation declaration.

1 Open or create the code that parses an XML document.

2 Type the code that creates the DTD handler class.

3 Type the code that creates the **notationDecl** method.

4 Type the code that creates the **unparsedEntityDecl** method.

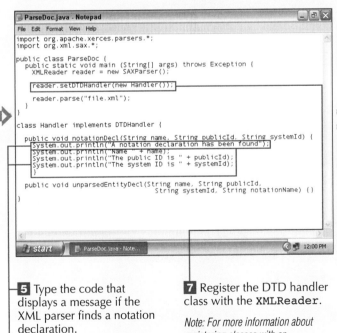

Apply It

You can use the other method of the DTD handler class, `unparsedEntityDecl`, to detect unparsed external entities, which you often use in conjunction with notation declarations. Create a DTD that contains `<!ENTITY owner SYSTEM "http://127.0.0.1/who.xml" NDATA txt>` and then type the following code.

TYPE THIS:

```
class Handler implements DTDHandler {
    public void notationDecl(String name, String publicId, String systemId) {
    }
    public void unparsedEntityDecl(String name, String publicId, String systemId,
                                   String notationName) {
        System.out.println("An Unparsed external entity has been found");
        System.out.println("Name " + name);
        System.out.println("The public ID is " + publicId);
        System.out.println("The system ID is " + systemId);
        System.out.println("The notation name is " + notationName);
    }
}
```

RESULT:

```
An Unparsed external entity has been found
Name owner
The public ID is null
The system ID is http://127.0.0.1/who.xml
The notation name is txt
```

5 Type the code that displays a message if the XML parser finds a notation declaration.

6 Type the code that displays the notation declaration information.

7 Register the DTD handler class with the **XMLReader**.

*Note: For more information about registering classes with an **XMLReader** object, see "Parse an XML Document."*

8 Compile and run your program.

Note: See Chapter 2 for instructions on compiling and running Java programs.

■ The name of the notation declaration and its details display.

CREATE A DECLARATION HANDLER

The DTD in an XML document contains declarations, such as element declarations, that describe the elements' format within the XML document. You can extract the information from the declarations in the DTD. You may want to retrieve the data in a DTD concerning declarations to reconstruct an XML document or to compile an analysis of the elements in an XML document.

You must create a declaration handler class to handle the callbacks that relate to declarations within the DTD. Each time the XML parser encounters a declaration in the DTD, the declaration handler makes a callback to a method. The method that the declaration handler calls depends on the type of declaration.

The declaration handler must implement the `DeclHandler` interface in the `org.xml.sax.ext` package. The `org.xml.sax.ext` package, which you must import prior to using the interface, contains extensions for use with most SAX-compliant XML parsers. The declaration handler that implements the `DeclHandler` package must define four

methods: `elementDecl`, which reports element declarations in the DTD; `attributeDecl`, which reports about attribute declarations; and `internalEntityDecl` and `externalEntityDecl`, which retrieve information about internal and external declarations in the DTD. You must define these four methods in the declaration handler class, even if you do not use all of the methods. The element declaration passes each method value that reflects the information within the declaration. For example, the element declaration in the DTD passes two string values that represent the name and content type to the `elementDecl` method.

You use the declaration handler in a slightly different manner than other content handlers. To use the declaration handler, a declaration handler object passes the `setProperty` method of the `XMLReader` object as a value to the http://www.xml.org/sax/properties/declaration-handler property. As with other properties, you may find the URI of the property quite long, so you should place it in a variable to make the property easier to manage.

CREATE A DECLARATION HANDLER

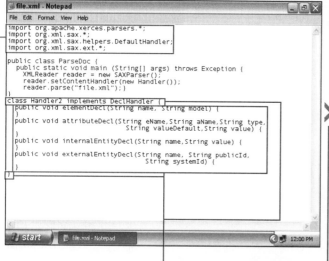

1 Open or create the code that parses an XML document.

Note: To generate the required results, you need to parse an XML document that includes element declarations.

2 Type the code that imports the required packages.

3 Type the code that creates the declaration handler class.

4 Type the code that creates the methods of the declaration handler class.

5 Type the code that displays the information that the XML parser passes to the `elementDecl` method.

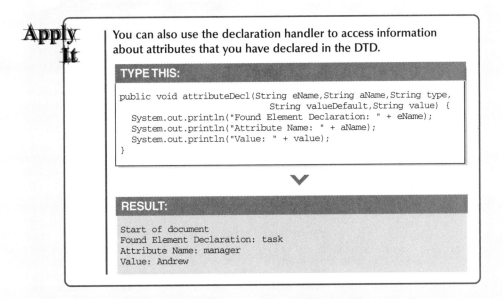

Apply It

You can also use the declaration handler to access information about attributes that you have declared in the DTD.

TYPE THIS:

```
public void attributeDecl(String eName,String aName,String type,
                          String valueDefault,String value) {
  System.out.println("Found Element Declaration: " + eName);
  System.out.println("Attribute Name: " + aName);
  System.out.println("Value: " + value);
}
```

RESULT:

```
Start of document
Found Element Declaration: task
Attribute Name: manager
Value: Andrew
```

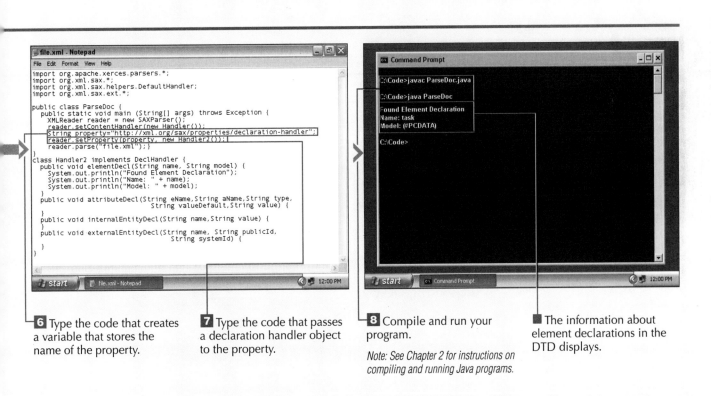

6 Type the code that creates a variable that stores the name of the property.

7 Type the code that passes a declaration handler object to the property.

8 Compile and run your program.

Note: See Chapter 2 for instructions on compiling and running Java programs.

■ The information about element declarations in the DTD displays.

CREATE A LEXICAL HANDLER

You can retrieve information from an XML document that does not make up part of the content of the XML document. For example, you can retrieve the comments and entity declarations that you have present in an XML document. You may find retrieving this type of information useful if you want to reconstruct an XML document or if you need to more closely examine the information within an XML document.

You use a lexical handler to access information about lexical events during the parsing of an XML document. As with other event handlers, the lexical handler contains methods that the XML parser calls when it encounters the corresponding event. For example, the parser calls the comment method of the lexical handler whenever it encounters a comment while parsing an XML document.

The lexical handler must implement the LexicalHandler interface as part of the org.xml.sax.ext package. The org.xml.sax.ext package contains extensions to the

SAX API and you typically find it included with most SAX-compliant parsers. The org.xml.sax.ext package must be imported prior to using the interface. For more information about importing a package, see Chapter 3.

The lexical handler must implement six methods: the comment method reports comments; startCDATA and endCDATA methods report the start and end of CDATA sections; the startDTD and endDTD methods report the start and end of the DTD; and the startEntity and endEntity methods report the start and end of any entities in the XML document.

You use the lexical handler by passing a lexical handler object to the property using the setProperty method of the XMLReader object. As with other properties, you may find the URI of the property to be quite long, so you may want to place it in a variable to make the property easier to handle.

CREATE A LEXICAL HANDLER

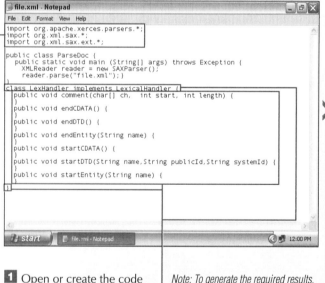

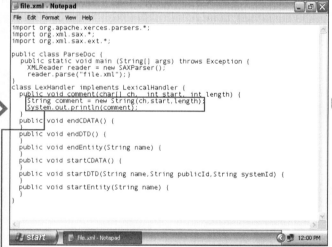

1 Open or create the code that parses an XML document.

2 Type the code that imports the required packages.

Note: To generate the required results, you need to parse an XML document that contains comments.

3 Type the code that creates the lexical handler class.

4 Type the code that creates the required methods of the lexical handler class.

5 Type the code that displays the information passed to the **comment** method.

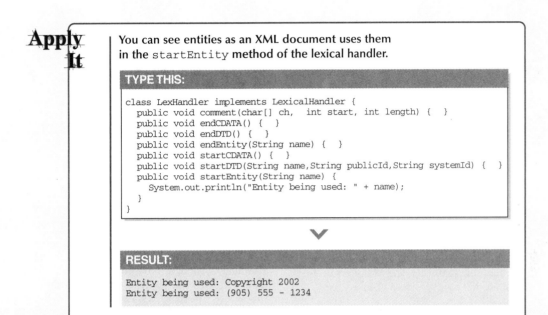

Apply It

You can see entities as an XML document uses them in the `startEntity` method of the lexical handler.

TYPE THIS:

```
class LexHandler implements LexicalHandler {
    public void comment(char[] ch,  int start, int length) {  }
    public void endCDATA() {  }
    public void endDTD() {  }
    public void endEntity(String name) {  }
    public void startCDATA() {  }
    public void startDTD(String name,String publicId,String systemId) {  }
    public void startEntity(String name) {
       System.out.println("Entity being used: " + name);
    }
}
```

RESULT:

```
Entity being used: Copyright 2002
Entity being used: (905) 555 - 1234
```

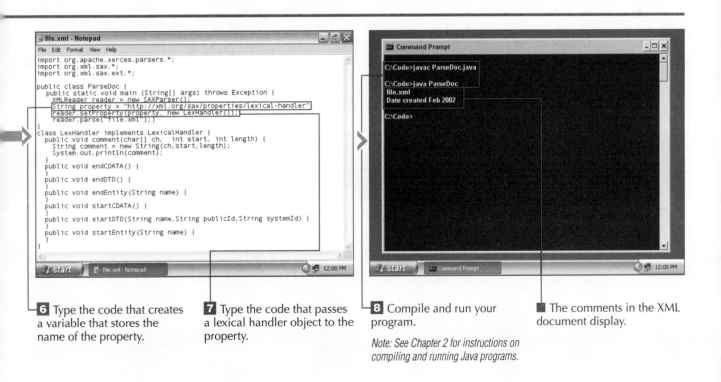

file.xml - Notepad

```
import org.apache.xerces.parsers.*;
import org.xml.sax.*;
import org.xml.sax.ext.*;

public class ParseDoc {
   public static void main (String[] args) throws Exception {
      XMLReader reader = new SAXParser();
      String property = "http://xml.org/sax/properties/lexical-handler";
      reader.setProperty(property, new LexHandler());
      reader.parse("file.xml");
   }
}
class LexHandler implements LexicalHandler {
   public void comment(char[] ch,  int start, int length) {
      String comment = new String(ch,start,length);
      System.out.println(comment);
   }
   public void endCDATA() {
   }
   public void endDTD() {
   }
   public void endEntity(String name) {
   }
   public void startCDATA() {
   }
   public void startDTD(String name,String publicId,String systemId) {
   }
   public void startEntity(String name) {
   }
}
```

Command Prompt

```
C:\Code>javac ParseDoc.java

C:\Code>java ParseDoc
file.xml
Date created Feb 2002

C:\Code>
```

■6 Type the code that creates a variable that stores the name of the property.

■7 Type the code that passes a lexical handler object to the property.

■8 Compile and run your program.

Note: See Chapter 2 for instructions on compiling and running Java programs.

■ The comments in the XML document display.

TURN ON VALIDATION

One of the most useful features of an XML parser involves checking the validity of XML documents. Valid XML documents must conform to a specific set of rules that governs their structure and make-up, thus maintaining the proper organization of information within XML documents. Validation also ensures the integrity of the data within an XML document, especially if the XML document makes use of XML Schemas. For more information about XML Schemas, see Chapter 6.

You can have either a validating or a non-validating parser. Non-validating parsers can verify the validity of an XML document. A validating parser allows you to either turn on or turn off the validating feature of the XML parser. By default, most validating XML parsers do not have their validating feature enabled.

With its validating feature enabled, the validating parser detects a non-valid document, generates an error, and stops parsing the XML document. In most cases, you check to

see if a parser considers an XML document valid before attempting to process the XML document.

You can turn the validating feature of the parser on or off by setting the http://www.xml.org/sax/features/validation feature. Setting the feature to `true` turns on the validation checking of XML documents, while setting this feature to `false` turns off validation. You must set the feature before you parse a document. You can turn the validation on for some documents and off for others.

All SAX-compliant XML parsers must support the validation feature, and they must all support the enabling and disabling of validation by using the http://www.xml.org/sax/features/validation feature setting. In addition to setting the validation feature, XML parsers may have the ability to enable or disable validation using other methods outside of your Java application.

TURN ON VALIDATION

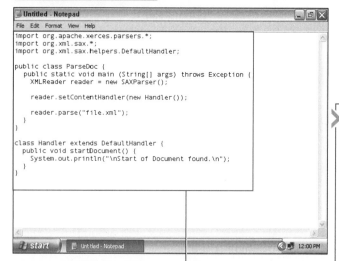

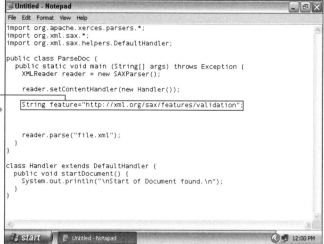

Note: For this example, you need to parse a non-valid XML document. For information about XML document validity, see Chapter 6.

1 Type the code that parses an XML document.

Note: You can use the code from the section "Parse an XML Document."

2 Type the code that assigns the name of the feature to a variable.

Apply
It

You may find the error message that the XML parser produces when it discovers a non-valid XML document to be very cryptic. You can provide a more detailed message by using an error handler.

TYPE THIS:

```java
public class ParseDoc {
  public static void main (String[] args) throws Exception {
    XMLReader reader = new SAXParser();
    reader.setContentHandler(new Handler());
    reader.setErrorHandler(new MyErrHandler());
    reader.parse("file.xml");}
}
class MyErrHandler implements ErrorHandler {
  public void warning(SAXParseException exception) {
  }
  public void error(SAXParseException exception) {
  }
  public void fatalError(SAXParseException exception) {
    System.out.println("\n\n There has been a serious error\n\n");
    System.out.println(" Please ensure your XML document is valid\n\n");
  }
}
```

RESULT:

```
There has been a serious error
Please ensure your XML document is valid
```

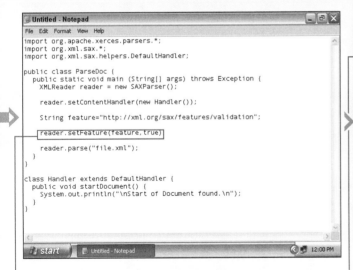

3 Type the code that enables the parser's validation feature.

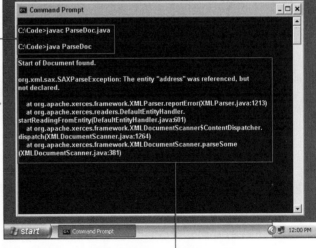

4 Compile and run your program.

Note: See Chapter 2 for instructions on compiling and running Java programs.

■ The parser generates an error if it does not find the XML document to be valid.

TOGGLE NAMESPACE AND PREFIX USAGE

Namespaces allow you to use tags in a single XML document that you have defined in a multitude of other documents. For example, you may have two elements called name in your XML document, where each name element belongs to a different namespace. For more information about namespaces, refer to Chapter 5.

You can instruct the XML parser to use namespaces if you use namespaces in your XML documents. You can set the http://www.xml.org/sax/features/namespaces feature to either true or false to turn the use of namespaces on or off.

XML parsers should have the ability to process XML documents that use namespaces, even if the parser does not support namespaces. Because of the format of the element names, the parser assumes that the namespace, colon, and element name are a single element name.

When you use namespaces in XML documents, you use xmlns declarations to indicate the location of the

namespace. For parsers that do not support namespaces, the xmlns declaration appears as just another attribute of an element.

You can turn the reporting of the xmlns declaration as an attribute on or off. You typically want to turn off the reporting of xmlns declarations as attributes when you have enabled the support for namespaces in your XML parser. You set the http://xml.org/sax/features/namespace-prefixes feature to either true or false to turn the prefix reporting on or off.

If you want to handle the namespaces within your own code, consider enabling the namespace prefix reporting. Older versions of SAX-compliant XML parsers do not include support for namespaces. The SAX API version 2, or simply SAX 2, supports the use of namespaces.

All SAX 2-compliant XML parsers support the enabling or disabling of namespace processing and namespace prefix reporting.

TOGGLE NAMESPACE AND PREFIX USAGE

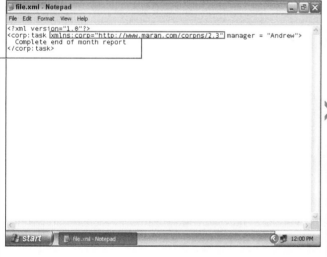

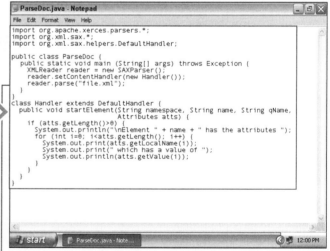

1 Open or create an XML document.

Note: See Chapter 5 for more information about namespaces.

2 Ensure the document uses namespaces.

3 Save the XML document.

4 Open or create the Java code that displays element attributes.

Note: You can use the code from the section "Determine the Value of Attributes."

Apply It

You can parse an XML document repeatedly, enabling or disabling namespace prefix reporting.

TYPE THIS:

```
public class ParseDoc {
   public static void main (String[] args) throws Exception {
      XMLReader reader = new SAXParser();
      reader.setContentHandler(new Handler());
      String feature="http://xml.org/sax/features/namespace-prefixes";
      reader.setFeature(feature, false);
      reader.parse("file.xml");
      feature="http://xml.org/sax/features/namespace-prefixes";
      reader.setFeature(feature, true);
      reader.parse("file.xml");
   }
}
```

RESULT:

```
Element task has the attributes
manager which has a value of Andrew

Element task has the attributes
corp which has a value of http://www.maran.com/corpns/2.3
manager which has a value of Andrew
```

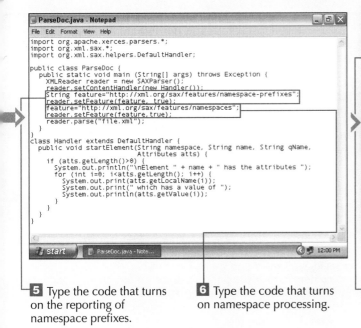

5 Type the code that turns on the reporting of namespace prefixes.

6 Type the code that turns on namespace processing.

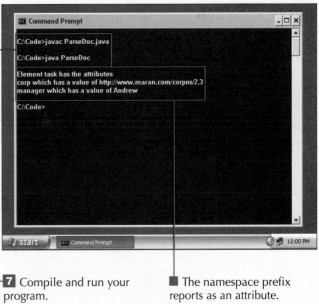

7 Compile and run your program.

■ The namespace prefix reports as an attribute.

Note: See Chapter 2 for instructions on compiling and running Java programs.

INTRODUCING THE DOM

You use the DOM, an Application Programming Interface (API), with the Java programming language and XML documents to allow communication between a DOM-compliant parser and Java applications. A specification developed by the World Wide Web Consortium (W3C), the W3C *Document Object Model*, or simply DOM, outlines a collection of interfaces which creates the objects that represent an XML document. The DOM API allows you to access XML documents, and, as with all Java APIs, consists of a collection of classes and interfaces that you access within your Java code. The DOM API files typically come with the application that you use with the XML documents. For example, most DOM-compliant XML parsers include the Java DOM API files.

DYNAMIC HTML

Although developed independently of XML, the DOM works with XML, and other similar markup languages like HTML. Originally conceived to permit the use of dynamic HTML, the DOM specification allows you to represent the structure of a Web page as objects. You can then modify, enable, or disable these objects at any time to create dynamic HTML. Not intended for exclusive use with applications you create with Java, DOM was developed for many different programming languages. Because Java is an object-oriented programming language, it works very efficiently with the DOM. Programming language- and platform-Independent, the environment and operating system have no bearing on the DOM specifications.

TREE STRUCTURE

You can use the DOM API to work with XML documents, and also with similar documents such as HTML, the code that creates Web pages. The DOM works by creating a tree structure with a document that you parse. For example, if you represent a Web page that contains two paragraphs in a DOM tree structure, DOM represents the Web page as a document object with two branches representing two paragraphs, with each paragraph containing one or more branches which contain text. Although initially perplexing, you may find representing documents and their contents as a tree structure to be a very effective way to work with data, particularly for large, complex documents. Utilizing a tree structure to represent data also makes it easier to manage your data when using an object-oriented programming language, such as Java.

TREE NODES

Called *nodes*, you use the individual items within a DOM tree structure to represent individual elements you find within an XML document. For example, you represent the text content of an element in an XML document by its own node within the DOM tree structure. Accessing and modifying the node information allows you to modify and access the actual text content of the elements within an XML document. You can make the XML document a pre-existing and previously parsed document, or a newly created XML document, which you generate using the information in a newly created DOM tree structure. For more information about nodes, see the section "Work with Nodes" in this chapter.

DIFFERENT APPROACHES

Each API that you use to access or create XML documents has its own strengths and weaknesses. Which API you choose to utilize from within your Java programs depends upon the type of application you create, the type of XML documents you access, and the size of those documents.

Analyzing XML documents involves parsing the documents and then representing each document as a tree structure. You must retrieve and analyze the complete XML documents prior to working with them

in the DOM API. This can create limitations depending on the available memory of the computer and the size of the XML documents. Other APIs can read XML documents sequentially from start to finish without having to store the complete XML documents in memory. Commonly, Java applications use multiple APIs when working with XML documents. You can easily use the DOM API alongside a different API, such as the SAX API, from within the same Java application that you create.

GENERATE XML DOCUMENTS

You use the DOM API to represent an XML document in a tree-like structure that conforms to specific rules. The DOM API does not specify how you use, save, or otherwise work with the data in the tree structure. If you want to save the information that a parser generates, you must create the code that extracts the data from the DOM tree, format that data, and save the

data to a file. The DOM allows you to work with portions of XML documents. For example, you can use the DOM API to read an XML document, then change a single element in that document, and create and save a new XML document containing the modified data. For more information about creating XML documents, see the section "Create an XML Document" in this chapter.

DOM-COMPLIANT PARSERS

To use the DOM API, you need a DOM-compliant XML parser and you need to create Java code that utilizes the API to communicate with the parser. You can issue instructions to, and receive information about, XML documents from an XML parser using the DOM API. While you have no specification that states that DOM-compliant applications must represent data parsed from an XML document as a tree structure, DOM-compliant applications do so.

Of the many DOM-compliant XML parsers, you can access one of the most popular ones, Xerces XML parser, on the Internet at http://www.apache.org, as well as through the companion CD-ROM to this book. For information about obtaining and installing the Xerces XML parser, refer to Chapter 7. The Xerces XML parser is the XML parser that the examples throughout the remainder of this chapter use. If you are using an XML parser other than the Xerces XML parser and you experience any difficulty with the examples in this chapter, you should refer to that parser's documentation.

OTHER PROGRAMMING LANGUAGES

Many other programming languages, such as Perl, in addition to Java use the DOM. Once you use the DOM API with one programming language, you should find it easy to use it with other programming languages. You

can download the DOM API separately, but you should use the DOM API files included with your XML application.

RETRIEVE THE ROOT ELEMENT NAME

To process an XML document, you must first determine the name of the document's root element. Because it encompasses all the other elements and contents of an XML document, you can only have one root element in a document. You should not confuse the root element with the XML declaration, which comprises the first line of every XML document. For more information about XML declarations, see Chapter 5.

To process an XML document, you create a DOMParser object. You then use the parse method of the DOMParser object to specify the name of the XML document to parse, as well as to initiate the actual parsing of the XML document. If you use the Xerces XML parser, the package org.apache.xerces.parsers contains the DOMParser class that creates DOMParser objects.

You must create a document object, which represents an XML document as an object, to determine the name of the root element. You can access almost all information about an XML document via a document object. The document

interface is part of the package org.w3c.dom, which you must import in order to use the document interface in your Java code. For more information about importing packages, see Chapter 3.

You create an element object to contain information about an element. You can then access information about the element, such as the element's name.

The getDocumentElement method of the document object returns an element object that represents the first child node of the document. You must always make the root element of an XML document the only child node of the XML document, so the getDocumentElement method can create an element object that represents the root element.

You use the getTagName method of the element object to create a String value that contains the name of the element. This String value has the same name as the root element.

RETRIEVE THE ROOT ELEMENT NAME

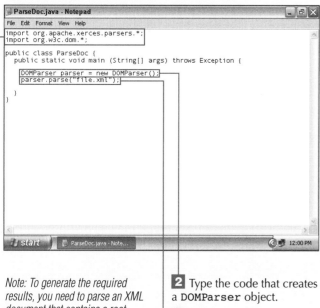

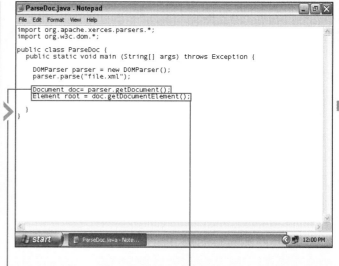

Note: To generate the required results, you need to parse an XML document that contains a root element.

1 Type the code that imports the required packages.

2 Type the code that creates a **DOMParser** object.

3 Type the code that initiates the parsing of an XML document.

4 Type the code that creates a document object based on the parsed XML document.

5 Type the code that creates an element object that represents the root element.

Apply It

You can reuse document objects when parsing multiple XML documents. This enables you to conserve resources when processing multiple XML documents.

TYPE THIS:

```
public static void main (String[] args) throws Exception {
  DOMParser parser = new DOMParser();
  parser.parse("file.xml");
  Document doc= parser.getDocument();
  Element root = doc.getDocumentElement();
  String rootElementName = (root.getTagName());
  System.out.println("The root element is " + rootElementName);
  parser.parse("file2.xml");
  doc= parser.getDocument();
  root = doc.getDocumentElement();
  rootElementName = (root.getTagName());
  System.out.println("The root element is " + rootElementName);
}
```

▼

RESULT:

```
The root element is task
The root element is todo
```

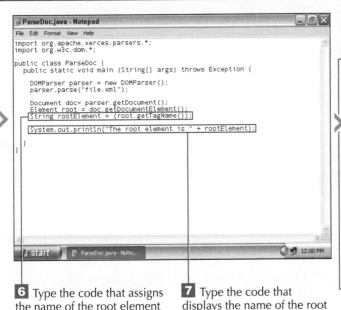

6 Type the code that assigns the name of the root element to a variable.

7 Type the code that displays the name of the root element.

8 Compile and run your program.

Note: See Chapter 2 for instructions on compiling and running Java programs.

■ The name of the root element displays.

DETERMINE NODE TYPE

You can use nodes, the primary way of working with information using the DOM API, to represent almost all the individual parts of an XML document. For example, you can represent an element, as well as the textual content of that element, as a node. At this time, the DOM tree structure does not contain a node that represents the XML declaration within a parsed XML document.

Because the type of information about a node changes depending on the type of node, you need to determine informational content. For example, if the current node represents an element, then you can use the getNodeName method to retrieve the name of the element. However, if the node represents the textual content of an element, then the getNodeName method simply returns the string #text, regardless of the value of the textual content of the element.

You use the getNodeType method of the Node interface to determine the type of node. The getNodeType method returns a short value that changes depending on the type of node. The Node interface defines a number of fields that you can use as constants that match the type of node for which you want to determine the node type. Because of the number of different types of nodes, the most efficient method for working with values that the getNodeType method returns involves using the Java switch construct. This construct allows you to execute a specific section of code depending on the node type. For more information about the switch construct, see Chapter 3.

You always make the root element of an XML document a node that represents an element. Therefore, you always make the node type value of the node representing the root element Node.ELEMENT_NODE.

DETERMINE NODE TYPE

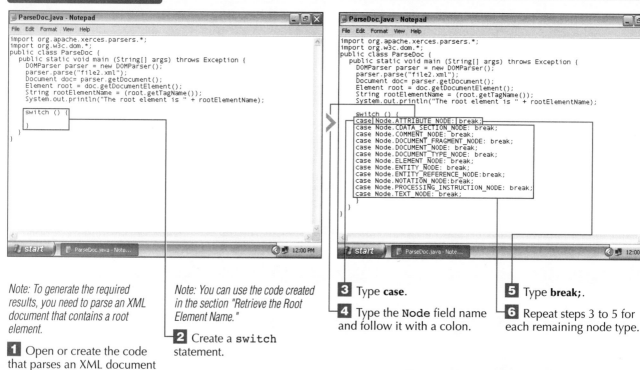

Note: To generate the required results, you need to parse an XML document that contains a root element.

1 Open or create the code that parses an XML document and implements an entity resolver class.

Note: You can use the code created in the section "Retrieve the Root Element Name."

2 Create a switch statement.

3 Type case.

4 Type the Node field name and follow it with a colon.

5 Type break;.

6 Repeat steps 3 to 5 for each remaining node type.

Extra

The DOM has 12 different types of nodes, each of which are represented with a field of the `Node` interface.

FIELD	TYPE
ATTRIBUTE_NODE	The attributes of an element.
CDATA_SECTION_NODE	A CDATA section.
COMMENT_NODE	An XML comment.
DOCUMENT_FRAGMENT_NODE	A portion of an XML document.
DOCUMENT_NODE	The complete XML document.
DOCUMENT_TYPE_NODE	A DOCTYPE declaration.
ELEMENT_NODE	An XML document element.
ENTITY_NODE	An entity.
ENTITY_REFERENCE_NODE	A reference to an entity.
NOTATION_NODE	A notation you declare in the DTD.
PROCESSING_INSTRUCTION_NODE	A processing instruction.
TEXT_NODE	Textual content within a tag.

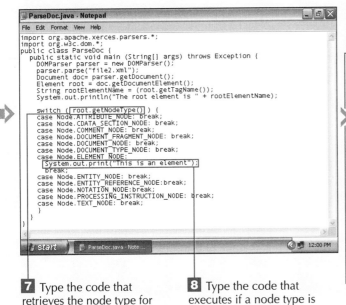

```
import org.apache.xerces.parsers.*;
import org.w3c.dom.*;
public class ParseDoc {
  public static void main (String[] args) throws Exception {
    DOMParser parser = new DOMParser();
    parser.parse("file2.xml");
    Document doc= parser.getDocument();
    Element root = doc.getDocumentElement();
    String rootElementName = (root.getTagName());
    System.out.println("The root element is " + rootElementName);

    switch ( root.getNodeType() ) {
    case Node.ATTRIBUTE_NODE: break;
    case Node.CDATA_SECTION_NODE: break;
    case Node.COMMENT_NODE: break;
    case Node.DOCUMENT_FRAGMENT_NODE: break;
    case Node.DOCUMENT_NODE: break;
    case Node.DOCUMENT_TYPE_NODE: break;
    case Node.ELEMENT_NODE:
      System.out.print("This is an element");
      break;
    case Node.ENTITY_NODE: break;
    case Node.ENTITY_REFERENCE_NODE:break;
    case Node.NOTATION_NODE:break;
    case Node.PROCESSING_INSTRUCTION_NODE: break;
    case Node.TEXT_NODE: break;
    }
  }
}
```

```
C:\Code>javac ParseDoc.java

C:\Code>java ParseDoc
The root element is todo
This is an element

C:\Code>
```

7 Type the code that retrieves the node type for the root element.

8 Type the code that executes if a node type is an element.

9 Compile and run your program.

Note: See Chapter 2 for instructions on compiling and running Java programs.

■ The name and type of the node displays.

WORK WITH NODES

You create the nodes that represent an XML document in a hierarchical manner. You do this because information that you represent in a hierarchical manner is easy to manage and access. Child nodes are nodes that are contained underneath another node, known as the parent node. In an XML document, the root element contains all the other elements in the XML document. You always represent the root element by a node that becomes the parent node of the child nodes, which represents the sub-elements of the root element in the XML document. Multiple child nodes are children of the parent element.

You can use the children of the root element node in order to access the elements and contents the root element contains. Once you represent the root element as a node, you can use the getChildNodes method to generate a NodeList object, which contains information about all the immediate child nodes of a node.

You use a NodeList object to create a collection of node objects. The NodeList object has two methods, getLength and item. The getLength method stores an int value that indicates the number of nodes in the NodeList. The item method allows you to access the node objects by specifying an index number representing the index of a node in a NodeList.

To transverse the nodes in a NodeList, you typically use a for loop to access each node in order. For more information about using a for loop, see Chapter 3.

As with any node object, you can use the node indicated by an item method of the NodeList object to access the name of the node using the getNodeName method. The value that the getNodeName method retrieves depends on the type of node.

WORK WITH NODES

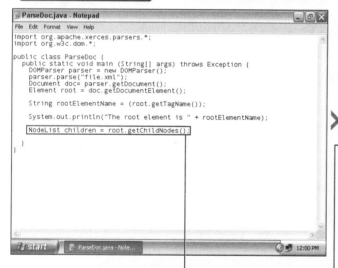

1 Open or create the code that parses an XML document and displays the root element name.

Note: You can use the code from the section "Retrieve the Root Element Name."

2 Type the code that creates a **NodeList** object containing the **child** nodes of the root node.

3 Type the code that displays the number of nodes in the **NodeList** collection.

Apply It

Depending on the structure of your XML document, elements may report an additional node containing text, even though the element does not contain textual data. This occurs because the XML parser interprets the element as containing an element, or elements, and whitespace, which it classifies as textual data, and thus as a text node. For more information about text nodes, see the section "Retrieve Text Information."

TYPE THIS:

```
<?xml version="1.0"?>
<todo>
   <task>
      <description>
            Back up Data
      </description>
   </task>
</todo>
```

RESULT:

```
The root element is todo
It has 3 child nodes

#text
task
#text
```

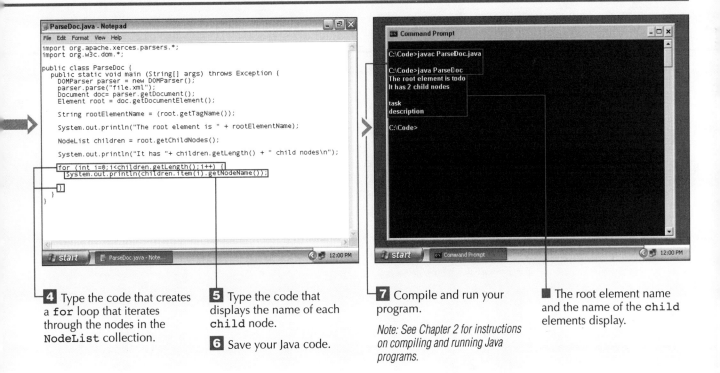

4 Type the code that creates a **for** loop that iterates through the nodes in the **NodeList** collection.

5 Type the code that displays the name of each **child** node.

6 Save your Java code.

7 Compile and run your program.

Note: See Chapter 2 for instructions on compiling and running Java programs.

■ The root element name and the name of the **child** elements display.

TRANSVERSE ALL ELEMENT NODES

When working with the DOM API, it converts an XML document into a structure consisting of multiple nodes. A very common task involves transversing all the nodes of the XML document after you parse it. Transversing the nodes of the documents allows you to iterate through the information within the XML document. As you transverse nodes, you can identify and access specific information about the XML document and the XML document's contents. Because the primary item in an XML document consists of elements, you commonly transverse all the nodes of a document to identify which nodes represent elements.

The first step in transversing the DOM element nodes involves identifying the node that represents the root element. You then transverse the children of the root element as well as any `child` elements to determine if they, too, have children. Using this method you can gradually transverse all the nodes that represent the elements of an XML document.

The easiest way to repeatedly transverse all the element nodes involves creating a method that you pass to a node, where the code within the method identifies if an element node has previously passed to the method. The method can then explore the `child` nodes of the node passed to it and call itself on any other element nodes that it finds. You access the information within the `child` nodes by creating a list of type `NodeList` using the `getChildNodes` method of the `node` object. Once you create the `NodeList`, you access individual nodes using the item method and an index number. If the method initially passes the node that represents the root element of an XML document, then the method eventually works its way through all the nodes of the document, identifying each element node as it finds them. Once you identify an element node, you can work with the node, for example, displaying the node name.

TRANSVERSE ALL ELEMENT NODES

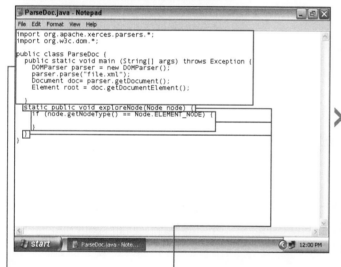

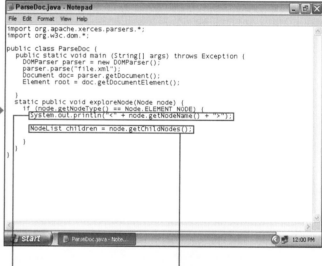

Note: To generate the required results, you need to parse an XML document that contains multiple elements.

1 Open or create the code that parses an XML document and creates an `element` object representing the root element.

Note: You can use the code created in the section "Retrieve the Root Element Name."

2 Create a method that accepts a node as an argument.

3 Type the code that determines if the node represents an element.

4 Type the code that displays the element name.

5 Type the code that attempts to create a `NodeList` of the node's children.

Extra

You can easily alter your code to display an element's start tag and end tag. You can also indent the tags to provide a better layout of your code.

Example:
```java
  static int level=0;
""  exploreNode(root);

  static public void exploreNode(Node node) {
    if (node.getNodeType() == Node.ELEMENT_NODE) {
      for (int x=0;x<level;x++) {
        System.out.print("   ");
      }
      System.out.println("<" + node.getNodeName() + ">");
      NodeList children = node.getChildNodes();
      for (int i=0;i<children.getLength();i++) {
        level++;
        exploreNode(children.item(i));
      }
      for (int x=0;x<level;x++) {
        System.out.print("   ");
      }
      System.out.println("</" + node.getNodeName() + ">");
    }
    level—;
  }
}
```

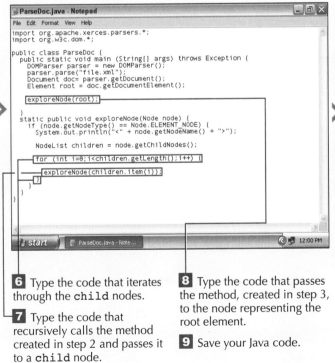

6 Type the code that iterates through the **child** nodes.

7 Type the code that recursively calls the method created in step 2 and passes it to a **child** node.

8 Type the code that passes the method, created in step 3, to the node representing the root element.

9 Save your Java code.

10 Compile and run your program.

Note: See Chapter 2 for instructions on compiling and running Java programs.

■ The names of the elements in the XML document display.

DETERMINE NAMES OF ATTRIBUTES

You can use an attribute as an additional item of information that you can associate with an element. For example, an element called 'fax' may have an attribute called 'code' that indicates the area code of the fax number that makes up the content of the fax element. If an element has an attribute, or attributes, you can access the names of the attributes. You can use the attribute's name to identify the attribute and its value, or simply to create other nodes using the same attributes. For more information about creating nodes with attributes, see the section "Add Attributes to an Element."

You represent the attributes of an element as nodes. To access the nodes that represent each attribute, you must create a `NamedNodeMap` object. An `NamedNodeMap` object contains a collection of nodes, specifically the nodes that represent attributes.

Similar to `NodeList`, the `NamedNodeMap` object uses the `getLength` method to determine the number of nodes in the collection, and hence the number of attributes that an

element has. The `NamedNodeMap` object also uses the `item` method with an index number to access each of the nodes in the collection.

You represent each attribute as a node in a `NamedNodeMap` collection, so you can use the `getNodeName` method to retrieve the name of the node, which becomes the name of the attribute.

Before you can access element attributes, you must create code that transverses the nodes of a document. For more information about transversing through the nodes of a DOM tree structure, see the section "Transverse All Element Nodes." This allows you to identify element nodes, which you can then use to access the attributes of that element.

You should note that the attributes do not appear in the `NamedNodeMap` collection in any predefined order. This means that the first attribute for an element may appear as the last node in the `NamedNodeMap` collection.

DETERMINE NAMES OF ATTRIBUTES

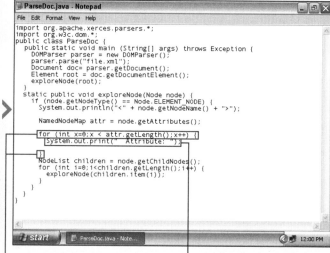

Note: To generate the required results, you need to parse an XML document that contains elements that have attributes.

1 Open or create the code that parses an XML document and identifies the element nodes.

Note: You can use the code created in the section "Transverse All Element Nodes."

2 Type the code that creates a `NamedNodeMap` object, following the code with an `=`.

3 Type the code that creates the `NamedNodeMap` object containing the element node's attributes.

4 Type the code that iterates through the attributes of an element node.

Note: For more information about iterating through the attributes of an element node, see the section "Transverse All Element Nodes" in this chapter.

5 Type the code that displays a text message describing the attribute.

Apply It

You can easily use the `getLength` method of the `NamedNodeMap` object to create an `if` statement to only display elements that have attributes.

TYPE THIS:

```java
static public void exploreNode(Node node) {
    if (node.getNodeType() == Node.ELEMENT_NODE) {
        NamedNodeMap attr = node.getAttributes();
        if (attr.getLength() > 0) {
            System.out.println("<" + node.getNodeName() + ">");
            for (int x=0;x < attr.getLength();x++) {
                System.out.print("  Attribute: ");
                System.out.println(attr.item(x).getNodeName());
            }
        }
        NodeList children = node.getChildNodes();
        for (int i=0;i<children.getLength();i++) {
            exploreNode(children.item(i));
        }
    }
}
```

RESULT:

```
<owner>
  Attribute: employeeID
  Attribute: managerID
<priority>
  Attribute: ignore
```

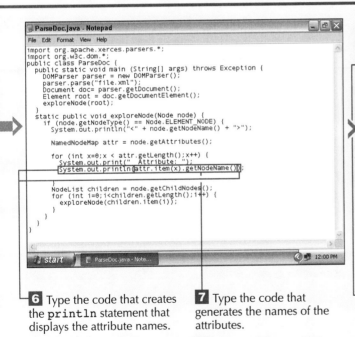

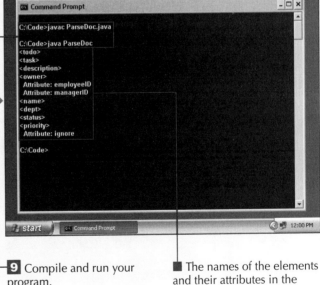

6 Type the code that creates the `println` statement that displays the attribute names.

7 Type the code that generates the names of the attributes.

8 Save your Java code.

9 Compile and run your program.

Note: See Chapter 2 for instructions on compiling and running Java programs.

■ The names of the elements and their attributes in the XML document display.

DETERMINE THE VALUES OF ATTRIBUTES

Attributes that you specify for an element consist of a name and a corresponding value. Once you determine the names of the attributes associated with an element in an XML document, you need to retrieve the values for those attributes.

A DOM tree structure represents each attribute as a node in a `NamedNodeMap` collection, so you can use the `getNodeName` method to retrieve the name of the node, which also becomes the name of the attribute. You use the `getNodeValue` method to retrieve the value of an attribute when you represent that attribute as a node in a `getNodeName` collection.

You not only use the `getNodeName` and `getNodeValue` methods to retrieve the names and values of element attributes, but also to retrieve information about other types of nodes. For example, the `getNodeValue` method returns a comment if you make the node type a comment. You should always ensure that you work with nodes that represent attributes if that is the type of data you need to access.

You may specify some attributes for an element that has a name but has no value assigned to the attribute. In this case, you can still retrieve the name of the attribute, but when you attempt to retrieve the value of the attribute, the `getNodeValue` method returns a `null` value. When creating your own code to access the attributes and their values, you need to check all the values that an attribute returns to make sure they exist. If the returned value of the attribute is not a `null` value, indicating that no value is currently assigned to the attribute, the value of the attribute returns as a `String` value.

DETERMINE THE VALUES OF ATTRIBUTES

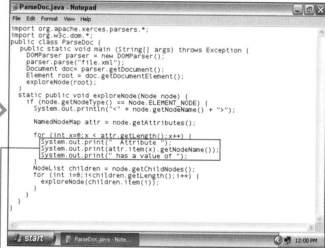

Note: To generate the required results, you need to parse an XML document that contains elements that have attributes.

Note: You can use the code created in the section "Determine Name of Attributes."

1 Open or create the code that parses an XML document and displays the name of the attributes.

2 Type the code that displays a message about an attribute's value.

Apply It

Once you determine the names and values of attributes, you can easily generate an element's start and end tag, including the attributes.

TYPE THIS:

```
static public void exploreNode(Node node) {
    if (node.getNodeType() == Node.ELEMENT_NODE) {
        System.out.print("<" + node.getNodeName());
        NamedNodeMap attr = node.getAttributes();
        for (int x=0;x < attr.getLength();x++) {
            System.out.print(" " +attr.item(x).getNodeName() + "=\"");
            System.out.print(attr.item(x).getNodeValue() +"\"" );
        }
        System.out.println("></" + node.getNodeName() + ">");
        NodeList children = node.getChildNodes();
        for (int i=0;i<children.getLength();i++) {
            exploreNode(children.item(i));
        }
    }
}
```

RESULT:

```
<todo></todo>
<task></task>
<description></description>
<owner employeeID="none"⏎
 managerID="543"></owner>
<name></name>
<dept></dept>
<status></status>
<priority ignore="yes"></priority>
```

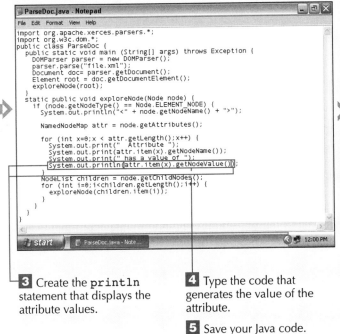

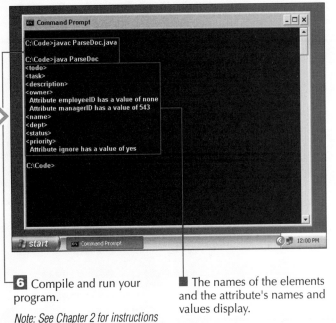

3 Create the `println` statement that displays the attribute values.

4 Type the code that generates the value of the attribute.

5 Save your Java code.

6 Compile and run your program.

Note: See Chapter 2 for instructions on compiling and running Java programs.

■ The names of the elements and the attribute's names and values display.

WORK WITH PROCESSING INSTRUCTIONS

You place *processing instructions* in XML documents so that an application can perform actions on those XML documents. Processing instructions on their own do not perform any action; you must create the code that can detect the processing instruction and then perform specific actions based on information in the processing instruction. When transversing the nodes of an XML document, you commonly start with the node that represents the root element of the XML document and then recurse through all the other nodes in the document from this starting point. This approach works fine for nodes that the root element node encompasses, but it does not transverse any nodes outside of the root element, such as processing instructions.

Although you can include some processing instructions within the body of an XML document, you place most instructions after the XML declaration — the first line of an XML document. When you include instructions in this manner and represent them in a hierarchical way, the processing instructions reside on the same level as the root element.

If you have created code that recurses nodes, once it is given a starting node, then you can recurse all nodes in the XML document by using the Document object as the primary node. The DOM treats items in an XML document as nodes, and this includes the XML document itself. To be sure that you recurse all nodes in an XML document, including all the processing instruction nodes, recurse the node representing the whole document as your starting point.

You can easily check a node to determine if it is a processing instruction by using the Node.PROCESSING_INSTRUCTION_NODE constant. Once you detect the processing instruction node, you can use the getNodeName method to retrieve the target and the getNodeValue method to retrieve the text of the processing instruction.

WORK WITH PROCESSING INSTRUCTIONS

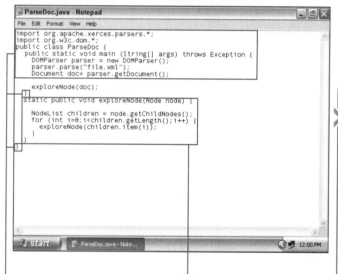

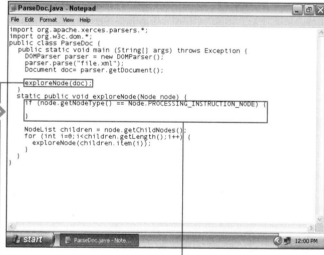

Note: To generate the required results, you need to parse an XML document that contains processing instructions.

1 Open or create the code that parses an XML document and creates a **Document** object.

2 Create a method that transverses the nodes of a DOM.

Note: For more information about transversing the nodes of a DOM, see the section "Transverse All Element Nodes."

3 Type the code that passes the **Document** object to the method created in step 2.

4 Type the code that checks if a node represents a processing instruction.

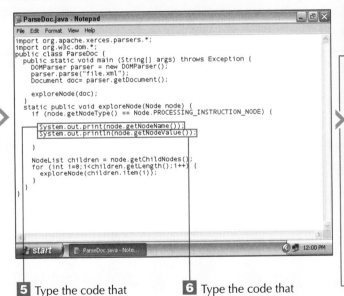

If you plan to work extensively with processing instructions, you can use the `ProcessingInstruction` interface to create objects that represent a processing instruction. For more detailed information about the `ProcessingInstruction` interface, refer to the DOM API documentation.

TYPE THIS:

```java
static public void exploreNode(Node node) {
    if (node.getNodeType() == Node.PROCESSING_INSTRUCTION_NODE) {
      ProcessingInstruction pi = (ProcessingInstruction) node;
      System.out.print(pi.getTarget());
      System.out.println(pi.getData());
    }
    NodeList children = node.getChildNodes();
    for (int i=0;i<children.getLength();i++) {
      exploreNode(children.item(i));
    }
}
```

RESULT:

```
myAppprinting="enable"
myAppprint="on"
myAppprint="off"
```

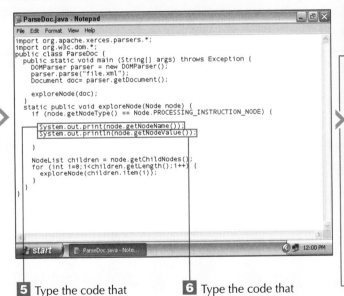
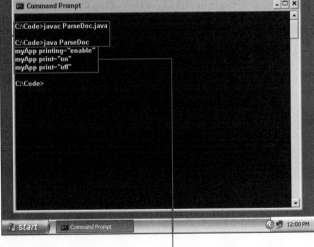

5 Type the code that displays the target of the processing instruction.

6 Type the code that displays the data of the processing instruction.

7 Save your Java code.

8 Compile and run your program.

Note: See Chapter 2 for instructions on compiling and running Java programs.

■ The processing instructions in the XML document display.

DETECT ENTITY REFERENCES

An entity allows you to use a string to represent a large amount of data in an XML document. You often use entities when you want to recycle a section of the same XML code within the document. For example, you may have a company's address or a copyright warning message multiple times in the same XML document.

When an XML document parses, nodes represent the entity references in the document, just as they represent most other elements of the XML document. You can determine the type of information that the node represents by analyzing the numerical value of specific fields of the node object. You can use the numerical constant Node.ENTITY_REFERENCE_NODE to identify when a node represents an entity reference in the collection of nodes that make up a DOM API tree structure.

Once you identify an entity reference node, you can use the getNodeValue method to determine the name for the

entity reference. The getNodeValue method returns a String value that becomes the name of the entity.

You cannot directly retrieve the value that replaces the entity reference in your XML document simply by accessing the entity reference node. You determine the value of the entity by examining the DTD's contents — the location where you define the entities. For more information about viewing the entities in the DTD, see the section "Detect General Entities in the DTD" in this chapter.

Some XML parsers may not return the names of entities when you use the getNodeName method and may, instead, return the value that the entity references. If you encounter problems accessing entity references, check the parser behavior in your XML parser documentation to determine how to resolve entity references.

DETECT ENTITY REFERENCES

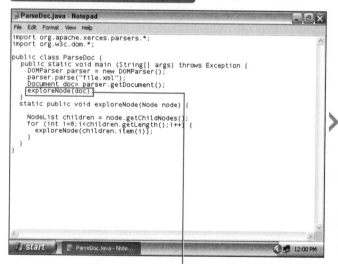

Note: To generate the required results, you need to parse an XML document that contains general entities.

1 Open or create the code that parses an XML document and iterates through the nodes of a DOM tree.

2 Ensure that iteration starts with the document node.

3 Type the code that checks if a node represents an entity reference.

Apply It

The `getNodeName` method returns the name of the entity. When you use the entity in an XML document, you precede the name with an ampersand and follow it with a semicolon. If you intend to output the entity name to another XML document, you must add these characters.

TYPE THIS:

```
static public void exploreNode(Node node) {
    if (node.getNodeType() == Node.ENTITY_REFERENCE_NODE) {
        System.out.print("&");
        System.out.print(node.getNodeName());
        System.out.println(";");
    }
```

RESULT:

```
&address;
&owner;
&owner;
```

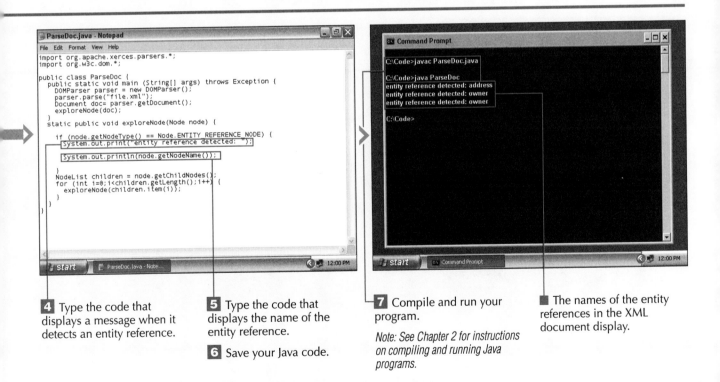

4 Type the code that displays a message when it detects an entity reference.

5 Type the code that displays the name of the entity reference.

6 Save your Java code.

7 Compile and run your program.

Note: See Chapter 2 for instructions on compiling and running Java programs.

■ The names of the entity references in the XML document display.

DETECT GENERAL ENTITIES IN THE DTD

You use entities to insert repetitive information into XML documents. You can define the information that you ascribe to an entity within the DTD itself, or you can link it to an external file. The entity declaration consists of the entity name and the entity definition. You must compose the name of the general entity out of a valid XML name. This includes letters, numbers, underscores, and colons, although programmers discourage the use of colons because a parser may confuse them with the namespaces.

You can extract the entity definition information from the DTD. You may want to extract the entity information to modify the definition of the entity within your code, or because the application that you utilize to access your XML documents does not resolve entities; you may have to resolve the entities yourself as you encounter them throughout the XML document.

You assess entities with the getEntities method of the DocumentType object. The getEntities method returns

a NamedNodeMap collection of nodes that correspond to each entity definition within the DTD.

Once you create the NamedNodeMap collection, you can determine the number of nodes in the NamedNodeMap collection with the getLength method. Because the number of nodes in a collection corresponds to the number of entity definitions in the DTD, the value that the getLength method returns reflects the number of general entity definitions within the DTD.

The getNodeName method of the node object returns the name of the entity. You store the entity definition information itself as child nodes of the items in the NamedNodeMap collection. To access the entity definitions, you can retrieve the value of each of the child nodes. You can use a simple for loop to iterate through the child nodes to retrieve the values.

DETECT GENERAL ENTITIES IN THE DTD

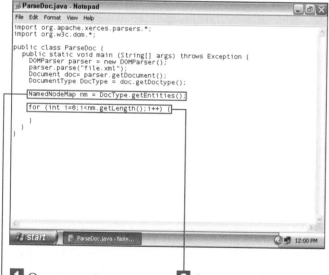

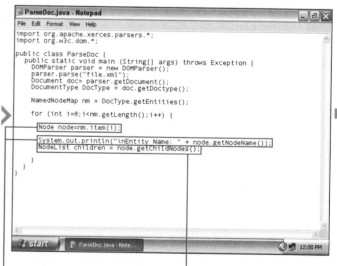

1 Open or create a document that parses an XML document.

2 Type the code that creates a NamedNodeMap collection of the nodes representing the entities.

3 Create a for loop to iterate through the nodes.

4 Type the code that creates a node from the NamedNodeMap collection.

5 Type the code that displays the name of the node.

6 Type the code that creates a NodeList of the child nodes.

Apply It

You can create an `Entity` object that accesses more information about an entity. For example, the `getSystemId` method of the `Entity` object displays the name of the file which an entity declaration references.

TYPE THIS:

```
for (int i=0;i<nm.getLength();i++) {
  Node node=nm.item(i);
  Entity ent=(Entity) nm.item(i);
  System.out.println("\nEntity Name: " + node.getNodeName());
  System.out.println("System ID:" + ent.getSystemId());
  NodeList children = node.getChildNodes();
  for (int x=0;x<children.getLength();x++) {
    System.out.println("Definition: " +
    children.item(x).getNodeValue());
  }
}
```

RESULT:

```
Entity Name: address
sysid: who.xml
Definition: null

Entity Name: owner
sysid: null
Definition: Andrew
```

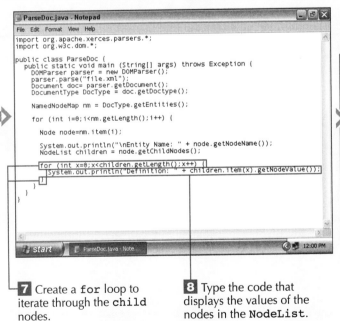

7 Create a `for` loop to iterate through the **child** nodes.

8 Type the code that displays the values of the nodes in the **NodeList**.

9 Save your Java code.

10 Compile and run your program.

Note: See Chapter 2 for instructions on compiling and running Java programs.

■ The names of the entity references and the definitions in the XML document display.

RETRIEVE DTD INFORMATION

You can access the information that the DTD of an XML document contains. The DTD can contain a wide variety of information. Accessing the information in the DTD allows you to directly access DTD information such as element and entity declarations.

When parsing an XML document, the parser creates a `DocumentType` object that can access some of the information available in the DTD. You can use the `getDoctype` method of the `Document` object to create a `DocumentType` object. Because the `DocumentType` interface is part of the `org.w3c.dom` package, you must import this package prior to using the `DocumentType` interface in your Java code. For more information about importing the package, see Chapter 3.

You can retrieve the name of a DTD — the same name as that of the root element of the XML document. You use the `getName` method of the `DocumentType` object to retrieve

the name of the DTD. The name of the DTD returns a `String` value from the `getName` method.

The `DocumentType` object also allows you to retrieve the rest of the information in the DTD. The information in the DTD returns as a `string` value corresponding to the information that you find in the DTD between the `[` and `]` delimiters. The `getInternalSubset` method retrieves the data.

Depending on the length of the information in the DTD and the type of XML parser in use, you may find it impossible to retrieve all the information in the DTD. You should not depend on the values that the `getInternalSubset` method returns, such as notation declarations, to retrieve information, but should instead use another more appropriate method to extract the information from the DTD. The information in a DTD becomes available regardless of whether the DTD you have is an inline DTD or an external DTD.

RETRIEVE DTD INFORMATION

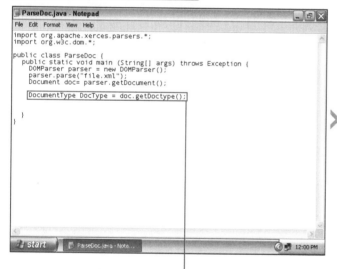

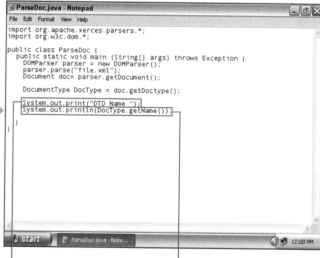

1 Open or create a program that parses an XML document.

2 Type the code that creates a **DocumentType** object.

3 Type the code that displays a descriptive message about the name of the DTD.

4 Type the code that displays the name of the **DocumentType** object.

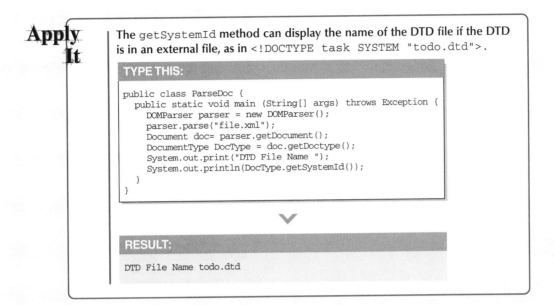

Apply It

The `getSystemId` method can display the name of the DTD file if the DTD is in an external file, as in `<!DOCTYPE task SYSTEM "todo.dtd">`.

TYPE THIS:

```
public class ParseDoc {
  public static void main (String[] args) throws Exception {
    DOMParser parser = new DOMParser();
    parser.parse("file.xml");
    Document doc= parser.getDocument();
    DocumentType DocType = doc.getDoctype();
    System.out.print("DTD File Name ");
    System.out.println(DocType.getSystemId());
  }
}
```

RESULT:

```
DTD File Name todo.dtd
```

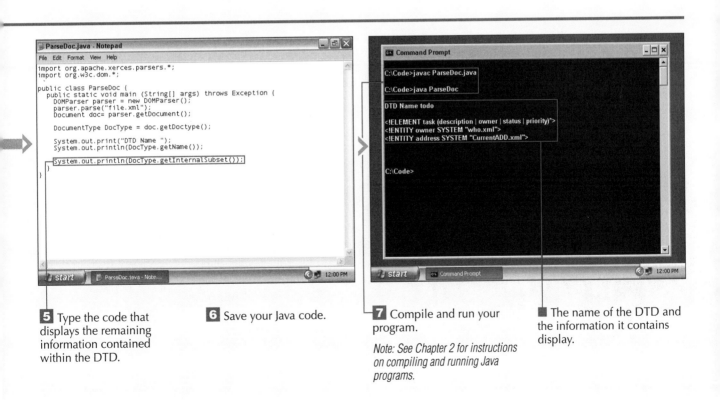

5 Type the code that displays the remaining information contained within the DTD.

6 Save your Java code.

7 Compile and run your program.

Note: See Chapter 2 for instructions on compiling and running Java programs.

■ The name of the DTD and the information it contains display.

RETRIEVE TEXT INFORMATION

Y ou can retrieve the contents of elements that contain text. Once you identify an element node, you can access the information in the element. In most cases, the type of content in an element of an XML document is textual data.

When using the DOM to access an XML document, you consider the content of an element node a child of the node. This way of treating an element's data maintains the strict tree structure that you must enforce when using the DOM API. Treating the textual content of an element node as a child node may initially appear an awkward way of organizing data, but in practice, it makes accessing this textual content quite easy as you access all the information in a DOM tree structure, regardless of information type, in the same hierarchical manner.

When extracting textual data from an element, you can identify the node as an element node. You can then check the type of node that you identify as the first child node of the element node to determine if it is a text node. You use a text node to contain textual data, and you can verify the type by checking the node type against the Node.TEXT_NODE constant.

Typically, you iterate through all the nodes in a DOM tree, and extract the text data from the nodes that contain text.

The information returned from the XML parser preserves all whitespace, such as new lines and tabs, within the text data. This also includes the whitespace that may surround child elements of an element that contains both text and elements. When creating code to retrieve text data, you probably want the code to detect and remove excess whitespace.

RETRIEVE TEXT INFORMATION

```
ParseDoc.java - Notepad
File  Edit  Format  View  Help
import org.apache.xerces.parsers.*;
import org.w3c.dom.*;

public class ParseDoc {
  public static void main (String[] args) throws Exception {
    DOMParser parser = new DOMParser();
    parser.parse("file.xml");
    Document doc= parser.getDocument();
    Element root = doc.getDocumentElement();
    exploreNode(root);
  }
  static public void exploreNode(Node node) {
    if (node.getNodeType() == Node.ELEMENT_NODE) {

    }

    NodeList children = node.getChildNodes();
    for (int i=0;i<children.getLength();i++) {
      exploreNode(children.item(i));
    }
  }
}

start        ParseDoc.java - Note...                    12:00 PM
```

```
ParseDoc.java - Notepad
File  Edit  Format  View  Help
import org.apache.xerces.parsers.*;
import org.w3c.dom.*;

public class ParseDoc {
  public static void main (String[] args) throws Exception {
    DOMParser parser = new DOMParser();
    parser.parse("file.xml");
    Document doc= parser.getDocument();
    Element root = doc.getDocumentElement();
    exploreNode(root);
  }
  static public void exploreNode(Node node) {
    if (node.getNodeType() == Node.ELEMENT_NODE) {

      if (node.getFirstChild().getNodeType() == Node.TEXT_NODE) {

      }
    }

    NodeList children = node.getChildNodes();
    for (int i=0;i<children.getLength();i++) {
      exploreNode(children.item(i));
    }
  }
}

start        ParseDoc.java - Note...                    12:00 PM
```

1 Open or create the code that parses an XML document and identifies the element nodes.

Note: You can use the code created in the section "Transverse All Element Nodes."

2 Type the code that determines if the first **child** node of the element is a text node.

Apply It

You can easily extract text data from only selected elements by expanding the if argument to match the name of the node with the name of the desired element.

TYPE THIS:

```
static public void exploreNode(Node node) {
   if (node.getNodeType() == Node.ELEMENT_NODE &&
       node.getNodeName().equals("description")) {
     if (node.getFirstChild().getNodeType() == Node.TEXT_NODE) {

       System.out.println(node.getFirstChild().getNodeValue());
     }
   }
   NodeList children = node.getChildNodes();
   for (int i=0;i<children.getLength();i++) {
     exploreNode(children.item(i));
   }
}
```

RESULT:

```
Backup sales data for last month
Complete end of month report
```

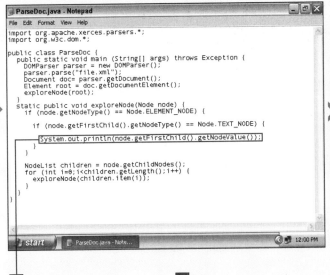

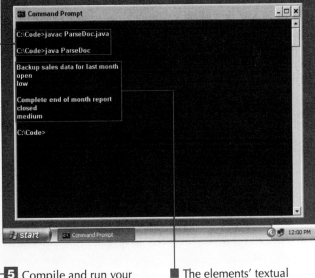

3 Type the code that displays the value of the text node.

4 Save your Java code.

5 Compile and run your program.

Note: See Chapter 2 for instructions on compiling and running Java programs.

■ The elements' textual content displays.

EXTRACT COMMENTS

You can retrieve information from an XML document that does not make up part of the content of the XML document. You may find retrieving this type of information useful if you want to reconstruct an XML document, or if you need to examine the information within an XML document more closely.

You often use comments to help explain a part of the XML document or to simply provide more background information, such as the name of the document's author. You may want to extract the comments from an XML document to strip out unneeded information before saving the XML document to a database or file system where space is at a premium. Removing the comments from an XML document does not affect the information or structure of the XML document.

As with most other types of data in an XML document, the parser creates a node that represents comments when it

finds a comment in an XML document. Locating all the comments in an XML document involves iterating through the nodes of the DOM tree and identifying the comment nodes. You can easily identify comment nodes by determining the node type of the current node and checking the type against the `Node.COMMENT_NODE` constant.

You retrieve the text that makes up the comment of a comment node by using the `getNodeValue` method of the `node` object. The `getNodeValue` method retrieves a `string` value, which can contain whitespace, such as new lines, spaces, and tabs.

While you can use information in comments for other purposes, such as creating a placeholder for data or passing information to an application, you should use more appropriate methods, such as entities and processing instructions, to accomplish these tasks.

EXTRACT COMMENTS

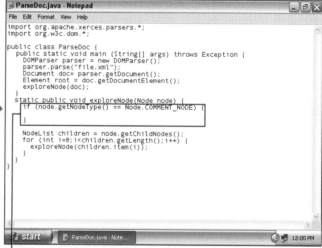

1 Open or create the code that parses an XML document and identifies the element nodes.

Note: You can use the code created in the section "Transverse All Element Nodes."

2 Type the code that determines if the first **child** node of the element is a comment node.

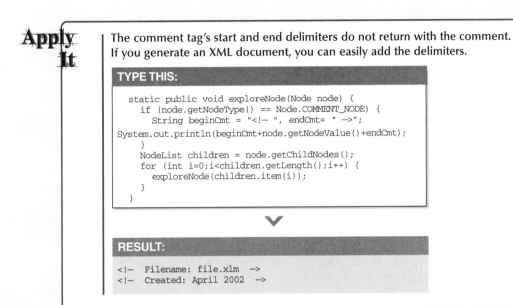

Apply It

The comment tag's start and end delimiters do not return with the comment.
If you generate an XML document, you can easily add the delimiters.

TYPE THIS:

```
static public void exploreNode(Node node) {
    if (node.getNodeType() == Node.COMMENT_NODE) {
        String beginCmt = "<!- ", endCmt= " ->";
System.out.println(beginCmt+node.getNodeValue()+endCmt);
    }
    NodeList children = node.getChildNodes();
    for (int i=0;i<children.getLength();i++) {
        exploreNode(children.item(i));
    }
}
```

RESULT:

```
<!-  Filename: file.xlm  ->
<!-  Created: April 2002  ->
```

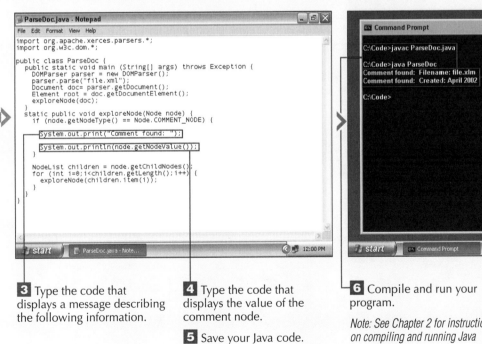

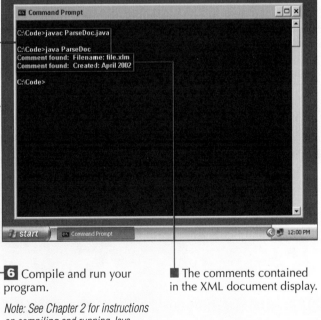

3 Type the code that displays a message describing the following information.

4 Type the code that displays the value of the comment node.

5 Save your Java code.

6 Compile and run your program.

Note: See Chapter 2 for instructions on compiling and running Java programs.

■ The comments contained in the XML document display.

EXTRACT CDATA SECTIONS

XML documents contain CDATA sections, into which you can place textual data. A CDATA section can contain any character. The character set, which the XML document establishes, determines the characters that you can use. You comprise the ending delimiter of a CDATA section as the characters]]>. Any information in the CDATA section except the ending delimiters is considered valid. If other sources, such as the information that makes up an image file, generate the information in a CDATA section, you must check the information to ensure that the ending delimiter does not appear as a valid part of the information.

You typically use CDATA sections to store text that contains markup tags, such as HTML code or fragments of XML documents. Placing markup information in a CDATA section prevents the XML parser from interpreting the tags in the information as part of the XML document. You represent

the CDATA sections in an XML document as a CDATA section node in the DOM tree structure.

You can determine a CDATA section by comparing the node type against the constant Node.CDATA_SECTION_NODE. You access the content of the CDATA section with the getNodeValue method of the node object. The getNodeValue method returns a string value. You do not include the CDATA delimiters with the returned string.

The string, which the getNodeValue method returns, includes any whitespace, such as new lines and tabs, that comprises part of the CDATA section in the document. Depending on the character set you use, the CDATA section may also contain some non-displayable characters, for which you may need to check, before you can store the data in a file or other storage format.

EXTRACT CDATA SECTIONS

1 Open or create the code that parses an XML document and identifies the element nodes.

Note: You can use the code created in the section "Transverse All Element Nodes."

Note: You need to parse an XML document that contains a CDATA section.

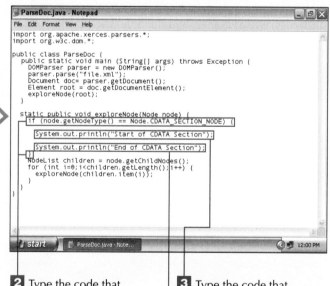

2 Type the code that determines if the first **child** node of the element is a **CDATA** section node.

3 Type the code that displays a message indicating the start of the **CDATA** section.

4 Type the code that displays a message indicating the end of the **CDATA** section.

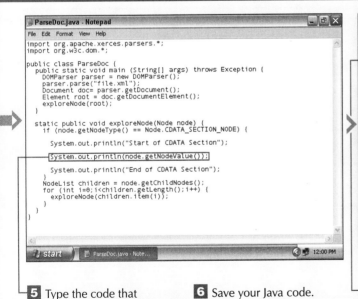

Apply It

You can create a CDATASection object to work with CDATASection nodes, for example, splitting the information in a node into two nodes. For more detailed information about CDATASection objects, refer to the DOM API documentation.

TYPE THIS:

```
if (node.getNodeType() == Node.CDATA_SECTION_NODE) {
    CDATASection node2 = (CDATASection) node;
    Node node3=node2.splitText(10);
    System.out.println("Start of CDATA Section");
    System.out.println(node.getNodeValue());
    System.out.println("End of CDATA Section");
}
```

RESULT:

```
Start of CDATA Section

    Ba
End of CDATA Section
Start of CDATA Section
Complete <
End of CDATA Section
```

5 Type the code that displays the value of the **CDATA** section node.

6 Save your Java code.

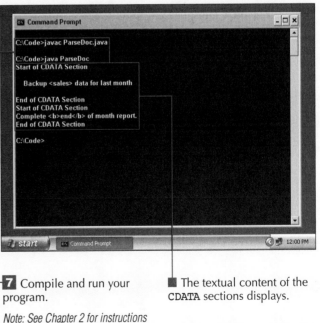

7 Compile and run your program.

Note: See Chapter 2 for instructions on compiling and running Java programs.

■ The textual content of the **CDATA** sections displays.

RETRIEVE NOTATION DECLARATIONS

You can use a notation declaration to let an application know that certain information within the XML document may require an external application for processing. You use the information in a notation declaration to determine what data or application your Java application may need to access to interpret the data in the XML document. For example, if you parse an XML document on computers that have different operating systems, you may need to access different image applications to interpret image data in the document.

You use the getDoctype method of the Document object to create a DocumentType object. Once you create an object, you can access defined entities in the DTD of an XML document. The getNotations method retrieves a collection of nodes that represent the notation declaration in a DTD and places the nodes into a NamedNodeMap collection.

You can iterate through a NamedNodeMap collection of nodes by determining the number of nodes in the

collection and then iterating through each node with a simple for loop. You determine the number of nodes in a NamedNodeMap collection with the getLength method of the NamedNodeMap object.

You access each node in the collection with the item method of the NamedNodeMap object by specifying an index number as the argument of the method. The Notation interface, which represents a previously declared notation in the DTD of an XML document, creates a Notation object. You create a Notation object from the nodes in the NamedNode collection.

Once you create a Notation object that represents individual notation declarations, you can retrieve the name of the notation with the getNodeName method. If the notation declaration refers to a local application, you can retrieve the specified name with the getSystemId method.

RETRIEVE NOTATION DECLARATIONS

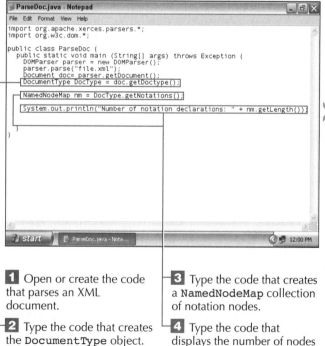

1 Open or create the code that parses an XML document.

2 Type the code that creates the DocumentType object.

3 Type the code that creates a NamedNodeMap collection of notation nodes.

4 Type the code that displays the number of nodes in the NamedNodeMap collection.

5 Create a **for** loop that iterates through the NamedNodeMap collection.

6 Type the code that creates a new **Notation** node from an item in the NamedNodeMap collection.

Apply It

If you only want to access the name of the notation node, you do not have to create a `Notation` object. The `node` object returns the name of the notation using the `getNodeName` method of the `node` object.

TYPE THIS:

```
import org.apache.xerces.parsers.*;
import org.w3c.dom.*;
public class ParseDoc {
   public static void main (String[] args) throws Exception {
      DOMParser parser = new DOMParser();
      parser.parse("file.xml");
      Document doc = parser.getDocument();
      DocumentType DocType = doc.getDoctype();
      NamedNodeMap nm = DocType.getNotations();
      System.out.println("Number of notation declarations: " + nm.getLength());
      for (int i=0;i<nm.getLength();i++) {
         System.out.println("\nName: " + nm.item(i).getNodeName());
      }
   }
}
```

RESULT:

```
Number of notation declarations: 2

Name: gif

Name: note
```

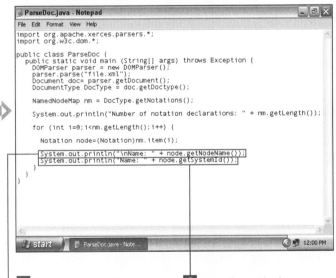

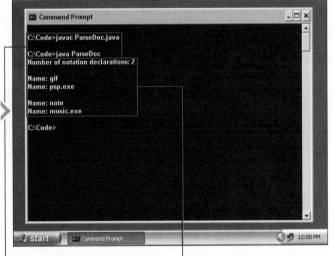

7 Type the code that displays the name of the notation node.

8 Type the code that displays the system ID of the notation node.

9 Save your Java code.

10 Compile and run your program.

Note: See Chapter 2 for instructions on compiling and running Java programs.

■ The number of notation declarations and the information contained in each notation declaration display.

NAVIGATE NODES

The primary element of the DOM tree structure is a node. You must navigate through the nodes in the tree structure to efficiently access parts of an XML document representation. You can use a number of `node` object methods to move from node to node.

You use the `getFirstChild` method to create a node that corresponds to the first `child` node of any known node. For example, if you create a node that represents the root element of an XML document, then you use the `getFirstChild` method to access the first element in the XML document other than the root element. Conversely, you use the `getLastChild` method to create a node that represents the last node — the child of the known node.

You use the `getNextSibling` method of the `node` object to retrieve the next node on the same level as the current

node. The `getPreviousSibling` method retrieves another node on the same level prior to the current node. When viewing the tree structure, the DOM's representation of an XML document, you define the same level as a node lateral to another node.

When using any of these methods to access nodes, you may find that a node that you want to create does not exist. For example, if an XML document only has a single element, the root element, then that node does not have any `child` nodes. Any attempt to navigate to a node that does not exist may result in the node-creating navigation method returning a `null` value. If you intend to navigate an XML document of unknown structure, you should create some checking code to determine that the nodes to which you attempt to navigate actually do exist.

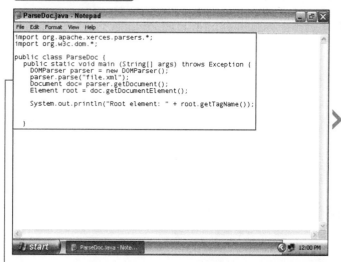

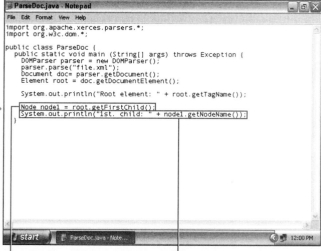

1 Open or create the code that parses an XML document and displays the root element name.

Note: You can use the code created in the section "Retrieve the Root Element Name."

Note: In this example, you need an XML document that contains a root element and two child elements, and that contains no whitespace.

2 Type the code that creates a node that represents the first **child** node of the root element.

3 Type the code that displays the name of the **child** node.

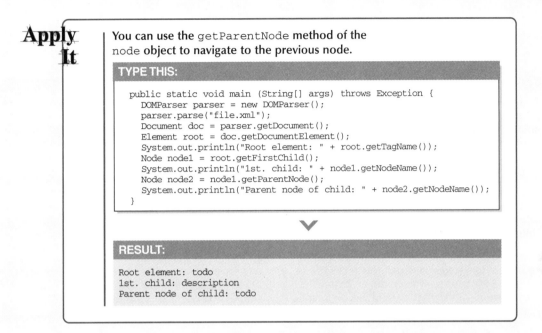

Apply
It

You can use the `getParentNode` method of the `node` object to navigate to the previous node.

TYPE THIS:

```
public static void main (String[] args) throws Exception {
    DOMParser parser = new DOMParser();
    parser.parse("file.xml");
    Document doc = parser.getDocument();
    Element root = doc.getDocumentElement();
    System.out.println("Root element: " + root.getTagName());
    Node node1 = root.getFirstChild();
    System.out.println("1st. child: " + node1.getNodeName());
    Node node2 = node1.getParentNode();
    System.out.println("Parent node of child: " + node2.getNodeName());
}
```

RESULT:

```
Root element: todo
1st. child: description
Parent node of child: todo
```

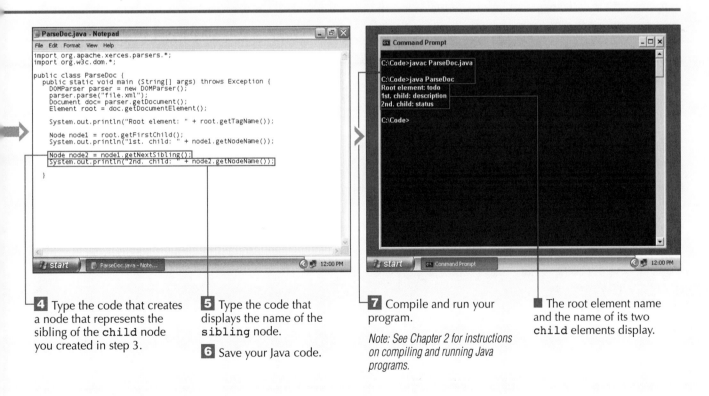

4 Type the code that creates a node that represents the sibling of the **child** node you created in step 3.

5 Type the code that displays the name of the **sibling** node.

6 Save your Java code.

7 Compile and run your program.

Note: See Chapter 2 for instructions on compiling and running Java programs.

■ The root element name and the name of its two **child** elements display.

CREATE AN XML DOCUMENT

You can create XML documents from within your Java applications, using the DOM API to construct the documents. Creating XML documents allows you to save information in a structured, easy-to-manage format.

You create a DOM tree structure and, in turn, you can output the DOM tree to a file. You represent existing XML documents with a DOM tree, modify them, and then write them back to an XML file. You can easily take multiple XML documents and, using the DOM API, merge these XML documents into a single XML document.

The first step in creating an XML document involves writing the XML declaration. Once you construct the declaration, you can write it to a file and use it to create an XML document. You must make the XML declaration the first line of an XML document.

Unfortunately, the DOM API does not yet provide a way of representing the XML declaration in a DOM tree structure.

To create an XML declaration, you must construct one from a string.

You use the `FileWriter` class of the `java.io` package to construct files from within Java code. You have to create a `FileWriter` object and pass to it the name of the file to create. XML documents should use the `.xml` file extension. The `write` method of the `FileWriter` object allows you to place information in the file. Once you finish working with the file, you can use the `close` method of the `FileWriter` object to close the file. You may not have access to the XML document from other applications while you still have the file open from within your Java code.

Once you save the XML document, you can view it using a simple text editor or another XML application.

CREATE AN XML DOCUMENT

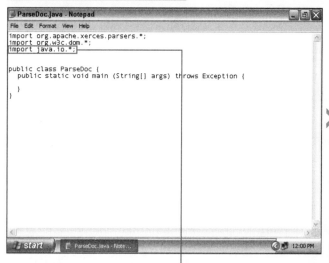

1 Create or open a Java program that allows you to work with the DOM API.

2 Ensure that you import the packages required to create the files.

3 Type the code that creates a new **FileWriter** object.

4 Type the code that writes the XML declaration to a file.

5 Type the code that prevents any more data from writing to the file.

6 Save your Java code.

Apply It

Quite commonly, you use a `String` value to represent a new line when creating data that you want to output. Using a `String` value to represent a new line allows you to easily change the new line character and to avoid using a multitude of escape sequences in your code.

TYPE THIS:

```
public class ParseDoc {
  public static void main (String[] args) throws Exception {
    FileWriter fw = new FileWriter("doc.xml");
    String newLine="\n";
    fw.write("<?xml version=\"1.0\"?>");
    fw.write(newLine);
    fw.write(newLine);
    fw.write("<!— Created by Andrew —>");
    fw.close();
  }
}
```

RESULT:

```
<?xml version="1.0"?>

<!— Created by Andrew —>
```

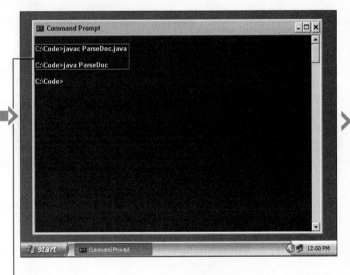

7 Compile and run your program.

Note: See Chapter 2 for instructions on compiling and running Java programs.

8 Open the XML document.

■ The XML declaration is the first line of the document.

CREATE A NEW DOM TREE WITH A ROOT ELEMENT

Y ou can create a DOM tree structure as if you had created the DOM tree from a parsed XML document. This enables you to create DOM tree structures from within your code and then work with the information within the structure using all the features of the DOM API.

You create a DOMImplementation object that facilitates the creation of a new document, as represented by a DOM tree structure. The DOMImplementationImpl class produces the new DOMImplementation object. The DOMImplementationImpl class is part of the org.apache.xerces.dom package, which you must import prior to using the DOMImplementationImpl class in your Java code. For more information about importing packages, see Chapter 3.

You use the createDocument method of the DOMImplentation object to make the new Document object. The createDocument method takes three arguments. The first and third arguments consist of the namespace of the document element and the document

type, respectively. For simple XML documents, you can specify them as null. The second argument consists of the name you use for the root element of the XML document.

You can easily verify that you have previously created the root element of the XML document by making a new node that represents the root element of the document.

You can create an XML document by writing an XML declaration, and the root element start and end tags, to a file. You create the root element's start and end tags by using the getNodeName method of the node object to output the name of the root element. You must place the start and end tag delimiters appropriately around the element name.

Once you create the XML document, you can easily view it with a simple text editor to confirm that you have created the document properly and that you have named the root element correctly.

CREATE A NEW DOM TREE WITH A ROOT ELEMENT

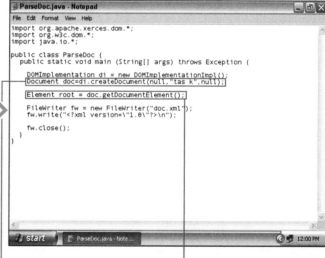

1 Create or open the code that can create an XML file containing an XML declaration.

Note: You can use the code created in "Create an XML document."

2 Type the code that creates a new **DOMImplementation** object.

3 Type the code that creates a new document object.

4 Type the code that creates a new element node that represents the root element of the XML document.

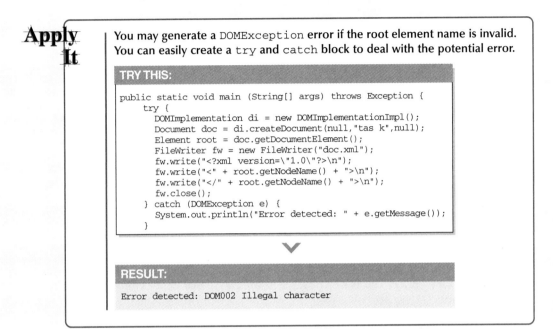

Apply It

You may generate a `DOMException` error if the root element name is invalid. You can easily create a `try` and `catch` block to deal with the potential error.

TRY THIS:

```java
public static void main (String[] args) throws Exception {
    try {
        DOMImplementation di = new DOMImplementationImpl();
        Document doc = di.createDocument(null,"tas k",null);
        Element root = doc.getDocumentElement();
        FileWriter fw = new FileWriter("doc.xml");
        fw.write("<?xml version=\"1.0\"?>\n");
        fw.write("<" + root.getNodeName() + ">\n");
        fw.write("</" + root.getNodeName() + ">\n");
        fw.close();
    } catch (DOMException e) {
        System.out.println("Error detected: " + e.getMessage());
    }
```

RESULT:

```
Error detected: DOM002 Illegal character
```

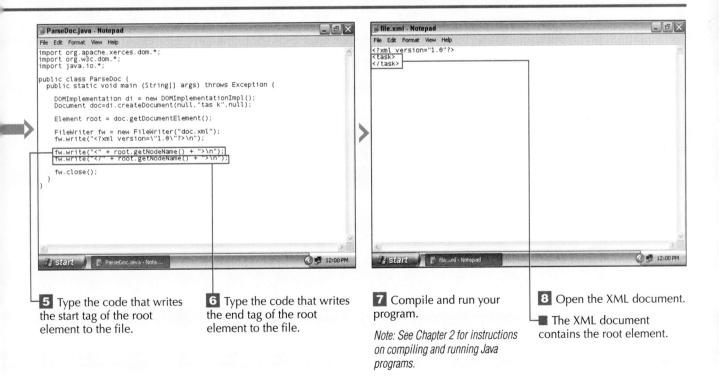

5 Type the code that writes the start tag of the root element to the file.

6 Type the code that writes the end tag of the root element to the file.

7 Compile and run your program.

Note: See Chapter 2 for instructions on compiling and running Java programs.

8 Open the XML document.

■ The XML document contains the root element.

ADD ATTRIBUTES TO AN ELEMENT

A part from the primary content of an element, such as text or other elements, elements can contain more information in the form of attributes. For example, an element called 'fax' may have an attribute called 'code,' which you use to indicate the area code of the fax number that makes up the content of the fax element.

You must first create the node that you want to add to the elements. You must make the node an element node, but you can also include the root element of the XML document. Once you create the element node, you can use the setAttribute method of the node object to add an attribute to an element.

The setAttribute method takes two arguments. The first argument consists of the attribute's name, and as with all attribute names, you must make it an invalid XML name. The second argument consists of the value that you want to specify for the attribute. You can state both arguments in the form of a string.

If you output an element and its associative attributes to an XML document, you need to format the information accordingly. For example, as with all attributes, you must enclose the attribute value within quotation marks when you save it in the XML document. You must also place the 'equals' symbol between the attribute name and the attribute value.

As with all attributes, when creating XML documents, you must place the attributes and their values within the start tag of an element.

You can access the attributes of an element node via the NamedNodeMap collection of nodes. When outputting the attributes of an element to an XML file, you can create a simple loop that iterates through the nodes in the NamedNodeMap collection.

ADD ATTRIBUTES TO AN ELEMENT

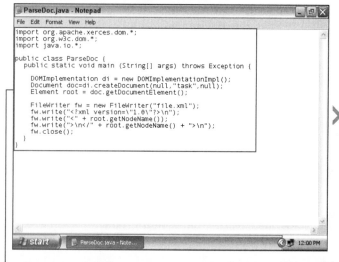

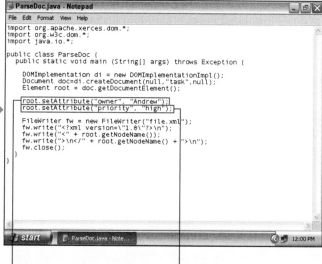

1 Open or create the code that creates an element node and creates an XML document.

Note: You can use the code from the section "Create a New DOM Tree with a Root Element."

2 Type the code that assigns the attribute name and value to the element node.

3 Repeat step 2 for each attribute you have to create.

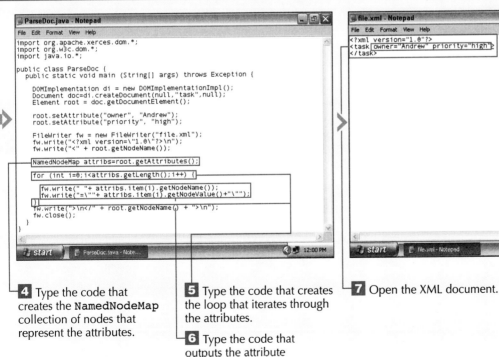

Apply It

Whether you want to output element nodes to an XML document, the display, or a database, you may find it more efficient to create a dedicated method that can output the element information from any element node and not just from the root element.

TYPE THIS:

```java
public static void main (String[] args) throws Exception {
  DOMImplementation di = new DOMImplementationImpl();
  Document doc = di.createDocument(null,"task",null);
  Element root = doc.getDocumentElement();
  root.setAttribute("owner", "Andrew");
  root.setAttribute("priority", "high");
  writeElement(root);
}
static void writeElement (Node node) {
  System.out.print("<" + node.getNodeName());
  NamedNodeMap attribs=node.getAttributes();
  for (int i=0;i<attribs.getLength();i++) {
    System.out.print(" "+ attribs.item(i).getNodeName());
    System.out.print("=\""+ attribs.item(i).getNodeValue()+"\"");
  }
  System.out.print(">\n</" + node.getNodeName() + ">\n");
}
```

RESULT:

```
<task owner="Andrew" priority="high">
</task>
```

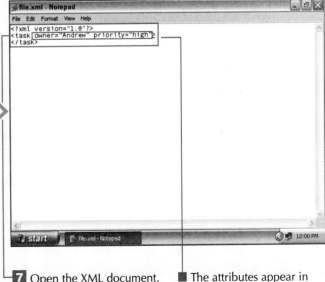

4 Type the code that creates the **NamedNodeMap** collection of nodes that represent the attributes.

5 Type the code that creates the loop that iterates through the attributes.

6 Type the code that outputs the attribute information.

7 Open the XML document.

■ The attributes appear in the element start tag.

ADD A CHILD ELEMENT

You can create child element nodes for any node in a DOM tree structure. You create child element nodes to build DOM tree structures of nodes that represent elements in an XML document. For example, you can create multiple child element nodes that add children to the root element of an XML document.

The first step in the process involves creating an element node with the desired name. Once you do this, you can append it to the node that becomes the parent node of the child element node. You use the createElement method to create a new node.

The parameter for the createElement method, a string value, becomes the name of the node, which also becomes the name of the element within the XML document. You therefore make the name you specify in the createElement method a valid element name within an XML document.

Once you create the new node, you can perform any operation on the node that you would on any other node, such as the node of a parsed XML document. For example, you can use the getNodeName method to retrieve the name of the new node. Once you build the new element, you can insert it into the DOM tree structure. You do this by appending the child node to an existing node in the DOM tree structure.

You use the appendChild method to append one node to another. The appendChild method is the method of the element object. The argument for the appendChild method becomes the name of the newly created element node.

When you append the new node, you can work with the nodes in the DOM tree structure as you would a DOM tree structure that a parsed XML document generates. In many cases, you want to display or otherwise output the XML document that the DOM tree structure represents.

ADD A CHILD ELEMENT

1 Open or create the code that parses an XML document and identifies the element nodes.

Note: You can use the code created in the section "Transverse All Element Nodes."

2 Type the code that creates a new element.

■ This example creates an element with the name "todo."

Apply It

Just as you can add attributes to the root element, you can add attributes to any element node in a DOM tree structure.

TYPE THIS:

```
public class ParseDoc {
  public static void main (String[] args) throws Exception {
    DOMImplementation di = new DOMImplementationImpl();
    Document doc = di.createDocument(null,"task",null);
    Element root = doc.getDocumentElement();
    Element todoElement = doc.createElement("todo");
    todoElement.setAttribute("owner", "Andrew");
    todoElement.setAttribute("priority", "high");
    root.appendChild(todoElement);
    exploreNode(root);
  }
```

RESULT:

```
<task>
  <todo owner="Andrew" priority="high">
  </todo>
</task>
```

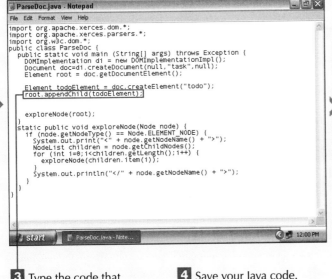

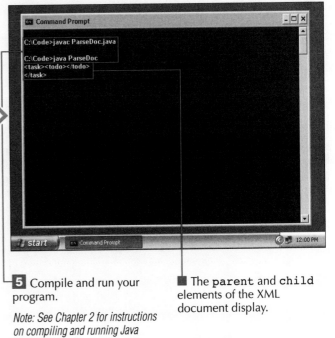

3 Type the code that appends the newly created node to the root node of the DOM tree structure.

4 Save your Java code.

5 Compile and run your program.

Note: See Chapter 2 for instructions on compiling and running Java programs.

■ The **parent** and **child** elements of the XML document display.

CREATE A TEXT NODE

A text node allows you to create elements that use textual data as the content within an XML document. Once you create an element node, you can generate a text node that stores textual data in an element of an XML document. For more information about creating element nodes, see the section "Add a Child Element" in this chapter.

As with any other newly created node, you can append a text node to another node. This is how you insert text nodes into a DOM tree structure. In most cases, you append text nodes to element nodes.

You use the createTextNode method, a method of the document object, to create the new text node. You can work with multiple documents within a single Java application, but you must ensure that the new text node uses the createTextNode method of the appropriate object.

The createTextNode method takes one argument — the textual content of the text node. When you create the element in an XML document, you place the argument of the createTextNode method between the start and end tags of the element, which consists of the parent node of the newly created text node.

Once you create text nodes, you typically write the code that outputs all the elements in the DOM tree structure to an XML document. You must create the specific code that recognizes element nodes, determines if they have child text nodes, retrieves the data from the nodes, formats it accordingly, and then outputs the data to an XML document. If you create an XML document that utilizes multiple node types, such as comment nodes, you must generate the code that identifies the node types and formats the output appropriately.

CREATE A TEXT NODE

1 Open or create the code that creates a root and **child** element and then parses the DOM tree structure and identifies the element nodes and their contents.

Note: You can use the code created in the section "Add a Child Element."

2 Type the code that identifies if the **child** node of an element contains text.

3 Type the code that displays the value of the text node.

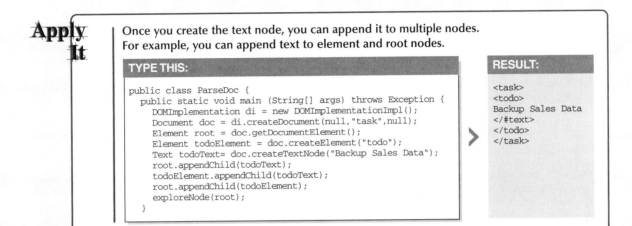

Apply It

Once you create the text node, you can append it to multiple nodes. For example, you can append text to element and root nodes.

TYPE THIS:

```
public class ParseDoc {
    public static void main (String[] args) throws Exception {
        DOMImplementation di = new DOMImplementationImpl();
        Document doc = di.createDocument(null,"task",null);
        Element root = doc.getDocumentElement();
        Element todoElement = doc.createElement("todo");
        Text todoText= doc.createTextNode("Backup Sales Data");
        root.appendChild(todoText);
        todoElement.appendChild(todoText);
        root.appendChild(todoElement);
        exploreNode(root);
    }
```

RESULT:

```
<task>
<todo>
Backup Sales Data
</#text>
</todo>
</task>
```

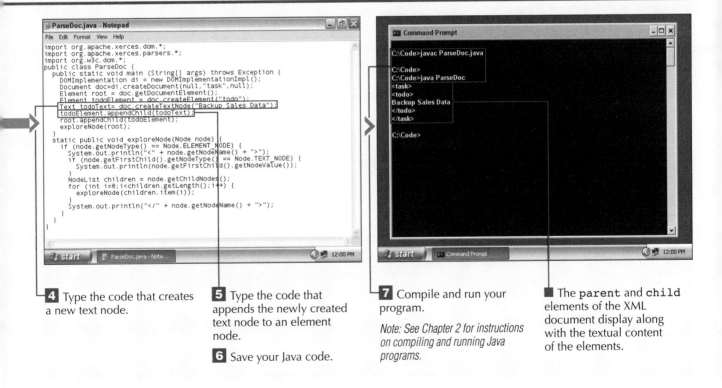

4 Type the code that creates a new text node.

5 Type the code that appends the newly created text node to an element node.

6 Save your Java code.

7 Compile and run your program.

Note: See Chapter 2 for instructions on compiling and running Java programs.

■ The **parent** and **child** elements of the XML document display along with the textual content of the elements.

CREATE OTHER NODE TYPES

Different node types allow you to add differing structural information and content to an XML document that you create from a DOM tree structure. Apart from element and text nodes, you have many other types of nodes that you can create and insert into the DOM tree structure. For more information about creating text elements, refer to "Create a Text Node" in this chapter.

You create nodes of types other than text and elements in the same manner — by creating a method of the document object. For example, the createCDATASection method creates a new CDATA section node. The object type corresponds to the type of node that you require; for example, a CDATA section node requires the creation of a CDATASection object.

Once you generate the node, you can insert it into the DOM tree structure by appending it as the child node of a pre-existing parent node in the DOM tree structure.

The arguments, which the node creation methods use, correspond to the previously created node type. For example, the createCDATASection method takes a String as its sole argument, and the String becomes the content of the CDATA section when it creates an XML document.

When creating nodes that place information into an XML document, you must create the code that formats the data appropriately. For example, if you create nodes that insert comments into an XML document, you must format the information that is used for the comments so that it does not contain the comment start or end delimiters. Once you create a node, you insert it into the DOM tree structure. The limitations of your computer's available resources determine the complexity and size of the DOM tree structure and the XML document you generate from the DOM tree structure.

CREATE OTHER NODE TYPES

```
ParseDoc.java - Notepad
File Edit Format View Help
import org.apache.xerces.dom.*;
import org.apache.xerces.parsers.*;
import org.w3c.dom.*;
public class ParseDoc {
  public static void main (String[] args) throws Exception {
    DOMImplementation di = new DOMImplementationImpl();
    Document doc=di.createDocument(null,"task",null);
    Element root = doc.getDocumentElement();
    Element todoElement = doc.createElement("todo");
    root.appendChild(todoElement);
    exploreNode(root);
  }
  static public void exploreNode(Node node) {
    if (node.getNodeType() == Node.CDATA_SECTION_NODE) {
      System.out.println("Start of CDATA Section");
      System.out.println(node.getNodeValue());
      System.out.println("End of CDATA Section");
    }
    NodeList children = node.getChildNodes();
    for (int i=0;i<children.getLength();i++) {
      exploreNode(children.item(i));
    }
  }
}
```

```
ParseDoc.java - Notepad
File Edit Format View Help
import org.apache.xerces.dom.*;
import org.apache.xerces.parsers.*;
import org.w3c.dom.*;
public class ParseDoc {
  public static void main (String[] args) throws Exception {
    DOMImplementation di = new DOMImplementationImpl();
    Document doc=di.createDocument(null,"task",null);
    Element root = doc.getDocumentElement();
    Element todoElement = doc.createElement("todo");

    CDATASection todoCDATA= doc.createCDATASection("Backup <b>Sales</b> Data"

    root.appendChild(todoElement);
    exploreNode(root);
  }
  static public void exploreNode(Node node) {
    if (node.getNodeType() == Node.CDATA_SECTION_NODE) {
      System.out.println("Start of CDATA Section");
      System.out.println(node.getNodeValue());
      System.out.println("End of CDATA Section");
    }
    NodeList children = node.getChildNodes();
    for (int i=0;i<children.getLength();i++) {
      exploreNode(children.item(i));
    }
  }
}
```

1 Open or create the code that creates a root and **child** element and then parses the DOM tree structure and identifies the CDATA section nodes.

■ This example adds a CDATA section node to a DOM tree structure.

2 Type the code that creates a new **node** object of the desired type.

Apply It

You can create many different types of nodes within a DOM tree structure.

COMMONLY USED NODE CREATION METHODS		
OBJECT	**METHOD**	**NODE TYPE**
`Attr`	`createAttribute(String)`	**Element attributes**
`CDATASection`	`createCDATASection(String)`	**A** CDATA **section**
`Comment`	`createComment(String)`	**A comment**
`DocumentFragment`	`createDocumentFragment()`	**A fragment of an XML document**
`Element`	`createElement(String)`	**An element**
`EntityReference`	`createEntityReference(String)`	**An entity reference**
`ProcessingInstruction`	`createProcessingInstruction (String target, String data)`	**A processing instruction containing the target and data**
`Text`	`createTextNode(String)`	**A text node**

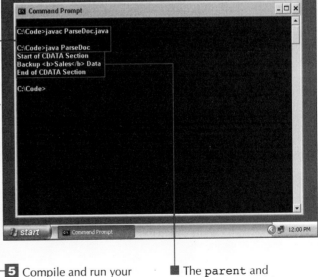

3 Type the code that appends the newly created node to an existing node in the DOM tree structure.

4 Save your Java code.

5 Compile and run your program.

Note: See Chapter 2 for instructions on compiling and running Java programs.

■ The **parent** and **child** elements of the XML document display along with the newly inserted content.

COPY NODES

You can copy nodes to rearrange the structure of an existing DOM tree structure or to copy a node from one DOM tree structure to another new or existing DOM tree structure. You can create exact duplicates of nodes that you may or may not have as part of the DOM tree structure.

You can create exact duplicates of the node by using the cloneNode method of a node object. The cloneNode method returns the node object. The cloneNode method takes one argument, a Boolean value that indicates whether or not to copy the node's underlying DOM tree structure.

You commonly utilize the cloneNode method to copy nodes between different DOM tree structures. Another use involves parsing XML documents and then copying an individual element from one XML document to another.

When copying nodes using the cloneNode method, you also copy any associated attributes of that node. Once you copy a node, you can append that node to another node in a DOM tree structure. This enables you to rearrange the XML documents with which you work. You can treat the copy of a node as any other previously created node using the DOM API. Once you make a copy of the node, you have no relationship between the original and the copy node; the copied node does not reflect any changes you make to the original node.

Depending on the type of XML parser, you can create copies of certain nodes using the cloneNode method. For example, some XML parsers may allow you to make copies of nodes that represent elements, but do not allow you to make a copy of a node that represents a document object. For more information about the types of nodes you can copy with a particular XML parser, refer to the XML parser's documentation.

COPY NODES

```
ParseDoc.java - Notepad
File  Edit  Format  View  Help
import org.apache.xerces.dom.*;
import org.apache.xerces.parsers.*;
import org.w3c.dom.*;
public class ParseDoc {
  public static void main (String[] args) throws Exception {
    DOMImplementation di = new DOMImplementationImpl();
    Document doc=di.createDocument(null,"task",null);
    Element root = doc.getDocumentElement();
    Element todoElement = doc.createElement("todo");
    exploreNode(root);
  }
  static public void exploreNode(Node node) {
    if (node.getNodeType() == Node.ELEMENT_NODE) {
      System.out.println("<" + node.getNodeName() + ">");
    }
    NodeList children = node.getChildNodes();
    for (int i=0;i<children.getLength();i++) {
      exploreNode(children.item(i));
    }
    System.out.println("</" + node.getNodeName() + ">");
  }
}
```
start   ParseDoc.java - Note...   12:00 PM

```
ParseDoc.java - Notepad
File  Edit  Format  View  Help
import org.apache.xerces.dom.*;
import org.apache.xerces.parsers.*;
import org.w3c.dom.*;
public class ParseDoc {
  public static void main (String[] args) throws Exception {
    DOMImplementation di = new DOMImplementationImpl();
    Document doc=di.createDocument(null,"task",null);
    Element root = doc.getDocumentElement();
    Element todoElement = doc.createElement("todo");

    Node nodeCopy = todoElement.cloneNode(false);

    exploreNode(root);
  }
  static public void exploreNode(Node node) {
    if (node.getNodeType() == Node.ELEMENT_NODE) {
      System.out.println("<" + node.getNodeName() + ">");
    }
    NodeList children = node.getChildNodes();
    for (int i=0;i<children.getLength();i++) {
      exploreNode(children.item(i));
    }
    System.out.println("</" + node.getNodeName() + ">");
  }
}
```
start   ParseDoc.java - Note...   12:00 PM

1 Open or create the code that creates a DOM tree structure with a root element and that can display the elements in the DOM tree structure.

2 Type the code that creates a node, which copies an existing node.

Apply It

You can create a copy of the node and any of its children by changing the argument of the `cloneNode` method to `true`.

TYPE THIS:

```
public static void main (String[] args) throws Exception {
    DOMImplementation di = new DOMImplementationImpl();
    Document doc = di.createDocument(null,"task",null);
    Element root = doc.getDocumentElement();
    Element todoElement = doc.createElement("todo");
    Text todoText= doc.createTextNode("Backup Sales Data");
    todoElement.appendChild(todoText);
    Node nodeCopy = todoElement.cloneNode(true);
    root.appendChild(todoElement);
    root.appendChild(nodeCopy);
    exploreNode(root);
}
```

RESULT:

```
<task>
  <todo>Backup Sales Data</todo>
  <todo>Backup Sales Data</todo>
</task>
```

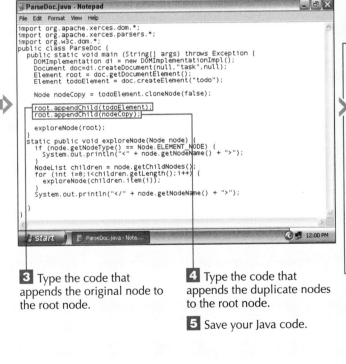

3 Type the code that appends the original node to the root node.

4 Type the code that appends the duplicate nodes to the root node.

5 Save your Java code.

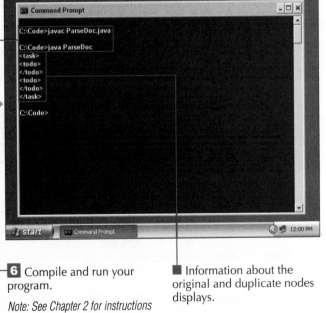

6 Compile and run your program.

Note: See Chapter 2 for instructions on compiling and running Java programs.

■ Information about the original and duplicate nodes displays.

INTRODUCING JDOM

Not actually an acronym for anything, JDOM is an application program interface, or API, that enables a Java application to communicate with an XML parser. You can use JDOM to create, manipulate, save, and display XML documents. As with all of the APIs that access XML parsers from within Java applications, the JDOM API

consists of a number of classes and packages. Similar to the DOM API, the JDOM API permits the representation of an XML document as a tree structure. Despite the similar names, do not confuse the JDOM API as a part of the DOM API or vice versa. For more on the DOM API, see Chapter 8.

JAVA COMPATIBLE

The concepts you use when working with the Java programming language are similar to those that you use when working with JDOM. Therefore, any developer familiar with Java has an easier task when learning and using the JDOM API. Created specifically with Java in mind, JDOM uses the very same object-oriented approach to working with XML information. For example, other APIs, such as SAX and DOM, provide their own classes that allow for the collection of items, such as the

node list classes in the DOM API. Instead of developing a specific list mechanism for people working with the JDOM API, JDOM can work with Java collections, which is a list mechanism that Java developers in other areas use. This compatibility makes it easier for Java developers to start using the JDOM API. In fact, the similarities between Java and JDOM make not only lists, but also other areas within the JDOM API, very easy to learn.

XML PARSERS

An XML parser is an application that you use to process XML documents in conjunction with Java programs that you create. Not a parser itself, the JDOM is simply an API that communicates with an XML parser. Many XML parsers now include the JDOM API as part of the package of files installed along with an XML parser. Although the files that make up the JDOM API are available as a separate package, if your XML parser includes a version of the JDOM API files, you should use this JDOM version when developing code to work with that specific XML parser. Using the JDOM files that

accompanied your XML parser ensures full compatibility between the version of the JDOM API you use and your XML parser. This chapter uses the Xerces parser when working with the JDOM API. If you want to work with another XML parser, you must consult the documentation that accompanied the XML parser for instructions on configuring and setting up the JDOM API to work with your particular parser. JDOM should work with any SAX- or DOM-compliant XML parser. For more information about installing the Xerces XML parser, see Chapter 7.

INSTALLATION

Before you can use the JDOM API, you must install the JDOM API files. If you acquired the JDOM API files with an XML parser, you should install those particular API files during the parser installation. The files that make up the JDOM API install with the XML parser if the JDOM API was included with the parser. If you acquired the JDOM API files elsewhere, you may have to copy the files to a specific directory on your computer, and adjust the

CLASSPATH environment variable for your operating system. For more information about setting the CLASSPATH environment variable on your computer, see Chapter 7. For complete installation instructions for the JDOM API, you should always refer to the installation instructions for your operating system that accompanied the JDOM API files. You can download the JDOM API files from the main JDOM Web site, http://www.jdom.org.

RESOURCES

The Internet offers many resources and a wide range of information for Java developers working with the JDOM API, including newsgroups, mailing lists, and Web sites. The most important of these resources is the primary JDOM Web site, available at http://www.jdom.org.

Not only does this site contain the JDOM API for download, it also contains a complete set of JDOM API documentation, background articles, and other relevant information.

SAX AND DOM

The JDOM API, which can process DOM tree structures, is compatible with SAX- and DOM-compliant parsers. You can also use SAX events with the JDOM API to process an XML document. Although JDOM can use a DOM-compliant parser to access XML documents, typically you use only a SAX-compliant parser to read XML documents, as SAX parsers process and read XML documents more efficiently and faster than JDOM. Allowing the JDOM API to work efficiently with both SAX and DOM enables you to use the best implementation of these technologies for any given scenario.

Using JDOM with SAX and DOM enables you to utilize the strengths of both the SAX and the DOM API without having to deal with their weaknesses. SAX is a great API for quickly reading an XML document, while the DOM API is more efficient at modifying and rearranging XML information. Using JDOM allows you to combine these strengths when working with complex XML documents. Although JDOM cannot replace the use of SAX or DOM APIs, it makes them easier to use. For more information about the SAX API, refer to Chapter 7. For more information about the DOM API, refer to Chapter 8.

VERSIONS

Due to constant development and revisions, JDOM continually phases out or adds features. You must always ensure that you use the latest version of the JDOM API. This guarantees you have access to the latest features and a longer life span for any applications that you create. If you acquire the JDOM API files with your

XML parser, you can verify the XML parser documentation to determine the version number of the JDOM API included with the XML parser. To determine the very latest version of the JDOM API, visit the main JDOM Web site at http://www.jdom.org.

COST

As with most things related to XML and Java development, the JDOM API is free to use. The JDOM API is open-source software, enabling you to use and

implement the JDOM API in your applications. You can also distribute those applications without charging a fee for them.

CREATE THE ROOT ELEMENT

You can create a root element in order to start building an XML document. The root element of an XML document is the first element within the document. Each XML document requires only one root element, which contains all the other elements within the document. To create the root element, you use an `Element` object, which allows the creation of the root element within the JDOM representation of an XML document. For more information about creating objects, see Chapter 3. The `Element` object is part of the main JDOM package called `org.jdom`, which you import to create `Element` objects.

Once you have the root element object, you create a document object using the root element as an argument of the document class.

You can list the XML documents created with JDOM on the display by using an `XMLOutputter` object. Once you create

the `XMLOutputter` object, you can use the output method to send the document object to the display. The output method of the `XMLOutputter` class takes two arguments. The first argument consists of the document object's name. The second argument, `System.out`, displays the output on the screen. The `XMLOutputter` class is part of the `org.jdom.output` package; you must import this package before creating `XMLOutputter` objects within your application.

If the root element of the document is empty, the JDOM generates a single element tag instead of separate start and end tags. When generating the output derived from the document object, JDOM automatically inserts the XML declaration, which you must always make the first line of any XML document.

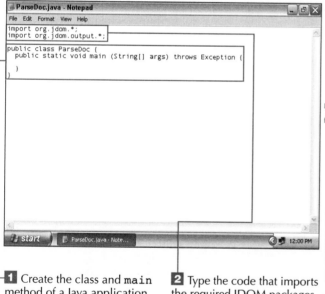

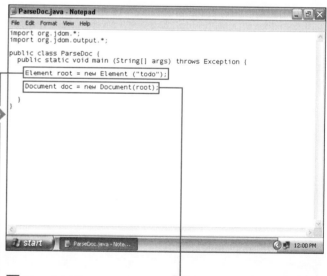

1 Create the class and **main** method of a Java application.

2 Type the code that imports the required JDOM packages.

3 Type the code that creates a new **Element** object with the root element name.

4 Type the code that creates a new document object using the root element.

You can check if an element is a root element
by using the `isRootElement` method of the
`Element` object.

TYPE THIS:

```
import org.jdom.*;
import org.jdom.output.*;
public class ParseDoc {
  public static void main (String[] args) throws Exception {
  Element root = new Element ("todo");
  Document doc = new Document(root);
  if(root.isRootElement() ){
    System.out.println("Root element has been created");
  }
}
}
```

RESULT:

Root element is
created.

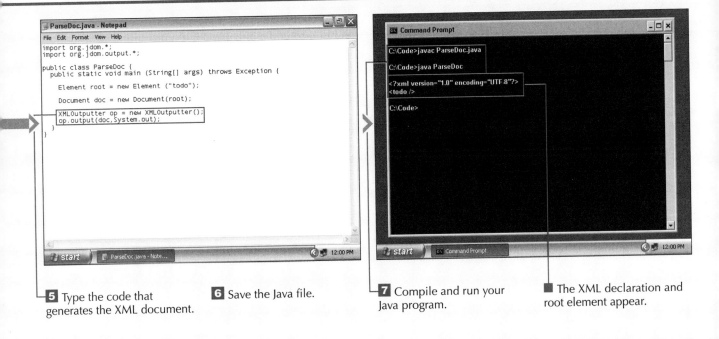

5 Type the code that generates the XML document.

6 Save the Java file.

7 Compile and run your Java program.

■ The XML declaration and root element appear.

ADD CONTENT TO THE ROOT ELEMENT

To create XML documents, you can create a root element and add content to that element. You can create root elements that have content using the JDOM API. You can use root elements to contain textual data. You can place textual data within an element by using the addContent method of the Element object. The addContent method takes as its argument a string value. After adding content to an element, you can append more textual data by calling the addContent method again. Each time you call the addContent method, and you have text for the argument of the addContent method, the data simply appends to the existing textual data of the element.

As with XML documents, you have no limitation, other than system resources, on the amount of textual data that you can place in any one element. For more information

about creating textual content for elements in an XML document, see Chapter 4.

You create an element using a new instance of an Element object and assigning the object the name of the element. You can make the element itself the root element, or more likely, you can make the element, which has text assigned to it, a sub-element of the root element. For more information about how to create child elements of the root element, see the section "Creating Child Elements" in this chapter. Once you assign textual data to the content of the root elements, you can display the XML document that includes the root element. You use the XMLOutputter class to display XML documents on your screen. If required, you can also save the XML document to a file. For more information, see "Save an XML Document" in this chapter.

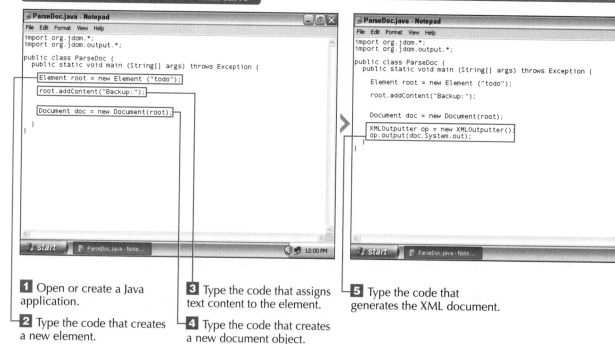

■1 Open or create a Java application.

■2 Type the code that creates a new element.

■3 Type the code that assigns text content to the element.

■4 Type the code that creates a new document object.

■5 Type the code that generates the XML document.

Apply It

You can use the setText method of the Element object to assign new text to an element. The difference between the setText method and the addContent method lies in the fact that the setText method replaces any existing textual data that you have assigned to the element.

TYPE THIS:

```
public static void main (String[] args) throws Exception {
    Element root = new Element ("todo");
    root.addContent("Backup:"); and
    root.addContent("Sales Data");
    root.setText("Print Sales Reports");
    Document doc = new Document(root);
    XMLOutputter op = new XMLOutputter();
    op.output(doc,System.out);
}
```

RESULT:

```
<?xml version="1.0" encoding="UTF-8"?>
<todo>Print Sales Reports</todo>
```

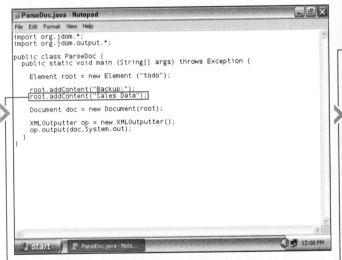

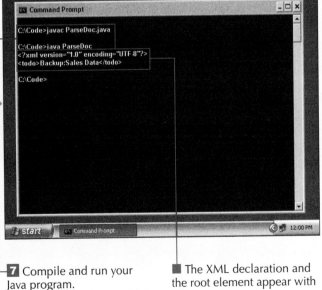

6 Repeat step 3 for any subsequent text you want to add to the element.

7 Compile and run your Java program.

■ The XML declaration and the root element appear with its contents.

CREATE CHILD ELEMENTS

Y ou can create child elements in order to build XML documents that contain multiple items of information. Apart from textual data, elements can also contain other elements. The root element of an XML document usually contains other elements. In this case, the root element is known as a *container* element and the elements that it contains are referred to as *children*, or *child* elements. For more information about creating child elements for an element in an XML document, see Chapter 4.

You can create elements and then assign them to a container element. You can alter the characteristics of any element before you make it a child element of another element. For example, you can create an element called "name" and assign it the text value of a person's name, and then assign that element as a child of an element called "identity."

You assign elements to other elements in the same manner that you add text to an element: You use the addContent method of the Element object to assign the element to its parent. For more information about adding textual content to an element, see the sections "Create the Root Elements" and "Add Content to the Root Element" in this chapter.

You can create multiple elements by using the addContent method to append each element to a single parent element.

When creating child elements of the root element, you can assign the elements to the root element and then create the document specifying the name of the root element. You can then create the XML document with the root element and the root element's child elements in place.

CREATE CHILD ELEMENTS

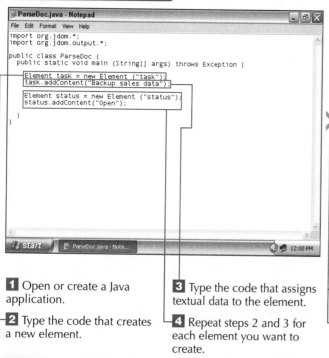

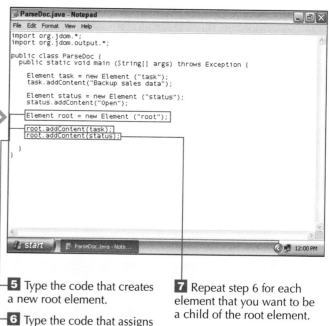

1 Open or create a Java application.

2 Type the code that creates a new element.

3 Type the code that assigns textual data to the element.

4 Repeat steps 2 and 3 for each element you want to create.

5 Type the code that creates a new root element.

6 Type the code that assigns the element you created in step 2 as a child element of the root.

7 Repeat step 6 for each element that you want to be a child of the root element.

Apply It

You can format the output that the XMLOutputter object generates to include an indent and new lines. You specify the characters for an indent as the first argument. Making the second argument a true value indicates that you want to use new lines when creating the XMLOutputter object.

TYPE THIS:

```
public static void main (String[] args) throws Exception {
    Element task = new Element ("task");
    task.addContent("Backup sales data");
    Element status = new Element ("status");
    status.addContent("Open");
    Element root = new Element ("root");
    root.addContent(task);
    root.addContent(status);
    Document doc = new Document(root);
    XMLOutputter op = new XMLOutputter("      ",true);
    op.output(doc,System.out);
}
```

RESULT:

```
<?xml version="1.0" encoding="UTF-8"?>
<root>
    <task>Backup sales data</task>
    <status>Open</status>
</root>
```

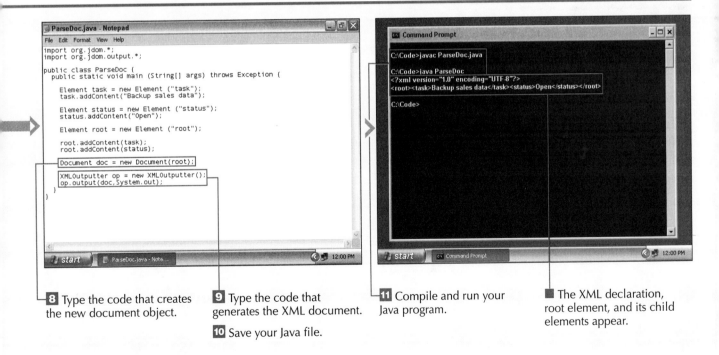

8 Type the code that creates the new document object.

9 Type the code that generates the XML document.

10 Save your Java file.

11 Compile and run your Java program.

■ The XML declaration, root element, and its child elements appear.

READ AN XML DOCUMENT

Y ou can use the JDOM API to read an XML document and extract information from that XML document. You can read XML documents and process them using JDOM. You find the classes that you use to parse an XML document in the package `org.jdom.input`. Before you can parse an XML document, you need to import this package. For more information about importing a package, see Chapter 3.

The `SAXBuilder` class uses a SAX-compliant parser to parse an XML document, and from that information, it creates a JDOM document object. The arguments you use when creating the `SAXBuilder` object depend on the XML parser that you have. If you have the Xerces XML parser, you do not have to specify any arguments to create a `SAXBuilder` object. For more information about installing the Xerces XML parser, see Chapter 7.

Once you create a new `SAXBuilder` object, you can use the `build` method to specify the name of the XML

documents that you want to read. The `build` method of a `SAXBuilder` object returns a JDOM document object, which you can then access to display the contents of the XML file.

To display the complete contents of the XML file, you can use the `XMLOutputter` object to display the JDOM document object. If required, you can also save the XML document to a new file. For more information, see the section "Save an XML Document" in this chapter.

Some XML parsers cannot process the XML declaration within an XML document. When the JDOM document object generates, the XML declaration, by default, becomes `<?xml version="1.0" encoding="UTF-8"?>`. If you read an XML document that contains a different XML declaration, such as `<?xml version="1.0"?>`, JDOM replaces the declaration when it appears.

READ AN XML DOCUMENT

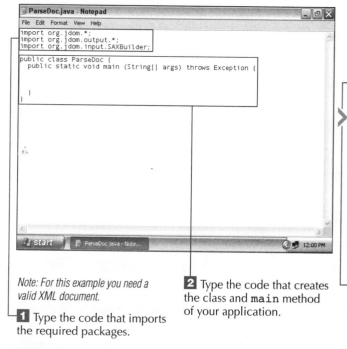

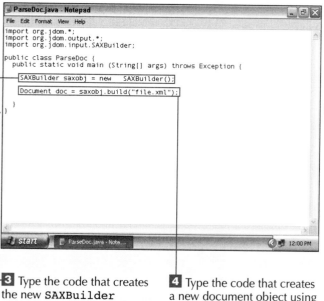

Note: For this example you need a valid XML document.

1 Type the code that imports the required packages.

2 Type the code that creates the class and **main** method of your application.

3 Type the code that creates the new **SAXBuilder** object.

4 Type the code that creates a new document object using the **build** method of the **SAXBuilder** object.

Apply It

You cannot perform the XML document validation before reading the XML document. You can enable validation by using the `Boolean` value `true` when creating a new `SAXBuilder` object. If you enable validation and attempt to read an XML document that is not valid, an error generates. If your code accesses XML documents whose validity you cannot verify, you should create your own error-handling code.

TYPE THIS:

```
public class ParseDoc {
  public static void main (String[] args) throws Exception {
    SAXBuilder saxobj = new SAXBuilder(true);
    Document doc = saxobj.build("file.xml");
    XMLOutputter op = new XMLOutputter();
    op.output(doc,System.out);

  }
```

▼

RESULT:

```
org.jdom.JDOMException: Error on line 19 of document ⏎
file:///C:/Code/file.xml: Attribute "priority" with ⏎
value "higher" must have a value from the list
"(low | high)".
```

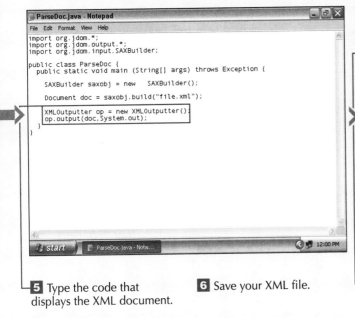

5 Type the code that displays the XML document.

6 Save your XML file.

7 Compile and run your Java program.

■ The XML document appears.

EXTRACT ELEMENT TEXT CONTENT

You can extract the information, stored as plain text, that an XML document contains. You can retrieve the content of elements that contain text. The content of an element consists of the data between the start and end tags of the element. Text data typically comprises the majority of content of elements you find in an XML document.

To extract the textual content from an element, you can create an `Element` object that represents the root element of the XML document. You can easily create an `Element` object from the root element of the XML document by using the `getRootElement` method of the document object.

Once you create an `Element` object, you can use the `getText` method to extract the textual data from the

element. The value returned from the `getText` method is a `string` value that also contains whitespace within the textual content of the element.

When displaying element data, you may also want to display the element's name, which you find between the start and end tags of the element within the XML data. The `getName` method of the `Element` object returns the name of the element as a `string` value.

What happens to the text data that makes up the contents of an element in an XML document depends on what you want your application to do with it. Some applications may simply display or print the text data, while other applications may want to execute other code depending on the actual contents of the text data.

EXTRACT ELEMENT TEXT CONTENT

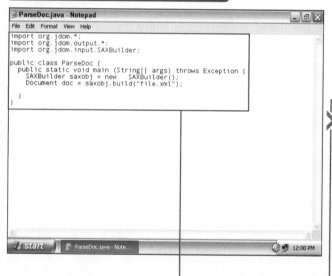

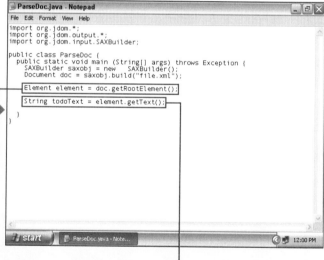

Note: For this example, you must create an XML document that has a root element that contains textual data and is called `file.xml`.

1 Open or create the code that will read an XML document.

2 Type the code that creates a new **Element** object from the information within the JDOM document object.

3 Type the code that retrieves the textual content of the element.

Apply It

You can use the `getTextTrim` method of the `Element` object to clean up any unnecessary white space that you may have within the textual content of an element.

TYPE THIS:

```
public class ParseDoc {
  public static void main (String[] args) throws Exception {
    SAXBuilder saxobj = new SAXBuilder();
    Document doc = saxobj.build("file.xml");
    Element element = doc.getRootElement();
    String todoText = element.getTextTrim();
    System.out.println("Element '" + element.getName() + ⏎
"' contains ");
    System.out.println(todoText);
  }
}
```

RESULT:

```
Element 'todo' contains
Backup Sales Data
```

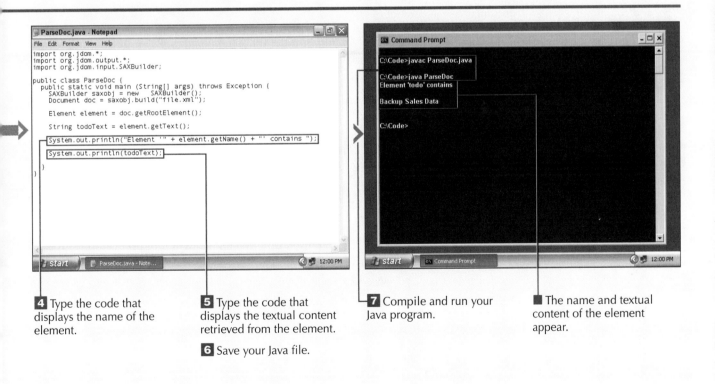

4 Type the code that displays the name of the element.

5 Type the code that displays the textual content retrieved from the element.

6 Save your Java file.

7 Compile and run your Java program.

■ The name and textual content of the element appear.

INSERT A COMMENT

You often use comments in XML documents to help explain a part of the document, or to simply provide more background information such as the name of the document's author.

To insert an XML comment into a document, you must first create a comment. You can specify the text string when creating the comment object. The text string becomes the string enclosed within the comment delimiters inside of the XML document.

You input the opening comment delimiter within an XML document as `<!--`. You input the ending delimiter as `-->`. Do not include any characters that one may interpret as the ending tags within the text you want to place within the XML document's comment.

When outputting the XML document using JDOM, the comment start and end delimiters automatically appear on either side of the text that makes up the comment. You can add comments to an XML document as the content of

elements by using the `addContent` method of the `Element` object. You can create child elements by this same method.

While you may find it possible to use information in comments for other purposes, such as creating a placeholder for data or to pass information to an application, consider using more appropriate methods, for example, entities and processing instructions, to accomplish these types of tasks. For more on entities, see the section "Insert Pre-Defined Entity References" in this chapter. For more on processing instructions, see the section "Add Processing Instructions" in this chapter.

The processing applications and XML parsers ignore comments you insert into XML documents unless you specifically identify and extract the information from the comments in the XML document. For more information about extracting comments from XML documents, see Chapter 8.

INSERT A COMMENT

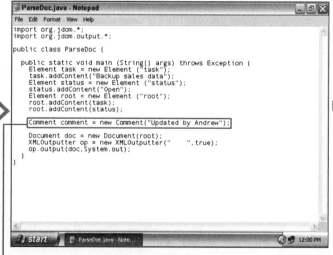

1 Open or create the code that constructs and displays an XML document with multiple elements.

Note: You can use the code from the section "Creating Child Elements."

2 Type the code that creates the new **comment** object.

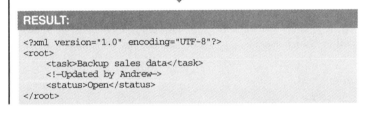

Apply It

You can adjust the placement of the comments in the XML document simply by moving the content method that inserts the comments to the desired location.

TYPE THIS:

```java
public class ParseDoc {
    public static void main (String[] args) throws Exception {
    Element task = new Element ("task");
    task.addContent("Backup sales data");
    Element status = new Element ("status");
    status.addContent("Open");
    Element root = new Element ("root");
    Comment comment = new Comment("Updated by Andrew");
    root.addContent(task);
    root.addContent(comment);
    root.addContent(status);
    Document doc = new Document(root);
    XMLOutputter op = new XMLOutputter("     ",true);
    op.output(doc,System.out);
  }
}
```

▼

RESULT:

```xml
<?xml version="1.0" encoding="UTF-8"?>
<root>
    <task>Backup sales data</task>
    <!--Updated by Andrew-->
    <status>Open</status>
</root>
```

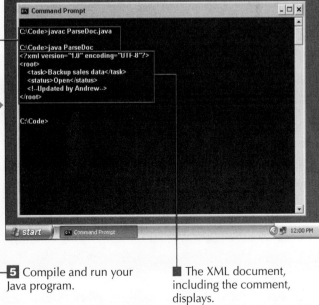

3 Type the code that adds the **comment** object to the contents of an element.

4 Save your Java file.

5 Compile and run your Java program.

■ The XML document, including the comment, displays.

INSERT A CDATA SECTION

The CDATA section enables you to incorporate large blocks of text containing special characters into an XML document without replacing each special character with an entity reference. You often use CDATA sections within an XML document to contain non-text information such as the data that makes up an image.

Within an XML document, a CDATA section starts with the characters <![CDATA[and ends with the characters]]>. Within the tag, you can include any text that may contain special characters. You can make the information in the CDATA section almost anything. The information can contain programming code, such as Java, or, more commonly, HTML. Any information in the CDATA section except the ending delimiters is considered valid, so you must be careful to ensure that any data that you want to place in a CDATA section does not contain the character

sequence]]>. You must create a CDATA object to add a CDATA section to an XML document. When creating a CDATA object, specify the content of the CDATA section information.

You often include CDATA sections in an XML document as the sole content of an element. You can use the Element object to create the element for storing this CDATA section. You can use the addContent method of the Element object to add the CDATA section object to that element. You use the addContent method of the Element object to add a child element to a parent element. Once you create the element with a CDATA section, you can insert it into the XML document. To do so, you use the addContent method of the element object that you want to make the parent element containing the CDATA section in the XML document.

INSERT A CDATA SECTION

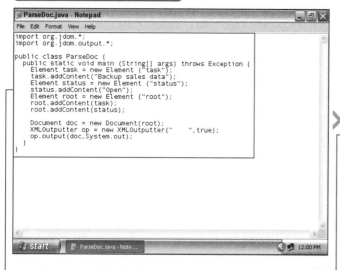

1 Open or create the code that constructs and displays an XML document with multiple elements.

Note: You can use the code from the section "Creating Child Elements."

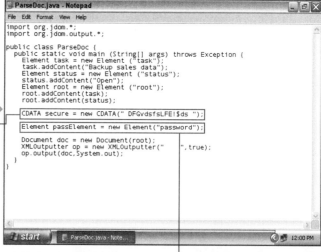

2 Type the code that creates the new **CDATA** object.

3 Type the code that creates the element that you want to contain the **CDATA** section.

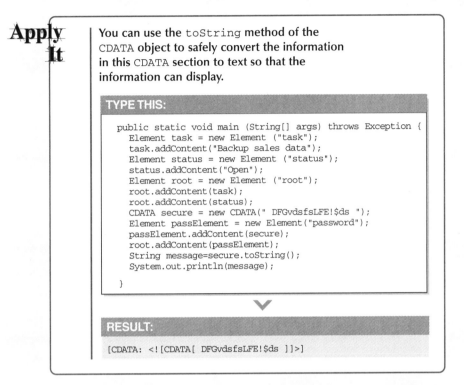

Apply It

You can use the toString method of the CDATA object to safely convert the information in this CDATA section to text so that the information can display.

TYPE THIS:

```
public static void main (String[] args) throws Exception {
   Element task = new Element ("task");
   task.addContent("Backup sales data");
   Element status = new Element ("status");
   status.addContent("Open");
   Element root = new Element ("root");
   root.addContent(task);
   root.addContent(status);
   CDATA secure = new CDATA(" DFGvdsfsLFE!$ds ");
   Element passElement = new Element("password");
   passElement.addContent(secure);
   root.addContent(passElement);
   String message=secure.toString();
   System.out.println(message);

}
```

RESULT:

```
[CDATA: <![CDATA[ DFGvdsfsLFE!$ds ]]>]
```

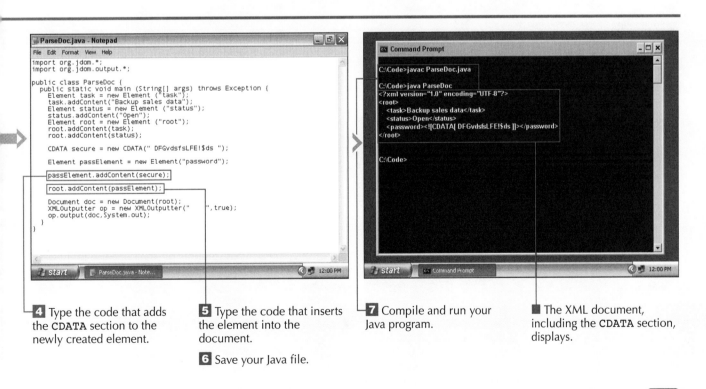

4 Type the code that adds the CDATA section to the newly created element.

5 Type the code that inserts the element into the document.

6 Save your Java file.

7 Compile and run your Java program.

■ The XML document, including the CDATA section, displays.

ADD PROCESSING INSTRUCTIONS

You use processing instructions to pass information to a specific application accessing an XML document. The application can then perform a task based on the values within the processing instructions or, if required, take no action at all.

Processing instructions consist of two parts. The *target* is typically the name of the application that reads the processing instruction. The *value* is a string that you may use to contain instructions. For example, you can contain a processing instruction called print with the value of `yes` or `no` to specify whether to print the XML document when your XML application processes it.

To add a processing instruction to your XML document, you must first create a processing instruction object and then add that object as the content of the document object. You can insert a processing instruction object as the content of

other elements in the XML document. More typically, you add processing instructions, as the content to the document object, on the same level as the root element. You specify two arguments, `string` values, when creating the processing instruction object. The first argument is the target and the second is the value of the processing instruction.

You make the ending delimiter of a processing instruction a question mark and you follow it with a greater-than symbol. You should make sure that the values for the target and the processing instruction do not contain these characters.

Processing instructions alone do not affect your XML documents during parsing. You must write your applications so that they recognize the processing instructions intended for them and then perform a task depending on the value of the processing instructions.

ADD PROCESSING INSTRUCTIONS

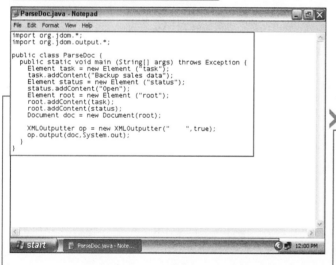

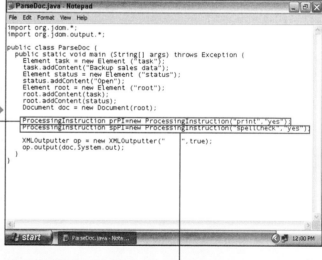

1 Open or create the code that constructs and displays an XML document with multiple elements.

Note: You can use the code from the section "Creating Child Elements."

2 Type the code that creates the new `ProcessingInstruction` object that you want to insert into the document.

3 Repeat step 2 for each processing instruction you want to create.

Apply It

If you have previously added a processing instruction to a document, you can move the processing instruction to another location in the XML document. You can use the `detach` method of the `ProcessingInstruction` object to remove the processing instruction from the `parent` element. You can then attach the processing instruction to another element.

TYPE THIS:

```
public class ParseDoc {
  public static void main (String[] args) throws Exception {
    Element task = new Element ("task");
    task.addContent("Backup sales data");
    Element status = new Element ("status");
    status.addContent("Open");
    Element root = new Element ("root");
    root.addContent(task);
    root.addContent(status);
    Document doc = new Document(root);
    ProcessingInstruction prPI=new ProcessingInstruction ⏎
    ("print","yes");
    root.addContent(prPI);
    prPI.detach();
    status.addContent(prPI);
    XMLOutputter op = new XMLOutputter("      ",true);
    op.output(doc,System.out);
  }
```

RESULT:

```
<?xml version="1.0" encoding="UTF-8"?>
<root>
    <task>Backup sales data</task>
    <status>
        Open
        <?print yes?>
    </status>
</root>
```

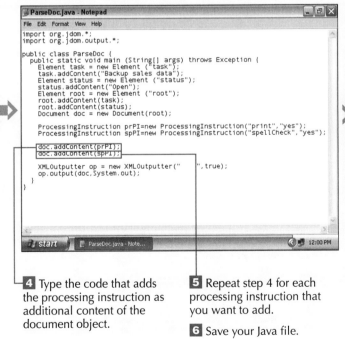

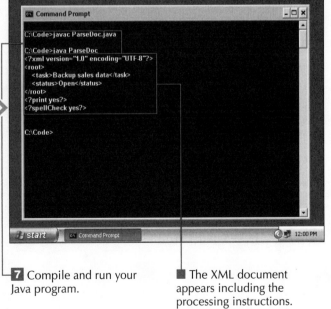

4 Type the code that adds the processing instruction as additional content of the document object.

5 Repeat step 4 for each processing instruction that you want to add.

6 Save your Java file.

7 Compile and run your Java program.

■ The XML document appears including the processing instructions.

ADD ATTRIBUTES TO AN ELEMENT

Most elements store data in the form of content, placed between the start and end tags of the element. As well as content, an element may also have attributes associated with the element that can hold data. Attributes provide additional information that you may want to specify about an element's content.

An attribute consists of the name and the value of the attribute. You separate the attribute name and value with the equal character and place them within the start tag of the element.

The setAttribute method of the Element object assigns an attribute to an element. The setAttribute method can take two arguments. The first argument consists of the attribute's name, and the second argument consists of the value you assign to the attribute. You must make both values, which the setAttribute method uses, string

values. You can assign multiple attributes to the same elements by simply recalling the setAttribute method on the same elements.

You separate attributes from other attributes, and the element name in the element's start tag, with spaces. You enclose the value of the attribute in quotes. When you output elements with attributes, JDOM automatically handles the spacing and quotation mark requirements.

You have no limits on the number of attributes that you can assign to a single element. If you try to use the setAttribute method to create an attribute with the same name as an attribute that already exists for the same elements, JDOM removes the existing attribute's value and specifies a new value. You can use attributes of the same name with different elements with no conflict.

ADD ATTRIBUTES TO AN ELEMENT

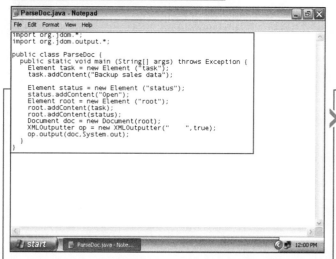

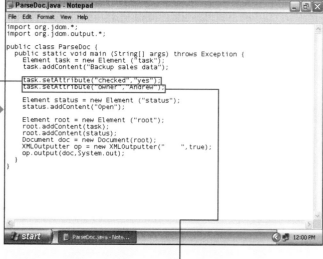

1 Open or create the code that constructs and displays an XML document with multiple elements.

Note: You can use the code from the section "Creating Child Elements."

2 Type the code that assigns a new attribute and its value to an element.

3 Repeat step 2 for each attribute that you want to add to the same elements.

Apply It

You can delete attributes previously assigned to an element using the `removeAttribute` method of the `Element` object.

TYPE THIS:

```java
public static void main (String[] args) throws Exception {
   Element task = new Element ("task");
   task.addContent("Backup sales data");
   task.setAttribute("checked","yes");
   task.setAttribute("owner","Andrew");
   task.removeAttribute("owner");
   Element status = new Element ("status");
   status.addContent("Open");
   status.setAttribute("checked","no");
   status.removeAttribute("checked");
   Element root = new Element ("root");
   root.addContent(task);
   root.addContent(status);
   Document doc = new Document(root);
   XMLOutputter op = new XMLOutputter("      ",true);
   op.output(doc,System.out);
}
```

RESULT:

```xml
<?xml version="1.0" encoding="UTF-8"?>
<root>
    <task checked="yes">Backup sales data</task>
    <status>Open</status>
</root>
```

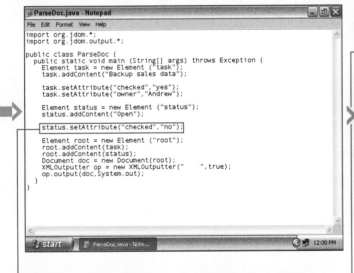

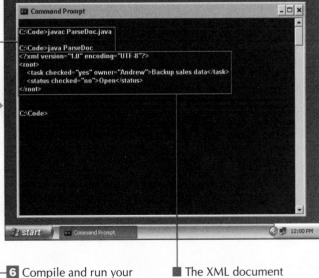

4 Repeat steps 2 and 3 for each element in which you want to assign attributes.

5 Save your Java file.

6 Compile and run your Java program.

■ The XML document appears containing elements and their attributes.

WORK WITH ATTRIBUTE OBJECTS

You can create Attribute objects to work more efficiently with attributes that you may have previously assigned to elements in an XML document. Attribute objects have their own methods that you can use to modify and manipulate the attribute names and values, as well as to create new Attribute objects.

You use Attribute objects to represent a name and value pair of an attribute. The setAttribute method of the Element object assigns the attribute name and value pair to an element in an XML document. The setAttribute method of the Element object takes as its argument the name of an Attribute object.

You can create duplicate Attribute objects from existing Attribute objects by using the clone method of the Attribute object. You may find this useful if you want to take an attribute name and value pair and then manipulate and reassign them to another element. Making a duplicate

of an Attribute object is also helpful if you have previously assigned an Attribute object to an element and you want to use it with another element.

Once you create an Attribute object, you can assign a new value to the Attribute object. When you assign the new value, it erases any existing values you assigned to the Attribute object, including the value assigned upon the object's creation. You use the setValue method of the Attribute object to assign the new value to the Attribute object.

As with any attribute, the name of an attribute must not contain whitespaces. Using whitespaces in the attribute name causes the code to generate an error when it executes. If you choose attribute names that describe the values the attributes contain, it will also help make you XML documents easier to read. For example, use the attribute name *firstname* as opposed to *name1*.

WORK WITH ATTRIBUTE OBJECTS

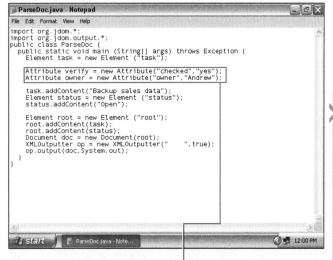

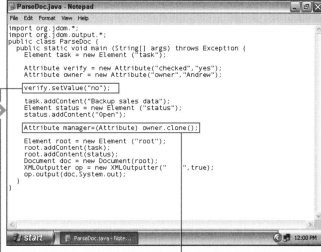

1 Open or create the code that constructs and displays an XML document with multiple elements.

Note: You can use the code from the section "Creating Child Elements."

2 Type the code that creates the **Attribute** objects for each attribute you want to use.

3 Type the code that changes the value of a previously created **Attribute** object.

4 Type the code that creates a duplicate **Attribute** object from an existing **Attribute** object.

Apply It

You can use the `setName` method of the `Attribute` object to change the name of the attribute after creating an `Attribute` object. Changing the name of the attribute does not re-create the attribute or change the value. It simply changes the name of the attribute as it appears within the start tag of the element within the XML document.

TYPE THIS:

```
public class ParseDoc {
  public static void main (String[] args) throws Exception {
    Element task = new Element ("task");
    Attribute owner = new Attribute("owner","Andrew");
    owner.setName("manager");
    task.setAttribute("owner");
    task.addContent("Backup sales data");
    Element root = new Element ("root");
    root.addContent(task);
    Document doc = new Document(root);
    XMLOutputter op = new XMLOutputter("      ",true);
    op.output(doc,System.out);
  }
```

▼

RESULT:

```
<?xml version="1.0" encoding="UTF-8"?>
<root>
    <task manager="Andrew">Backup sales data</task>
</root>
```

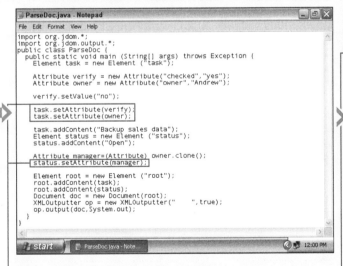

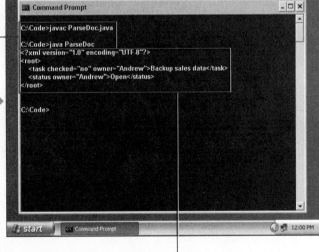

5 Type the code that assigns the **Attribute** objects to the elements that will use the attributes.

6 Save your Java file.

7 Compile and run your Java program.

■ The XML document appears containing elements and their attributes.

SAVE AN XML DOCUMENT

Y ou can create XML documents from within your Java applications, using the JDOM API to construct the documents, and then using standard Java procedures to save the information to a file. JDOM uses an XMLOutputter object to generate XML documents that you can save to a file.

To better format your XML documents, the XMLOutputter object can take two arguments. You only use the first argument to indent the code, and you typically make it two spaces. The second argument is a Boolean value that enables the inclusion of new lines; true enables new lines, while false turns off new line inclusion.

You can use the FileWriter class of the java.io package to create files from within Java code. Your Java program creates a FileWriter object and passes it the name of the file to create. XML documents should use the .xml file extension. The write method of the

FileWriter object allows you to place information in the file. Once you finish working with the file, you can use the close method of the FileWriter object to close the file. You generally cannot access the XML document from other applications when you have the file open from within your Java code.

Once you save the XML document, you can view the XML document using a simple text editor or another XML application.

Once you create a FileWriter object, it passes to the XMLOutputter object along with the JDOM document object that you want to save.

If the document which you want to create with the FileWriter object already exists, the new document overwrites the current document and you lose all the contents of the old file.

SAVE AN XML DOCUMENT

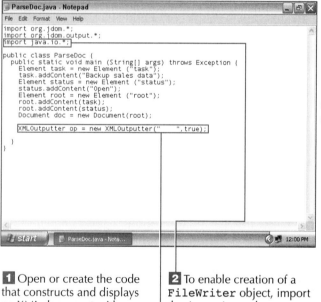

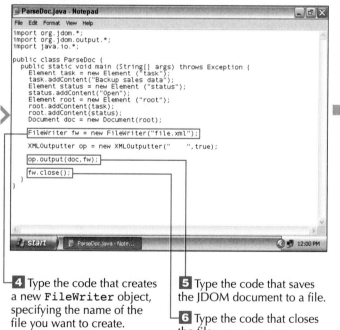

1 Open or create the code that constructs and displays an XML document with multiple elements.

Note: You can use the code from the section "Creating Child Elements."

2 To enable creation of a **FileWriter** object, import the **java.io** package.

3 Type the code that creates the new **XMLOutputter** object.

4 Type the code that creates a new **FileWriter** object, specifying the name of the file you want to create.

5 Type the code that saves the JDOM document to a file.

6 Type the code that closes the file.

Apply It

You can easily output the same JDOM document to a file and to your display simultaneously using the same XMLOutputter object.

TYPE THIS:

```
public class ParseDoc {
  public static void main (String[] args) throws Exception {
    Element task = new Element ("task");
    task.addContent("Backup sales data");
    Element status = new Element ("status1");
    status.addContent("Open");
    Element root = new Element ("root");
    root.addContent(task);
    root.addContent(status);
    Document doc = new Document(root);
    FileWriter fw = new FileWriter("doc.xml");
    XMLOutputter op = new XMLOutputter("    ",true);
    op.output(doc,fw);
    op.output(doc,System.out);
    fw.close();
  }
```

RESULT:

```
<?xml version="1.0" encoding="UTF-8"?>
<root>
    <task>Backup sales data</task>
    <status1>Open</status1>
</root>
```

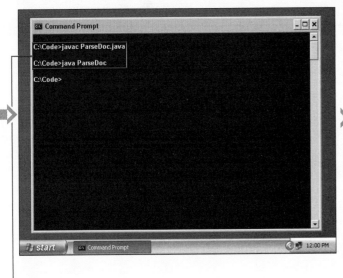

7 Save your Java file.

8 Compile and run your Java program.

■ The XML document is created.

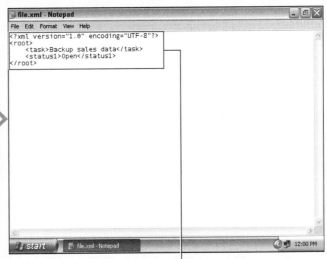

9 Open your text editor application.

10 Open the XML document specified in step 4.

■ The content of the XML document appears.

WORK WITH CHILD ELEMENTS

Container elements have some elements referred to as children, or child elements. You can manipulate the child element of an element if you know the child element name.

You can delete child elements from the JDOM document in order to delete the element from the resulting XML document. This allows you to read an XML document, manipulate the content of that document, and then redisplay the XML document. If required, you can also save the XML document to a file. For more information, see the section "Save an XML Document" in this chapter.

You use the removeChild method of the Element object to delete a sub-element. Once you remove the element, you cannot access the element, the element's attributes, or any content that you previously stored in the element.

To determine which element you want to delete, you can examine the content of an element and then make a decision to remove it or not. To make a decision, you can use an if statement to compare the content of an element to a known value. If the values do not match, you can remove the element. You may find this technique useful for removing redundant or outdated information from an XML document. For example, you may want to remove all references to a model number of a discontinued item in an XML document that stores the model numbers of items currently in stock at a store. For more information about using the if statement, see Chapter 3.

The getChild method of the Element object allows you to access sub-elements given the element name. You can access the textual data of a child element by using the getText method of the Element object.

WORK WITH CHILD ELEMENTS

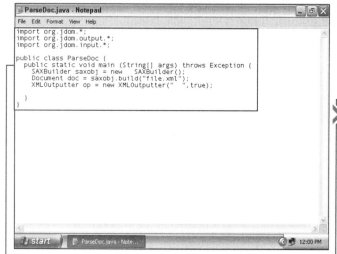

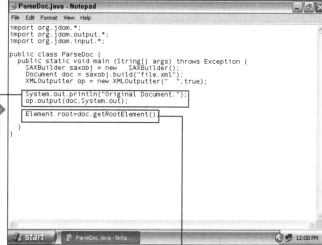

1 Create an XML document that reads an XML file and creates an **XMLOutputter** object.

Note: You can use the code created in the section "Read an XML Document."

Note: In this example, you need to access an XML document that contains a root element and child elements called ***task*** *and* ***status***. *You should make the contents of the* ***status*** *element 'Closed.'*

2 Type the code that displays the XML document.

3 Type the code that creates a new **Element** object based on the root element of the XML document.

Apply It

You can determine the parent of a child element by using the `getParent` method of the `Element` object.

TYPE THIS:

```
public static void main (String[] args) throws Exception {
    SAXBuilder saxobj = new SAXBuilder();
    Document doc = saxobj.build("file.xml");
    Element root=doc.getRootElement();
    Element childElement=root.getChild("status");
    System.out.print("The parent element of ");
    System.out.print(childElement.getName() + " is ");
    System.out.println(childElement.getParent().getName());
}
```

RESULT:

The parent element of status is root.

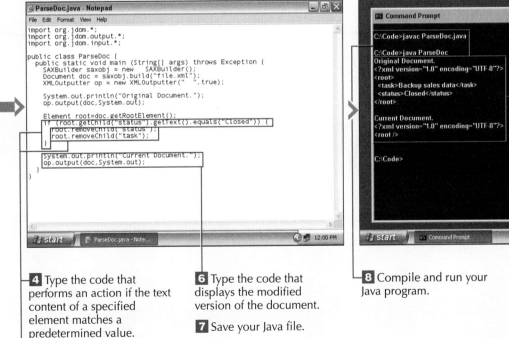

-4 Type the code that performs an action if the text content of a specified element matches a predetermined value.

-5 Type the code that removes specific child elements from the document.

6 Type the code that displays the modified version of the document.

7 Save your Java file.

-8 Compile and run your Java program.

■ The XML document appears showing before and after the elements are removed.

INSERT PRE-DEFINED ENTITY REFERENCES

The XML applications processing your XML document may incorrectly interpret some special characters that you place into element content as XML markup tags. For example, the text "is x < y" contains a less-than symbol that the XML parser interprets as the opening delimiter of a tag, even though the symbol is part of an element's content. You can incorporate special characters into XML data using predefined XML entities.

To enable you to define data containing special characters, like angle brackets and ampersands, XML uses pre-defined entities to differentiate between symbols that have special meaning in XML, such as the left angle bracket, and those same symbols embedded in a text string.

You can create a special EntityRef object and use it to represent a pre-defined entity reference, which you can insert into the content of an element within an XML document.

When you create the EntityRef object, you can specify a single string argument to represent the name of the

entity reference. When you insert the entity reference name into the XML document, you precede the name with an ampersand and you follow it with a semicolon. When creating the EntityRef object, you do not have to specify the ampersand or the semicolon when you specify the name of the entity reference. The application parsing the XML document converts the pre-defined entity reference into the appropriate symbol before processing or displaying the XML document that contains that pre-defined entity reference.

Once you create the EntityRef object, you can add it to the content of an element using the addContent method of the Element object.

When you view an XML document that contains a pre-defined entity reference with Microsoft Internet Explorer, the entity reference resolves into the symbol indicated by the entity reference.

INSERT PRE-DEFINED ENTITY REFERENCES

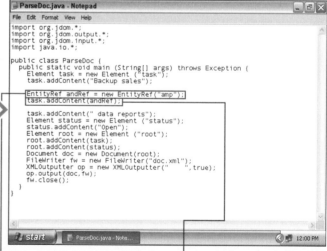

ParseDoc.java - Notepad
File Edit Format View Help
```
import org.jdom.*;
import org.jdom.output.*;
import org.jdom.input.*;
import java.io.*;

public class ParseDoc {
  public static void main (String[] args) throws Exception {
    Element task = new Element ("task");
    task.addContent("Backup sales");
    task.addContent(" data reports");
    Element status = new Element ("status");
    status.addContent("Open");
    Element root = new Element ("root");
    root.addContent(task);
    root.addContent(status);
    Document doc = new Document(root);
    FileWriter fw = new FileWriter("doc.xml");
    XMLOutputter op = new XMLOutputter("    ",true);
    op.output(doc,fw);
    fw.close();
  }
}
```

ParseDoc.java - Notepad
File Edit Format View Help
```
import org.jdom.*;
import org.jdom.output.*;
import org.jdom.input.*;
import java.io.*;

public class ParseDoc {
  public static void main (String[] args) throws Exception {
    Element task = new Element ("task");
    task.addContent("Backup sales");

    EntityRef andRef = new EntityRef("amp");
    task.addContent(andRef);

    task.addContent(" data reports");
    Element status = new Element ("status");
    status.addContent("Open");
    Element root = new Element ("root");
    root.addContent(task);
    root.addContent(status);
    Document doc = new Document(root);
    FileWriter fw = new FileWriter("doc.xml");
    XMLOutputter op = new XMLOutputter("    ",true);
    op.output(doc,fw);
    fw.close();
  }
}
```

1 Open or create the code that saves an XML document.

Note: You can use the code created in the section "Save an XML Document."

2 Type the code that creates the new entity reference object using the name of a pre-defined entity.

3 Type the code that inserts the entity reference object into the content of an existing element.

Extra

XML supports five pre-defined entities. You precede each entity with an ampersand and follow it with a semicolon when you place them into an XML document. All XML parsers have the ability to recognize pre-defined entities, also referred to as pre-defined internal entities.

PRE-DEFINED ENTITY	DESCRIPTION	EXAMPLE
&lt;	Less-than character (<)	Is X < Y
&gt;	Greater-than character (>)	Is X > Y
&amp;	Ampersand (&)	Peaches & Cream
&apos;	Apostrophe (')	Tom's Diner
&quot;	Quotation mark (")	He said &quotHi&quot

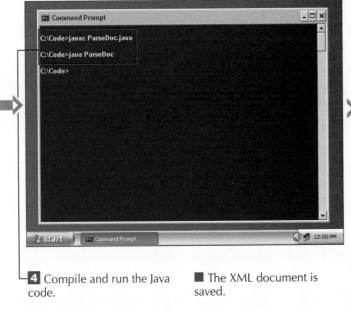

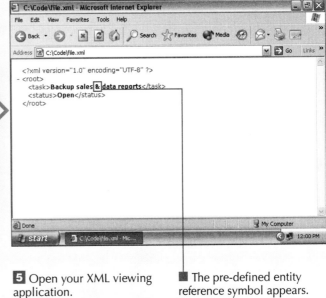

4 Compile and run the Java code.

■ The XML document is saved.

5 Open your XML viewing application.

■ The pre-defined entity reference symbol appears.

Note: This example uses Microsoft Internet Explorer.

DETERMINE ELEMENT TYPE

When using the JDOM API to analyze an XML document or the contents of the JDOM tree, you may want to identify what kind of content each element stores. For example, when trying to locate the occurrence of the processing instructions in the XML document, you need to find element types that contain processing instructions, and you can ignore all other element types, such as text or comments.

The easiest way to examine element types is to place the elements in a List. You use a List to store a sequence of objects that you can easily iterate through using standard Java procedures. You can import the java.util package to create a List. The getContent method of the Element object creates a List that stores the contents of the element. You can then iterate through the contents in the List, extracting each element as an object, and then analyzing the object to determine what type of object it is. For example, the contents of the root element are typically

child elements. When you create a List from the contents of the root element, you can create a List that contains items that you can use to create objects, which JDOM interprets as Element objects. You can use the instanceof keyword in a simple if statement to determine the type of object and then to perform any required code when JDOM finds an object of a specified type.

If you intend to analyze all the contents of every element in an XML document, you need to create the code that transverses through the contents of the document, testing each element to see what type it is and then performing an action based on the type of element.

For more information about Java Lists and the methods you use to manipulate the contents of a List, refer to the Java API documentation.

DETERMINE ELEMENT TYPE

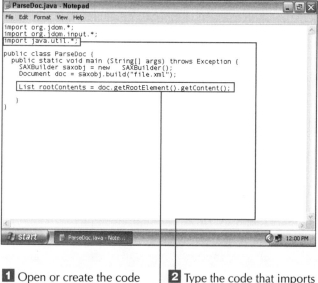

1 Open or create the code that reads an XML document.

Note: In this example, you need to read an XML document that contains a root element and two child elements.

2 Type the code that imports the package required to create a List.

3 Type the code that creates a List using the contents of the root element.

4 Type the code that iterates through all the objects in the List.

5 Type the code that retrieves each object from the List.

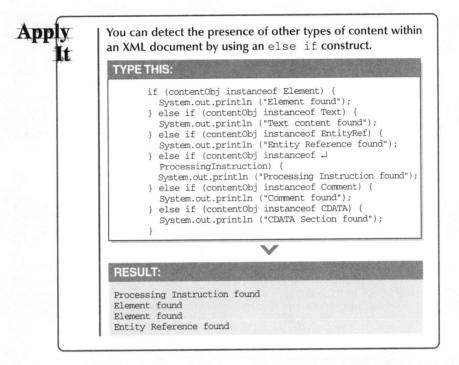

Apply It

You can detect the presence of other types of content within an XML document by using an `else if` construct.

TYPE THIS:

```
        if (contentObj instanceof Element) {
          System.out.println ("Element found");
        } else if (contentObj instanceof Text) {
          System.out.println ("Text content found");
        } else if (contentObj instanceof EntityRef) {
          System.out.println ("Entity Reference found");
        } else if (contentObj instanceof ⏎
          ProcessingInstruction) {
          System.out.println ("Processing Instruction found");
        } else if (contentObj instanceof Comment) {
          System.out.println ("Comment found");
        } else if (contentObj instanceof CDATA) {
          System.out.println ("CDATA Section found");
        }
```

RESULT:

```
Processing Instruction found
Element found
Element found
Entity Reference found
```

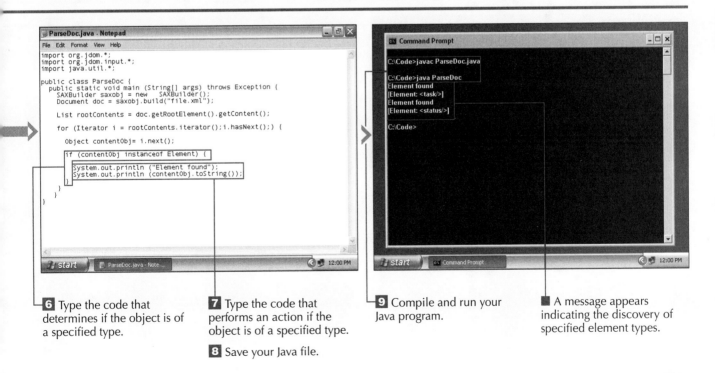

6 Type the code that determines if the object is of a specified type.

7 Type the code that performs an action if the object is of a specified type.

8 Save your Java file.

9 Compile and run your Java program.

■ A message appears indicating the discovery of specified element types.

OUTPUT A DOM TREE USING JDOM

When reading XML files and working with them within JDOM, you can use a SAXBuilder class or a DOMBuilder class to process XML documents from files or other sources. In almost all cases you should use a SAXBuilder class to process files because it is much faster than a DOMBuilder class. You can use a DOMBuilder class to process DOM tree structures that already exist within your application using JDOM. It is not unusual to use many different APIs, including both DOM and JDOM, within the same application. You can easily convert a DOM tree structure into a JDOM document that you can work with using the JDOM API.

The JDOM API is more efficient at outputting formatted XML documents than the DOM API, so you may find it easier to convert a DOM tree structure to a JDOM

document and output it than to try and output formatted XML documents using the DOM API.

After you use DOM to create a DOM tree, you must create a DOMBuilder object to convert that DOM document object to a JDOM document object. You create a JDOM document object by using the build method of the DOMBuilder object, which takes as its argument the DOM document object. DOMBuilder is part of the org.jdom .input package; therefore, to create DOMBuilder objects, you must import the org.jdom.input package. For more information about importing packages, see Chapter 3.

Once you convert a DOM document to a JDOM document, you can work with the information using the JDOM API. For example, you can very easily output that document to a file or to the display.

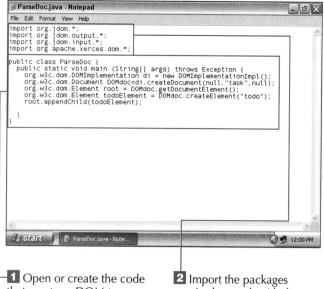

1 Open or create the code that creates a DOM tree structure.

2 Import the packages required to work with the JDOM API.

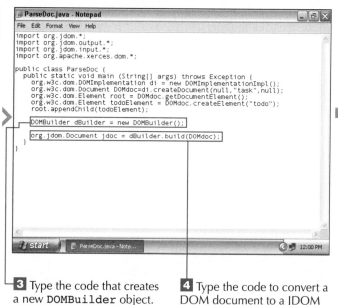

3 Type the code that creates a new **DOMBuilder** object.

4 Type the code to convert a DOM document to a JDOM document.

Apply It

You can also use the `DOMBuilder` object to convert elements in a DOM tree structure to elements in a JDOM tree structure.

TYPE THIS:

```
public class ParseDoc {
  public static void main (String[] args) throws Exception {
    org.w3c.dom.DOMImplementation di = new ↵
DOMImplementationImpl();
    org.w3c.dom.Document DOMdoc = ↵
 di.createDocument(null,"task",null);
    org.w3c.dom.Element root = DOMdoc.getDocumentElement();
    org.w3c.dom.Element todoElement = DOMdoc. ↵
createElement("todo");
    root.appendChild(todoElement);
    DOMBuilder dBuilder = new DOMBuilder();
    org.jdom.Document jdoc = dBuilder.build(DOMdoc);
    org.w3c.dom.Element newElement = DOMdoc.↵
createElement("owner");
    org.jdom.Element jElement = dBuilder.build(newElement);
    jElement.detach();
    Element jroot = jdoc.getRootElement();
    jroot.addContent(jElement);
    XMLOutputter op = new XMLOutputter();
    op.output(jdoc,System.out);
  }
}
```

RESULT:

```
<?xml version="1.0" encoding= ↵
"UTF-8"?>

<task><todo /><owner /></task>
```

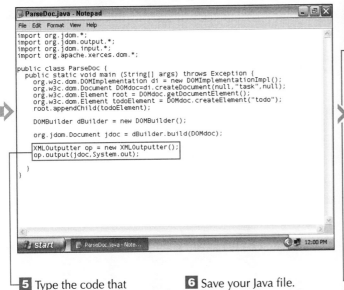

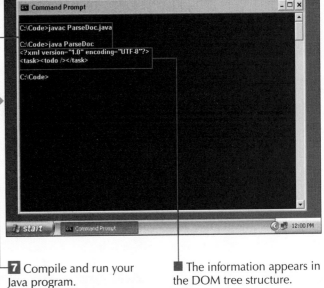

5 Type the code that displays the JDOM document.

6 Save your Java file.

7 Compile and run your Java program.

■ The information appears in the DOM tree structure.

INTRODUCING JAXP

The Java API for XML parsing, simply called JAXP, is an API that allows your Java applications to communicate with an XML parser so that the parser can read, process, and generate XML documents. JAXP itself is not a parser and it does not facilitate XML document parsing. You must use JAXP with another API that facilitates XML parsing, such as the SAX or the DOM API. The JAXP API allows you to interact with another XML-parsing API. An XML parser with which APIs, such as SAX, communicate still does the actual parsing of an XML document.

ABSTRACTION

Frequently, the different levels of API usage make it difficult to understand the purpose of using JAXP. The benefit of JAXP stems from the fact that you can create code that requires fewer changes should you make changes to the underlying XML parsing structures of your Java applications. Because you can think of JAXP as working on top of another API, programmers often refer to it as an *abstraction layer*, because it provides another level of separation from the underlying API.

SAX AND DOM

JAXP requires access to either the DOM or SAX APIs. Typically, JAXP accesses both SAX and DOM APIs for most efficient use. Although JAXP is an API itself, you must still install one of these two APIs and make them accessible to JAXP before you can use the JAXP API with an XML parser. Some installations of the DOM and SAX APIs interact with the underlying XML parser in ways specific to the accessed parser. Accessing the parser using these types of proprietary methods can lead to greater difficulty when you want to update or modify your code or the underlying XML parser. Because JAXP provides a method of interfacing with the DOM and SAX APIs, it allows you to perform the same functions without having to create proprietary techniques for interacting with the parser.

PARSERS FOR JAXP

Many XML parsers now include the JAXP API with the parser, and many XML parsers allow you to use the JAXP API. The most popular XML parser that can work with the JAXP API is the Xerces XML parser, available from the Apache organization at http://www.apache.org. This chapter uses the Xerces XML parser to generate its examples. It is recommended to install the Xerces XML parser prior to creating the examples and sample code illustrated in this chapter. You can download the Xerces XML parser, or you can install a copy from this book's companion CD-ROM. See Appendix D for more information on the CD-ROM.

ACQUIRING JAXP

You have several options for acquiring a copy of JAXP. For the latest version of JAXP, you can download the required files from Sun Microsystem's main JAXP Web site at http://java.sun.com/xml/jaxp/. The most common way of acquiring JAXP files, however, is by using an XML parser that includes the required JAXP installation files with the parser. This is the best method for acquiring JAX. You can safely assume that this version of JAXP is completely compatible with the XML parser that you access using JAXP. The companion CD-ROM with this book has a copy of the JAXP API available. See Appendix D for more information on the CD-ROM.

As well as the core JAXP API files, the JAXP has a collection of documentation. Typically, this documentation comes with the JAXP API files you acquire. Depending on how you acquire the JAXP files, you may find the API files separate from the documentation. This separation facilitates ease of transfer over networks.

You should always ensure that you have the correct documentation for the version of JAXP files installed on your computer. You have no better reference for any API including JAXP than the authoritative documentation that accompanies the JAXP API installation.

INSTALLATION

A simple procedure, installing the JAXP API files involves copying them to a specific directory on your computer, typically within the directory structure of the Java SDK installation. Once you copy the appropriate files to the target destination, you may have to adjust the `CLASSPATH` environment variable to reflect the location of the installed JAXP files. For more information about how to change the `CLASSPATH` environment variable in your computer, see Chapter 7. If you have the JAXP API files included with your XML parser, you can install the required JAXP API files when you install the XML parser

itself. To ensure that you have the correct installation method for your version of the JAXP API, and that you place the files in the correct directories, you should always consult the documentation for the proper installation and configuration procedures. Although most JAXP APIs install the same way, some parsers, or associated XML applications, may require that you install the JAXP API in a different location. For most installations, you install the JAXP API files when you install the Java API itself.

VERSIONS

The first released version of the JAXP API was JAXP version 1.0. Although the oldest version, you can still routinely find JAXP version 1.0 in many installations. When creating code using an existing JAXP installation, you should not assume that the latest version of the JAXP API has been installed. Currently the most popular version of JAXP is 1.1, which includes some improvements over JAXP 1.0, such as support for later versions of the SAX and DOM APIs. When the API deals with the reading, processing, and generating of XML documents, you find very little difference between JAXP

1.0 and JAXP 1.1. Any code you create with JAXP 1.0 should work equally well when you use it with an installation of JAXP 1.1. As with all APIs and specifications, over time, you may encounter improvements and modifications made to the API, resulting in a changed version number. If possible, you should always use the very latest version of the API to have access to the complete functionality and advantages that the JAXP API offers. To view a list of the differences between JAXP API versions 1.0 and 1.1, visit Sun's main JAXP Web site at http://java.sun.com/xml/jaxp/.

PARSE AN XML DOCUMENT

*P*arsing an XML document is the process of reading the XML document and extracting the content and structural information from the XML document. You can use JAXP to initiate the parsing of an XML document and then to access the information in the XML document.

You can easily use JAXP to communicate with an underlying SAX parser to parse an XML document with the SAXParser object. The first step in using JAXP with a SAX-compliant parser involves creating a SAXParserFactory object. Part of the package javax.xml.parsers, a SAXParserFactory object provides the method newSAXParser, which enables you to create an instance of the SAX XML parser that you can use to access an XML document. You use the newInstance method of the SAXParserFactory class to create the new SAXParserFactory object.

Once you create the SAXParser object, you can use the parse method to start parsing an XML document.

The parse method has two arguments. The first argument consists of the name of the XML document that you want to parse. The second argument is an instance of a handler class. You use that handler class to contain the methods that are called when the SAX-compliant parser encounters specific events during the parsing of an XML document. The handler class extends the DefaultHandler class when accessing the SAXParser using the SAX API. You can find the DefaultHandler class in the org.xml.sax.helpers package, which you must import prior to creating the handler class. For more information about extending classes and importing a package, see Chapter 3.

Within the handler class you can create a startDocument method. The startDocument method executes code when the parser encounters the start of an XML document. The startDocument method displays a brief message, which indicates when the parser started processing the document. For more information about creating the DefaultHandler class, see the section "Detect Events" in this chapter.

PARSE AN XML DOCUMENT

1 Type the code that imports the required packages.

2 Create the `main` method and class declarations for the application.

Note: This example requires a valid XML document. For more on creating a valid XML document, see Chapter 6.

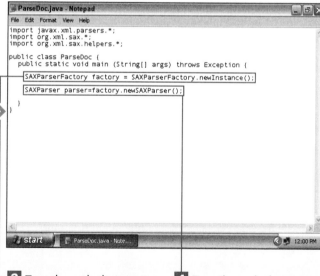

3 Type the code that creates a new **SAXParserFactory** object.

4 Type the code that creates the new **SAXParser** object.

Most XML parsers, such as Xerces, allow you to easily change the underlying parser by using the `SAXParserFactoryImpl` class that extends a `SAXParserFactory` object. You can access information about the parser implementation you are using with the `parser.getClass().getName()` method. The following example illustrates how to use an implementation-specific SAX parser.

Apply It

TYPE THIS:

```
import javax.xml.parsers.*;
import org.xml.sax.*;
import org.xml.sax.helpers.*;
import org.apache.xerces.jaxp.*;

public class ParseDoc {
  public static void main (String[] args) throws Exception {
    SAXParserFactory factory = new SAXParserFactoryImpl();
    SAXParser parser=factory.newSAXParser();
    parser.parse("file.xml", new Handler());
    System.out.println("Parser implementation;");
    System.out.println(parser.getClass().getName());
  }
}
```

RESULT:

```
Start of document detected
Parser implementation;
org.apache.xerces.jaxp.SAXParserImpl
```

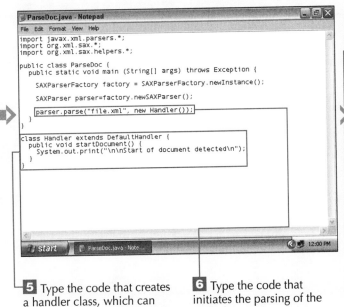

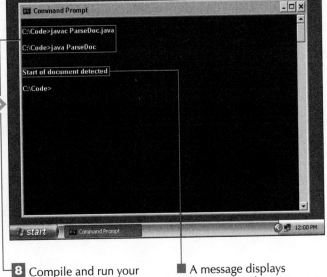

5 Type the code that creates a handler class, which can generate a message when the parser detects the start of the XML document during parsing.

6 Type the code that initiates the parsing of the XML document.

7 Save your Java file.

8 Compile and run your Java code.

■ A message displays indicating that the parser has parsed the document.

DETECT EVENTS

You can detect events to identify and extract information from an XML document. When parsing an XML document, the parser processes specific characteristics of the XML document, such as the beginning of the document or the start and end of an element. When an XML parser encounters one of these specific characteristics, such as the start tag of an element, you refer to it as an *event*. In event-based XML parsing, the parser can execute specific code when it encounters one of these events.

One of the first steps in processing an XML document in an application involves locating specific elements in the XML document. Once the parser detects an element in an XML document, it makes a callback to the appropriate method of the handler class. Once you register the event handler object with the parser object, the parser object uses the

callback methods in the registered event handler class with that instance of the parser.

You can create event callback methods within the event handler class that display a message whenever the parser encounters the start and end tags of an element when it parses an XML document.

The XML parser calls the startElement method of the event handler class whenever the XMLReader detects a tag that it identifies as the start tag of an element. The XML parser calls the endElement method of the event handler class whenever the XMLReader detects a tag that it identifies as the end tag of an element. For more detailed information about events and how they work within event handlers, refer to Chapter 7.

DETECT EVENTS

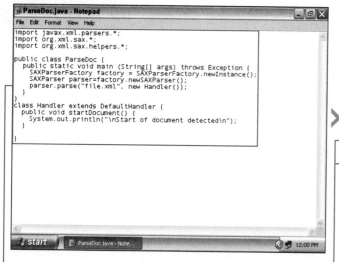

1 Open or create the code that parses an XML document.

Note: You can use the code from the section "Parse an XML Document."

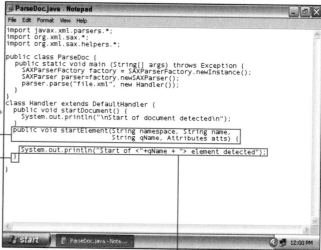

2 Type the code to create the method you want to call when the parser detects the start of an element.

3 Type the code you want to execute when the parser detects the start of an element.

Extra

The parser detects many types of events when you use a SAX-compliant parser under JAXP. You can add the appropriate method to the event handler class to execute code when the parser encounters certain XML document characteristics in an XML document.

For more detailed information about handler methods and how they work within event handlers, refer to Chapter 7.

METHOD	PURPOSE
characters	Character data
endDocument	End of an XML document
endElement	End of an XML element
endPrefixMapping	End of prefix mapping section
ignorableWhitespace	Non-needed whitespace
processingInstruction	A processing instruction
setDocumentLocator	Locator object to determine parsing position
startDocument	Start of an XML document
startElement	Start of an XML element
startPrefixMapping	Start of prefix mapping section

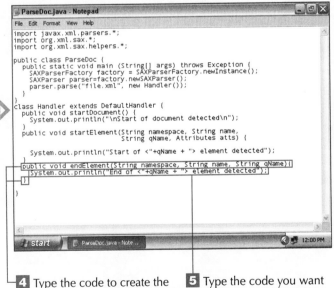

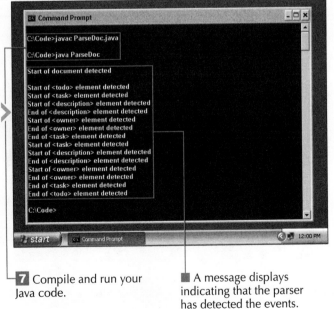

4 Type the code to create the method you want to call when the parser detects the end tag of an element.

5 Type the code you want to execute when the parser detects the end tag of an element.

6 Save your Java code.

7 Compile and run your Java code.

■ A message displays indicating that the parser has detected the events.

CONFIGURE FACTORY SETTINGS

A *factory* is a class file that you use to create objects. You can alter some of the characteristics of a factory object, which then impact all the objects subsequently created from that factory. For example, when using JAXP to create a new SAXParser object using the SAXParserFactory class, you can enable validation of any XML documents that you want to parse by setting a feature of the factory class prior to creating the new SAXParser object. Enabling validation requires that you make all XML documents, which your application parses with the instance of the SAXParser, valid or your code will generate an error.

Once you enable a feature with the factory class, any objects you create using a factory class have those enabled features. Commonly, you utilize a factory class to create multiple related objects for use within the same application. You can enable or disable most features of a factory class,

so you can enable a feature prior to creating some objects, then disable a feature and continue to create objects using the same factory class but with a feature now disabled.

Typically, the objects you create from a factory class have a corresponding method to indicate whether you have enabled or disabled the feature on the new object. For example, to determine whether you have the validation enabled on a new SAXParser object, the isValidating method returns a value of true or false to indicate whether the parser will or will not validate any XML documents that it parses.

You can configure some settings for the factory class, such as enabling namespaces, whether you use the DOM or the SAX API with JAXP. For more information about the parser features that you can access using JAXP, see Appendix A.

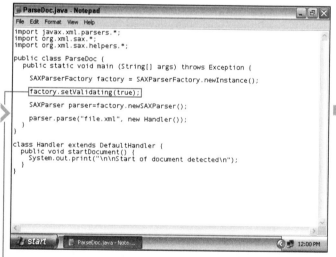

1 Open or create the code that parses an XML document.

Note: You can use the code from the section "Parse an XML Document."

2 Type the code that configures the factory object settings.

■ This example uses the isValidating method to enable the creation of validating parsers.

Apply It

A namespace aware XML parser can correctly process XML documents that make use of namespaces. For more information about namespaces, see Chapter 5.

You can use the `setNamespaceAware` method to enable parsers that you created with a factory to be aware of namespaces in XML documents. You can check to see if a parser is namespace-aware by using the `isNamespaceAware` method of the parser object.

TYPE THIS:

```
public static void main (String[] args) throws Exception {
  SAXParserFactory factory = SAXParserFactory.newInstance();
  factory.setValidating(true);
  factory.setNamespaceAware(true);
  SAXParser parser = factory.newSAXParser();

  if (parser.isValidating()) {
    System.out.println("Validation is enabled");
  }
  if (parser.isNamespaceAware()) {
    System.out.println("Parser is namespace aware");
  }
  parser.parse("file.xml", new Handler());
}
```

RESULT:

```
Validation is enabled
Parser is namespace aware


Start of document detected
```

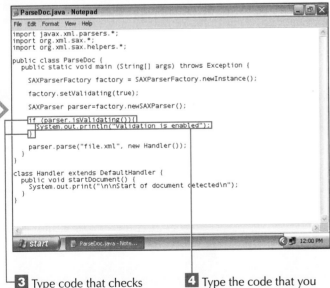

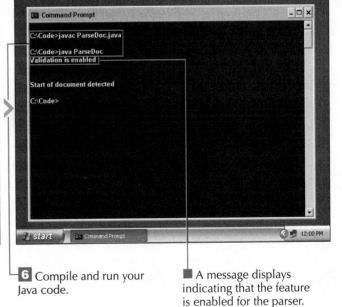

3 Type code that checks whether you have enabled the feature for the newly created parser object.

4 Type the code that you want to execute if you have the feature enabled.

5 Save your Java file.

6 Compile and run your Java code.

■ A message displays indicating that the feature is enabled for the parser.

SET SAXPARSER FEATURES

XML parsers have their own configuration choices, which can help you determine if you can access a specific function or feature of your application. You refer to the settings of an XML parser as the features of the parser.

Represented by URLs, features of an XML parser typically consist of very long strings. The `setFeature` method of the `SAXParserFactory` class allows you to enable or disable a feature by specifying the URL of the feature. After the URI, you place a `boolean` value of `true` or `false`. Located at http://xml.org/sax/features/validation, one of the more common features of SAX-compliant XML parsers indicates whether you have enabled validation.

The `getFeature` method of the `SAXParserFactory` class allows you to determine the value associated with a feature of the parser. The `getFeature` method returns a value of either `true` or `false`, indicating whether the feature is enabled or not.

Not all XML parsers allow you to modify the features available to a parser. The SAX API specifies some features that all SAX-compliant XML parsers must support. You may only have other features and properties available to you when using the SAX API with a specific XML parser. You have only the SAX-specified features and properties available to you on all SAX-compliant parsers.

You should not depend too heavily on features or properties specific to one parser in your code. If you have to change the parser or even change to a different version of the same XML parser at some time in the future, the features available in one version may become unavailable in another version of the same parser. One reason for using JAXP stems from its ability to change the underlying parser without you having to modify your code; you should avoid using implementation-specific features of the parser whenever possible.

SET SAXPARSER FEATURES

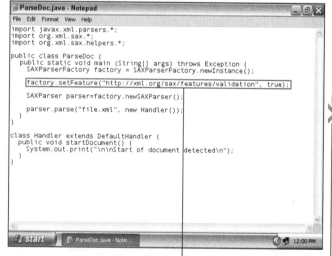

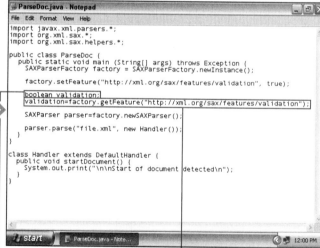

1 Open or create the code that parses an XML document.

Note: You can use the code from the section "Parse an XML Document."

2 Type the code that enables a feature on the underlying **SAXParser**.

3 Type the code to declare a **boolean** variable.

4 Type the code that returns a value, after checking that a feature is set, and assigns the value to a variable.

Apply it

If you try to set a feature of a `SAXParser` that does not exist, a `SAXNotRecognizedException` error may generate. You can use a simple `try` and `catch` block to isolate the error and deal with the failure of setting the feature.

TYPE THIS:

```
try {
    factory.setFeature("http://xml.org/sax/features/edit", false);
} catch (SAXNotRecognizedException e) {
    System.out.println("The feature ");
    System.out.println(e.getMessage());
    System.out.println("cannot be set. ");
}
```

RESULT:

```
The feature
http://xml.org/sax/features/edit
cannot be set.
```

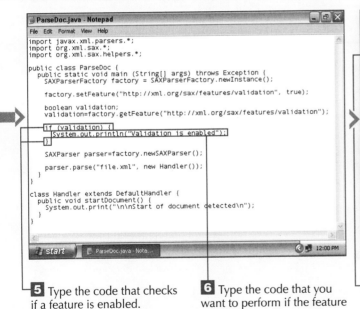

5 Type the code that checks if a feature is enabled.

6 Type the code that you want to perform if the feature is enabled.

7 Save your Java code.

8 Compile and run your Java code.

■ A message displays if the feature is enabled successfully.

PARSE A DOCUMENT USING DOM

Although SAX is typically the most popular API to use with JAXP, you can just as easily use the DOM API to interact with an underlying XML parser. The DOM API provides you with another way of working with XML documents, allowing you more flexibility when creating your Java applications.

The first step involves creating a `DocumentBuilderFactory` object, using the `newInstance` method of the `DocumentBuilderFactory` class. Once you create the `DocumentBuilderFactory` object, you can utilize the `newDocumentBuilder` method to create a `DocumentBuilder` object, which you use to parse a document. The `DocumentBuilder` object allows you to use the parse method to specify the name of the XML document you want to parse. The return type of the parse method is a DOM document type. Once you create a DOM

document object, you can use the DOM API to access the information in that object. Before using the DOM API, you must ensure that you import the appropriate DOM API packages. For more information about working with the DOM API, refer to Chapter 8.

Part of the reason you use the JAXP API stems from the fact that it provides an additional level of abstraction when you have different parsers. You can use both DOM- and SAX-compliant parsers and access the parsers with their respective APIs, while still using the same methods to access that data. For example, the `SAXParser` class and the `DocumentBuilder` class both use the parse method to initiate the parsing of a document. By simply changing a limited number of class files, you can completely change the way your Java application interacts with an XML parser, without having to completely rewrite your code.

PARSE A DOCUMENT USING DOM

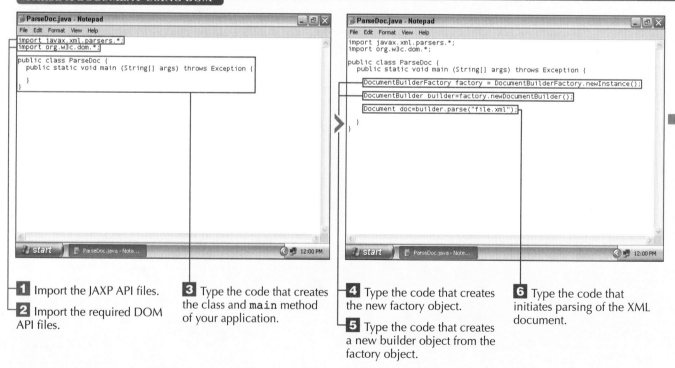

1 Import the JAXP API files.

2 Import the required DOM API files.

3 Type the code that creates the class and **main** method of your application.

4 Type the code that creates the new factory object.

5 Type the code that creates a new builder object from the factory object.

6 Type the code that initiates parsing of the XML document.

Regardless of whether you use the SAX or DOM API, JAXP still allows you to access similar methods to set the same features. For example, the `setValidation` and `setNamespaceAware` settings are the same for both APIs.

TYPE THIS:

```
public static void main (String[] args) throws Exception {
    DocumentBuilderFactory factory = DocumentBuilderFactory.newInstance();
    factory.setValidating(true);
    factory.setNamespaceAware(true);
    DocumentBuilder builder = factory.newDocumentBuilder();
    if (builder.isValidating()) {
      System.out.println("Validation is enabled");
    }
    if (builder.isNamespaceAware()) {
      System.out.println("Parser is namespace aware");
    }
    Document doc = builder.parse("file.xml");
    Element root = doc.getDocumentElement();
    String rootElementName = (root.getTagName());
    System.out.println("The root element name is " + rootElementName);

}
```

RESULT:

```
Validation is enabled
Parser is namespace aware
The root element name is todo
```

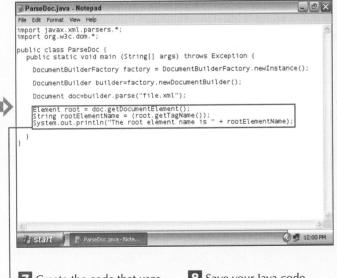

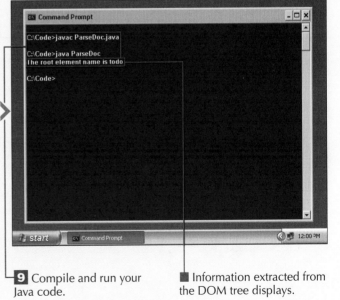

7 Create the code that uses the DOM API to interact with the XML document.

8 Save your Java code.

9 Compile and run your Java code.

■ Information extracted from the DOM tree displays.

CREATE AN ERROR HANDLER FOR USE WITH DOM

E ven if you are using the DOM API with JAXP, you can utilize the more efficient error handling capabilities of the SAX API to handle the errors the XML parser generates. When dealing with SAX API errors you must use an error handler class to handle the errors. You can use the setErrorHandler method of the DOM builder class to register an error handler class with a DOM builder object.

The error handler class you create and register with the DOM builder object must implement the ErrorHandler interface of the org.xml.sax package. For more information about creating a SAX error handling class, see Chapter 7.

The error handler class you create must implement three methods: warning, error, and fatalError.

The application calls each method whenever code in the XML document generates the corresponding error. A call to

the fatalError method often means that the parser finds it impossible to properly parse an XML document, if, for example, you failed to include the required start or end element tags in the XML document. Warnings are errors that the error or fatalError methods do not catch. You can typically continue parsing an XML document after the application generates a warning. You use the error method with the types of errors from which you commonly recover. For example, the application calls this method if the XML document is not a valid XML document.

You should always develop every application that you create to handle whatever errors the application may generate when it executes your code. You typically create error-handling code for all of the methods in the error handling class. For more information about handling errors in Java code, see Chapter 3.

CREATE AN ERROR HANDLER FOR USE WITH DOM

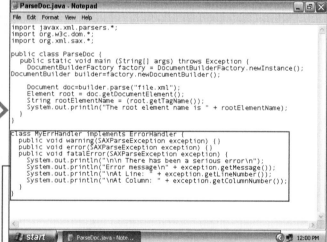

Note: To generate the required error for this example, you need to parse an XML document that has an element with a missing end tag.

1 Type or create the code that uses JAXP and the DOM API to parse a document.

Note: You can use the code from the section "Parse a Document Using DOM."

2 Import the SAX files you require to create the error handler class.

3 Create the error handler class that displays a message when the application encounters a fatal error.

Note: You can use the code from "Create a Custom Error Message" in Chapter 7.

The application may also generate `SAXException` errors which you can handle using a simple `try` and `catch` block within your Java code.

TYPE THIS:

```
public static void main (String[] args) throws Exception {
    DocumentBuilderFactory factory = DocumentBuilderFactory.newInstance();
    DocumentBuilder builder = factory.newDocumentBuilder();
    builder.setErrorHandler(new MyErrHandler());
    try {
        Document doc = builder.parse("file.xml");
        Element root = doc.getDocumentElement();
        String rootElementName = (root.getTagName());
        System.out.println("The root element name is " + rootElementName);
    } catch (SAXException e) {
        System.out.println("Program execution has been terminated");
    }
}
```

RESULT:

```
There has been a serious error

Error message
The element type "status" must be terminated by the matching end-tag "</status>".

At Line: 12

At Column: 7
Program execution has been terminated
```

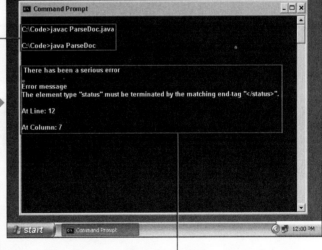

4 Type the code that registers the error handler class with the **DOMBuilder** object.

5 Save your Java code.

6 Compile and run your Java program.

■ An error message displays.

SAX API QUICK REFERENCE

The SAX API contains a complex array of interfaces, classes, and methods. For detailed information about the SAX API, always consult the documentation that comes with your version of the SAX API. The following tables give a quick reference for some of the more commonly used features of the SAX API.

PRIMARY INTERFACES

NAME	DESCRIPTION
Attributes	Accesses XML attributes.
ContentHandler	Handles differing content in an XML document.
DTDHandler	Accesses the declarations present in a DTD.
EntityResolver	Resolves entities.
ErrorHandler	Handles SAX errors.
Locator	Locates a position in an XML document.
XMLFilter	Use when employing XML filters.
XMLReader	Use for accessing XML documents.

THE ERRORHANDLER INTERFACE

RETURN TYPE	METHOD	DESCRIPTION
void	error(SAXParseException exception)	Receives notification of a recoverable error.
void	fatalError(SAXParseException exception)	Receives notification of a non-recoverable error.
void	warning(SAXParseException exception)	Receives notification of a warning.

THE ATTRIBUTE INTERFACE

RETURN TYPE	METHOD	DESCRIPTION
int	getIndex(String qName)	Looks up the index of an attribute by XML 1.0 qualified name.
int	getIndex(String uri, String localPart)	Looks up the index of an attribute by namespace name.
int	getLength()	Returns the number of attributes in a list.
String	getLocalName(int index)	Looks up an attribute's local name by index.
String	getQName(int index)	Looks up an attribute's XML 1.0 qualified name by index.
String	getType(int index)	Looks up an attribute's type by index.
String	getType(String qName)	Looks up an attribute's type by XML 1.0 qualified name.
String	getType(String uri, String localName)	Looks up an attribute's type by namespace name.
String	getURI(int index)	Looks up an attribute's namespace URI by index.
String	getValue(int index)	Looks up an attribute's value by index.
String	getValue(String qName)	Looks up an attribute's value by XML 1.0 qualified name.
String	getValue(String uri, String localName)	Looks up an attribute's value by namespace name.

THE CONTENTHANDLER INTERFACE

RETURN TYPE	METHOD	DESCRIPTION
void	characters(char[] ch, int start, int length)	Receives notification of character data.
void	endDocument()	Receives notification of the end of a document.
void	endElement(String namespaceURI, String localName, String qName)	Receives notification of the end of an element.
void	endPrefixMapping(String prefix)	Ends the scope of a prefix-URI mapping.
void	ignorableWhitespace(char[] ch, int start, int length)	Receives notification of ignorable whitespace in element content.
void	processingInstruction(String target, String data)	Receives notification of a processing instruction.
void	setDocumentLocator(Locator locator)	Receives an object for locating the origin of SAX document events.
void	skippedEntity(String name)	Receives notification of a skipped entity.
void	startDocument()	Receives notification of the beginning of a document.
void	startElement(String namespaceURI, String localName, String qName, Attributes atts)	Receives notification of the beginning of an element.
void	startPrefixMapping(String prefix, String uri)	Begins the scope of a prefix-URI namespace mapping.

THE XMLREADER INTERFACE

RETURN TYPE	METHOD	DESCRIPTION
ContentHandler	getContentHandler()	Returns the current content handler.
DTDHandler	getDTDHandler()	Returns the current DTD handler.
EntityResolver	getEntityResolver()	Returns the current entity resolver.
ErrorHandler	getErrorHandler()	Returns the current error handler.
boolean	getFeature(String name)	Looks up the value of a feature.
Object	getProperty(String name)	Looks up the value of a property.
void	parse(InputSource input)	Parses an XML document.
void	parse(String systemId)	Parses an XML document from a system identifier (URI).
void	setContentHandler(ContentHandler handler)	Allows an application to register a content event handler.
void	setDTDHandler(DTDHandler handler)	Allows an application to register a DTD event handler.
void	setEntityResolver(EntityResolver resolver)	Allows an application to register an entity resolver.
void	setErrorHandler(ErrorHandler handler)	Allows an application to register an error event handler.
void	setFeature(String name, boolean value)	Sets the state of a feature.
void	setProperty(String name, Object value)	Sets the value of a property.

DOM API QUICK REFERENCE

The DOM API contains a complex array of interfaces, classes, and methods. For detailed information about the DOM API, you should always consult the documentation that came with the version of the DOM API you are using. The following tables give a quick reference for some of the more commonly used features of the DOM API.

THE DOCUMENTTYPE INTERFACE

RETURN TYPE	METHOD	DESCRIPTION
Attr	createAttribute(String name)	Creates an Attr object of the given name.
Attr	createAttributeNS(String namespaceURI,String qualifiedName)	Creates an attribute of the given qualified name and namespace URI.
CDATASection	createCDATASection(String data)	Creates a CDATASection node whose value is the specified string.
Comment	createComment(String data)	Creates a Comment node given the specified string.
DocumentFragment	createDocumentFragment()	Creates an empty DocumentFragment object.
Element	createElement(String tagName)	Creates an element of the type specified.
Element	createElementNS(String namespaceURI, String qualifiedName)	Creates an element of the given qualified name and namespace URI.
EntityReference	createEntityReference(String name)	Creates an EntityReference object.
ProcessingInstruction	createProcessingInstruction (String target, String data)	Creates a ProcessingInstruction node given the specified name and data strings.
Text	createTextNode(String data)	Creates a Text node given the specified string.
DocumentType	getDoctype()	The Document Type Declaration associated with this document.
Element	getDocumentElement()	This is a convenience attribute that allows direct access to the child node that is the root element of the document.
Element	getElementById(String elementId)	Returns the element whose ID is given by elementId.
NodeList	getElementsByTagName (String tagname)	Returns a NodeList of all the elements with a given tag name in the order in which they are encountered in a preorder traversal of the document tree.
NodeList	getElementsByTagNameNS(String namespaceURI, String localName)	Returns a NodeList of all the elements with a given local name and namespace URI in the order in which they are encountered in a preorder traversal of the Document tree.
DOMImplementation	getImplementation()	The DOMImplementation object that handles this document.
Node	importNode(Node importedNode, boolean deep)	Imports a node from another document to this document.

RETURN TYPE	METHOD	DESCRIPTION
String	getAttribute(String name)	Retrieves an attribute value by name.
Attr	getAttributeNode(String name)	Retrieves an attribute node by name.
Attr	getAttributeNodeNS(String namespaceURI, String localName)	Retrieves an Attr node by local name and namespace URI.
String	getAttributeNS(String namespaceURI, String localName)	Retrieves an attribute value by local name and namespace URI.
NodeList	getElementsByTagName(String name)	Returns a `NodeList` of all descendant elements with a given tag name, in the order in which they are encountered in a preorder traversal of this element tree.
NodeList	getElementsByTagNameNS(String namespaceURI, String localName)	Returns a NodeList of all the descendant elements with a given local name and namespace URI in the order in which they are encountered in a preorder traversal of this element tree.
String	getTagName()	The name of the element.
boolean	hasAttribute(String name)	Returns true when an attribute with a given name is specified on this element or has a default value, false otherwise.
boolean	hasAttributeNS(String namespaceURI, String localName)	Returns true when an attribute with a given local name and namespace URI is specified on this element or has a default value, false otherwise.
void	removeAttribute(String name)	Removes an attribute by name.
Attr	removeAttributeNode(Attr oldAttr)	Removes the specified attribute node.
void	removeAttributeNS(String namespaceURI, String localName)	Removes an attribute by local name and namespace URI.
void	setAttribute(String name, String value)	Adds a new attribute.
Attr	setAttributeNode(Attr newAttr)	Adds a new attribute node.
Attr	setAttributeNodeNS(Attr newAttr)	Adds a new attribute.
void	setAttributeNS(String namespaceURI, String qualifiedName, String value)	Adds a new attribute.

DOM API QUICK REFERENCE (CONTINUED)

THE NODE INTERFACE

RETURN TYPE	METHOD	DESCRIPTION
Node	appendChild(Node newChild)	Adds the node newChild to the end of the list of children of this node.
Node	cloneNode(boolean deep)	Returns a duplicate of this node. For example, it serves as a generic copy constructor for nodes.
NamedNodeMap	getAttributes()	A NamedNodeMap containing the attributes of this node (if it is an element) or null otherwise.
NodeList	getChildNodes()	A NodeList that contains all children of this node.
Node	getFirstChild()	The first child of this node.
Node	getLastChild()	The last child of this node.
String	getLocalName()	Returns the local part of the qualified name of this node.
String	getNamespaceURI()	The namespace URI of this node, or null if it is unspecified.
Node	getNextSibling()	The node immediately following this node.
String	getNodeName()	The name of this node.
Short	getNodeType()	A code representing the type of the underlying object, as defined above.
String	getNodeValue()	The value of this node.
Document	getOwnerDocument()	The Document object associated with this node.
Node	getParentNode()	The parent of this node.
String	getPrefix()	The namespace prefix of this node, or null if it is unspecified.
Node	getPreviousSibling()	The node immediately preceding this node.
Boolean	hasAttributes()	Returns whether this node (if it is an element) has any attributes.
Boolean	hasChildNodes()	Returns whether this node has any children.
Node	insertBefore(Node newChild, Node refChild)	Inserts the node newChild before the existing child node refChild.
Boolean	isSupported(String feature, String version)	Tests whether the DOM implementation creates a specific feature and whether that feature is supported by this node.
Node	removeChild(Node oldChild)	Removes the child node indicated by oldChild from the list of children, and returns it.
Node	replaceChild(Node newChild, Node oldChild)	Replaces the child node oldChild with newChild in the list of children, and returns the oldChild node.

JDOM QUICK REFERENCE

J DOM uses many packages and class files. For complete details about the class files and their methods, fields, and

constructors, refer to the JDOM API documentation that accompanies your JDOM installation.

The org.jom package is the principal package of the JDOM API.

CLASS SUMMARY	
CLASS NAME	DESCRIPTION
Text	Allows for the manipulation of textual data.
ProcessingInstruction	Creates and manipulates processing instructions.
EntityRef	Defines an entity reference.
Element	Creates and manipulates elements of an XML document.
Document	Allows representation of an XML document.
DocType	Creates an XML docType object.
Comment	Creates and manipulates XML document comments.
CDATA	Creates and manipulates CDATA sections of an XML document.
Attribute	Creates and manipulates element attributes.

The Document class allows you to represent an XML document as an object.

COMMONLY USED METHODS		
RETURN TYPE	METHOD	DESCRIPTION
Document	addContent(commentcomment)	Adds a comment.
Document	addContent(ProcessingInstructionpi)	Inserts a processing instruction.
Object	clone()	Creates a copy of the document.
boolean	equals(Objectob)	Determines if documents are the same.
List	getContent()	Retrieves the content of the document.
DocType	getDocType()	Retrieves the DocType declaration.
Element	getRootElement()	Retrieves the root element.
boolean	removeContent(Commentcomment)	Deletes a comment.
boolean	removeContent(ProcessingInstructionpi)	Deletes a processing instruction.
Document	setContent(ListnewContent)	Creates content from a list.
Document	setDocType(DocTypedocType)	Sets the DocType declaration.
Document	setRootElement(ElementrootElement)	Sets the root element.
String	toString()	Converts the document to a string.

JDOM QUICK REFERENCE (CONTINUED).

THE TEXT CLASS

You can use the Text class to represent textual information, as it stores in an XML document.

COMMONLY USED METHODS		
RETURN TYPE	**METHOD**	**DESCRIPTION**
void	append(StringstringValue)	Appends textual data.
Object	clone()	Copies a text node.
boolean	equals(Objectob)	Determines if objects are the same.
Document	getDocument()	Retrieves the document to which the text belongs.
Element	getParent()	Retrieves the parent element.
String	getValue()	Retrieves the value of the text.
void	getValue(StringstringValue)	Sets the text value.
String	toString()	Converts the text information to a string.

THE ELEMENT CLASS

The Element class is one of the most used and important classes when working with the JDOM API. A wide range of methods reflect the versatility and complexity of the Element class.

COMMONLY USED METHODS		
RETURN TYPE	**METHOD**	**DESCRIPTION**
Element	addContent(CDATAcdata)	Adds a CDATA section.
Element	addContent(Commentcomment)	Adds a comment to the element.
Element	addContent(Elementelement)	Adds an element content to the element.
Element	addContent(EntityRefentity)	Adds an entity content to this element.
Element	addContent(ProcessingInstructionpi)	Adds a processing instruction to the element.
Element	addContent(Stringtext)	Adds a textual content to the element.
Object	clone()	Creates a copy of the element.
Element	detach()	Detaches the element from its parent.
Attribute	getAttribute(Stringname)	Retrieves an attribute.
List	getAttributes()	Retrieves a list of the elements attributes.
String	getAttributeValue(Stringname)	Retrieves the value of an attribute.

THE ELEMENT CLASS

COMMONLY USED METHODS		
RETURN TYPE	**METHOD**	**DESCRIPTION**
Element	getChild(Stringname)	Retrieves the first child element.
List	getChildren()	Retrieves a list of all the child elements.
List	getChildren(Stringname)	Retrieves a list of all the specified child elements.
String	getChildText(Stringname)	Retrieves the text of a child element.
String	getChildTextTrim(Stringname)	Retrieves the trimmed text of a child element.
List	getContent()	Retrieves a list of the elements content.
Document	getDocument()	Retrieves the document the element belongs to.
String	getName()	The element name.
Element	getParent()	Retrieves the parent element.
String	getText()	Retrieves the textual content of the element.
String	getTextNormalize()	Retrieves the textual content of the element with the whitespace condensed.
String	getTextTrim()	Retrieves the textual content of the element without the whitespace.
boolean	hasChildren()	Determines if an element has children.
boolean	isRootElement()	Determines if an element is a root element.
boolean	removeAttribute(Stringname)	Removes an attribute.
boolean	hasChild(Stringname)	Deletes first child element.
boolean	removeChildren()	Deletes all child elements.
boolean	removeChildren(Stringname)	Removes specified child element.
boolean	removeContent(CDATAcdata)	Removes a CDATA section.
boolean	removeContent(Commentcomment)	Removes a comment.
boolean	removeContent(Elementelement)	Removes an element.
boolean	removeContent(EntityRefentity)	Removes an EnityRef.
boolean	removeContent(ProcessingInstructionpi)	Removes a ProcessingInstruction.
Element	setAttribute(Attributeattribute)	Sets an attribute for the element.
Element	setAttribute(Stringname,Stringvalue)	Sets an attribute value for the element.
Element	setAttributes(Listattributes)	Sets the attributes for an element from a list.
Element	setChildren(Listchildren)	Creates child elements from a list.
Element	setContent(ListnewContent)	Creates element content from a list.
Element	setName(Stringname)	Specifies the name of the element.
Element	settext(Stringtext)	Specifies textual content for the element
String	toString()	Converts element data into a string.

JAXP QUICK REFERENCE

The JAXP API contains various classes and methods that you can use. For detailed information about the JAXP API, always consult the documentation that comes with the version of the SAX API you are using. This quick reference gives some of the more commonly used features of the JAXP API. The JAXP API is contained in the package `javax.xml.parsers`.

CLASS SUMMARY

CLASS NAME	PURPOSE
DocumentBuilderFactory	Creates DOM factory objects.
DocumentBuilder	A parser object that uses DOM.
SAXParserFactory	Creates SAX factory objects.
SAXParser	A parser object that uses SAX.

DOCUMENTBUILDER METHOD SUMMARY

RETURN TYPE	METHOD	DESCRIPTION
DOMImplementation	getDOMImplementation()	Creates a DOM Implementation object.
boolean	isNamespaceAware()	Determines if a parser understands namespaces.
boolean	isValidating()	Determines if a parser will validate XML documents.
Document	newDocument()	Creates a new DOM Document object.
Document	parse(file)	Initiates the parsing of a file.
void	setEntityResolver (EntityResolver er)	Sets the entity resolver that you want to use.
void	setErrorHandler (ErrorHandler eh)	Sets the error handler resolver that you want to use.

DOCUMENTBUILDERFACTORY METHOD SUMMARY

RETURN TYPE	METHOD	DESCRIPTION
Object	getAttribute(java.lang. String name)	Retrieves attributes.
boolean	isCoalescing()	Determines if a parser coverts CDATA to text nodes.
boolean	isExpandEntityReferences()	Determines if a parser resolves entity references.
boolean	isIgnoringComments()	Determines if a parser ignores comments.
boolean	isIgnoringElementContent Whitespace()	Determines if a parser ignores whitespace.
boolean	isNamespaceAware()	Determines if a parser recognizes namespace usage.
boolean	isValidating()	Determines if a parser validates XML documents.
DocumentBuilder	newDocumentBuilder()	Creates a new DocumentBuilder object.
DocumentBuilderFactory	newInstance()	Creates a new DocumentBuilderFactory object.

DOCUMENTBUILDERFACTORY METHOD SUMMARY (CONTINUED)

RETURN TYPE	METHOD	DESCRIPTION
void	setAttribute(java.lang.String name,java.lang.Object value)	Sets parser attributes.
void	setCoalescing(boolean coalescing)	Configures new parsers to convert CDATA to text nodes.
void	setExpandEntityReferences (boolean expandEntityRef)	Configures new parsers to resolve entity references.
void	setIgnoringComments (booleanignoreComments)	Configures new parsers to ignore comments.
void	setIgnoringElementContent Whitespace(booleanwhitespace)	Configures new parsers to ignore whitespace.
void	setNamespaceAware(booleanawareness)	Configures new parsers to recognize namespace.
void	setValidating(booleanvalidating)	Configures new parsers to validate XML documents.

SAXPARSERFACTORY METHOD SUMMARY

RETURN TYPE	METHOD	DESCRIPTION
boolean	getFeature(java.lang. String name)	Determines parser feature setting.
boolean	isNamespaceAware()	Determines if a parser to be created is aware of namespace usage.
boolean	isValidating()	Determines if a parser to be created will validate XML documents.
SAXParserFactory	newInstance()	Creates a new SAXParserFactory object.
SAXParser	newSAXParser()	Creates a new SAXParser object.
void	setFeature(java.lang. String name, boolean value)	Configures the features of new parsers.
void	setNamespaceAware (boolean awareness)	Configures new parsers to be namespace aware.
void	setValidating(boolean validating)	Configure new parsers to validate XML documents.

SAXPARSER METHOD SUMMARY

RETURN TYPE	METHOD	DESCRIPTION
Parser	getParser()	Creates a Parser object.
Object	getProperty(java.lang.String name)	Retrieves property objects.
XMLReader	getXMLReader()	Generates an XMLReader object.
boolean	isNamespaceAware()	Determines if parser recognizes namespace.
boolean	isValidating()	Determines if parser validates XML documents.
void	parse(File, DefaultHandler dh)	Parses a file and registers the default content handler for callbacks.
void	setProperty(java.lang.String name, java.lang.Object value)	Sets a parser's property.

JAVA QUICK REFERENCE

This appendix contains some useful tabular information,
as well as a quick reference to control structures in Java.

JAVA KEYWORDS

abstract	boolean	break	byte	case
catch	char	class	const*	continue
default	do	double	else	extends
final	finally	float	for	goto*
if	implements	import	instanceof	int
interface	long	native	new	null
package	private	protected	public	return
short	static	strictfp	super	switch
synchronized	this	throw	throws	transient
try	void	volatile	while	

*const and goto are reserved but not used.

BUILT-IN TYPES

INTEGRAL TYPES

TYPE	SIZE IN BITS	MAXIMUM VALUE	MINIMUM VALUE
byte	8	127	-128
char	16	65535	0
short	16	32767	-32768
int	32	2147483647	-2147483648
long	64	9223372036854775807	-9223372036854775808

FLOATING-POINT TYPES

TYPE	SIZE IN BITS	MAXIMUM VALUE	SMALLEST POSITIVE VALUE
float	32	$3.403 \times 10^{+38}$	1.401×10^{-45}
double	64	$1.798 \times 10^{+308}$	4.900×10^{-324}

CHARACTER ESCAPE SEQUENCES

You can use these character escape sequences to embed special characters in quoted strings.

ESCAPE SEQUENCE	MEANING
\b	backspace
\f	formfeed
\n	newline
\r	carriage return
\t	tab
\"	double quote
\'	single quote
\\	backslash
\unnnn	any Unicode character (n are hexadecimal digits)

OPERATORS

The following tables list all the operators defined by the Java language.

COMPARISON AND BOOLEAN LOGIC

>	<	==	<=	>=
!	?:	&&	||	!=
instanceof				

ARITHMETIC

+	-	*	/	%
++	—			

SHIFTS AND BITWISE LOGIC

&	|	^	<<	>>>
>>	~			

ASSIGNMENT

=	&=	|=	^=	<<=
>>=	>>	+=	-=	*=
/=	%=			

OTHER

.	[]	(*typename*)	new

JAVA QUICK REFERENCE (CONTINUED)

CONTROL FLOW

The following sections describe each of the control structures available in Java. You can choose the most appropriate one for each programming situation.

The `while` **loop**

```
while (condition)
  {
     statement1;
     statement2;
  }
```

Java evaluates the condition, and if it is true, executes the statements. It repeats this process until the condition becomes false.

The `do-while` **loop**

```
do
  {
     statement1;
     statement2;
     ...
  }
while (condition);
```

Java executes the statements while the condition is true. It always executes the statements at least once.

The `for` **loop**

```
for (initialization; condition; advance)
  {
     statement1;
     statement2;
     ...
  }
```

Java executes the initialization statement, and then evaluates the condition. If the condition is true, Java executes the statements, and then the advance clause. Java then re-evaluates the condition, and if it is true, it executes the statements again, then executes the advance clause. This sequence continues until the condition evaluates to false. Java may execute the statements zero or more times.

The `switch` **statement**

```
switch (integral-value)
{
 case constant1:
    statement1;

 case constant2:
    statement2;

  ...

 default:
    statementn;
}
```

Java evaluates the value, and if it matches one of the constants, executes the statements starting with the next one following that constant. If a case includes no `break` statement, execution falls through to the next statement, even if the code contains an intervening label.

The `if` **statement**

```
if (condition)
   {
      statement1;
      statement2;
      ...
   }
[else
   {
      statement3;
      statement4;
      ...
   }]
```

Java evaluates the condition; if it is true, Java executes the statements in the following block. If the condition is false and the optional else block is present, Java executes the statements in the else block.

CONTROL FLOW (CONTINUED)

The try/catch/finally
statement

```
try
  {
     statement1;
     statement2;
     ...
  }
catch (throwable1 t1)
  {
     statement3;
     statement4;
     ...
  }
catch (throwable2 t2)
  {
     statement5;
     statement6;
     ...
  }
finally
  {
     statement6;
     statement7;
     ...
  }
```

Java executes the statements in the try block. If an exception occurs, Java checks each catch block in order until it finds a variable of the given type to which it can assign a value of the exception object's type. If such a block exists, Java executes its statements. Regardless of whether Java throws an exception, after it can no longer execute statements in the try block or any catch block, Java executes the statements in the finally block.

Zero or more catch blocks and zero or one finally block may follow a try block; at least one catch or one finally block must follow a try.

The break **and** continue
statements

```
break [label];
```

With no label, Java exits any enclosing while, for, or switch statement. With a label, Java exits any number of nested do, while, for, or switch statements until it encounters the one labeled with the corresponding name; Java then continues execution with the statement immediately after that loop.

```
continue [label];
```

With no label, Java begins the next iteration of the enclosing do, while, or for loop by evaluating the loop condition. With a label, Java breaks out of any number of enclosing do, while, or for loops until it encounters the one that the label names; Java continues by evaluating the condition for that loop.

USEFUL WEB SITES

www.javasoft.com

Java's home page. From here, you can find Java software and documentation, news, helpful hints, and a lot more.

www.javasoft.com/docs/books/tutorial/?frontpage

Sun's online Java tutorial. A wealth of examples and explanations are available here.

www.afu.com/javafaq.htm

The Java programming Frequently Asked Questions list. A great resource when you have a "How do I . . . ?" question.

www.javaworld.com

Java World, an online magazine for Java programmers. This site has many useful technical articles.

www.alphaworks.ibm.com/

IBM's AlphaWorks site. It offers a huge selection of interesting Java tools for free trial and commercial licensing.

**www.10.software.ibm.com/developerworks/
opensource/jikes/project/**

The home page for Jikes, IBM's fast, compliant open-source Java compiler.

www.sys-con.com/java/

The Web site for Java Developer's Journal, another print and online Java magazine.

XML QUICK REFERENCE

While XML allows for the creation of large, complex documents, the XML language itself is quite compact and easy to learn. Here is a quick reference of the XML language that you can use when creating your XML documents and applications.

THE XML DECLARATION

Syntax

```
<?xml version="1.0"  encoding="UTF-8" standalone="no"  ?>
```

`version` is the version of XML.

`encoding` is the character coding of the document, usually `UTF-8`, but it can also be:

`UTF-16`

`EUC-JP`

`ISO10646-UCS2`

`standalone` indicates if an external DTD is to be used. Can be `"yes"` or `"no"`.

THE DOCUMENT-TYPE DECLARATION

Syntax

```
<!DOCTYPE    docname    External-ID       [  declarations            ]  >
```

Starts with the word `DOCTYPE`. `docname` is the name of the document type. `External-ID` is the location of an external file.

`declarations` is the optional DTD declarations.

THE NOTATION DECLARATION

Syntax

```
<!NOTATION        name          External-ID   >
```

Starts with the word `NOTATION`. `name` is the unique name of the format. `External-ID` identifies the notation.

COMMENTS

Syntax

```
<--          comment          -->
```

`comment` **can be any string of characters, but must not contain '–'.**

PROCESSING INSTRUCTIONS

Syntax

```
<?target        value        ?>
```

`target` **is typically the name of the intended application.** `value` **is the textual data to pass to the target application.**

PREDEFINED GENERAL ENTITIES

DESCRIPTION	ENTITY	SYMBOL	VALUE
Ampersand	&amp;	&	&#38;
Less than	&lt;	<	&#60;
Greater than	&gt;	>	&#62;
Apostrophe	&apos;	'	&#39;
Quote	&quot;	"	&#34;

INTERNAL ENTITIES

Syntax

```
<!ENTITY      name      "   replacement text      "   >
```

Starts with the word `ENTITY`. `name` **is the name of the entity.** `replacement text` **is the value of the entity.**

EXTERNAL ENTITIES

Syntax

```
<!ENTITY          name          External-ID   NDATA      notname >
```

Starts with the word `ENTITY`. `name` **is the name of the entity.** `External-ID` **is the location of a file.** `notname` **is the name of a notation.**

XML QUICK REFERENCE (CONTINUED)

INTERNAL PARAMETER ENTITIES

Syntax

```
<!ENTITY  %  name     "  replacement text      "   >
```

Starts with the word ENTITY. name is the name of the entity. replacement text is the value of the entity.

EXTERNAL PARAMETER ENTITIES

Syntax

```
<!ENTITY       %      name          External-ID  >
```

Starts with the word ENTITY. name is the name of the entity. External-ID is the location of a file.

CDATA SECTIONS

Syntax

```
<![CDATA [           textual data             ]]>
```

textual data can be any string of characters, but must not contain ']]'.

ELEMENT TAGS

Element with Content

```
<element>content</element>
```

element is the name of the element.

content is the content model of the element.

Empty Element

```
<element/ >
```

```
<element name="value">content</element>
```

name is the name of the attribute.

value is the string value of the attribute. You can use double quotes, as this example shows, or, alternatively, single quotes.

ELEMENT DECLARATIONS

Syntax

```
<!ELEMENT    name    (content)>
```

Starts with the word ENTITY. name is the name of the element.

content is the type of data in the element; it can be:

ANY	any type of data
EMPTY	no data
#PCDATA	parsed character data

ATTRIBUTE DECLARATIONS

Syntax

<!ATTLIST   element   name   value   default >

Starts with the word ATTLIST. element is the name of the element. name is the name of the attribute. value indicates the type of value; it can be:

CDATA	character data
NMTOKEN	single name token
NMTOKENS	multiple name tokens
ID	unique element identifier
ENTITY	an entity reference

default is the default value for the attribute.

WHAT'S ON THE CD-ROM

The CD-ROM included in this book contains many useful files and programs. Before installing any of the programs on the disc, make sure that you do not already have a newer version of the program already installed on your computer. For information on installing different versions of the same program, contact the program's manufacturer. For the latest and greatest information, please refer to the ReadMe file located at the root level of the CD-ROM.

SYSTEM REQUIREMENTS

To use the contents of the CD-ROM, your computer must have the following hardware and software:

- A PC with a Pentium or faster processor
- Microsoft Windows 95, 98, ME, NT 4.0, 2000, or XP
- At least 128MB of physical RAM installed on your computer
- A double-speed (8x) or faster CD-ROM drive
- A monitor capable of displaying at least 256 colors or grayscale
- A network card

AUTHOR'S SOURCE CODE

These files contain all the sample code from the book. You can browse the files directly from the CD-ROM, or you can copy them to your hard drive and use them as the basis for your own projects. To find the files on the CD-ROM, open the D:\Samples folder.

ACROBAT VERSION

The CD-ROM contains an e-version of this book that you can view and search using Adobe Acrobat Reader. You cannot print the pages or copy text from the Acrobat files. The CD-ROM includes an evaluation version of Adobe Acrobat Reader.

INSTALLING AND USING THE SOFTWARE

For your convenience, the software titles appearing on the CD-ROM are listed alphabetically.

Acrobat Reader

For Windows 95/98/NT/2000 and Linux. Freeware.

Adobe Acrobat Reader allows you to view the online version of this book. For more information on using Acrobat Reader, see the section "Using the e-Version of this Book" in this Appendix. For more information about Acrobat Reader and Adobe Systems, see www.adobe.com.

Crimson

For all platforms. Open Source.

Crimson is a Java XML parser that you can access from within the Java code you create. The Crimson XML parser supports JAXP, SAX, and the DOM API. For more information about the Crimson XML parser, see http://xml.apache.org/crimson/.

GNU JAXP

For all platforms. GNU Public License.

GNU JAXP is a no-cost version of the standard XML processing API, SAX, DOM, and JAXP, for Java. For more information and updates, and for the latest version of GNU JAXP, see http://www.gnu.org/software/classpathx/jaxp/.

Java 2 SDK, Standard Edition v1.3.1

For Windows 95/98/NT/2000/XP and Linux. Sun Microsystems Public License.

You can use the standard edition of the Java 2 platform by Sun Microsystems to create, execute, and assist in deploying Java applications. For more information, see http://java.sun.com/j2se/.

JDOM

For Windows 95/98/NT/2000/XP and Linux. Open Source.

JDOM is a programming API that accesses XML documents from within your Java code. For more information and the latest updates, see http://www.jdom.org/.

JPad Pro

For Windows 95/98/NT/2000/XP. Shareware.

JPad Pro is an integrated development environment that creates, compiles, and executes Java applications. For more information, see http://www.modelworks.com/products.html.

UltraEdit

For Windows 95/98/NT/2000/XP. Shareware.

UltraEdit is a text editor that creates code in many languages, including Java and XML. UltraEdit has many features to make coding easier and more efficient. For more information, see http://www.ultraedit.com/.

Xerces Java Parser

For all platforms. Open Source.

Xerces is an XML parser that you can access from within your Java applications. Xerces is currently the most popular XML parser for use with Java applications. For more information and updates, see http://xml.apache.org/xerces-j/.

XML Pro

For Windows 95/98/NT/2000/XP. Shareware.

XML Pro is an XML editor that you can use to create XML documents. As well as having a full range of editing capabilities, XML Pro fully supports the Java SDK. For more information, see http://www.vervet.com/demo.html.

XML Spy Suite

For Windows 95/98/NT/2000/XP. Shareware.

XML Spy is an application that creates and validates XML documents including DTDs and schemas. For more information, see http://www.xmlspy.com.

TROUBLESHOOTING

The programs on the CD-ROM should work on computers with the minimum of system requirements. However, some programs may not work properly.

The two most likely reasons for the programs not working properly include not having enough memory (RAM) for the programs you want to use, or having other programs running that affect the installation or running of a program. If you receive error messages such as Not enough memory or Setup cannot continue, try one or more of the methods below and then try using the software again:

- Turn off any anti-virus software
- Close all running programs
- In Windows, close the CD-ROM interface and run demos or installations directly from Windows Explorer
- Have your local computer store add more RAM to your computer

If you still have trouble installing the items from the CD-ROM, call the Wiley Publishing Customer Service phone number: 800-762-2974 (outside the U.S.: 317-572-3994). You can also contact Wiley Publishing Customer Service by e-mail at techsupdum@wiley.com.

USING THE E-VERSION OF THIS BOOK

You can view *Java and XML: Your visual blueprint for creating Java-enhanced Web programs* on your screen using the CD-ROM included at the back of this book. The CD-ROM allows you to search the contents of each chapter of the book for a specific word or phrase. The CD-ROM also provides a convenient way of keeping the book handy while traveling.

You must install Adobe Acrobat Reader on your computer before you can view the book on the CD-ROM. The

CD-ROM includes this program for your convenience. Acrobat Reader allows you to view Portable Document Format (PDF) files, which can display books and magazines on your screen exactly as they appear in printed form.

To view the content of this book using Acrobat Reader, display the contents of the CD-ROM. Double-click the Book folder to display the contents of the folder. In the window that appears, double-click the icon for the chapter of the book you want to review.

USING THE E-VERSION OF THE BOOK

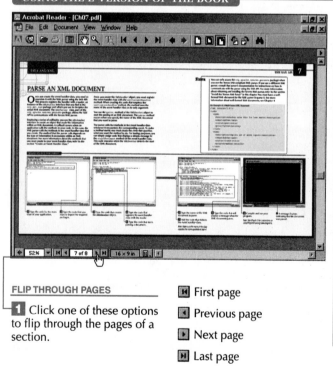

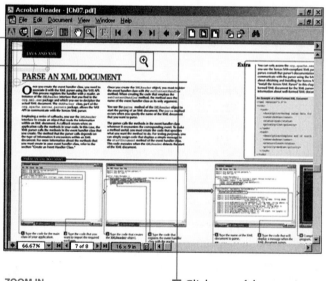

FLIP THROUGH PAGES

-1 Click one of these options to flip through the pages of a section.

- First page
- Previous page
- Next page
- Last page

ZOOM IN

-1 Click to magnify an area of the page.

-2 Click the area of the page you want to magnify.

■ Click one of these options to display the page at 100% magnification (□) or to fit the entire page inside the window (□).

Extra

To install Acrobat Reader, insert the CD-ROM into a drive. In the screen that appears, click Software. Click Acrobat Reader and then follow the instructions on your screen to install the program.

You can make searching the book more convenient by copying the PDF files to your computer. To do this, display the contents of the CD-ROM and then copy the Book folder from the CD-ROM to your hard drive. This allows you to easily access the contents of the book at any time.

Acrobat Reader is a popular and useful program. There are many files available on the Web that are designed to be viewed using Acrobat Reader. Look for files with the .pdf extension. For more information about Acrobat Reader, visit the www.adobe.com/products/acrobat/readermain.html Web site.

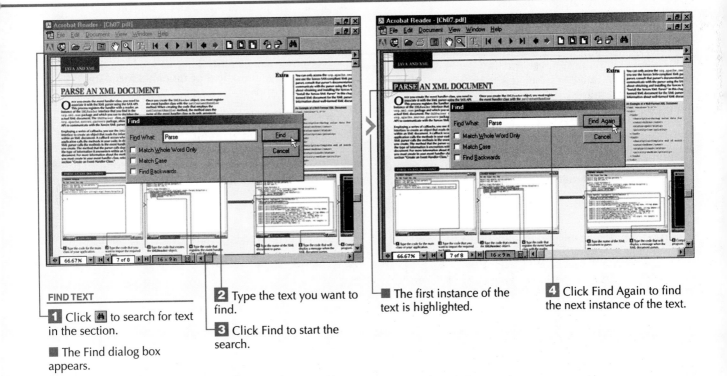

FIND TEXT

1 Click 🔍 to search for text in the section.

■ The Find dialog box appears.

2 Type the text you want to find.

3 Click Find to start the search.

■ The first instance of the text is highlighted.

4 Click Find Again to find the next instance of the text.

APPENDIX

END-USER LICENSE AGREEMENT

READ THIS. You should carefully read these terms and conditions before opening the software packet(s) included with *Java and XML: Your visual blueprint for creating Java-enhanced Web programs*. This is a license agreement ("Agreement") between you and "Wiley Publishing". By opening the accompanying software packet(s), you acknowledge that you have read and accept the following terms and conditions. If you do not agree and do not want to be bound by such terms and conditions, promptly return the Book and the unopened software packet(s) to the place you obtained them from for a full refund.

1. License Grant. Wiley Publishing grants to you (either an individual or entity) a nonexclusive license to use one copy of the enclosed software program(s) (collectively, the "Software") solely for your own personal or business purposes on a single computer (whether a standard computer or a workstation component of a multi-user network). The Software is in use on a computer when it is loaded into temporary memory (RAM) or installed into permanent memory (hard disc, CD-ROM, or other storage device). Wiley Publishing reserves all rights not expressly granted herein.

2. Ownership. Wiley Publishing is the owner of all right, title, and interest, including copyright, in and to the compilation of the Software recorded on the disc(s) or CD-ROM ("Software Media"). Copyright to the individual programs recorded on the Software Media is owned by the author, or other authorized copyright owner of each program. Ownership of the Software and all proprietary rights relating thereto remain with Wiley Publishing and its licensers.

3. Restrictions on Use and Transfer.

(a) You may only (i) make one copy of the Software for backup or archival purposes, or (ii) transfer the Software to a single hard disc, provided that you keep the original for backup or archival purposes. You may not (i) rent or lease the Software, (ii) copy or reproduce the Software through a LAN or other network system or through any computer subscriber system or bulletin-board system, or (iii) modify, adapt, or create derivative works based on the Software.

(b) You may not reverse engineer, decompile, or disassemble the Software. You may transfer the Software and user documentation on a permanent basis, provided that the transferee agrees to accept the terms and conditions of this Agreement and you retain no copies. If the Software is an update or has been updated, any transfer must include the most recent update and all prior versions.

4. Restrictions on Use of Individual Programs. You must follow the individual requirements and restrictions detailed for each individual program in Appendix D of this Book. These limitations are also contained in the individual license agreements recorded on the Software Media. These limitations may include a requirement that after using the program for a specified period of time, the user must pay a registration fee or discontinue use. By opening the Software packet(s), you will be agreeing to abide by the licenses and restrictions for these individual programs that are detailed in Appendix D and on the Software Media. None of the material on this Software Media or listed in this Book may ever be redistributed, in original or modified form, for commercial purposes.

5. Limited Warranty.

(a) Wiley Publishing warrants that the Software and Software Media are free from defects in materials and workmanship under normal use for a period of sixty (60) days from the date of purchase of this Book. If Wiley Publishing receives notification within the warranty period of defects in materials or workmanship, Wiley Publishing will replace the defective Software Media.

(b) WILEY PUBLISHING AND THE AUTHOR OF THE BOOK DISCLAIM ALL OTHER WARRANTIES, EXPRESS OR IMPLIED, INCLUDING WITHOUT LIMITATION IMPLIED WARRANTIES OF MERCHANTABILITY AND FITNESS FOR A PARTICULAR PURPOSE, WITH RESPECT TO THE SOFTWARE, THE PROGRAMS, THE SOURCE

CODE CONTAINED THEREIN, AND/OR THE TECHNIQUES DESCRIBED IN THIS BOOK. WILEY PUBLISHING DOES NOT WARRANT THAT THE FUNCTIONS CONTAINED IN THE SOFTWARE WILL MEET YOUR REQUIREMENTS OR THAT THE OPERATION OF THE SOFTWARE WILL BE ERROR FREE.

(c) This limited warranty gives you specific legal rights, and you may have other rights that vary from jurisdiction to jurisdiction.

6.   Remedies.

(a) Wiley Publishing's entire liability and your exclusive remedy for defects in materials and workmanship shall be limited to replacement of the Software Media, which may be returned to Wiley Publishing with a copy of your receipt at the following address: Software Media Fulfillment Department, Attn.: Java and XML: Your visual blueprint for creating Java-enhanced Web programs, Wiley Publishing, Inc., 10475 Crosspoint Blvd., Indianapolis, IN 46256, or call 1-800-762-2974. Please allow four to six weeks for delivery. This Limited Warranty is void if failure of the Software Media has resulted from accident, abuse or misapplication. Any replacement Software Media will be warranted for the remainder of the original warranty period or thirty (30) days, whichever is longer.

(b) In no event shall Wiley Publishing or the author be liable for any damages whatsoever (including without limitation damages for loss of business profits, business interruption, loss of business information, or any other pecuniary loss) arising from the use of or inability to use the Book or the Software, even if Wiley Publishing has been advised of the possibility of such damages.

(c) Because some jurisdictions do not allow the exclusion or limitation of liability for consequential or incidental damages, the above limitation or exclusion may not apply to you.

7.   U.S. Government Restricted Rights. Use, duplication, or disclosure of the Software for or on behalf of the United States of America, its agencies and/or

instrumentalities (the "U.S. Government") is subject to restrictions as stated in paragraph (c)(1)(ii) of the Rights in Technical Data and Computer Software clause of DFARS 252.227-7013, or subparagraphs (c) (1) and (2) of the Commercial Computer Software - Restricted Rights clause at FAR 52.227-19, and in similar clauses in the NASA FAR supplement, as applicable.

8.   General. This Agreement constitutes the entire understanding of the parties and revokes and supersedes all prior agreements, oral or written, between them and may not be modified or amended except in a writing signed by both parties hereto that specifically refers to this Agreement. This Agreement shall take precedence over any other documents that may be in conflict herewith. If any one or more provisions contained in this Agreement are held by any court or tribunal to be invalid, illegal, or otherwise unenforceable, each and every other provision shall remain in full force and effect.

JAVA™ END-USER LICENSE AGREEMENT

FORTE FOR JAVA, RELEASE 3.0, COMMUNITY EDITION, ENGLISH

SUN MICROSYSTEMS, INC.
BINARY CODE LICENSE AGREEMENT

To obtain Forte for Java, release 3.0, Community Edition, English, you must agree to the software license below.

READ THE TERMS OF THIS AGREEMENT AND ANY PROVIDED SUPPLEMENTAL LICENSE TERMS (COLLECTIVELY "AGREEMENT") CAREFULLY BEFORE OPENING THE SOFTWARE MEDIA PACKAGE. BY OPENING THE SOFTWARE MEDIA PACKAGE, YOU AGREE TO THE TERMS OF THIS AGREEMENT. IF YOU ARE ACCESSING THE SOFTWARE ELECTRONICALLY, INDICATE YOUR ACCEPTANCE OF THESE TERMS BY SELECTING THE "ACCEPT" BUTTON AT THE END OF THIS AGREEMENT. IF YOU DO NOT AGREE TO ALL THESE TERMS, PROMPTLY RETURN THE UNUSED SOFTWARE TO YOUR PLACE OF PURCHASE FOR A REFUND OR, IF THE SOFTWARE IS ACCESSED ELECTRONICALLY, SELECT THE "DECLINE" BUTTON AT THE END OF THIS AGREEMENT.

1. **LICENSE TO USE.** Sun grants you a non-exclusive and non-transferable license for the internal use only of the accompanying software and documentation and any error corrections provided by Sun (collectively "Software"), by the number of users and the class of computer hardware for which the corresponding fee has been paid.

2. **RESTRICTIONS.** Software is confidential and copyrighted. Title to Software and all associated intellectual property rights is retained by Sun and/or its licensors. Except as specifically authorized in any Supplemental License Terms, you may not make copies of Software, other than a single copy of Software for archival purposes. Unless enforcement is prohibited by applicable law, you may not modify, decompile, or reverse engineer Software. You acknowledge that Software is not designed, licensed or intended for use in the design, construction, operation or maintenance of any nuclear facility. Sun disclaims any express or implied warranty of fitness for such uses. No right, title or interest in or to any trademark, service mark, logo or trade name of Sun or its licensors is granted under this Agreement.

3. **LIMITED WARRANTY.** Sun warrants to you that for a period of ninety (90) days from the date of purchase, as evidenced by a copy of the receipt, the media on which Software is furnished (if any) will be free of defects in materials and workmanship under normal use. Except for the foregoing, Software is provided "AS IS". Your exclusive remedy and Sun's entire liability under this limited warranty will be at Sun's option to replace Software media or refund the fee paid for Software.

4. **DISCLAIMER OF WARRANTY.** UNLESS SPECIFIED IN THIS AGREEMENT, ALL EXPRESS OR IMPLIED CONDITIONS, REPRESENTATIONS AND WARRANTIES, INCLUDING ANY IMPLIED WARRANTY OF MERCHANTABILITY, FITNESS FOR A PARTICULAR PURPOSE OR NON-INFRINGEMENT ARE DISCLAIMED, EXCEPT TO THE EXTENT THAT THESE DISCLAIMERS ARE HELD TO BE LEGALLY INVALID.

5. **LIMITATION OF LIABILITY.** TO THE EXTENT NOT PROHIBITED BY LAW, IN NO EVENT WILL SUN OR ITS LICENSORS BE LIABLE FOR ANY LOST REVENUE, PROFIT OR DATA, OR FOR SPECIAL, INDIRECT, CONSEQUENTIAL, INCIDENTAL OR PUNITIVE DAMAGES, HOWEVER CAUSED REGARDLESS OF THE THEORY OF LIABILITY, ARISING OUT OF OR RELATED TO THE USE OF OR INABILITY TO USE SOFTWARE, EVEN IF SUN HAS BEEN ADVISED OF THE POSSIBILITY OF SUCH DAMAGES. In no event will Sun's liability to you, whether in contract, tort (including negligence), or otherwise, exceed the amount paid by you for Software under this Agreement. The foregoing limitations will apply even if the above stated warranty fails of its essential purpose.

6. **Termination.** This Agreement is effective until terminated. You may terminate this Agreement at any time by destroying all copies of Software. This Agreement will terminate immediately without notice from Sun if you fail to comply with any provision of this Agreement. Upon Termination, you must destroy all copies of Software.

7. **Export Regulations.** All Software and technical data delivered under this Agreement are subject to US export control laws and may be subject to export or import regulations in other countries. You agree to comply strictly with all such laws and regulations and acknowledge that you have the responsibility to obtain such licenses to export, re-export, or import as may be required after delivery to you.

8. **U.S. Government Restricted Rights.** If Software is being acquired by or on behalf of the U.S. Government or by a U.S. Government prime contractor or subcontractor (at any tier), then the Government's rights in Software and accompanying documentation will be only as set forth in this Agreement; this is in accordance with 48 CFR 227.7201 through 227.7202-4 (for Department of Defense (DOD) acquisitions) and with 48 CFR 2.101 and 12.212 (for non-DOD acquisitions).

9. **Governing Law.** Any action related to this Agreement will be governed by California law and controlling U.S. federal law. No choice of law rules of any jurisdiction will apply.

10. **Severability.** If any provision of this Agreement is held to be unenforceable, this Agreement will remain in effect with the provision omitted, unless omission would frustrate the intent of the parties, in which case this Agreement will immediately terminate.

11. **Integration.** This Agreement is the entire agreement between you and Sun relating to its subject matter. It supersedes all prior or contemporaneous oral or written communications, proposals, representations and warranties and prevails over any conflicting or additional terms of any quote, order, acknowledgment, or other communication between the parties relating to its subject matter during the term of this Agreement. No modification of this Agreement will be binding, unless in writing and signed by an authorized representative of each party.

FORTE™ FOR JAVA™, RELEASE 3.0, COMMUNITY EDITION

SUPPLEMENTAL LICENSE TERMS

These supplemental license terms ("Supplemental Terms") add to or modify the terms of the Binary Code License Agreement (collectively, the "Agreement"). Capitalized terms not defined in these Supplemental Terms shall have the same meanings ascribed to them in the Agreement. These Supplemental Terms shall supersede any inconsistent or conflicting terms in the Agreement, or in any license contained within the Software.

1. **Software Internal Use and Development License Grant.** Subject to the terms and conditions of this Agreement, including, but not limited to Section 4 (Java™ Technology Restrictions) of these Supplemental Terms, Sun grants you a non-exclusive, non-transferable, limited license to reproduce internally and use internally the binary form of the Software complete and unmodified for the sole purpose of designing, developing and testing your Java applets and applications intended to run on the Java platform ("Programs").

2. **License to Distribute Software.** Subject to the terms and conditions of this Agreement, including, but not limited to Section 4 (Java™ Technology Restrictions) of these Supplemental Terms, Sun grants you a non-exclusive, non-transferable, limited license to reproduce and distribute the Software in binary code form only, provided that (i) you distribute the Software complete and unmodified and only bundled as part of, and for the sole purpose of running, your Programs, (ii) the Programs add significant and primary functionality to the Software, (iii) you do not distribute additional software intended to replace any component(s) of the Software, (iv) for a particular version of the Java platform, any executable output generated by a compiler that is contained in the Software must (a) only be compiled from source code that conforms to the corresponding version of the OEM Java Language Specification; (b) be in the class file format defined by the corresponding version of the OEM Java Virtual Machine Specification; and (c) execute properly on a reference runtime, as specified by Sun, associated with such version of the Java platform, (v) you do not remove or alter any proprietary legends or notices contained in the Software, (v) you only distribute the Software subject to a license agreement that protects Sun's interests consistent with the terms contained in this Agreement, and (vi) you agree to defend and indemnify Sun and its licensors from and against any damages, costs, liabilities, settlement amounts and/or expenses (including attorneys' fees) incurred in connection with any claim, lawsuit or action by any third party that arises or results from the use or distribution of any and all Programs and/or Software.

3. **License to Distribute Redistributables.** Subject to the terms and conditions of this Agreement, including but not limited to Section 4 (Java Technology Restrictions) of these Supplemental Terms, Sun grants you a non-

exclusive, non-transferable, limited license to reproduce and distribute the binary form of those files specifically identified as redistributable in the Software "RELEASE NOTES" file ("Redistributables") provided that: (i) you distribute the Redistributables complete and unmodified (unless otherwise specified in the applicable RELEASE NOTES file), and only bundled as part of Programs, (ii) you do not distribute additional software intended to supersede any component(s) of the Redistributables, (iii) you do not remove or alter any proprietary legends or notices contained in or on the Redistributables, (iv) for a particular version of the Java platform, any executable output generated by a compiler that is contained in the Software must (a) only be compiled from source code that conforms to the corresponding version of the OEM Java Language Specification; (b) be in the class file format defined by the corresponding version of the OEM Java Virtual Machine Specification; and (c) execute properly on a reference runtime, as specified by Sun, associated with such version of the Java platform, (v) you only distribute the Redistributables pursuant to a license agreement that protects Sun's interests consistent with the terms contained in the Agreement, and (v) you agree to defend and indemnify Sun and its licensors from and against any damages, costs, liabilities, settlement amounts and/or expenses (including attorneys' fees) incurred in connection with any claim, lawsuit or action by any third party that arises or results from the use or distribution of any and all Programs and/or Software.

4. **Java Technology Restrictions.** You may not modify the Java Platform Interface ("JPI, identified as classes contained within the "java" package or any subpackages of the "java" package), by creating additional classes within the JPI or otherwise causing the addition to or modification of the classes in the JPI. In the event that you create an additional class and associated API(s) which (i) extends the functionality of the Java platform, and (ii) is exposed to third party software developers for the purpose of developing additional software which invokes such additional API, you must promptly publish broadly an accurate specification for such API for free use by all developers. You may not create, or authorize your licensees to create, additional classes, interfaces, or subpackages that are in any way identified as "java", "javax", "sun" or similar convention as specified by Sun in any naming convention designation.

5. **Java Runtime Availability.** Refer to the appropriate version of the Java Runtime Environment binary code license (currently located at http://www.java.sun.com/jdk/index.html) for the availability of runtime code which may be distributed with Java applets and applications.

6. **Trademarks and Logos.** You acknowledge and agree as between you and Sun that Sun owns the SUN, SOLARIS, JAVA, JINI, FORTE, and iPLANET trademarks and all SUN, SOLARIS, JAVA, JINI, FORTE, and iPLANET-related trademarks, service marks, logos and other brand designations ("Sun Marks"), and you agree to comply with the Sun Trademark and Logo Usage Requirements currently located at http://www.sun.com/policies/trademarks. Any use you make of the Sun Marks inures to Sun's benefit.

7. **Source Code.** Software may contain source code that is provided solely for reference purposes pursuant to the terms of this Agreement. Source code may not be redistributed unless expressly provided for in this Agreement.

8. **Termination for Infringement.** Either party may terminate this Agreement immediately should any Software become, or in either party's opinion be likely to become, the subject of a claim of infringement of any intellectual property right.

For inquiries please contact: Sun Microsystems, Inc. 901

San Antonio Road, Palo Alto, California 94303

(LFI#91205/Form ID#011801)

TERMS AND CONDITIONS OF THE LICENSE & EXPORT FOR JAVA™ 2 SDK, STANDARD EDITION 1.4.0 SUN MICROSYSTEMS, INC.
BINARY CODE LICENSE AGREEMENT
READ THE TERMS OF THIS AGREEMENT AND ANY PROVIDED SUPPLEMENTAL LICENSE TERMS (COLLECTIVELY "AGREEMENT") CAREFULLY BEFORE OPENING THE SOFTWARE MEDIA PACKAGE. BY OPENING THE SOFTWARE MEDIA PACKAGE, YOU AGREE TO THE TERMS OF THIS AGREEMENT. IF YOU ARE ACCESSING THE SOFTWARE ELECTRONICALLY, INDICATE YOUR ACCEPTANCE OF THESE TERMS BY SELECTING THE "ACCEPT" BUTTON AT THE END OF THIS AGREEMENT. IF YOU DO NOT AGREE TO ALL THESE TERMS, PROMPTLY RETURN THE

UNUSED SOFTWARE TO YOUR PLACE OF PURCHASE FOR A REFUND OR, IF THE SOFTWARE IS ACCESSED ELECTRONICALLY, SELECT THE "DECLINE" BUTTON AT THE END OF THIS AGREEMENT.

1. **LICENSE TO USE.** Sun grants you a non-exclusive and non-transferable license for the internal use only of the accompanying software and documentation and any error corrections provided by Sun (collectively "Software"), by the number of users and the class of computer hardware for which the corresponding fee has been paid.

2. **RESTRICTIONS.** Software is confidential and copyrighted. Title to Software and all associated intellectual property rights is retained by Sun and/or its licensors. Except as specifically authorized in any Supplemental License Terms, you may not make copies of Software, other than a single copy of Software for archival purposes. Unless enforcement is prohibited by applicable law, you may not modify, decompile, or reverse engineer Software. You acknowledge that Software is not designed, licensed or intended for use in the design, construction, operation or maintenance of any nuclear facility. Sun disclaims any express or implied warranty of fitness for such uses. No right, title or interest in or to any trademark, service mark, logo or trade name of Sun or its licensors is granted under this Agreement.

3. **LIMITED WARRANTY.** Sun warrants to you that for a period of ninety (90) days from the date of purchase, as evidenced by a copy of the receipt, the media on which Software is furnished (if any) will be free of defects in materials and workmanship under normal use. Except for the foregoing, Software is provided "AS IS". Your exclusive remedy and Sun's entire liability under this limited warranty will be at Sun's option to replace Software media or refund the fee paid for Software.

4. **DISCLAIMER OF WARRANTY.** UNLESS SPECIFIED IN THIS AGREEMENT, ALL EXPRESS OR IMPLIED CONDITIONS, REPRESENTATIONS AND WARRANTIES, INCLUDING ANY IMPLIED WARRANTY OF MERCHANTABILITY, FITNESS FOR A PARTICULAR PURPOSE OR NON-INFRINGEMENT ARE DISCLAIMED, EXCEPT TO THE EXTENT THAT THESE DISCLAIMERS ARE HELD TO BE LEGALLY INVALID.

5. **LIMITATION OF LIABILITY.** TO THE EXTENT NOT PROHIBITED BY LAW, IN NO EVENT WILL SUN OR ITS LICENSORS BE LIABLE FOR ANY LOST REVENUE, PROFIT OR DATA, OR FOR SPECIAL, INDIRECT, CONSEQUENTIAL, INCIDENTAL OR PUNITIVE DAMAGES, HOWEVER CAUSED REGARDLESS OF THE THEORY OF LIABILITY, ARISING OUT OF OR RELATED TO THE USE OF OR INABILITY TO USE SOFTWARE, EVEN IF SUN HAS BEEN ADVISED OF THE POSSIBILITY OF SUCH DAMAGES. In no event will Sun's liability to you, whether in contract, tort (including negligence), or otherwise, exceed the amount paid by you for Software under this Agreement. The foregoing limitations will apply even if the above stated warranty fails of its essential purpose.

6. **Termination.** This Agreement is effective until terminated. You may terminate this Agreement at any time by destroying all copies of Software. This Agreement will terminate immediately without notice from Sun if you fail to comply with any provision of this Agreement. Upon Termination, you must destroy all copies of Software.

7. **Export Regulations.** All Software and technical data delivered under this Agreement are subject to US export control laws and may be subject to export or import regulations in other countries. You agree to comply strictly with all such laws and regulations and acknowledge that you have the responsibility to obtain such licenses to export, re-export, or import as may be required after delivery to you.

8. **U.S. Government Restricted Rights.** If Software is being acquired by or on behalf of the U.S. Government or by a U.S. Government prime contractor or subcontractor (at any tier), then the Government's rights in Software and accompanying documentation will be only as set forth in this Agreement; this is in accordance with 48 CFR 227.7201 through 227.7202-4 (for Department of Defense (DOD) acquisitions) and with 48 CFR 2.101 and 12.212 (for non-DOD acquisitions).

9. **Governing Law.** Any action related to this Agreement will be governed by California law and controlling U.S. federal law. No choice of law rules of any jurisdiction will apply.

10. **Severability.** If any provision of this Agreement is held to be unenforceable, this Agreement will remain in effect with the provision omitted, unless omission would frustrate the intent of the parties, in which case this Agreement will immediately terminate.

11. Integration. This Agreement is the entire agreement between you and Sun relating to its subject matter. It supersedes all prior or contemporaneous oral or written communications, proposals, representations and warranties and prevails over any conflicting or additional terms of any quote, order, acknowledgment, or other communication between the parties relating to its subject matter during the term of this Agreement. No modification of this Agreement will be binding, unless in writing and signed by an authorized representative of each party.

JAVATM 2 SOFTWARE DEVELOPMENT KIT (J2SDK), STANDARD EDITION, VERSION 1.4.X
SUPPLEMENTAL LICENSE TERMS

These supplemental license terms ("Supplemental Terms") add to or modify the terms of the Binary Code License Agreement (collectively, the "Agreement"). Capitalized terms not defined in these Supplemental Terms shall have the same meanings ascribed to them in the Agreement. These Supplemental Terms shall supersede any inconsistent or conflicting terms in the Agreement, or in any license contained within the Software.

1. Software Internal Use and Development License Grant. Subject to the terms and conditions of this Agreement, including, but not limited to Section 4 (Java Technology Restrictions) of these Supplemental Terms, Sun grants you a non-exclusive, non-transferable, limited license to reproduce internally and use internally the binary form of the Software complete and unmodified for the sole purpose of designing, developing and testing your Java applets and applications intended to run on the Java platform ("Programs").

2. License to Distribute Software. Subject to the terms and conditions of this Agreement, including, but not limited to Section 4 (Java Technology Restrictions) of these Supplemental Terms, Sun grants you a non-exclusive, non-transferable, limited license to reproduce and distribute the Software, provided that (i) you distribute the Software complete and unmodified (unless otherwise specified in the applicable README file) and only bundled as part of, and for the sole purpose of running, your Programs, (ii) the Programs add significant and primary functionality to the Software, (iii) you do not distribute additional software intended to replace any component(s) of the Software (unless otherwise specified in the applicable README file), (iv) you do not remove or alter any proprietary legends or notices contained in the Software, (v) you only distribute the Software subject to a license agreement that protects Sun's interests consistent with the terms contained in this Agreement, and (vi) you agree to defend and indemnify Sun and its licensors from and against any damages, costs, liabilities, settlement amounts and/or expenses (including attorneys' fees) incurred in connection with any claim, lawsuit or action by any third party that arises or results from the use or distribution of any and all Programs and/or Software. (vi) include the following statement as part of product documentation (whether hard copy or electronic), as a part of a copyright page or proprietary rights notice page, in an "About" box or in any other form reasonably designed to make the statement visible to users of the Software: "This product includes code licensed from RSA Security, Inc.", and (vii) include the statement, "Some portions licensed from IBM are available at http://oss.software.ibm.com/icu4j/".

3. License to Distribute Redistributables. Subject to the terms and conditions of this Agreement, including but not limited to Section 4 (Java Technology Restrictions) of these Supplemental Terms, Sun grants you a non-exclusive, non-transferable, limited license to reproduce and distribute those files specifically identified as redistributable in the Software "README" file ("Redistributables") provided that: (i) you distribute the Redistributables complete and unmodified (unless otherwise specified in the applicable README file), and only bundled as part of Programs, (ii) you do not distribute additional software intended to supersede any component(s) of the Redistributables (unless otherwise specified in the applicable README file), (iii) you do not remove or alter any proprietary legends or notices contained in or on the Redistributables, (iv) you only distribute the Redistributables pursuant to a license agreement that protects Sun's interests consistent with the terms contained in the Agreement, (v) you agree to defend and indemnify Sun and its licensors from and against any damages, costs, liabilities, settlement amounts and/or expenses (including attorneys' fees) incurred in connection with any claim, lawsuit or action by any third party that arises or results from the use or distribution of any and all Programs and/or Software, (vi) include the following statement as part of product documentation (whether hard copy or electronic), as a part of a copyright page or proprietary rights notice page, in an "About" box or in any

other form reasonably designed to make the statement visible to users of the Software: "This product includes code licensed from RSA Security, Inc.", and (vii) include the statement, "Some portions licensed from IBM are available at http://oss.software.ibm.com/icu4j/".

4. Java Technology Restrictions. You may not modify the Java Platform Interface ("JPI", identified as classes contained within the "java" package or any subpackages of the "java" package), by creating additional classes within the JPI or otherwise causing the addition to or modification of the classes in the JPI. In the event that you create an additional class and associated API(s) which (i) extends the functionality of the Java platform, and (ii) is exposed to third party software developers for the purpose of developing additional software which invokes such additional API, you must promptly publish broadly an accurate specification for such API for free use by all developers. You may not create, or authorize your licensees to create, additional classes, interfaces, or subpackages that are in any way identified as "java", "javax", "sun" or similar convention as specified by Sun in any naming convention designation.

5. Notice of Automatic Software Updates from Sun. You acknowledge that the Software may automatically download, install, and execute applets, applications, software extensions, and updated versions of the Software from Sun ("Software Updates"), which may require you to accept updated terms and conditions for installation. If additional terms and conditions are not presented on installation, the Software Updates will be considered part of the Software and subject to the terms and conditions of the Agreement.

6. Notice of Automatic Downloads. You acknowledge that, by your use of the Software and/or by requesting services that require use of the Software, the Software may automatically download, install, and execute software applications from sources other than Sun ("Other Software"). Sun makes no representations of a relationship of any kind to licensors of Other Software. TO THE EXTENT NOT PROHIBITED BY LAW, IN NO EVENT WILL SUN OR ITS LICENSORS BE LIABLE FOR ANY LOST REVENUE, PROFIT OR DATA, OR FOR SPECIAL, INDIRECT, CONSEQUENTIAL, INCIDENTAL OR PUNITIVE DAMAGES, HOWEVER CAUSED REGARDLESS OF THE THEORY OF LIABILITY, ARISING OUT OF OR RELATED TO THE USE OF OR INABILITY TO USE OTHER SOFTWARE, EVEN IF SUN HAS BEEN ADVISED OF THE POSSIBILITY OF SUCH DAMAGES.

7. Trademarks and Logos. You acknowledge and agree as between you and Sun that Sun owns the SUN, SOLARIS, JAVA, JINI, FORTE, and iPLANET trademarks and all SUN, SOLARIS, JAVA, JINI, FORTE, and iPLANET-related trademarks, service marks, logos and other brand designations ("Sun Marks"), and you agree to comply with the Sun Trademark and Logo Usage Requirements currently located at http://www.sun.com/policies/trademarks. Any use you make of the Sun Marks inures to Sun's benefit.

8. Source Code. Software may contain source code that is provided solely for reference purposes pursuant to the terms of this Agreement. Source code may not be redistributed unless expressly provided for in this Agreement.

9. Termination for Infringement. Either party may terminate this Agreement immediately should any Software become, or in either party's opinion be likely to become, the subject of a claim of infringement of any intellectual property right.

For inquiries please contact: Sun Microsystems, Inc. 901 San Antonio Road, Palo Alto, California 94303

(LFI#109998/Form ID#011801)

TERMS AND CONDITIONS OF THE LICENSE & EXPORT FOR JAVA™ 2 MICRO EDITION WIRELESS TOOLKIT 1.0.3 SUN MICROSYSTEMS, INC.
BINARY CODE LICENSE AGREEMENT

READ THE TERMS OF THIS AGREEMENT AND ANY PROVIDED SUPPLEMENTAL LICENSE TERMS (COLLECTIVELY "AGREEMENT") CAREFULLY BEFORE OPENING THE SOFTWARE MEDIA PACKAGE. BY OPENING THE SOFTWARE MEDIA PACKAGE, YOU AGREE TO THE TERMS OF THIS AGREEMENT. IF YOU ARE ACCESSING THE SOFTWARE ELECTRONICALLY, INDICATE YOUR ACCEPTANCE OF THESE TERMS BY SELECTING THE "ACCEPT" BUTTON AT THE END OF THIS AGREEMENT. IF YOU DO NOT AGREE TO ALL THESE TERMS, PROMPTLY RETURN THE UNUSED SOFTWARE TO YOUR PLACE OF PURCHASE FOR A REFUND OR, IF THE SOFTWARE IS ACCESSED ELECTRONICALLY, SELECT THE "DECLINE" BUTTON AT THE END OF THIS AGREEMENT.

1. LICENSE TO USE. Sun grants you a non-exclusive and non-transferable license for the internal use only of the accompanying software and documentation and any error corrections provided by Sun (collectively "Software"), by the number of users and the class of computer hardware for which the corresponding fee has been paid.

2. RESTRICTIONS. Software is confidential and copyrighted. Title to Software and all associated intellectual property rights is retained by Sun and/or its licensors. Except as specifically authorized in any Supplemental License Terms, you may not make copies of Software, other than a single copy of Software for archival purposes. Unless enforcement is prohibited by applicable law, you may not modify, decompile, or reverse engineer Software. You acknowledge that Software is not designed, licensed or intended for use in the design, construction, operation or maintenance of any nuclear facility. Sun disclaims any express or implied warranty of fitness for such uses. No right, title or interest in or to any trademark, service mark, logo or trade name of Sun or its licensors is granted under this Agreement.

3. LIMITED WARRANTY. Sun warrants to you that for a period of ninety (90) days from the date of purchase, as evidenced by a copy of the receipt, the media on which Software is furnished (if any) will be free of defects in materials and workmanship under normal use. Except for the foregoing, Software is provided "AS IS". Your exclusive remedy and Sun's entire liability under this limited warranty will be at Sun's option to replace Software media or refund the fee paid for Software.

4. DISCLAIMER OF WARRANTY. UNLESS SPECIFIED IN THIS AGREEMENT, ALL EXPRESS OR IMPLIED CONDITIONS, REPRESENTATIONS AND WARRANTIES, INCLUDING ANY IMPLIED WARRANTY OF MERCHANTABILITY, FITNESS FOR A PARTICULAR PURPOSE OR NON-INFRINGEMENT ARE DISCLAIMED, EXCEPT TO THE EXTENT THAT THESE DISCLAIMERS ARE HELD TO BE LEGALLY INVALID.

5. LIMITATION OF LIABILITY. TO THE EXTENT NOT PROHIBITED BY LAW, IN NO EVENT WILL SUN OR ITS LICENSORS BE LIABLE FOR ANY LOST REVENUE, PROFIT OR DATA, OR FOR SPECIAL, INDIRECT, CONSEQUENTIAL, INCIDENTAL OR PUNITIVE DAMAGES, HOWEVER CAUSED REGARDLESS OF THE THEORY OF LIABILITY, ARISING OUT OF OR RELATED TO THE USE OF OR INABILITY TO USE SOFTWARE, EVEN IF SUN HAS BEEN ADVISED OF THE POSSIBILITY OF SUCH DAMAGES. In no event will Sun's liability to you, whether in contract, tort (including negligence), or otherwise, exceed the amount paid by you for Software under this Agreement. The foregoing limitations will apply even if the above stated warranty fails of its essential purpose.

6. Termination. This Agreement is effective until terminated. You may terminate this Agreement at any time by destroying all copies of Software. This Agreement will terminate immediately without notice from Sun if you fail to comply with any provision of this Agreement. Upon Termination, you must destroy all copies of Software.

7. Export Regulations. All Software and technical data delivered under this Agreement are subject to US export control laws and may be subject to export or import regulations in other countries. You agree to comply strictly with all such laws and regulations and acknowledge that you have the responsibility to obtain such licenses to export, re-export, or import as may be required after delivery to you.

8. U.S. Government Restricted Rights. If Software is being acquired by or on behalf of the U.S. Government or by a U.S. Government prime contractor or subcontractor (at any tier), then the Government's rights in Software and accompanying documentation will be only as set forth in this Agreement; this is in accordance with 48 CFR 227.7201 through 227.7202-4 (for Department of Defense (DOD) acquisitions) and with 48 CFR 2.101 and 12.212 (for non-DOD acquisitions).

9. Governing Law. Any action related to this Agreement will be governed by California law and controlling U.S. federal law. No choice of law rules of any jurisdiction will apply.

10. Severability. If any provision of this Agreement is held to be unenforceable, this Agreement will remain in effect with the provision omitted, unless omission would frustrate the intent of the parties, in which case this Agreement will immediately terminate.

11. Integration. This Agreement is the entire agreement between you and Sun relating to its subject matter. It supersedes all prior or contemporaneous oral or written communications, proposals, representations and warranties

and prevails over any conflicting or additional terms of any quote, order, acknowledgment, or other communication between the parties relating to its subject matter during the term of this Agreement. No modification of this Agreement will be binding, unless in writing and signed by an authorized representative of each party.

JAVA™ DEVELOPMENT TOOLS J2ME™ WIRELESS TOOLKIT (J2ME WTK), VERSION 1.0.X
SUPPLEMENTAL LICENSE TERMS

These supplemental license terms ("Supplemental Terms") add to or modify the terms of the Binary Code License Agreement (collectively, the "Agreement"). Capitalized terms not defined in these Supplemental Terms shall have the same meanings ascribed to them in the Agreement. These Supplemental Terms shall supersede any inconsistent or conflicting terms in the Agreement, or in any license contained within the Software.

1. Software Internal Use and Development License Grant. Subject to the terms and conditions of this Agreement, including, but not limited to Section 2 (Java™ Technology Restrictions) of these Supplemental Terms, Sun grants you a non-exclusive, non-transferable, limited license to reproduce internally and use internally the binary form of the Software complete and unmodified for the sole purpose of designing, developing and testing your Java applets and applications intended to run on the Java platform ("Programs") provided that any executable output generated by a compiler that is contained in the Software must (a) only be compiled from source code that conforms to the corresponding version of the OEM Java Language Specification; (b) be in the class file format defined by the corresponding version of the OEM Java Virtual Machine Specification; and (c) execute properly on a reference runtime, as specified by Sun, associated with such version of the Java platform.

2. Java Technology Restrictions. You may not modify the Java Platform Interface ("JPI", identified as classes contained within the "java" package or any subpackages of the "java" package), by creating additional classes within the JPI or otherwise causing the addition to or modification of the classes in the JPI. In the event that you create an additional class and associated API(s) which (i) extends the functionality of the Java platform, and (ii) is exposed to third party software developers for the purpose of developing additional software which invokes such additional API, you must promptly publish broadly an accurate specification for such API for free use by all developers. You may not create, or authorize your licensees to create, additional classes, interfaces, or subpackages that are in any way identified as "java", "javax", "sun" or similar convention as specified by Sun in any naming convention designation.

3. Java Runtime Availability. Refer to the appropriate version of the Java Runtime Environment binary code license (currently located at http://www.java.sun.com/jdk/index.html) for the availability of runtime code which may be distributed with Java applets and applications.

4. Trademarks and Logos. You acknowledge and agree as between you and Sun that Sun owns the SUN, SOLARIS, JAVA, JINI, FORTE, and iPLANET trademarks and all SUN, SOLARIS, JAVA, JINI, FORTE, and iPLANET-related trademarks, service marks, logos and other brand designations ("Sun Marks"), and you agree to comply with the Sun Trademark and Logo Usage Requirements currently located at http://www.sun.com/policies/trademarks. Any use you make of the Sun Marks inures to Sun's benefit.

5. Source Code. Software may contain source code that is provided solely for reference purposes pursuant to the terms of this Agreement. Source code may not be redistributed unless expressly provided for in this Agreement.

6. Termination for Infringement. Either party may terminate this Agreement immediately should any Software become, or in either party's opinion be likely to become, the subject of a claim of infringement of any intellectual property right.

For inquiries please contact: Sun Microsystems, Inc. 901 San Antonio Road, Palo Alto, California 94303

(LFI#101620/Form ID#011801)

INDEX

Java™ and XML:
Your visual blueprint for creating
Java-enhanced Web programs

D

E

INDEX

Java™ and XML:
Your visual blueprint for creating
Java-enhanced Web programs

INDEX

Java™ and XML:
Your visual blueprint for creating
Java-enhanced Web programs

with these two-color Visual™ guides

The Complete Visual Reference

"Master It" tips provide additional topic coverage.

Title	ISBN	Price
Master Active Directory™ VISUALLY™	0-7645-3425-4	$39.99
Master Microsoft® Access 2000 VISUALLY™	0-7645-6048-4	$39.99
Master Microsoft® Office 2000 VISUALLY™	0-7645-6050-6	$39.99
Master Microsoft® Word 2000 VISUALLY™	0-7645-6046-8	$39.99
Master Office 97 VISUALLY™	0-7645-6036-0	$39.99
Master Photoshop® 5.5 VISUALLY™	0-7645-6045-X	$39.99
Master Red Hat® Linux® VISUALLY™	0-7645-3436-X	$39.99
Master VISUALLY™ Adobe® Photoshop®, Illustrator®, Premiere®, and After Effects®	0-7645-3668-0	$39.99
Master VISUALLY™ Dreamweaver® 4 and Flash™ 5	0-7645-0855-5	$39.99
Master VISUALLY™ FrontPage® 2002	0-7645-3580-3	$39.99
Master VISUALLY™ HTML 4 & XHTML™ 1	0-7645-3454-8	$39.99
Master VISUALLY™ Microsoft® Windows® Me Millennium Edition	0-7645-3496-3	$39.99
Master VISUALLY™ Office XP	0-7645-3599-4	$39.99
Master VISUALLY™ Photoshop® 6	0-7645-3541-2	$39.99
Master VISUALLY™ Web Design	0-7645-3610-9	$39.99
Master VISUALLY™ Windows® 2000 Server	0-7645-3426-2	$39.99
Master VISUALLY™ Windows® XP	0-7645-3621-4	$39.99
Master Windows® 95 VISUALLY™	0-7645-6024-7	$39.99
Master Windows® 98 VISUALLY™	0-7645-6034-4	$39.99
Master Windows® 2000 Professional VISUALLY™	0-7645-3421-1	$39.99

Java® and XML:
Your visual blueprint for creating
Java-enhanced Web programs

CD-ROM INSTALLATION INSTRUCTIONS

The CD-ROM included in this book contains many useful files and programs. Before installing any of the programs on the disc, make sure that you do not already have a newer version of the program already installed on your computer. For information on installing different versions of the same program, contact the program's manufacturer. For the latest and greatest information, please refer to the ReadMe file located at the root level of the CD-ROM.

System Requirements

To use the contents of the CD-ROM, your computer must have the following hardware and software:

- A PC with a Pentium or faster processor

- Microsoft Windows 95, 98, ME, NT 4.0, 2000, or XP

- At least 128MB of physical RAM installed on your computer

- A double-speed (8x) or faster CD-ROM drive

- A monitor capable of displaying at least 256 colors or grayscale;

- A network card.

For a full listing of the CD-ROM's contents, the e-Version of the book, troubleshooting instructions, and End User Licensing Agreements, see Appendix D.

Java 2 Platform Installations

Use of the Java 2 Platform Micro Edition, Wireless Toolkit 1.03, (J2ME), Java 2 Platform, Standard Edition (J2SE) version 1.4 for Windows and Forte for Java are subject to the Sun Microsystems, Inc. Binary Code License agreement on pages 298-301 of the accompanying book. Read this agreement carefully. By opening the CD package, you are agreeing to be bound by the terms and conditions of this agreement.